Investigative
Interviews
of Children

Investigative Interviews of Children

A GUIDE FOR HELPING PROFESSIONALS

Debra A. Poole
Michael E. Lamb

American Psychological Association
Washington, DC

Third printing January 2002

Published by
American Psychological Association
750 First Street, NE
Washington, DC 20002

Copies may be ordered from
APA Order Department
P.O. Box 92984
Washington, DC 20090-2984

In the United Kingdom, Europe, Africa, and the Middle East, copies may be ordered from
American Psychological Association
3 Henrietta Street
Covent Garden
London WC2E 8LU
England

Typeset in Goudy by EPS Group Inc., Easton, MD

Printer: Sheridan Books, Inc., Ann Arbor, MI
Jacket designer: Minker Design, Bethesda, MD
Jacket illustrator: Elizabeth Wolf, Boise, ID
Technical/production editor: Valerie Montenegro

Library of Congress Cataloging-in-Publication Data
Poole, Debra A.
    Investigative interviews of children : a guide for helping
professionals / Debra A. Poole and Michael E. Lamb.
      p.   cm.
    Includes bibliographical references and index.
    ISBN 1-55798-500-6 (cloth : acid-free paper)
    ISBN 1-55798-684-3 (pbk : acid-free paper)
    1. Interviewing in child abuse. 2. Child abuse—Investigation.
3. Child witnesses. 4. Child witnesses—Psychology. I. Lamb,
Michael E., 1953– . II. Title.
    HV8079.C46P66 1998
    363.25′95554—dc21
                                      98-16385
                                        CIP

British Library Cataloguing-in-Publication Data
A CIP record is available from the British Library.

Printed in the United States of America

This book is dedicated to our teachers,
past and present.

CONTENTS

PREFACE

We began writing this book in 1995, when widespread efforts to develop and implement investigative interviewing protocols created a need for summary documents and training materials. Unfortunately, the guidelines available at that time often blended research results with hunches or working hypotheses in ways that made it difficult for helping professionals to distinguish one from the other. Because intuitions about best practice often are dramatically wrong, we set out to summarize the empirical literature in order to distill best-practice guidelines based on currently available knowledge. Unfortunately, little empirical research had actually been conducted on many of the topics that are important to interviewers, and thus we have had to suppress the urge to wait just 3 or perhaps 5 more years, when the results of conclusive studies would be available, and accept the fact that this book would be a call for research as much as a summary of useful recommendations.

The information in this book actually began to take shape in the mid-1980s, when high-profile media coverage of day care abuse cases, unforeseen calls from attorneys, and experiences with their own children prompted many developmental researchers to make connections between basic research and the growing need for data on children's reactions to interviews and interviewers. Interest in children's eyewitness testimony grew rapidly as some scientists seized the opportunity to test basic principles of memory and concept formation in more complex contexts, other scientists welcomed the chance to demonstrate the applicability, generalizability, and policy relevance of their research, and most scientists hoped that their work ultimately would benefit children.

Our approach to the topic reflects our backgrounds as developmental psychologists who have begun to work with and train investigative interviewers. It also reflects our lives as parents and our experiences as university professors. The early 1980s coincided with the birth of Deb's children, and many of her studies were prompted by casual and contrived conversations with her son and daughter, Bret and Lin. During this time, Deb codirected a women's studies program at Beloit College, beginning a tradition of interdisciplinary teaching that she continues by team-teaching regularly with Len Lieberman (a sociologist and physical anthropologist) as a professor of psychology at Central Michigan University. Michael, meanwhile, likewise was beginning to raise the first of his five children while working as a professor of psychology, psychiatry, and pediatrics at the University of Utah, where colleagues and students in the medical school were particularly insistent that he address the challenges they faced in their clinics each day. In the summer of 1985, Udo Undeutsch, a German forensic psychologist, conducted a multiday seminar in Salt Lake City on the evaluation of children's credibility, and this whetted Michael's interest in this topic. Later, fortuitous meetings with Ilana Karniel, then head of the youth investigative services in Israel, and with Phillip Esplin, an American forensic psychologist, permitted Michael and Kathy Sternberg to begin a program of research on investigative interviewing that continues to this day.

We describe our personal backgrounds both to help explain what this book is and to emphasize what it is not. Our academic interests and backgrounds have led us to view interviewing as an activity that is influenced not only by children's developmental levels but also by other recent interviews and conversations they have had, their home situations, and the ways in which the behavior and values of those around them influence their interpretations of the purpose and content of the interview. This perspective prevents us from believing, even for a moment, that there is one right way to interview children regardless of their social and cultural contexts. In this book, we address topics that concerned researchers when a particular convergence of social realities in the 1980s and early 1990s made those topics especially intriguing, and the resulting principles are actually rather simple: To be accurate informants, children must attend, they must be motivated to talk and be informative, they must understand what adults are asking them, and their own memories must be protected from potentially distorting information. Reflecting our backgrounds as teachers, we have organized the book so that individual chapters can stand alone as nontechnical summaries of specific topics, although the book as a whole also can be used to supplement interview training courses.

In Part I ("The Backdrop for Investigative Interviews"), we discuss the social problems and research findings that shaped the structure and emphases of interviewing protocols. In Part II ("Interview Protocols"), we review several prominent interviewing protocols and describe a flexible protocol that represents areas of consensus. Because interviewers who follow a protocol will always need to decide which specific questions and interviewing aids are most appropriate for each child, we review research on language development and ancillary aids in Part III ("Customizing Interviews"). Finally, in Part IV ("Professional Development Issues"), we address the need to stay abreast of new findings by explaining topics in judgment and decision making that are especially relevant for helping professionals, and we discuss strategies for locating current reference materials.

There are many topics that we do not discuss, however, simply because relevant empirical data are not yet available, and we felt uncomfortable offering opinions in their absence. We are wary of self-appointed "experts" who have long sold their products to helping professionals as though their advice alone should be sufficient to direct the actions of others, an attitude that is at best condescending and at worst dangerous. Thus, we avoid offering casual advice except when practical considerations make some discussion necessary. (For example, there are no studies on the impact of room size or type of furniture on the quality of children's testimonies, but interviewers who are required to capture interviews on videotape need to encourage children to stay in a fixed space, and this sets some limits on the types of environments that will work.) In our experience, most professionals enjoy grappling with thorny or highly technical issues even when those issues are outside the scope of their formal training, and therefore we believe that the best strategy is to present the issues and data as they are, lean though the research may be on some topics, so that professionals can better discriminate advice that is based on a solid foundation from advice that is clearly more tentative. For example, our recommendations about rapport-building strategies derive from only a few systematic studies, and thus future research is likely to refine guidelines for this portion of the interview. Professionals who find themselves defending their expertise in court might be comforted by the lesson we faced numerous times while writing this book: Oftentimes, "I don't know" is the most informed answer.

We have many people to thank for their mentoring and support during the past years, including those who worked with us on projects and those who reviewed our drafts. Deb gratefully acknowledges Maggie Bruck, Stephen Ceci, Steve Lindsay, Ray Bull, Amina Memon, Ron Fisher, Robyn Dawes, Amye Warren, Mel Pipe, Narina Nightingale, Chuck Brainerd, Martine Powell, and the steering committee of the Michigan Child Investigative Interviewing Pilot Project (Terry Beurer, Vickie Nimmo, Jim Beougher, Larry Leik, Jim Nye, and Bill Patrick). Michael's research has been made possible by collaboration with the Israeli Department of Youth Investigation, especially Dvora Horowitz, Meir Hovav, and Ilana Karniel, and many colleagues in the United States, Israel, and Europe, including Tascha Boychuk, Ray Bull, David Chadwick, Graham Davies, Phillip Esplin, Robyn Fivush, Irit Hershkowitz, Steve Horowitz, David Jones, Yael Orbach, David Raskin, Kathy Sternberg, and Udo Undeutsch.

I

THE BACKDROP FOR
INVESTIGATIVE
INTERVIEWS

INTRODUCTION

THE BACKDROP FOR INVESTIGATIVE INTERVIEWS

The study of human experience has long been intertwined with the art and science of conversation. Freudian psychoanalysis, a forerunner of modern psychotherapy, popularized the "talking cure." Early efforts to understand children's cognitive development, inspired by Jean Piaget and his followers, used the "clinical method" of questioning children. Numerous studies—whether focused on the social behavior of popular and unpopular children, the differing classroom experiences of male and female students, or the dynamics of romantic relationships—have involved analyses of conversation. It is therefore ironic that helping professionals had so little to guide them when a dramatic increase in child abuse allegations forced them to address a deceptively simple question: What is the best way to ask children about their experiences?

The primary purpose of this book is to summarize research on interviewing children, distilling guidelines to help practitioners who conduct investigative interviews. Because the goal of investigative interviewing is to help children relate their experiences accurately and completely, the principles of investigative interviewing also are useful for other professionals who work with children and frequently have reason to question them about their feelings and experiences, including teachers, physicians, and mental health practitioners. A simple "how-to" book would fail to address the complex issues that arise when conversations with children have legal implications, however. Professionals who talk with children make numerous decisions before, during, and after their conversations—decisions about which topics to raise, how to tailor questions to children's individual cir-

3

cumstances, and how to interpret children's responses. These decisions are influenced by our assumptions about the social contexts in which children live and our expectations about their skills and developmental limitations. Consider how these assumptions affect interviews about possible sexual abuse, the problem that motivated much of the research on interviewing and is thus a central focus of this book.

Children are interviewed about sexual abuse when they disclose abuse or adults suspect that abuse might have occurred. Suspicions can arise when medical examinations yield findings often associated with abuse, adults observe sexualized behavior, children make spontaneous comments that raise concerns, or they acknowledge abuse after direct questioning (e.g., "Did Bobby touch you there?"), and all such indications can be present in children who have not been sexually abused. As a result, investigative professionals must adopt a hypothesis-testing approach, generating and systematically testing each of several plausible explanations for the suspicious behavior, condition, or utterance. Unless the interview is conducted "blind" (i.e., without prior knowledge of the circumstances surrounding the allegation), interviewers typically can generate alternative hypotheses about the source of any allegation (see chap. 4). For example, if a mother reports that her 4-year-old daughter accused "Daddy" of sticking a finger in her "butt" during a custodial visit, the interviewer could generate at least five plausible hypotheses: (a) the child experienced digital penetration or fondling by her biological father, (b) the child calls another male "Daddy," (c) "Daddy" touched the child in a nonabusive way in the context of caretaking or medical treatment, (e) the mother misunderstood a partial description of an innocuous event (such as the father's repairing the child's feed-and-wet doll), or (f) the child never made the accusation as reported by her mother.

In general, how do interviewers generate alternative hypotheses about the origin of allegations? Interviewers are informed by current social circumstances that affect the occurrence and awareness of abuse, by factors related to unfounded suspicions of abuse, and by their understanding of variation in children's knowledge of sexuality and normative sexual behavior. Unless they understand the myriad reasons why the number of allegations increased so dramatically during the 1980s, however, interviewers may have difficulty developing plausible hypotheses to direct their interviews. Consequently, interviewer training courses should include the basic information on abuse that is briefly reviewed in chapter 1 ("Children as Witnesses: The Tragedy and the Dilemma"). Information about rates and patterns of abuse can prevent professionals from prematurely dismissing reports because they consider abuse unlikely, whereas knowledge of the factors associated with unfounded suspicions or accusations can help professionals develop and test alternative hypotheses.

In addition to testing alternative hypotheses about the origins of allegations, interviewers also should consider alternative interpretations about the meaning of children's behavior and comments during interviews. Imagine, for example, that 5-year-old Evan just described how he was fondled by a teacher and then, after a lengthy pause, piped up, "And Nanna just said, 'Don't do that again!'" A naive interviewer might assume that Evan had told his grandmother about the abuse. An experienced interviewer, however, would realize that Evan could be off topic. In this example, a follow-up question would be necessary to determine whether the grandmother's comment was related to the alleged touching. It takes a sophisticated understanding of cognitive and social development to formulate appropriate alternative hypotheses about children's behavior and language during an interview. To this end, in chapter 2 ("Strengths and Weaknesses of Children as Witnesses: Implications for Developmentally Sensitive Interviewing") we describe how children develop the basic skills they need to participate in an interview, and discuss various factors associated with accurate and inaccurate testimony.

The information we present in Part I is designed not only to help interviewers adopt a hypothesis-testing approach but also to help professionals modify their behavior to accommodate the nuances of specific cases. It would be easy to train interviewers if we could simply hand them a short list of questions to ask, but such an approach would be woefully inadequate. Professionals converse with children of various ages for a variety of reasons, and they encounter children with dramatically different personalities and reactions to questioning by unfamiliar adults. The risks and potential benefits of specific interview techniques are a function of children's life experiences, their levels of cognitive maturity, and the potential impact of the information on other individuals. Making decisions to meet the unique needs of each child requires considerable knowledge about the topics discussed in chapters 1 and 2, topics that provide the "backdrop" for investigative interviews.

1

CHILDREN AS WITNESSES:
THE TRAGEDY AND THE DILEMMA

It follows that, whether the threat be war and conflict or economic marginalization, children should, as far as is humanly possible, be protected from the worst mistakes and malignancies of the adult world.

James P. Grant
The State of the World's Children 1995

In the 1980s, a collection of social problems combined to produce a crisis in child protection. Allegations of child abuse flooded the social service system and overwhelmed available resources. Professionals who had little relevant experience suddenly found themselves investigating claims of physical and sexual abuse, claims that sometimes involved bizarre forms of abuse and often involved preschoolers caught up in a system designed for older children and adults. Experienced professionals also faced changing demands and expectations. A population of sexually naive children had somehow been transformed into a diverse group that included children who were surprisingly knowledgeable about sexual matters. In the absence of investigative protocols, therapeutic strategies designed for the assessment and treatment of victimized children, such as playroom environments and reinforcing dialogue, were rapidly co-opted for forensic purposes, often with unforeseen and disturbing results.

By the early 1990s, the media implied that experts had divided them-selves into two opposing camps: child advocates who believed that children never lie and skeptics who warned that children are highly suggestible. Professionals who had dedicated their lives to protecting children were accused of eliciting false allegations of abuse by using coercive and sugges-tive procedures. The stress on evaluators was enormous, leading Berliner (1990) to comment that some professionals were "virtually paralyzed, re-

7

luctant to ask any questions for fear of ruining a case" (p. 6). Conversely, researchers who hoped to improve the quality of investigations were often accused of defending perpetrators. Two vastly different positions—that children accurately report abuse and that children are highly suggestible— were honed by an adversarial legal system that discourages compromise and qualified conclusions.

Unfortunately, an important concept often was missing from the acrimonious debates about child witnesses: the notion that social interventions, such as investigative interviews, always reflect general social circumstances. As a result, there may be no "right" way to interview children that is independent of the social and historical milieu that necessitates those interviews. For example, the notion that children never lie about sexual abuse may once have been a largely accurate assumption, particularly when countering the "commonsense" belief that sexual abuse is rare or that children cannot be trusted. Changes in social circumstances have since made this assumption dangerously simplistic, however.

Increasingly, helping professionals are called on to make decisions that require an enormous amount of technical knowledge about children— knowledge about cognitive and language development, normative sexual behavior, characteristics of accidental versus nonaccidental injuries, and cultural variation. Practitioners who interview children also are expected to adjust their procedures continually to accommodate changes in social circumstances and rapid increases in knowledge. In the midst of these pressures, however, many important questions remain unanswered. Thus the recommendations offered in this book are not designed to canonize a new set of procedures, but rather to help minimize the most flagrant problems that occur when legal decisions are made that involve children. Professionals still need to consider the life circumstances of individual children and adapt their methods accordingly. Decisions about individual cases require an understanding of the many factors that created the controversy about interviewing children. This chapter is a summary of those factors.

THE TRAGEDY OF CHILD ABUSE

Training courses for investigative interviewers often provide information about the incidence and prevalence of childhood victimization,[1] both to raise awareness about the extent of child abuse and to dispel myths about the characteristics of perpetrators and their victims. Of course, actual rates of abuse are unknown, but frequency estimates can be derived from

---

[1]*Incidence* refers to the number of new occurrences and is usually expressed in terms of a fixed time period (e.g., the number of abuse reports per year). *Prevalence* refers to the total number of cases in a population (e.g., the percentage of adults who experienced sexual abuse in childhood).

several sources, including reports to child protective service agencies and retrospective studies of adults who are asked about events they experienced as children. Although such estimates undoubtedly are influenced by society's changing attitudes about abuse, they consistently confirm that child maltreatment is a widespread problem that cuts across social classes and historical periods.

Historical Perspectives on Child Abuse

Although recognition of child abuse has increased dramatically since 1960, there is little evidence that children are at greater risk today than they were during earlier historical periods. Economic and physical hardship have always been associated with declines in the quality of care offered to children. According to Kessen (1965), however, attitudes toward children have changed dramatically since the 17th century for three major reasons: improved medical care, the industrial revolution, and Darwin's theory of evolution.

Before the 17th century, there were few standards for rearing children and little public interest in the early years of life. During the 17th century, however, records became sufficiently detailed to arouse widespread concern about child welfare. As Kessen (1965) explained in *The Child*, "physicians avoided the child so long because he seemed hopelessly resistant to medical intervention. It was only yesterday in human history that the majority of children could be expected to live beyond their fifth year" (p. 7). Before 1750, for example, the odds were three to one against a child in London reaching 5 years of age. In addition to death by disease, children faced a huge risk of abandonment and little hope of surviving the "foundling" homes that were set up to handle the "dropping" of babies. According to Kessen, only 45 out of 10,272 infants survived in a Dublin foundling home during the late 18th century. Not knowing how to improve the survival rate of young children, society expressed little interest in this period of life. Though harsh, conditions during this time represented the continuation of a long history of child maltreatment that included practices such as infanticide and ritual mutilation (Zigler & Hall, 1991).

Gradually, improved understanding of disease, hygiene, and infant care reduced complacency about early mortality and prompted advocacy on behalf of children's health and safety. But these efforts faced new challenges in the 19th century when the industrial revolution increased the demand for child labor. Brutal conditions for young workers prompted new debates about society's obligations toward children and fostered efforts to regulate their working conditions. The history of child labor law is an interesting record of how definitions of child maltreatment have evolved. For example, consider a law passed to "protect" children in 1833: This law "prohibited night work to persons under 18 in cotton, woollen, and other factories, and provided that children from 9 to 13 were not to work more than 48 hours a week and those from 13 to 18 not more than 68 hours a week. Children under 9 were not to be employed at all" (Kessen, 1965, pp. 43–44). Unfortunately, this law did not apply to children who worked in mines, often beginning at 5 years of age.[2]

In Kessen's analysis, children's roles in society were transformed further when Darwin fostered the development of child psychology as a formal discipline, thereby converting children from the focus of reformers, like physicians and clergymen, into objects of scientific study. Darwin's notion that species develop over generations (phylogeny) gave new importance to the study of individual development (ontogeny) and prompted frequent analogies between "animal and child, between primitive man and child, between early human history and child" (p. 115). Indeed, an interesting analogy between a particular child and the animal kingdom occupies a special place in the history of child welfare. Many social historians trace the widespread recognition of child maltreatment in the United States to 1874, when a New York City social worker found 8-year-old Mary Ellen Wilson chained and beaten. The case went to trial through the efforts of Henry Berg, founder of the Society for the Prevention of Cruelty to Animals. Because laws did not address the abuse of children by their caretakers, legal protection was offered on the grounds that Mary Ellen was a member of the animal kingdom (Westman, 1979; Zigler & Hall, 1991).

The first half of the 20th century was marked by increased advocacy on behalf of children, including the creation of the Child Welfare League of America and a mandate for welfare services in the Social Security Act (Tower, 1996). By the 1980s, however, national statistics had raised concerns that rates of child abuse might be increasing. It is misleading to consider reporting rates, however, without considering the significant social and legislative changes that began in the 1960s. A symposium on child abuse convened by C. Henry Kempe and his colleagues for the annual meeting of the American Academy of Pediatrics in 1961 was especially influential (Cicchetti & Carlson, 1991). Alarmed by radiological evidence of nonaccidental injuries, Kempe and his colleagues coined a term, *the battered child syndrome* (Kempe, Silverman, Steele, Droegemueller, & Silver, 1962), which quickly captured public attention and prompted legislative changes. Mandatory reporting laws were passed by all 50 states before 1970,

---

[2]Grisly tales about maltreatment in the past remind us that there are no absolute standards defining child abuse. Recently, human rights activists have been rallying against American distributors who market clothing made by children in other countries, and one state representative has promoted a voluntary "No Sweat" label for child-labor-free products. (For a brief discussion, see an essay by syndicated columnist Ellen Goodman from *The Boston Globe*, July 18, 1996). Similarly, a recent but failed effort in Michigan to raise the age of compulsory school attendance to 18 shows how the gradual shift away from an agricultural economy has modified our beliefs about childhood and about the competing interests of parents and society at large.

and in 1974 the federal Child Abuse Prevention and Treatment Act, Section 3, broadened the definition of child abuse to include "the physical or mental injury, sexual abuse, negligent treatment, or maltreatment of a child under the age of 18 by a person who is responsible for the child's welfare under circumstances which indicate the child's health or welfare is harmed or threatened," thereby completing the shift in focus from infant mortality and maternal health to physical abuse and, finally, to a broader concern that also encompassed emotional and sexual abuse. Prompted by the Child Abuse Prevention and Treatment Act, the states also gradually broadened the list of professionals who were expected to report suspected cases of abuse. Amidst controversy about these broadened definitions and reporting responsibilities (Kalichman, 1993; Levine & Doueck, 1995), a new federal agency, the National Center on Child Abuse and Neglect (NCCAN), was established to expand public awareness and fund research and demonstration projects. During this period, child abuse became "a common household word" (Giovannoni, 1991, p. 10).

Although the child welfare movement initially focused on physical abuse and neglect, advocacy in behalf of sexually abused children also has a long history. The Bible contains proscriptions against incest, and laws protecting children against forcible sex were passed as early as the 16th century. Nonetheless, confused and contradictory attitudes about sexual relations between adults and children have long persisted. In a brief review of sexual exploitation, Tower (1996) reminded us that sexual contact between adult males and boys was condoned in early Greece and that child prostitution and sexual intercourse with young slaves were common during the 19th century. Even today, children are exploited by incest (sexual activity between relatives or members of the child's nuclear family), pedophilia (sexual activity with adults who have a sexual interest in children), pederasty (sexual relations between teenage boys and adult males who advocate consensual sex between boys and men), child pornography, and child prostitution.

Society currently conveys mixed messages about children and sexuality. As Tower (1996) noted,

> On the one hand, we state that children should not be exploited sexually; on the other hand, child pornography thrives and the courts are often more likely to believe molesting adults than molested children. Television commercials use nubile girls posed seductively. Such practices can only give molesters and children a mixed message about what society believes about sexual abuse and the sexual exploitation of children. (p. 7)

Tolerance for sexual relationships between children and adults has been advocated by organizations such as the North American Man Boy Love Association, and child pornography remains a flourishing business (see

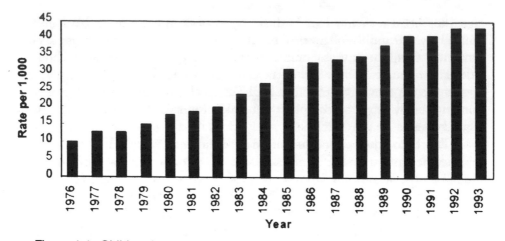

Figure 1.1. Child maltreatment reporting trends: 1976–1993. Adapted from data presented in *Child Maltreatment 1993: Reports From the States to the National Center on Child Abuse and Neglect* (U.S. Department of Health and Human Services, 1995).

de Young, 1988, for qualitative analysis of publications from pedophilic organizations).

The recent changes in child advocacy, including mandatory reporting legislation, created additional dilemmas for professionals who work with children and left them vulnerable to criticism about the techniques they use to make decisions about children's risk of abuse. Although current definitions of child maltreatment span a wide range of social problems, criticisms of child protection strategies initially focused on a particular type of case that represented only a small proportion of abuse reports: sexual abuse allegations involving very young children who reported unusual forms of abuse, often after investigative or therapeutic interactions with numerous adults (Ceci & Bruck, 1995). Highly publicized trials such as the McMartin and Little Rascals preschool cases had a disproportionate influence on public perceptions of child protection, the types of questions researchers sought to answer with their studies of interviewing, and consequently, the problems addressed by current interviewing protocols. To understand how interviewing protocols evolved into their present form, it is helpful to review how recent changes in reporting patterns created new challenges for investigative interviewers.

Recent Reporting Trends

The NCCAN compiles data on child abuse and neglect referrals and their disposition following investigation. The 1993 summary, reproduced in Figure 1.1, shows a steady increase in referrals between 1976 and 1992, with the 1992 and 1993 figures at 43 reports per 1,000 U.S. children under age 18 (U.S. Department of Health and Human Services, 1995). Stated differently, 2.9 million reports of maltreatment in 1993 prompted approximately 1.6 million investigations, most of which were conducted without adequate resources to respond effectively. For example, although the number of reports grew tremendously between 1985 and 1991, 35 states held funding steady or reduced support for child protective services during this period (Pence & Wilson, 1994).

Efforts to advocate on behalf of children were complicated not only by the increased number of referrals but also by the changing nature of these reports. Four trends during the 1980s and early 1990s influenced the focus and content of interviewing protocols: a disproportionate increase in allegations of sexual abuse, increased publicity about reports of severe or bizarre abuse, referrals from a wide range of professional and nonprofessional sources, and an increased number of very young alleged victims.

The Increased Prominence of Sexual Abuse

In 1981, approximately 7% of the abuse and neglect reports involved sexual abuse, a figure that doubled by 1993. Despite the fact that other types of abuse continued to be much more common than sexual abuse,[3] sexual abuse became the focus of criticism about incompetent interviewing (e.g., Underwager & Wakefield, 1990), perhaps because sexual abuse charges pose special difficulties for investigators. As Pence and Wilson (1994) pointed out, neglect sometimes can be identified during a single home visit, and physical abuse is likely to leave visible evidence. In contrast, the word of a child or guardian often is the only available evidence of sexual abuse, and careful investigations can consume an enormous amount of resources. Pence and Wilson concluded, "In the final analysis, investigating sexual abuse means interviewing all of the principals, sometimes more than once—a process that is, at best, time-consuming and requires the skillful application of the available knowledge" (p. 5).

To what extent did the increased number of reports reflect an increased *risk* to children as opposed to an increased *awareness* of abuse? Because social expectations play a large role in the identification of maltreatment, there probably is no definitive answer to this question. On the one hand, the past two decades were characterized by increases in the number of single-parent households, a risk factor for sexual abuse. On the other hand, changing awareness of abuse and mandated reporting also may have fueled the increasing reporting rates. For example, Ceci and Bruck (1995) argued that younger and older adults seem equally likely to have

---

[3]In 1993, 49% of all reports were for neglect, 24% for physical abuse, 14% for sexual abuse, and 22% for other types of maltreatment, including emotional maltreatment, medical neglect, abandonment, and congenital drug addiction. (Figures do not add to 100% because the same child can experience more than one type of abuse; U.S. Department of Health and Human Services, National Center on Child Abuse and Neglect, 1995).

been sexually abused as children, suggesting that there have been no dramatic changes in prevalence. In addition, although many more cases are reported, the number of cases that are classified as "substantiated" has remained steady or dropped slightly (Besharov, 1990; Ceci & Bruck, 1995). Nonetheless, the number of arrests for sexual offenses has increased markedly, from approximately 159,200 in 1976 to more than 247,000 in 1991 (U.S. Department of Justice, 1978, 1992).

Today, most interview training workshops focus predominantly on sexual abuse allegations, despite the fact that child protection workers spend more time assessing children's risk of physical abuse and neglect. Fortunately, the sorts of protocols described in this book should help structure conversations for a variety of purposes and across a variety of professional settings.

Increased Publicity for Bizarre Abuse

The increased awareness of sexual abuse has paralleled increased publicity about the most violent and unusual forms of child maltreatment. Many professional publications in the 1980s and early 1990s focused on the tragedy of child fatalities, noting that one half of all fatalities occurred in families that were already known to social service agencies or other helping professionals (Korbin, 1994). Thousands of stranger abductions were reported annually (Finkelhor, Hotaling, & Sedlak, 1990), prompting public service announcements that encouraged parents and children to use "code words" to prevent kidnapping. (See Best, 1989, for a critical look at the politics of social problem statistics.) Children in the inner cities were exposed to violence with alarming frequency. For example, interviews with parents determined that 51% of fifth graders in New Orleans and 32% of 6- to 10-year-olds in Washington, DC, had been victims of violence (see Osofsky, 1995, for a review). These portraits of an increasingly violent world altered adults' perceptions of what was possible or even likely. Media publicity contributed to this perception through coverage of highly publicized trials involving references to ritualistic features such as baby killing, animal sacrifice, religious candles, and other objects of ritual worship (see Ceci & Bruck, 1995, for case studies). In addition, professional workshops on ritualistic/satanic abuse increased dramatically (Nathan & Snedeker, 1995).

Because reports of highly unusual abuse could seldom be corroborated (Bottoms & Davis, 1997; Nathan & Snedeker, 1995), psychologists with an interest in memory and social influence initiated studies to determine whether suggestions actually could distort beliefs about significant life events. Some of the studies reviewed in chapter 2 indeed showed that adults have more influence on children's memories than many professionals had previously realized, and this prompted a focus on suggestibility rather than on other important issues, such as reluctance to disclose abuse. Interviewers were advised to help children describe events in their own words, avoiding contamination by adults.

The Changing Source of Reports

According to NCCAN's annual compilation, educators are by far the most frequent source of referrals to child protective services, accounting for 16% of all reports. They are followed, in order of prominence, by legal/justice (12%), social service (12%), and medical (11%) professionals, with friends and neighbors (10%), other relatives (10%), parents (7%), child care providers (2%), and even victims and perpetrators (2%) providing the remaining reports (11% are anonymous or unknown, and 7% are listed as "other").

Unfortunately, many adults converse with alleged victims before investigative interviews take place, and each conversation provides an opportunity for adults to influence a child's report. On the one hand, adults may encourage children to deny abuse, either by making explicit threats or by expressing disapproval or doubt. On the other hand, adults' suspicions of abuse can affect how suggestively they question children and, ultimately, the quality of information on which decisions must be based. As McGough explained (1996), legal and social service professionals often faced the "Humpty-Dumpty effect"—an inability to piece together what really had happened to children whose accounts had been contaminated—and this problem was exacerbated when referrals came from varied sources.

Concerns about previous conversations fostered research designed to determine how resistant children actually were to repeated suggestions from adults, and the results of this research prompted some professionals to urge that investigative interviews be videotaped routinely to provide a record of as many abuse-related conversations as possible (Lamb, 1994). Furthermore, current investigative guidelines, such as those for children's advocacy centers written by Sorenson, Bottoms, and Perona (1997), recommend limiting the number of adults who speak with alleged victims by encouraging interagency cooperation and using trained interviewers who can effectively elicit information in a single investigative interview.

The Increased Involvement of Young Children in the Legal Arena

As awareness of sexual abuse increased, the problems associated with prosecuting these crimes prompted procedural changes to accommodate children's involvement in the legal system. The process began in 1982, when the American Bar Association's National Legal Resource Center for Child Advocacy and Protection published a list of proposed legal reforms that included altering courtroom environments to minimize children's distress, interagency cooperation to reduce the number of interviews, and changes in the rules of evidence governing the presentation of information at trial (see McGough, 1994, for a review). Changes in the rules of evidence were most controversial because they involved minimizing competency evaluations for child witnesses and permitting the use of children's hearsay statements.[4] As McGough indicated, "The creation of special rules of evidence that apply only to child victims of sexual abuse [represented] an astonishing detour from the traditional path of the law" (p. 16).

There are a number of reasons why researchers have focused on interviews with young children. First, legal reforms have removed barriers that previously impeded the prosecution of cases involving very young children. Indeed, Gray (1993) reported that in one sample sexual abuse cases involving preschool children were disproportionately likely to progress to trial. Second, researchers have been fascinated by evidence that preschoolers can be amazingly accurate under some conditions but that they are more likely than older children or adults to succumb to suggestions (Ceci & Bruck, 1993). Finally, the fear that adults might misunderstand young children's comments or overreact to their sexualized behavior has fueled concern that referrals involving young children are more likely to be invalid. The interviewing protocols that evolved during this period reflected the need to accommodate younger children, suggesting the use of developmentally appropriate language (to ensure that young children understand interviewers' questions; see chap. 5) and avoidance of representational aids such as dolls (because some young children do not use props accurately to report events; see chap. 6). Unfortunately, research and guidelines for meeting the special needs of other groups, such as adolescents, have lagged behind.

In sum, societal perceptions of child abuse changed dramatically in the 1980s. Expanded awareness, coupled with mandatory reporting laws, meant that professionals who interacted with children were increasingly responsible for deciding whether abuse might have occurred. To make these decisions, they relied on information from professional sources and the media about the indicators of abuse, and their judgments fed reports of suspected abuse into social service and legal systems that were largely unprepared to deal with the volume of allegations, the frequency of cases without corroborating evidence, or the impact of legal reforms that increased the involvement of very young children in our courts of law. In short, helping professionals suddenly faced what McGough (1994) called "the child witness revolution" (p. 8).

---

[4]*Hearsay* refers to out-of-court statements, such as those made to parents or physicians. In the American and British legal systems, hearsay was traditionally considered less reliable than in-court pronouncements, although there are numerous exceptions to the exclusion of hearsay (McGough, 1994, chap. 7).

THE DILEMMA OF CHILDREN AS WITNESSES

Numerous methodological problems hamper attempts to estimate the prevalence of child maltreatment. Estimates of childhood sexual abuse, for example, range from 3% to 31% for boys and from 6% to 62% for girls (Kuehnle, 1996). Although there are no undisputed figures, available statistics leave little doubt that child abuse is widespread. The dilemma for professionals who work with children, however, is that a nontrivial but unknown percentage of the reported suspicions are unfounded. Until recently, little was known about the mechanisms underlying false allegations, there was little research on valid indicators of abuse, and no interview protocols emphasized the need to make reasoned distinctions between true and false reports. As a result, some interviewers viewed conversations with children as procedures for confirming that abuse had taken place. Children who denied abuse were sometimes badgered in dozens of suggestive and coercive interviews, leading critics to claim that helping professionals were merely perpetrating a form of institutionalized abuse (e.g., Wakefield & Underwager, 1994a). Although concerns about suggestibility began to resurface in the professional literature during the 1980s (Ceci & Bruck, 1993), analyses of actual investigative interviews and courtroom transcripts from the 1980s and early 1990s illuminated alarming injustices that eroded the public's trust in the child protection system (see Ceci & Bruck, 1995, for a discussion of some such cases). Consequently, the current demand for forensic guidelines can be understood better by considering how recent social changes complicated the process of distinguishing between true and false reports of abuse.

False Allegations

It is difficult to estimate how many false allegations are made, because rarely is there certainty about what really happened. In the case of sexual abuse, external evidence in the form of a confession, consistent medical findings, or other evidence (e.g., pornographic pictures of the child) is very seldom available (e.g., Elliott & Briere, 1994; Lamb et al., 1997). Despite the methodological barriers to estimating false allegation rates, it frequently has been claimed that only approximately 5–8% of sexual abuse allegations are false. This estimate has appeared in numerous articles (e.g., Sink, 1988), was underscored by the American Professional Society on the Abuse of Children (APSAC, 1993), and has been cited by experts in court (Ceci & Bruck, 1995). Several authors, however (e.g., Ceci & Bruck, 1995; Robin, 1991; Wakefield & Underwager, 1991), have argued that this rate is misleadingly low because it includes only deliberate attempts to deceive rather than cases in which honest errors were made (e.g., premature judgments about a genital rash or misinterpretations of children's comments).

When the latter are included, estimates jump from 6% to 23% for one comprehensive study (Jones & McGraw, 1987), with rates of approximately 35% or higher when allegations arising in the context of divorce or custody proceedings are included (e.g., Benedik & Schetky, cited in Jones & Seig, 1988; Faller, 1991; Thoennes & Tjaden, 1990).[5]

Unfortunately, the term *false allegation* often is used to describe unwarranted suspicions on the part of a neighbor or misinterpretations of children's statements, regardless of whether the children actually made any allegations. In our view, the term *false allegation* should be used only when children make an explicit allegation that is false, but we cannot ignore the fact that investigations *are* prompted by unsubstantiated suspicions, claims, or reports by others on children's behalf. In Sorensen and Snow's (1991) study of children referred for sexual abuse therapy, for example, sexualized behavior or time spent with an alleged perpetrator was the impetus for suspicions of abuse in 42% of the sample. Similarly, 51% of the children in a sample studied by Keary and Fitzpatrick (1994) were referred because of emotional or behavior problems, sexualized behavior, or physical signs suggestive of abuse. Because many children are interviewed when adults have concerns about abuse, and initial "disclosures" sometimes involve little more than head nods after a series of specific questions, interviewers have a serious responsibility when conducting investigations to consider the possibility that suspicions of abuse may be unfounded.

Recognition that false allegations occur has dispelled the notion that children never lie about sexual abuse. Consider this recent comment by the San Diego County Grand Jury:

> Members of the San Diego County Grand Jury recently learned of fourth-graders using false allegations of sexual abuse against their substitute teacher. The teacher told police his fourth-grade class on Chicago's South Side became unruly during his May 9, 1994 assignment. When the substitute threatened to report their misbehavior, a nine year old girl offered to pay 10 of her classmates one dollar each if they falsely claimed that the substitute fondled them. Fortunately the substitute was never charged but he also has yet to receive another teaching assignment. Police cleared him after some of the 10 children, nine

[5]Discussions about false allegations made in the context of divorce and custody proceedings often imply that sexual abuse allegations commonly arise in this context. In a 1990 study of 9,000 divorces, however, allegations arose in less than 2% of the divorces in which child custody was contested (Thoennes & Tjaden, 1990). Although low in absolute terms, this rate is six times higher than expected on the basis of national reporting statistics. Thoennes and Pearson (1988) concluded that such cases draw attention because they are more vexing for court professionals and are among the most time consuming to investigate, rather than because the rates of false allegations are higher. Other authors have argued that rates of false allegations *are* higher in cases involving divorce or custody, although as many as 50% of these reports may be valid (Ceci & Bruck, 1995). There is good agreement that false allegations are more common when reports are initiated by parents rather than by children and that false allegations often involve parents who sincerely are concerned about the possibility of abuse (Robin, 1991).

girls and one boy, made inconsistent statements. A spokesperson for the Chicago Teachers Union said, *"What's so scary—and so sad—is that you've got nine year-olds sophisticated enough to know they can get a teacher by saying he fondled them."* (pp. 28–29; italics in the original)

Although some children do lie about abuse, spontaneous lies from young children are believed to be rare, and documented cases of intentional lying generally involve adults or older children.[6] For example, one therapist (Smith, 1991) reported that on the fourth visit to his office, Stephanie, age 17, brought a letter describing how her mother had instructed her at age 6 to report that her dad touched her in "places that were nasty." Stephanie had been told that her father was sick but would receive the treatment he needed if she made the allegation. At age 12, she discovered that her father was imprisoned for child molestation. Stephanie subsequently died from a self-inflicted overdose of her mother's sleeping medication.

False allegations also can originate from misinterpretations, or over-interpretations, of young children's comments. While investigating Kelly Michaels, a former employee of the Wee Care Nursery School, in Maplewood, New Jersey, for example, investigators made insufficient efforts to consider alternative interpretations of children's spontaneous comments. A 4-year-old former student of Michaels was having his temperature taken rectally when he said to a nurse, "That's what my teacher does to me at nap time at school" (Rosenthal, 1995, p. 248). When he was asked to explain, he continued, "Her takes my temperature" (Ceci & Bruck, 1995, p. 12). Subsequent interviews of this boy and other children blossomed into a series of allegations, including charges that Michaels had raped the children with knives and other objects and licked peanut butter off their genitals. Kelly Michaels was convicted of 115 counts of sexual abuse and served 5 years in prison before the conviction was reversed by the Appeals Court of New Jersey. (See Rosenthal, 1995, for a brief description of this case, and other articles in the same volume for commentaries.)

Many clinicians believe that misinterpretations are more common than total fabrications even when there are family conflicts such as divorce or custody problems (Robin, 1991). Especially during the preschool period, children say things that can unsettle even the most well-intentioned parents, as illustrated by this anecdote from MacFarlane (1986):

> When a 4-year-old asked her mother to "lick her tushee," her mother became very alarmed and demanded to know where the child had done

---

[6]Everson and Boat (1989) asked child protective service (CPS) workers in North Carolina to identify cases in which a child or adolescent made an allegation that the worker believed was false. Common reasons for identifying an allegation as false were improbable, inconsistent, or recanted reports. In 59% of these cases, respondents concluded that the child or adolescent had deliberately fabricated in order to obtain secondary gains, such as changes in living arrangements, or to retaliate against a parent.

that before. When the child responded "at Daddy's house," the mother became too upset to ask further questions and proceeded to take legal action against the father. Meanwhile, the child kept asking to go to Daddy's house to get her tushee licked. After considerable furor and outrage on both sides, it was discovered, in the course of the evaluation, that the child *had* been engaging in sex play at her father's house but the perpetrator was actually his new puppy. Unbelievable as it seemed at first, the child's detailed description of the incidents (once she was finally encouraged to tell the whole story) were confirmed by direct observation of the child playing with the dog. (pp. 130–131; italics in the original)

False allegations also can develop when unscientific beliefs about the indicators of sexual abuse are combined with poor interviewing practices. One such case, typical of many that have been reported, was described by Wakefield and Underwager (1994a):

A seven-year-old boy was brought to us for therapy. He had trouble sleeping and was deathly frightened of two older boys who lived up the block. He didn't want to leave his mother or leave his home so he was school phobic. He had an acute anxiety attack every time he heard a siren or saw a police car. When he was four-and-one-half years old, during the bitter divorce of his parents, a day-care worker thought he was too aggressive in his play. He was playing by having cars crash together and TV characters fighting with swords. She had read lists of behavioral indicators of sexual abuse and thought the boy was showing signs of abuse, so she reported it. Two social workers came to the day-care center, interrogated the child using anatomical dolls, concluded he was abused, and took him into protective custody. When his mother came to pick him up that afternoon, she was told he had been taken away but nobody would tell her where. It took nine months before the child was returned, nine months during which he was repeatedly interrogated by social workers and police. He was physically examined three times, including, for example, having the physician stick two fingers up his anus while asking him if Mommy did this. He was in one children's hospital, two foster holding homes, and three treatment foster homes. When he was first returned to his mother, he didn't leave her side for three days. (pp. 12–13)

As Wakefield and Underwager concluded, "If adults make a mistake and treat nonabused children as if they had been abused, this is not innocuous or benign. It can amount to child abuse" (p. 13).

The fact that the number of undetected victims of abuse vastly exceeds the number of false allegations does not reduce the need to determine why it became difficult to assess sexual abuse in the 1980s. Understanding how problems develop can help professionals recognize features that are associated with false reports and suggest strategies for testing alternative explanations of alleged events. In this way, we can construct a more responsive and informed system for investigating all types of child maltreatment.

The Social Environment of the 1980s

Over the years, research on the causes of child maltreatment has focused less on parental psychopathology and more on broader social factors, such as societal attitudes and structures (Cicchetti & Carlson, 1991). This focus on social context also is useful for analyzing why concerns developed about investigative interviewing. Six factors are especially relevant: (a) the economic climate of the 1980s, (b) a revival of conservative politics in the media, (c) a therapeutic focus on childhood victimization, (d) the increased exposure of children to sexual material at a time when beliefs about the indicators of abuse were changing, (e) changing conceptions of sexual abuse, and (f) inattention to the differences between therapy and investigation when helping professionals were trained.

The Economic Climate of the 1980s

In the view of many critics, the 1980s represented a period of widespread economic violence against children. As described by Kevin Phillips in his provocative *The Politics of Rich and Poor* (1990), the decade of the 1980s was one of three major historical periods in which wealth was redistributed from one income bracket to another.[7] Between 1980 and 1989, for example, the combined salaries of people earning $1 million or more a year increased 2,184%, whereas those of people earning between $20,000 and $50,000 increased only 44% (Barlett & Steele, 1992). A gradual shrinking of the "working middle class" (Barlett & Steele, 1992, p. 4) left the United States with a gap between the lower and upper income brackets that was larger than that of any other industrial nation (Phillips, 1990). This trend had a direct effect on children in the United States: By 1991, the poverty rate had hit the highest level in 20 years while public assistance programs for poor children were being cut (Strawn, 1992). In 1991, 21.8% of U.S. children were living in poverty, with the rate being one out of every four for children under 6 years of age. Poverty rates for African American and Hispanic children were more than double those for European American children (Huston, 1994).

These economic trends correlated with increases in the number of single-parent households. As summarized by Hernandez (1994), "Studies

---

[7]The other two were the post–Civil War Gilded Age and the Roaring Twenties.

of divorce have shown that instability in husbands' work, declines in family income, and a low ratio of family income-to-needs lead to increased hostility between husbands and wives, decreased marital quality, and increased risk of divorce" (p. 9). Hernandez argued that each of the three economic recessions between 1970 and 1982 led to increases in the number of female-headed households, accounting for approximately 30% of the overall increase in the number of these families between 1968 and 1988. The number of children living without a father in the home almost tripled, from about 7% between 1940 and 1960 to 20% by 1990, and was projected to keep growing. Demographers estimated that approximately 80% of African American children would spend some time in a home with fewer than two parents (Hernandez, 1994).

Although controversy persists over the effects of poverty and single parenthood on child maltreatment (Coulton, Korbin, Su, & Chow, 1995), there is reason to expect that such stresses lead to increases in the number of reports. Reporting rates generally are higher for groups that are under the close scrutiny of public agencies, so that circumstances that place families under observation are likely to increase the detection of sexual abuse. In some locations, for example, investigators responding to complaints of physical abuse or neglect are required to ask children about sexual abuse as well.

Although economic hardship might have contributed to the rise in abuse and neglect reports, families across the economic spectrum have been affected by the increased divorce rate and the growing participation of mothers in the labor force (affecting from 10% of all children in 1940 to almost 60% by 1990; Hernandez, 1994). These changes meant that children were spending more time in the care of adults other than their biological parents, which increases both the risk of actual abuse as well as the likelihood that there will be concerns. Young children are much more likely to be physically or sexually abused when their families contain step-parents (Daly & Wilson, 1996; Finkelhor, Hotaling, Lewis, & Smith, 1990),[8] and reduced parental supervision is associated with an increased likelihood of sexual abuse outside the home (Finkelhor & Baron, 1986). Reflecting this reality, popular culture has long expressed fear about non-parental caregivers (Daly & Wilson, 1996), and media publicity about the link between societal changes and children's well-being probably has made parents increasingly vigilant about the possibility of abuse. Critics of investigative practices often mentioned multivictim day care cases or allegations in the context of divorce or custody conflicts, both enabled by

---

[8] In a review of physical violence against stepchildren, Daly and Wilson (1996) reviewed evidence that young children are seven times more likely to be abused in step-plus-genetic-parent homes than in homes with two genetic parents. Furthermore, fatality rates increase about 100-fold in stepparent homes.

recent changes in family structure and caregiving arrangements that cut across social classes.[9]

Conservative Politics in the Media

At a time when children were becoming increasingly dependent on single mothers for their economic support, economic progress for women was screeching to a halt. As summarized in Faludi's (1991) *Backlash: The Undeclared War Against American Women*, women in the 1980s were exposed to messages that celebrated their hard-won equality at a time when equality was far from achieved. Faludi's book is a depressing list of statistics on such aspects of female inequality as economic hardship, workplace discrimination, unequal representation in government and our courts of law, and gender inequities at home.

Women who were struggling to understand why their lives failed to match the expectations of the 1980s found little solace in the media. Most relevant to the crisis about sexual abuse was the constant attack on day care. As Faludi (1991) summarized, day care was referred to as the "Thalidomide of the 80's" (p. 42) and was the frequent target of headlines such as, "'MOMMY, DON'T LEAVE ME HERE!' THE DAY CARE PARENTS DON'T SEE. DAY CARE CAN BE DANGEROUS TO YOUR CHILD'S HEALTH. WHEN CHILD CARE BECOMES CHILD MOLESTING: IT HAPPENS MORE OFTEN THAN PARENTS LIKE TO THINK" (pp. 41–42). In 1984, *Newsweek* ran a feature article (Beck, 1984) on "an epidemic" of child abuse in day-care settings. Despite data showing that children were at much higher risk in their own homes than in alternate care settings (Finkelhor, Williams, & Burns, 1988), continued media coverage led vigilant parents and child care providers to discuss abuse with their children, and hundreds of thousands of children were exposed to sexual abuse prevention programs at school (Kohl, 1993). Although heightened awareness of sexual abuse was beneficial to the thousands of children who brought their victimization to the attention of an adult, rel-

---

[9]Many authors have noted how moral panics and resulting controversies often develop during periods of rapid social change. For example, Robin (1991) wrote an insightful essay on how American individualism favors solutions to social problems that focus on individual deviance rather than changes in the basic organization of society. Furthermore, he noted how changes in sexuality, sexual identity, and family roles threatened the traditional family and allowed child abuse to become "a convenient focus for public anxiety about changing social conditions related to the family" (p. 9). Similarly, Tavris (1992) argued that some women who became entangled in the "survivor" movement in the absence of prior concerns about their childhood identified with the sexual-victim culture because it provided "a lightning rod for the inchoate feelings of victimization they have as a result of their status in society at large. It provides a clearer focus than such vague enemies as 'the system,' sexism, deadening work, welfare, or boredom" (p. 321). These and other system-level critiques do not deny the reality of abuse or minimize its consequences. Rather, they attempt to understand the moral panic in recent decades that has fostered increased concerns about false allegations.

atively little concern was expressed about the risk that such publicity might foster false allegations.[10]

The media also were awash during the past decade with sensationalized accounts of ritualistic and satanic abuse. As with most examples of social hysteria, this coverage had its origins in real phenomena. Religion is sometimes used to justify physical abuse, sexual abuse, and medical neglect, and relationships with religious authorities provide opportunities for abuse to occur (Bottoms, Shaver, Goodman, & Qin, 1995). There also is no doubt that some perpetrators engage in abusive acts that involve religious or satanic symbols and activities. Despite the plethora of books, articles, and seminars designed to convince therapists that satanic cults exist, however, organized networks of satanic abusers were never documented (Bottoms & Davis, 1997; Nathan & Snedeker, 1995). Nonetheless, the intense publicity led many adults to accept such bizarre tales uncritically. Thus when young children described penetration by knives or claimed to have witnessed sacrifices in the absence of physical evidence, adults sometimes failed to consider that the children might have been influenced by sources of information other than personal experience. Instead, the children's comments seemed to increase the adults' confidence that abuse had occurred, leading to detailed questions that further escalated the severity of the allegations.

Therapeutic Focus on Childhood Victimization

During the past decades, the challenges women confronted fueled a market for pop psychology, self-help books written by professionals, and therapy by licensed professionals. In many of these forums, women's depression and anxiety were explained as consequences of individual personalities, decisions, or life experiences rather than as predictable responses to social and economic circumstances.

The tendency to attribute women's problems to their individual experiences is reflected in the intense controversy over repressed memories of childhood sexual abuse. Some of the women who flooded into therapy during the past decade for depression, anxiety, and relationship problems were told that their difficulties resembled those of women who had been

---

[10]During the 1980s, one of us (Debra Poole) attended a meeting to view a sexual abuse prevention film that was being reviewed for possible adoption by a local preschool. The film, with actors dressed in animal costumes, depicted a child who experienced fondling but was reinforced for informing an adult. Parents who attended the meeting voted not to adopt the film because they were concerned that children would learn about fondling from the film. Because fondling other children raises suspicions of abuse, the prevention program itself might have made it more difficult to distinguish between children who were abused outside the preschool and children who were simply modeling a behavior they had recently viewed. These concerns have serious legal parallels. In 1993, for example, the Supreme Court of Minnesota overturned a father's conviction for criminal sexual assault, concluding that the child had been improperly influenced by a highly suggestive abuse-prevention book (for a summary of that decision, see Ewing, 1994).

sexually abused. Clinicians sometimes used special techniques to help their clients recall abusive experiences—including hypnosis, dream interpretation, and guided imagery—under the assumption that the presumed abuse must be remembered before therapy could be successful. In one study, 25% of the doctoral-level therapists surveyed reported that (a) they sometimes concluded after only one session that clients who did not report abuse had in fact been abused as children, (b) abused clients needed to acknowledge or remember their abuse for therapy to be effective, and (c) they used two or more therapeutic techniques specifically to help clients remember childhood sexual abuse (Poole, Lindsay, Memon, & Bull, 1995). By their own estimates, these American and British therapists often were successful in retrieving memories of abuse. Extrapolation to the population of therapists from which the sample had been drawn suggested that during the 2-year period examined by the survey, hundreds of thousands of women were exposed to therapists who held such beliefs (see also Polusny & Follette, 1996).

Although people sometimes recall traumatic events they have not thought about for many years (Lindsay & Read, 1994; Read & Lindsay, 1997), there are startling differences between the typical profiles of abuse that always has been remembered and memories that are recovered following therapy (Wakefield & Underwager, 1994a), and this has fueled concern that some memories recovered in the course of therapy might be false. By 1992, the False Memory Syndrome Foundation was organized to address claims of false memories, and several critiques of repressed memory phenomena hit the bookstores (e.g., Loftus & Ketcham, 1994; Ofshe & Watters, 1994; Wright, 1994; Yapko, 1994).

Media publicity, combined with reliance by some therapists on potentially suggestive practices, drew support for a "social contagion" model of false allegations. For example, Coons (1994) tracked the frequency with which satanic ritual abuse was reported by patients at a dissociative disorders clinic: Reports were especially common in the 2 years after a televised Geraldo Rivera show on such abuse and during the year after a professional workshop on ritual abuse. In most cases, memories had been elicited using hypnosis (48%), dreamwork (34%), and regressive therapies (28%).

In summary, surveys of therapeutic practices suggest that increasing numbers of adults have been alerted to the possibility that they were abused as children, a social phenomenon that could have contributed to increased parental vigilance about the risks of abuse. Of course, awareness of child maltreatment does not necessarily lead to false allegations. Changes in family life and increased publicity about abuse were accompanied by a cultural milieu that bombarded young children with sexual information at the same time that it redefined standards of abuse. Together, these influences set the stage for social chaos.

Children's Exposure to Sexuality and "Indicators" of Abuse

Concern about undetected sexual abuse led practitioners and researchers to look for behavioral and emotional indicators to help them identify abused children. Throughout the 1980s, numerous so-called indicators of sexual abuse were reported, including behaviors frequently manifested by children who have not been abused (e.g., sleep problems and somatic complaints). Although evidence about indicators has been systematically challenged on the grounds that it is scientifically unfounded (see Poole & Lindsay, 1998, for a review), mandated reporters frequently were exposed to articles that cataloged unreliable methods for "identifying" abuse (e.g., see Riordan & Verdel, 1991, Table 1: "Indicators of Sexual Abuse in Human Figure Drawing").

Sexually abused children as a group do have more behavioral disorders than community controls (e.g., Dubowitz, Black, Harrington, & Verchoore, 1993) but fewer symptoms than children seen at clinics for other reasons (e.g., Cohen & Mannarino, 1988). Furthermore, parents of abused children often rate their children as more disturbed than do parents of nonabused children, although children's self-ratings do not show dramatic differences as a function of abuse status (Cohen & Mannarino, 1988; Elliott & Tarnowski, 1990). Throughout the literature, however, only one behavior consistently differentiates sexually abused from nonabused children: As a group, sexually abused children are unusually knowledgeable about sex and more often act out sexually (Friedrich, 1993; Friedrich et al., 1992; Slusser, 1995).

Coupled with a belief that nonabused children know little about adult sexual behavior, the findings on sexual behavior in abused children led practitioners to place great reliance on sexual acting out as an indicator of abuse. In fact, inappropriate sexual knowledge often prompted suspicions that precipitated investigations (Keary & Fitzpatrick, 1994; Sorensen & Snow, 1991). Assumptions about "normal" sexual knowledge were not entirely unwarranted, because children's tested knowledge of sexual behavior appears very limited (Gordon, Schroeder, & Abrams, 1990a, 1990b), but the frequency of sexual behavior in normative samples is nonetheless quite high. For example, after concluding that nonabused 2- to 7-year-olds did poorly when questioned about sexuality, Gordon et al. (1990a) noted that 28.5% of the parents admitted that these children had been exposed to sexually explicit materials such as R-rated movies, soap operas, or adult magazines, and 30% indicated that their children had engaged in exploratory sexual play. Similarly, 85% of the adults surveyed by Lamb and Coakley (1993) reported playing sexual games as children, with adults discovering these games approximately 44% of the time (most often through direct observation or physical evidence; e.g., pen marks around the genital area; see also Haugaard, 1996).

Despite the fact that sexual acting out is more common among abused than nonabused children, experts caution that the differences are too small to rely on sexual behavior alone when identifying abuse (Friedrich et al., 1992). The usefulness of sexual behavior as an indicator of abuse is limited by the fact that children today often are exposed to explicit sexual material, and exposure sometimes leads to increased sexual knowledge and behavior. For example, in a large-scale, community-based survey of 2- through 12-year-old children who had been screened to exclude those who could be identified as having a sexual abuse history, 3.6% to 5.8% of the children (depending on their age and sex) reportedly had drawn genitals on pictures during the past 6 months (Friedrich, Grambsch, Broughton, Kuiper, & Beilke, 1991), and their sexual behavior was significantly related to family experiences such as exposure to nudity or sexual intercourse (most often accidentally).

The increased focus on children's sexual behavior occurred at a time when changing standards regarding sex education and obscenity in the media increased children's exposure to sexually explicit materials. Parents were increasingly likely to endorse open attitudes about sex education and to speak frankly even with very young children, but sex education did not always include discussions about acceptable public displays of sexuality. One amusing example of how parental openness can translate into questionable behavior involved a preschool-aged girl who happily exclaimed to her mother, "Momma, I made the marbles disappear!" The child, who was allowed to watch her mother change tampons, had proudly experimented with a creative hiding place. This illustrates how the task of interpreting spontaneous behavior is complicated by the diversity of children's home environments and experiences.

Professionals might also be surprised by the information that children encounter at school, sometimes in formal presentations. In an article entitled "The Failure of Sex Education," Barbara Dafoe Whitehead (1994) described a sex education textbook aimed at kindergartners through third graders that follows the experiences of a fictional class of school children as they experience such life events as a teacher's pregnancy and a visit to a child's HIV-infected uncle. Excerpts from the book include quotes such as "A clitoris is a small sensitive part that only girls have, and it sometimes makes you feel good" (p. 60) and "To have sex, the man and the woman lie very close to each other so that their bodies are touching. Usually it happens in bed and they don't have any clothes on" (p. 60). Although few school districts adopted such explicit material, it is clear that cultural changes have made it impossible to assert what children should or should not know about sex.

Sexual content became increasingly prominent in the televised media as well. One content analysis of soap operas that aired during 1979, for example, found an average of 7 sexual behaviors per hour, with two of the most popular shows averaging 14 and 16 behaviors per hour. In this study, the most frequent categories involved talk about sex and erotic touching, although there were no explicit depictions of heterosexual intercourse, prostitution, or aggressive sexual contact (Lowry, Love, & Kirby, 1981). In a later content analysis of 1992–1993 prime-time shows that were popular with youngsters, Ward (1995) calculated that 29% of all interactions involved sexualized talk, with some shows averaging as high as 49%.

In summary, variability in parental openness about sexuality, increased discussion of sexuality in school, and sexual depictions in movies and television made it increasingly difficult to distinguish between typical and atypical sexual knowledge. Nonetheless, many books and articles have warned parents and professionals that inappropriate knowledge is a strong indicator of abuse, and these warnings undoubtedly increased the number of unwarranted suspicions.

The Changing Definition of Sexual Abuse

Just when the presentation of explicit sexual information was increasing, attitudes about permissible sexuality seemed to become more conservative. In a discussion of "antisexuality" in the child abuse system, for example, critics Wakefield and Underwager (1994a) described the conviction for sexual abuse of a man who had patted a boy on the buttocks during a bedtime kiss and a poll in which 20% of mental health and legal professionals responded that frequent hugging of a 10-year-old child by parents required intervention. Similarly, the labeling of young children as "perpetrators" for behavior that in the past would have been considered normal sexual exploratory play represented a new code of sexual ethics.

Conservative attitudes about sexuality were not encouraged by child developmentalists and pediatricians, who continued to show a great deal of tolerance for childhood sexual curiosity. For example, the 1976 edition of Spock's *Baby and Child Care* informed parents that "Babies in the last part of the first year discover their genitals the way they discover their fingers and toes, and handle them the same way, too" (p. 409). Of 3-, 4-, and 5-year-olds, Spock stated,

> They are interested in each other's bodies, occasionally have the desire to see and touch each other. This is one reason why they like to play doctor. If you realize that his early interest in sex is a natural part of the slow process of growing up and that it occurs to a degree in all wholesome children, you can take a sensible view of it. (p. 410)

Spock attributed excessive masturbation in 3-year-olds to worry about the differences between girls and boys, and casually discussed how, through peer pressure, even children between the ages of 6 years and puberty might become involved in sex play. He suggested gentle verbal tactics for inhibiting public exhibitions of sexuality, stating that "part of my discomfort would come from not wanting the neighbors to disapprove of my child" (p. 412). Likewise, child psychiatrists Chess and Hassibi (1986) began their discussion of sexual behavior in childhood with a reference to penile erections in infancy, further noting that approximately 50% of the children between the ages of 2 and 5 years engage in genital manipulation. They described sexual games as "quite common" among young children and explained how adult disapproval, rather than loss of interest, was primarily responsible for the apparent disappearance of overt sexual expression by the school years. Citing a 1943 study, however, Chess and Hassibi indicated that the frequency of masturbation and heterosexual interest and play all *increase* gradually between the ages of 7 and 13 years. In distinguishing between normal and abnormal play, these authors advised, "Although there is no rule by which the normal frequency can be judged, a child who engages in repeated daily autostimulation or prefers sexual games to all other activities is in need of a psychiatric evaluation" (p. 240).

Despite the fact that normative sexual experiences are covered in most introductory books on life-span development and adolescence, discrepancies exist between the beliefs of some professionals and the realities of children's lives. For example, one recent evaluation of an alleged sexual offender mentioned that he had experienced an incident of same-sex fondling as a teenager, a fact the evaluator presumably felt was relevant for estimating the likelihood that the alleged offender was guilty. Same-sex experiences are more common than the evaluator might have realized, however. In a recent national survey, 9% of male respondents reported having had sex with a man at least once since puberty (Michael, Gagnon, Laumann, & Kolata, 1994), 13% of male respondents in another prominent survey reported childhood sexual experiences with a male that they considered abusive (Finkelhor, Hotaling, Lewis, & Smith, 1990), and textbooks on adolescence state that it is not unusual for teens to engage in homosexual experimentation (e.g., Santrock, 1993; see Laumann, Gagnon, Michael, and Michaels, 1994, for additional data on sexual touching experiences during childhood).[11] It is clear that societal standards do not

[11]Rates of homosexual experimentation were higher in Kinsey, Pomeroy, and Martin's (1948) earlier data. For example, these authors reported that more than 20% of adolescent boys disclosed a same-sex experience leading to orgasm by age 16. Critics have noted that Kinsey's sampling procedures overrepresented groups that engage in higher rates of homosexual activity (e.g., volunteers from prisons and reform schools), but they also have acknowledged that Kinsey's interviewing practices might have encouraged disclosures more effectively than the recent structured surveys (e.g., Laumann et al., 1994). Methodological questions notwithstanding, professionals who have not read the book by Kinsey et al. (1948) will find it enormously rich and illuminating. About sexual experiences with peers, for example, Kinsey et al. pointed out,

On a specific calculation of our data, it may be stated that at least 85 per cent of the younger male population could be convicted as sex offenders if law enforcement officials were as efficient as most people expect them to be. The stray boy who is caught and brought before a court may not be different from most of his fellows, but the public, not knowing of the near universality of adolescent sexual activity, heaps the penalty for the whole group upon the shoulders of the one boy who happens to be apprehended. This situation presents a considerable dilemma for law enforcement officials and for students of the social organization as a whole. (p. 224)

always reflect awareness of how common sexual activity and experimentation by children really is. As a result, professionals sometimes have reacted with undue alarm to children's sexual behavior.

Coordination Between Training and Responsibilities in the Helping Professions

Professionals who investigate child abuse should collect data that help them distinguish between abused and nonabused children, but many professionals who become involved in legal proceedings (such as clinical psychologists or physicians) were trained to treat victims rather than to identify them. In a provocative essay, Dawes (1996; used with permission) noted that many professionals testify about the characteristics of abused children on the basis of their experience but report that they have little or no experience with children who were not abused but who at some point claimed to have been. According to Dawes, such statements "should automatically *disqualify* them as having any experienced-based expertise in the matter of most urgent interest to the court, which is the rational determination of whether or not the child has been abused as claimed" (pp. 6–7).

In addition, many of the professionals who report or investigate abuse do not have sufficient training in child development, child abuse, memory functions, or interviewing (Feld, 1994; Robin, 1991). According to Robin (1991), qualified child protective services (CPS) staff often quit because the working conditions are too difficult, and high staff turnover has hampered efforts to provide sufficient training.

How might inadequate training have contributed to controversies about child abuse assessments? Consider the many professional publications that offer advice on how to identify abuse, using such "symptoms" as "fear of doctor's office and/or shots," "fear of dying," "nightmares," and "fear of small places or closets" (San Diego County Grand Jury, 1994, p. 18). Basic training in diagnostic decision making would have made it clear that characteristics such as these, which are typical of most children, do not help to discriminate between abused and nonabused children. Likewise, misuse of the child sexual abuse accommodation syndrome (Summit, 1983) and other syndrome evidence also arose when descriptions of various clinical populations were treated as lists of features that could discriminate clinical from nonclinical groups (Poole & Lindsay, 1998). Furthermore, because sexually abused children sometimes retract their allegations, retraction has been identified by some professionals as *proof* that the original allegation was true. As one critic commented, "There is something fundamentally strange about saying that since the child denies that the event occurred, it must have occurred" (cited in Myers, 1987, p. 158). Such lapses in logic led critics to charge that interviewers were biased toward collecting data that would confirm abuse rather than also seeking information that potentially could disconfirm abuse.

Unfortunately, we still do not know enough about the characteristics of true and false allegations to draft clear guidelines on how professionals should evaluate the information they obtain or how they should modify interviewing strategies to accommodate differences among children. Because critical research is still being conducted (and society will continually pose new challenges), it is especially important that professionals learn how to interpret research findings so that they can update their decision-making strategies. Chapters 7 and 8 have been written with this goal in mind.

Summary

Interviewing strategies and techniques became controversial at a time when adults were increasingly attentive to the possibility of abuse. Many of the children who were interviewed had not made explicit reports of sexual abuse but were instead evaluated because their behaviors or comments raised suspicions, because they had been in contact with potential abusers, or because they were considered "at risk" because physical abuse or neglect had been alleged. The task of distinguishing between abused and nonabused children was complicated by a variety of factors that were beyond the control of investigative interviewers, including the increased exposure of children to sexual information, increases in the number of caretaking environments in which abuse might have occurred, and the possibility that conversations with concerned adults—primed by media coverage or their own life experiences—might have influenced or contaminated the children's accounts. Research on the impact of social influences, and the corresponding interviewing guidelines, reflect efforts to determine how such experiences might influence children's answers to questions about abuse.

IMPLICATIONS FOR INTERVIEWING

Society's awareness of abuse and the legal obligations of helping professionals to respond to abuse have both changed rapidly in the last few decades. The history of child maltreatment, however, reminds us that the concept of abuse is "a product of social negotiation between individual values and beliefs, social norms, and professional knowledge about children, child development, and family relationships" (Robin, 1991, p. 3). In recent years, society has been renegotiating basic expectations about how professionals should adapt to changing values, scientific knowledge, and family relationships. The emerging consensus involves two major themes.

First, helping professionals need to ask whether other factors could plausibly explain the apparent symptoms of abuse, perhaps beginning this investigation by considering *who* reported the abuse and *why*. For example, sexual acting out by a child should raise questions about the context and frequency of the behavior, and about possible exposure to sexual information. Likewise, when a report is based on an alarming comment by a child, helping professionals should consider whether the comment might have an innocent explanation. In practice, the extent to which individuals can appropriately collect such information is a function of their professional roles. Mandated reporters such as teachers or therapists, for example, should not assume an investigative role, but it is not inconsistent with their roles to ask for clarifying information (see Kalichman, 1993, for a thorough review of ethics, law, and policy regarding mandated reporting).

Second, professionals should collect information from children in ways that minimize distortion attributable to the interview itself. To help identify these influences, researchers have studied children's eyewitness accuracy under various conditions. The results of these studies, which provide the foundation for interview protocols, are the focus of the next chapter.

2

STRENGTHS AND WEAKNESSES OF CHILDREN AS WITNESSES: IMPLICATIONS FOR DEVELOPMENTALLY SENSITIVE INTERVIEWING

Lin: Bret, did you make lemonade?

Bret: No.

Lin: [Silence]

Bret: Lin, we're playing child testimony. You have to keep asking me, "Did you make lemonade?"

Lin: Did you make lemonade?

Bret: No.[1]

The conversation above illustrates that children have a tremendous capacity to monitor the activities and ideas of significant adults in their lives. However, this talent for mimicking adults raises serious questions about their ability to provide independent testimony on matters relevant to the courts. In the early 1900s, some psychologists portrayed children as the most "dangerous of all witnesses" because they were often influenced by social pressures and suggestion (Baginsky, cited by Goodman, 1984). By the 1980s a burgeoning awareness of physical and sexual abuse had prompted researchers to adopt more optimistic views of children's testimony. In a new generation of studies, researchers found that children were often very accurate when describing personally experienced events and that they resisted adult suggestions under many circumstances (e.g., Saywitz, Goodman, Nicholas, & Moan, 1991; Tobey & Goodman, 1992). It is now

---

[1]Conversation between Lin, age 11, and Bret, age 13, overheard August 15, 1995, 1 year after their mother had completed a series of papers on question repetition and children's eyewitness testimony. Used with the children's permission.

apparent that accuracy varies enormously, depending on the cognitive demands of the situation, including the characteristics of the events in question (such as how long ago they took place) and the circumstances surrounding their recall (such as whether the interviewer uses questions that children understand). Accuracy also depends on emotional and social factors, such as children's motivation to tell the truth and to please the interviewer.

Of course, it is not very helpful to conclude that children can be both highly accurate and wildly inaccurate in describing their experiences unless we can specify the conditions that are associated with reliable as opposed to unreliable testimony. To date, the most startling demonstrations of false reporting have involved children who were exposed to repeated misleading suggestions outside the interview environment or to highly suggestive interviews (e.g., Bruck, Ceci, Francoeur, & Renick, 1995; Garven, Wood, Malpass, & Shaw, in press; Poole & Lindsay, 1995). These findings have led some experts to argue that "adults are greater sources of distortion than any underlying deficits in children's cognitive capabilities" (McGough, 1996). As Michael Lamb and his colleagues (1995) concluded,

> The demonstrable fact that investigative interviews with young children can be rendered worthless by inept practice should not blind us to the substantial literature demonstrating that reliable information can be elicited from young children who are competently interviewed. ... This emphasis reflects our firm belief that the informativeness of interviews with child victims is strongly influenced by the skill and expertise of the interviewer and that interviewer characteristics, unlike the characteristics and abilities of the child, can be (and must be) improved. (p. 446)

The capacity of adults to elicit accurate accounts from children depends in large part on the extent to which they understand children's abilities and limitations. Appreciating children's strengths and weaknesses requires knowledge about when children develop the fundamental skills they need to report autobiographical events during an interview and knowing how children's accounts can be influenced by interviewers' behaviors and questioning styles. Regarding the development of fundamental skills, we describe developmental trends in attention, conversational remembering, and memory source monitoring in the first section of this chapter. Because some jurisdictions require investigative interviewers to instruct children about the need to tell the truth, we also briefly discuss research on children's understanding of truth and lies. In the second section we review research on eyewitness testimony. These studies have charted children's performance as a function of their age, the type of information requested, the interviewing methods, and children's exposure to misinformation outside the interview setting. Research on the development of basic skills and eyewitness testimony has motivated psychologists, legal professionals, and child protection specialists to recommend a variety of general guidelines that we introduce in this chapter and discuss more fully in subsequent chapters.

FUNDAMENTAL SKILLS FOR REPORTING
AUTOBIOGRAPHICAL EVENTS

An understanding of developmental trends in attention, memory, concept formation, and language can help interviewers appreciate why particular interview environments, questions, and assessment aids affect children differently, depending on their age. Most of these topics are discussed in this chapter, but two are sufficiently complex that they are discussed in Part 3 ("Customizing Interviews"). Specifically, knowledge of language development is necessary when formulating questions during an interview, and this topic is considered in chapter 5. Because the ability to understand representations affects the validity of information obtained using ancillary aids such as dolls and drawings, this topic is considered in chapter 6. Other developmental trends that broadly affect children's performance during an interview are discussed here.

The Development of Attention

To report events accurately, children first must attend to important features of the target events. During later interviews, they must attend to interviewers' instructions and questions. Remarkably, there is no evidence that young children are less aware of their surroundings than older children or adults; in fact, general alertness does not change much after the first few months of life (Gibson & Radner, 1979). Children *do* become better at focusing on information that allows them to achieve specific goals, however, and thus attentional development involves the coordination of perception with specific tasks or goals.

A visit to any school room is sufficient to demonstrate that young children are easily distracted by stimuli that adults consider irrelevant. Developmental deficits in selective attention also are readily apparent in the laboratory. In the "incidental learning" paradigm, for example, children are shown pairs of pictures and are instructed to learn one member of each pair but ignore the other. As expected, young children recall fewer of the target pictures than older children or adults do, although they often recall as many or more of the distracter stimuli (Bjorklund & Harnishfeger, 1995; Hagen & Hale, 1973; Lane & Pearson, 1982). Despite clear instructions from adults, young children's performance often suffers because their attention frequently shifts to information that cannot help them accomplish the task at hand.

Both biological maturation and prior experiences affect the extent to which children attend to task-irrelevant stimuli. One reason that young children have difficulty inhibiting unproductive behavior is that part of the brain called the *prefrontal cortex* is not fully developed. The prefrontal cortex is one of the last regions of the brain to develop in humans (Luria, 1973), with a developmental spurt between birth and 2 years of age and another between approximately 4 and 7 years, followed by gradual growth into young adulthood (see Bjorklund & Harnishfeger, 1995, for a review). Young children, like adults or animals with damage to this region, show a variety of problems associated with failures to inhibit or suppress behavior, including perseverance of prior responses that are no longer relevant and difficulty inhibiting actions to irrelevant stimuli. Neurological development is thus one of the reasons why children show dramatic improvements in their ability to sustain attention and focus on instructions from adults at approximately 6–7 years of age (Paris & Lindauer, 1982).

Despite their neurological immaturity, children show amazing persistence when they are engrossed in activities that interest them. As with most areas of cognitive development, performance on attentional tasks is highly "domain specific," or dependent on children's understanding of the task and materials (Ceci, 1996). Some psychologists have studied the relationship between children's knowledge and their attentional strategies by observing them during familiar tasks such as watching television, for example, and these studies have shown that even preschool children successfully divide attention between television and ongoing play by monitoring soundtrack features that signal topic changes. Their strategies are much less sophisticated when they are not familiar with the content, however, and therefore children's attention declines considerably when the televised dialogue is too advanced (Anderson, Alwitt, Lorch, & Levin, 1979; Anderson, Lorch, Field, Collins, & Nathan, 1986; Anderson, Lorch, Field, & Sanders, 1981).

Research on attentional development suggests several strategies for improving children's performance during investigative interviews. First, interviewers need to modify the environment to minimize distractions and help focus children's attention. Cluttered play rooms designed for therapy or diagnostic observation are not appropriate for investigative interviews because they are overly distracting. As described in chapter 4, interviewing rooms should be cheerful and nonthreatening but simple and uncluttered. Second, because young children tend to be interested in any particular conversation for only a short period of time, interviewers should carefully review their goals before the interview begins. Although they may want to undertake lengthy developmental assessments of preschool children, for example, interviewers need to weigh the value of the information gained against the fact that their conversational partners will rapidly lose interest in talking with them. Because assessments may be obtained at the expense of the investigative interview, interviewers should consider devoting separate sessions to developmental assessments of very young or special-needs children unless critical assessment questions can be integrated quickly into early phases of the investigative interview.

Finally, the relationship between language comprehension and attention suggests that children might attend better when they have a better understanding of the interview process. This is one reason why current guidelines (such as those described in chaps. 3 and 4) instruct interviewers to introduce themselves, their roles, and the rules for the interview itself as clearly as possible (Lamb et al., 1995; Steward, Bussey, Goodman, & Saywitz, 1993). Because inattentiveness can indicate a lack of understanding, interviewers need to reiterate the purpose of their questions and state them more simply when children appear to be drifting off task.

To summarize, research on the development of attention explains why it is more challenging to interview young children but suggests that even young preschoolers can be interviewed successfully if their needs are taken into account. Unfortunately, there is insufficient research on how the ability to sustain attention actually varies as a function of the interview environment and the interviewer's initial instructions. Many interviewers resist removing toys or activities from interview rooms on the grounds that it is easier for children to disclose when they can shift their attention to other tasks. Although this might be a useful strategy for some older children, extraneous activities such as coloring might be counterproductive for younger children. Unfortunately, we do not yet know how to balance the need to keep children task-oriented with the need to reduce their levels of stress. In an innovative study, Steward, Farquhar, Driskill, and Steward (1996) developed a computer-assisted interview procedure to reduce the emotional impact of disclosing to strange adults while helping children attend to the interviewers' questions. Computer-assisted interviews led 3- to 6-year-old children to look at the interview material more, look at other objects in the room less, and manipulate other objects in the room less than children interviewed with the assistance of anatomical drawings. According to Steward et al., computer-assisted interviews might also help less experienced interviewers maintain confidence and assist in data recording. Because children are increasingly familiar with computer technology, such techniques represent exciting innovations that deserve further study.

Developmental Trends in Conversational Remembering

In recent years, researchers have acknowledged what parents have known for years: As soon as children begin to chatter, they discuss past experiences. For example, 2½-year-olds not only talk about significant family events, they can recall some of these events as much as 14 months later (Fivush & Hamond, 1990). Even children below 2 years of age are sensitive to the temporal and causal relationships in event sequences, indicating that they remember events as organized wholes (Bauer & Mandler, 1990). Moreover, the delayed reports of very young children can be forensically meaningful, as illustrated by one 3½-year-old who testified 6½ months after an abduction experience (Jones & Krugman, 1986). Despite these impressive demonstrations of event memory, however, there are important differences between the autobiographical reports of preschool children and the reports of school-aged children. These differences probably reflect developmental differences in a variety of processes, including attention, forgetting, and children's understanding of conversational rules and conventions.

First, younger children have more difficulty than older children or adults in recognizing what event is under discussion. In a telling example, Steward and Steward (1996) described how difficult it was to get 3- to 6-year-olds to begin talking about a medical examination when interviewers did not explicitly ask about the visit itself:

> To parallel investigative interviewing strategies (Myers, 1992) and avoid unduly influencing the children with leading questions (Ceci & Bruck, 1993, 1995), our interviewers opened with a broad invitation to children to tell us "What did you do today? What has happened to you?" During the initial interview, children had a hard time understanding just what it was that we wanted them to talk about, an observation also made by Fivush and Shukat (1995) when they offered no prompts or cues beyond general open-ended questions. Only 26.9% of the children began immediately to tell us about the medical visit. Many children began with details of breakfast and preparation for school, while a few children began their narrative even further back in time with descriptions of their bedtime rituals the night before. ... A second prompt, "What else happened to you today?" brought another 10.8% on board. It wasn't until the third, very direct question, "Did you visit the doctor today?" that the majority of children understood what the topic of conversation was to be. In response to the direct question, seven children denied that they had visited the doctor, notwithstanding that the fact that they were still on the grounds of the medical center obviously contradicted their statements. (p. 119)

Preschool children sometimes remain off topic even when they are cued with specific prompts such as, "I'm going to ask now about what happened when you were playing in the science room" (Poole & Lindsay, 1995, 1996), and therefore interviewers cannot assume that young children are "on board" even when their answers seem to make sense. For example, only about half of the preschoolers in one study were able to report any information at all about an event they had previously discussed with an adult, but half of the children who "missed" the target began a discussion about a related event (e.g., a different party event; Fivush & Shukat, 1995). Although many children who are involved in ongoing sexual abuse investigations know why they are being interviewed and respond immediately to open-ended prompts (Sternberg et al., 1997), these studies illustrate why interviewers might have difficulty focusing children's attention on the target topic: Young children are not adept at inferring adults' intents, and they sometimes answer general questions in ways that can cause their responses to be misinterpreted.

Second, even when children begin talking about target events, they often shift focus as questioning continues. After a series of questions about a play session with "Mr. Science," for example, interviewers in one study delivered the final prompt, "Think about what you told me. Is there something you didn't tell me that you can tell me now?" (Poole & Lindsay, 1996). Inexplicably, the children did not always assume that this question referred to the play session that was the focus of the four previous questions. Instead, some children began talking about family events or other unrelated issues, apparently returning to the casual conversation that had characterized earlier rapport building. The following dialogue between an interviewer (I) and an 8-year-old boy (C), taken from laboratory transcripts, illustrates this phenomenon:

> I: I am going to ask now about what happened today in the science room. Start with the first thing that happened and tell me everything you can, even things you don't think are very important. But don't guess or make anything up. Just tell me what you saw or heard or did in the science room, so I will know about them, too.

> C: First we had this balloon filled with baking soda and the balloon blowed up.

> I: Can you tell me more so that I will know all about what happened in the science room, too?

> C: We had these tubes and put this, I don't know what it was, drainer that we had on the tubes and we had to listen to each other.

> I: Sometimes we remember a lot about how things looked. Think about all of the things that were in the science room. Tell me how everything looked.

> C: The balloon was red and the two drainers were red and blue, and we had a Coca-Cola can that we were doing with the balloons.

> I: Sometimes we remember a lot about sounds or things that people said. Tell me about all of the things you heard in the science room.

> C: I heard fuzz when we were doing the balloons. And when we were doing the tubes, I heard Mr. Science talking.

> I: Think about what you told me. Is there something you didn't tell me that you can tell me now?

C: We have two dogs and two cats in our family, and we used to have a fish, but it died.

Children who deviated from the established topic to answer this final prompt often gave no warning that they were addressing a different subject, as illustrated by this comment from a 4-year-old:

C: Well, I touched Sophie and I thought I could make my cold disappear if I, I thought somebody was dead back there. Some of our cats. I touched one of my cats and all the fuzz come off their, off their back and their, off of their head and if it's, if it was trick or treat time I would be the little fairy. But if it's not trick or treat time I cannot be a little fairy.

Topic drifts such as this one can have serious implications in forensic contexts, leading to bizarre interpretations of the child's experiences or even false accusations of other adults who happen to be mentioned. Topic drift might also lead adults to consider the child an unreliable witness. Interviewers therefore must be especially careful to ensure that children start, and stay, on topic. A simple strategy is to reword ambiguous prompts (e.g., "Can you tell me more?") into topic-focused prompts (e.g., "Can you tell me more about that time at the cottage?").

Third, young children provide less information about events than do older children, so they often require retrieval cues, such as specific questions (e.g., "Where did that happen?"), to flesh out a narrative that adults consider complete. This is problematic because, as discussed later in this chapter, specific cues often dramatically increase the amount of inaccurate information that children report. Despite the relative lack of detail in their reports, however, even preschoolers nonetheless recall a wide variety of information about actions, objects, appearance, locations, and even internal states, and their autobiographical narratives can be coherent, with information that orients events temporally and spatially. Although young children's narratives are "not exactly stellar stories," their reports of meaningful events make sense to adults (Fivush & Shukat, 1995, p. 14). As children develop, their narratives become increasingly complex and coherent (Fivush, Haden, & Adam, 1995).

Fourth, repeated accounts of the same events tend to be less consistent when provided by younger than by older children, because younger children are more likely to address different topics in different interviews. For example, Fivush and Shukat (1995) arranged for children to talk about significant events (as defined by the parents) when they averaged 3 years 4 months, 3 years 10 months, 4 years 10 months, and 5 years 10 months of age. An interviewer asked each child about three events in the second through fourth interviews, one of which was discussed during the previous interview. Content analyses of the children's narratives surprisingly revealed no decrease across sessions in either the total amount of information or the amount of descriptive information recalled, even after a 1-year delay.

The children reported different pieces of information across sessions, however, recalling less than 10% of their information during each of two consecutive sessions. This pattern of session-to-session inconsistency is a well-documented pattern. Fivush and Hamond (1990) likewise found that 2½-year-olds recalled less than 20% of the information in each of two interviews, spaced 14 months apart, although parents judged that 90% of what they recalled was accurate (for a discussion of this phenomenon, see Fivush & Schwarzmueller, 1995).

In contrast to conversational-remembering studies, in which session-to-session variability in information did not seem to predict inaccuracy, studies of recall for events that were staged by an investigator have found that information reported for the first time during a second interview is less accurate on average than information recalled in the first interview as well. For example, Salmon and Pipe (1997) found that 97% of the information children recalled after both a 3-day and a 1-year delay was accurate, compared with only 54% of the information that was unique to the 1-year delay, and a similar pattern was obtained in another study (i.e., 95% vs. 51%; Salmon & Pipe, 1998). Reminiscences (i.e., new information) in eyewitness studies may be less accurate than experiences reported in studies of conversational remembering because the target experiences were less memorable or because the interviewers in laboratory studies prompted children for details. Nevertheless, both types of studies show that information is not necessarily unreliable simply because it was not mentioned earlier.

Fifth, children as young as 2 years of age sometimes retain information about specific events for more than 1 year, but the fact remains that few older children or adults have any memory of events that occurred before their third birthdays, and some individuals remember little that happened before the age of 8 years (Nelson, 1990). Although there is no consensus about why early memories are not recalled later in development (e.g., Bauer & Wewerka, 1995; Howe & Courage, 1993), memory researchers generally are suspicious of "memories" that predate an individual's third birthday. Anecdotal claims by people recalling very early events often can be traced to conversations about these events or other reminders, and these early memories are especially prone to errors. The fact that early memories tend not to "survive the transition" from infancy to early childhood (Bauer & Wewerka, 1995), however, does not mean that some events experienced at 3 to 4 years of age are not recalled after 2 or 3 years (Fivush, Haden, & Adam, 1995) and occasionally much later (Pillemer, Picariello, & Pruett, 1994). Still, as a general rule young children tend not to recall specific events unless they are reminded of them within a particular window of time (Rovee-Collier, 1995), and for this reason the richest descriptions of personal events often are provided by children whose parents chat with them about their experiences (Reese, Haden, & Fivush, 1993).

In summary, young children can display impressive autobiographical memories, but they are more likely to require specific cues before they begin discussing target events, and they are more likely than older children to drift off topic during conversations. They also relate less information about events and tend to include different details in separate conversations about the same events. These characteristics of children's narratives have motivated a number of specific interviewing recommendations that we discuss in chapters 4 and 5, such as using rapport-building techniques that encourage longer narratives from children, marking topics explicitly in questions (e.g., "Where were you when he touched you?" rather than "Where were you?"), and asking questions to ensure that children are on topic.

To capitalize on children's strengths, it also is useful to distinguish between recall for specific or one-time events and recall for scripted events. A script is simply a generic description of a repeated event, such as a general description of "going to the grocery store" or "getting ready in the morning." Both children and adults recall repeated events in much the same way, with information temporally and causally connected (Bauer & Fivush, 1992). This is why it can be useful to ask children script questions such as "Tell me what usually happens when Sam gives you a bath" or "Tell me what usually happens when Mommy is mad at you." One problem with repeated events, however, is that information about specific episodes may be lost once a script is formed. For example, because adults park their cars at work in about the same place every day, they often cannot remember exactly where they parked on any particular day. Young children seem to have more difficulty than older children isolating specific examples of repeated events (Farrar & Goodman, 1990; Powell & Thomson, 1996, 1997a). Once a script has been formed, however, children often remember exceptions or details that are atypical (e.g., the shop was out of orange juice; Hudson, 1988; Hudson, Fivush, & Kuebli, 1992). The distinction between memory for a specific event and memory for repeated events is an important one for investigative interviewers, because expectations about anchoring specific incidents in time and space are relaxed in some jurisdictions when young children claim that abuse was repeated over a long period of time. In these cases, script-format questions *may* elicit longer narratives from children than questions about individual events, although researchers have not yet directly compared the quality of children's answers with script-based and temporally specific questions in forensic contexts. (See Powell, Thomson, & Dietze, 1997, for recommendations about how interviewers should probe for information about repeated events.)

Memory Source Monitoring

Source monitoring—the process of identifying the origin of one's knowledge or event memories—is an aspect of memory that is especially important for understanding how children's accounts can be contaminated by interactions with other children or adults. Source monitoring is involved in deciding whether John or Michael told you a joke, whether you attended a concert or only watched it on television, and whether you really turned off the stove or only planned to do so. Faulty source monitoring could lead children to report that they experienced events or saw objects that they had only heard about from an adult, saw on television, or imagined.

Adults are more likely to make source-monitoring errors when the sources are highly similar to one another, when memory information is less complete, or when decisions are made rapidly and without deliberation (Johnson, Hashtroudi, & Lindsay, 1993). Children are likewise more apt to confuse memories when the discrimination between possible sources is difficult because the sources are similar or the memory traces have degraded (Lindsay, Johnson, & Kwon, 1991). In one study, for example, 9-year-olds had more difficulty than adults in remembering whether they had actually performed an action or only imagined themselves doing so, but even 6-year-olds were as accurate as adults in indicating which of two persons had performed a particular action (Foley & Johnson, 1985). In another study, kindergartners and fourth graders made more source identification errors when 2 weeks had transpired between presentation and testing than when they were tested immediately (Parker, 1995).

Although the source-monitoring accuracy of children and adults varies across situations, young children are more likely than older children and adults to have difficulty in determining whether they had obtained information from their own experiences or from other sources.[2] Recent demonstrations of this limitation in preschool children are striking. In one study, for example, 4- and 5-year-olds were exposed to novel and familiar facts and then, only minutes later, asked to identify the information they had learned in the experimental setting (Taylor, Esbensen, & Bennett, 1994). Four-year-olds in particular tended to say that they always knew what they had just learned. Likewise, 3-year-olds who learned about the contents of a drawer visually, by verbal instruction, or by inference were very inaccurate in reporting the source of their knowledge (Gopnik & Graf, 1988).

Why are young preschoolers especially challenged by tasks that require them to indicate the source of their knowledge? Schacter, Kagan, and Leichtman (1995) suggested that immature frontal lobe development—a

---

[2]Developmental improvements in source monitoring are not simply artifacts of changes in response biases or general improvements in memory for the target events themselves. For example, Parker (1995) noted that source discrimination scores generally did not correlate with old/new recognition judgments, meaning that the ability to remember events did not predict children's ability to remember the source of events they did remember. Similarly, Poole and Lindsay (1997) found that source monitoring scores significantly predicted suggestibility even after individual differences in recall and acquiescence (i.e., the tendency to say "yes") were partialled out statistically. Furthermore, patterns of responses to source questions indicate that response bias is not a likely explanation for age-related improvements in source monitoring (e.g., Ackil & Zaragoza, 1995; Poole & Lindsay, 1997).

neurological mechanism we mentioned earlier with regard to attentional development—may explain why source-monitoring errors occur so commonly at this age. As with attentional development, however, neurological changes alone cannot fully explain children's source-monitoring performance, because the frequency of errors is dependent on the type of questions adults ask. For example, Roberts and Blades (1996) found that 4-year-olds who had witnessed one event and saw another event on television were as accurate as 10-year-olds and adults in their initial recall of the events, but the preschoolers more often confused events when the interviewer asked specific questions. Other researchers also have documented that children are more likely to intrude information from the wrong source when adults ask closed questions (e.g., "Did he . . .") rather than open-ended questions (e.g., "Tell me what happened;" Poole & Lindsay, 1995, 1996).

Although 3- and 4-year-olds are especially poor at source monitoring, this skill continues to develop during the elementary-school years. Brainerd and Reyna (1996), for example, asked kindergartners and third graders to learn a list of words and then tested their memory with two recognition tests. For each test, the children indicated whether the test words had been studied. On the final test, kindergartners were more likely than third graders to say that they had previously studied words that had appeared only in the prior memory test. Furthermore, when Ackil and Zaragoza (1995) exposed children and adults to misleading interview questions, even some adults came to believe that they had actually *seen* the suggested information, but first graders made more source errors than did third and fifth graders, who in turn made more errors than college students. Similarly, Poole and Lindsay (1996) arranged for parents to read stories that described some events their children had experienced as well as some novel events. After an initial interview, interviewers acknowledged the existence of the misleading story and asked children to report which events had really happened. Source monitoring improved between 3 and 8 years of age, but as we describe later in this chapter, even some older children reported entire events that never occurred, including two events that involved touching.

Overall, research on source monitoring explains why children might come to believe they actually experienced events that were only described by their parents or mentioned by interviewers. Interview protocols therefore caution interviewers not to mention specific names, objects, or actions *before* children have mentioned the information. Children who erroneously report information from the wrong source sometimes can reconstruct what they actually experienced when interviewers explicitly ask them to do so, but this ability is limited at ages 3 and 4 years (Lindsay, Gonzales, & Eso, 1995; Poole & Lindsay, 1996). Older children who remember the source of their knowledge may still describe events they only heard about from adults because they view the interview as an opportunity to demonstrate their knowledge, and therefore interviewers need to take special care to clarify the purpose of their questions.

Researchers have yet to determine how interviewers should ask children about the source of their knowledge. Laboratory research has not shed much light on this issue, because the set of possible sources is known in studies, and therefore researchers have simply asked children to distinguish between two or more predetermined sources (e.g., "Did the girl touch her nose or did you imagine the girl touching her nose?"). Investigative interviewers, of course, do not have such knowledge. When interviewers have reason to suspect that an adult only told the child about an event, they sometimes ask whether the target event "really" happened. A possible problem with this approach is illustrated by an anecdote reported to us by an investigator interviewer. A young girl, when asked whether the events she reported had "really" happened, replied "yes." Then, after a pause, she added, "Mommy told me." For children, evidently, information obtained from parents and other sources is "real," and therefore references to "what really happened" do not always prompt the distinction between information obtained by personal experience and information that was only heard. It is difficult to rephrase such questions, however, because many young children have not yet mastered the distinctions among mental verbs such as *remember, know,* and *guess* (Abbeduto & Rosenberg, 1985; Johnson & Wellman, 1980). Other possible strategies also are problematic. For example, questions such as "Did anybody tell you to say that . . . ?" are problematic because parents of victims often instruct them to be cooperative during the interview and "Just tell everything that happened." Consequently, a "yes" response to such questions is not very informative and may discredit a child unjustly. Researchers currently are attempting to develop practical source-monitoring procedures, but for the time being we cannot say which questions might work best for children of various age groups.

Understanding Truth and Lies

Some states in the United States retain the competency *voir dire,* or the requirement that children prove their competency to testify in court by responding to a series of questions designed to test their ability to report information and to convey their understanding of the duty to tell the truth. (See McGough, 1994, for a discussion of this requirement and recommendations for redirecting the focus of competency evaluations.) Because of this requirement, some interviewers test children's understanding of the words *truth* and *lie* before instructing them to talk about things that are true.

It is hard to say when children understand the difference between lies and the truth, because the concept of a lie is multifaceted. For adults, a statement is a lie not only because it is false, but because the speaker knows it is false and intends to deceive someone. There are numerous exceptions to this general rule: Certain jokes that meet these criteria are not judged to be lies by most adults, and an individual can lie when telling the truth (because it was a partial truth, or the individual inadvertently told the truth; Flanagan, 1992). It is not surprising, then, that children's understanding of the truth seems to vary, depending on how adults ask them questions.

Children's understanding of truth and lies improves noticeably at approximately age 4 and continues to develop gradually for many years afterward (see Ceci, Leichtman, & Putnick, 1992, for reviews). At about 3 or 4 years of age, most children define a lie in terms of objective reality: Truth matches reality and lies do not. Around 8 to 9 years, children often consider the speaker's intent to deceive and realize that honest mistakes are not lies. The ability to use intent in defining a lie is highly dependent on the specific task, however. In one study, even 4-year-olds considered intent when deciding whether or not a speaker deserved a reward (Wimmer, Gruber, & Perner, 1984), yet in another study it was not until a verbal age of 17 that the belief of the speaker was weighed more heavily than factuality in judging what was a lie (Burton & Strichartz, 1992).

Most important, the ability to distinguish between lies and the truth varies as a function of two factors: the form of the questions asked and the topic selected for discussion. For example, Siegal and Peterson (1996) found that 3- to 5-year-olds did poorly when asked whether a bear had "lied or not lied," but they performed above chance when asked whether the bear "lied or was mistaken." Children also performed better when asked to judge the validity of statements about food contamination (e.g., whether saying that moldy bread was safe to eat was a lie) than statements about another danger (e.g., whether saying it was okay to enter a clubhouse that contained a dangerous snake was a lie). Research on children's understanding of these concepts has shown that interviewers can improve children's perceived competency by asking them concrete questions about the truth (e.g., Interviewer: "What color is your shirt?" Child: "Red." Interviewer: "Okay, if I said your shirt was blue, would that be the truth or a lie?"), rather than asking them to define the truth. Abstract questions that are not grounded in a content domain, such as "What does it mean to tell the truth?", may confuse even school-aged children. (See chap. 4 and Walker, 1994, for further examples of questions that might be used with children of various ages.)

Although interviewers can improve children's performance on truth/lie questions by asking simple, concrete questions, researchers have identified three major limitations to incorporating truth/lie discussions into investigative interviews. First, some researchers have shown that children who pass such questions are not more accurate or less suggestible than same-aged peers who fail, and thus these discussions do not seem to predict which children will be accurate informants (Goodman, Aman, & Hirschman, 1987; Pipe & Wilson, 1994). Second, there is no evidence that typical truth/lie discussions encourage children to filter out inaccurate information. In a recent study, Huffman, Warren, and Frazier (1997) arranged for preschool children to witness a series of activities led by a visitor to their school. The children were subsequently interviewed with nonleading questions and some leading questions that introduced misinformation about what had occurred. Each child was assigned to one of three conditions for the final interview: no truth/lie discussion, a standard truth/lie discussion that assessed his or her ability to identify what was the truth and what was a lie, and an elaborated truth/lie discussion that involved considerable training and explanation. Children in the elaborated condition *were* more accurate than children in the other conditions, indicating that even preschool children respond to initial instructions, but children who engaged in standard truth/lie discussions (see examples in chap. 4) reported as much suggested information as children who had received no instructions at all.

A third criticism of truth/lie discussions helps explain why standard instructions might have limited value: When young children misreport events, it often is because they misunderstand the purpose of the questions or fail to monitor the source of their knowledge. In other words, errors due to complying with the perceived demands of the interview situation and memory errors may account for inaccurate testimony more often than intentional deception. When this is the case, truth/lie discussions probably will not make reports more accurate. A study by Haugaard (1993) illustrates this point. Haugaard arranged for preschoolers through third graders to watch one of two videotapes in which either a boy or his mother lied by saying that a girl had hit the boy. Haugaard was interested in whether the children would accurately identify the target statement as a lie, whether they would consider it a lie if the mother failed to correct the boy's false statement to a neighbor, and whether they would consider it a lie if the boy corroborated his mother's false statement when she told the lie. The children were highly accurate in labeling the lie. Among those children who remembered that the girl had not hit the boy, 95% who heard the boy lie said that he had lied; furthermore, 79% of these children classified his mother's silence as a lie. Similarly, among those children who remembered that the girl had not hit the boy and who heard the mother tell a lie, 86% said that the mother's statement was a lie, and 97% of these children considered it a lie when the boy falsely corroborated that story. Thus most of the children understood the concept of lying well enough to accurately identify a concrete example. It was disturbing how poorly the younger children recalled the critical theme of the videotape, however. When asked two preliminary questions about whether the girl had hit the boy, 42% of the preschoolers and 18% of the kindergartners stated that this had occurred, but none of the older children made this error. The children gave various explanations for how they "knew" that the boy had been hit: Some children believed that they had seen this event in the videotape, others believed that the liar must have been telling the truth, and some gave other reasons or no reason at all.

Haugaard's study illustrates why there is a controversy over whether children should be required to demonstrate "competency" to testify: Current competency procedures do not address many of the reasons why children sometimes misreport events. Some experts believe that a limited *voir dire* is appropriate, provided that it focuses on relevant issues such as memory and suggestibility (McGough, 1994). Unfortunately, there is not yet sufficient research on this issue to recommend a substitute for the truth/lie discussion.

Summary

Trends in cognitive development do not dictate that children must reach a specific age before they can be interviewed. As soon as they begin talking, even young children are attentive to their environment and can relate autobiographical events. Disagreement about whether it is justifiable to single out children as a special class of witness hinges not on their ability to participate in an interview but rather on the reliability of the information they provide. Concerns revolve around two issues: whether children's testimony is less reliable because they forget more rapidly and whether they are more suggestible (McGough, 1994). We turn to these issues in the following section.

CHILDREN'S EYEWITNESS ACCURACY AND SUGGESTIBILITY

There has been an explosion of research on children's eyewitness testimony in the past 15 years, with the focus predominantly on children's accuracy and suggestibility. *Accuracy* refers to the amount of correct versus incorrect information in children's answers, and memory researchers talk about accuracy when errors stem from the witnesses themselves (i.e., when errors are attributable to memory failure or misunderstanding of the questions). In contrast, *suggestibility* generally refers to errors that arise when witnesses are exposed to information that is false or to social pressures that encourage particular types of answers.[3] In our discussion, we adopt a broad definition of suggestibility that includes both cognitive factors (such as integrating false postevent information into event narratives because of

---

[3]An exception to this convention is the term *autosuggestibility*, which refers to memory errors that result from an individual's own reasoning errors (e.g., Brainerd & Reyna, 1995b).

source-monitoring failures) and social factors (such as acquiescing to what one believes the interviewer wants to hear).

It is difficult to summarize the data on children's accuracy and suggestibility because eyewitness performance varies tremendously, depending on the amount of time since the event, the interview procedures, and the extent of exposure to misinformation from earlier formal interviews or from other sources. We therefore use these factors to organize our review of the evidence. Across these variables, age differences are generally more pronounced under less optimal circumstances (such as when interviews are delayed, conducted inexpertly, or conducted after children have been exposed to misinformation), and all age groups perform better when the target events are highly salient.

Time Since the Event

Citing delays of between 2 and 10 months between referral for prosecution and trial or other disposition, Whitcomb (1992) identified the length of the adjudication process as one of the two "most frustrating aspects of our criminal justice system" (p. 135). Similar delays characterize proceedings in other countries. In Scotland, for example, child witnesses wait an average of 5 to 7 months between witnessing the offense and being examined in court (Flin, Bull, Boon, & Knox, 1990; Flin, Davies, & Tarrant, 1988). Although legislation has been enacted to expedite trials involving children, prosecutors and judges remain reluctant to invoke procedural exceptions for cases involving child witnesses (Whitcomb, 1992), and these realities have fostered interest in how children's event memories survive over time.

What impact do extended delays have on children's recall of meaningful events? The most optimistic data come from studies of conversational remembering. For example, Fivush and Schwarzmueller (1995) showed that young preschoolers can describe events months or years after they took place. There are several reasons why children's performance in eyewitness studies is often less impressive, however. First, as Fivush and Shukat emphasized (1995) in one study of recall for naturally occurring events, only about half of the children who were asked about a previously discussed event recounted any information about that target after 6-month and 1-year delays. It is important to remember that impressive descriptions of children's autobiographical recall refer only to those events they *did* recall, but that such studies tell us nothing about what happens when children are prompted for information they do not initially discuss. Second, research on recall in naturalistic settings is typically concerned with events that adults thought were especially memorable, events that probably prompted conversations between the children and their parents or teachers. Although some forensically relevant events may be highly salient and reinforced by conversations with adults, others may not be. Third, many of the autobiographical events that researchers have discussed with children are long, multifaceted events about which children acquire knowledge as they develop (e.g., theme parks, airplane rides), and this may affect the amount of detail reported after long delays. These caveats notwithstanding, the research on conversational remembering suggests that children may not recall events after lengthy intervals, but if they do, their reports can be very detailed, accurate, and coherent. Other research suggests much less optimistic conclusions about delayed recall. Consider several examples.

In a study by Poole and White (1991), 4-, 6-, and 8-year-old children and adults were drawing a picture when an unfamiliar man snatched their pen and instigated a good-natured fight with the female research assistant. When they were interviewed 1 week after the event, the children and adults were equivalently accurate, averaging only 7% errors. But 2 years later (Poole & White, 1993), 20% of the information the children reported was inaccurate, compared with only 7% of the information provided by the adults. In response to open-ended questions, the children made errors that involved distortions or confusions rather than gross confabulations: No child misreported the main pen-snatching event, but 21% of the children attributed at least one action to the wrong assistant. Moreover, whereas few children attempted to answer a specific question they had no basis for answering (i.e., "What did the man do for a living, what was his job?") after the 1-week delay, 19% of the children did so after the long delay. The children volunteered a variety of detailed but false answers to this "impossible" question, including "secretary," "works at a lumber company," and "worked with my daddy."

In this study, the accuracy of the children's accounts varied, depending on whether they spontaneously reported the main theme (pen snatching) before being prompted with a specific question that mentioned the pen. Children who spontaneously mentioned the pen averaged only 14% errors, whereas 25% of the information from children who had not spontaneously recalled the pen was inaccurate. Furthermore, only 1 child (4%) who spontaneously mentioned the pen associated various actions with the wrong assistant, whereas 12 (32%) of the other children seemed confused. Like the responses concerning the actors' occupation, these findings indicate that specific questions are especially problematic when children's memories are no longer fresh.

Many researchers have shown that children forget more rapidly than adults do (Brainerd & Reyna, 1995a; Brainerd, Reyna, Howe, & Kingma, 1990). Poole and White's research showed not only that children report less than do adults after a long delay but also that what they do report is less accurate. Accuracy declined in response to questions about the actor's appearance and also in response to general questions about the central event (e.g., "Tell me what happened when he came into the room").

Delayed recall also is problematic when children are asked about somewhat stressful events. For example, Goodman, Hirschman, Hepps, and Rudy (1991) reinterviewed 3- to 7-year-olds 1 year after a clinic visit in which they had received inoculations. The amount of accurate information in children's free recall declined during the course of the year, whereas the amount of inaccurate information remained stable, yielding a 1% error rate initially and a 10% error rate after the 1-year delay. In the later interview, the children were especially inaccurate when responding to specific questions about actions, and they were more likely to comply with suggestions in misleading questions. Performance was troublesome: 27% of the responses to specific action questions were wrong, as were 51% of the responses to misleading questions. When the children were asked to identify the nurse from photos, errors increased from 50% initially to 86% after the 1-year delay.

In a study of bystander witnesses, Flin, Boon, Knox, and Bull (1992) arranged for 6- and 9-year-old children and adults to witness a talk on foot hygiene followed by a fight between the assistants who were in charge of the slides. One day and 5 months after the event, the witnesses answered general open-ended questions (e.g., "Tell me all about it as I was not there") and questions about specific aspects of the event (e.g., "Can you describe who was arguing?"). As others had found previously, the amount of accurate information reported by the children declined between the 1-day and 5-month interviews, whereas the amount of inaccurate information did not. Translated into percentages, the rates of inaccurate information at the two time periods (10% and 8%, respectively) were similar for adults, whereas the proportion of inaccurate information reported by the children increased from 9% initially to 18% after 5 months.

It is not surprising that children's reports deteriorate after delays of between 5 months and 2 years. But how long is too long to obtain a reasonably accurate narrative? Developmental trends are not as clear when delays are briefer, because accuracy varies considerably as a function of the type of event and the type of interview. In general, preschool children are most affected by delay and by the subtle suggestions contained in specific questions, and this is particularly true when the target events were not particularly distinctive. For example, when children were questioned about a pediatric examination, 3-year-olds forgot information by a 1-week delay, but 5- and 7-year-olds did not. The 3-year-olds also were more likely to acquiesce to suggestions about events that had not happened, but the rate of false assertions (12%) did not change significantly even when there was a 6-week delay between the first and second interviews (Baker-Ward, Gordon, Ornstein, Larus, & Clubb, 1993). In a similar study, the performance of 6-year-olds was consistent across a 3-week interval, but the 3-year-olds showed declines in accuracy and increases in false assertions after the 1-week delay (to a high of 50%; Ornstein, Gordon, & Larus, 1992). The accuracy of 3- to 7-year-olds was more impressive when they were questioned about a procedure called VCUG (voiding cystourethrogram), an invasive test administered to children with recurrent urinary-tract infections. These children correctly identified 83% of the event features after 6 weeks and falsely acknowledged only 7% of the nonexperienced events. Furthermore, neither index of accuracy changed significantly over the 6-week period in this study, suggesting that the salience of the target event has an important impact on memory (Merritt, Ornstein, & Spicker, 1994).

In summary, accuracy declines over time, but the rate of decline is a function of age, the types of questions that interviewers ask, and the salience of the event. It usually is best to interview as soon as possible, because both children and adults begin to forget details shortly after an event (Brainerd & Reyna, 1990). Regardless of the delay, children report central information more accurately than peripheral information and respond more accurately to general questions than to specific questions. It is especially important to avoid specific probes when recall is delayed because, as we explain in the following section, it is less likely that children will remember specific details after a delay, but nonetheless, they often try to answer specific questions.

Overview of Interview Procedures

Open-Ended Versus Specific Questions

There is no universally accepted way to categorize questions, but for our purposes the term *open-ended question* refers to questions that require a multiple-word response (e.g., initial free-recall questions such as, "Tell me about that," or more focused questions such as, "Tell me about all the things you saw in the house"). In contrast, specific questions ask about a particular detail or concept and often can be answered in a single word (e.g., "What color was her hair?"). The term *closed question* refers to specific questions that have a limited number of response alternatives, including multiple-choice and yes–no questions. Open-ended questions can be quite focused, such as "Tell me about his eyes," but in general open-ended questions deal with broader topics than do specific questions, and open-ended questions allow children more flexibility to choose which aspects of an event they will describe (e.g., "Tell me about his eyes" is more open than "What color were his eyes?").

Although individual specific questions elicit much less information than individual open-ended prompts (Lamb, Hershkowitz, Sternberg, Boat, & Everson, 1996; Lamb, Hershkowitz, Sternberg, Esplin, et al., 1996; Sternberg, Lamb, Hershkowitz, Esplin, et al., 1996), researchers consistently have shown that children provide fewer details in response to open-ended questions than in response to a series of specific questions. As a result, a carefully planned series of specific questions can yield a more complete account of an incident. Children's responses to specific questions are much less accurate than their responses to open-ended questions, however. For example, Dent and Stephenson (1979) reported that 9% of the information provided by 10- to 11-year-olds in response to free-recall questions was inaccurate, compared with 19% in response to specific questions. In addition, specific questions are much more likely to be suggestive, and the risks are compounded when interviewers ask many specific questions. *Regardless of the experimental procedures, the ages studied, the cognitive capacity of the subjects, or the length of the delay between events and the interview, open-ended questions are more likely to elicit accurate accounts* (Dent, 1991; Hershkowitz, 1997; Hershkowitz, Lamb, Sternberg, & Esplin, 1997; Lamb et al., 1994, 1995).

Why are specific questions so risky? First, children choose what information they will report in response to open-ended questions, whereas specific questions may focus on details that were never encoded or are no longer remembered. This raises the risk of error, especially because both children and adults show poorer memories as the critical details become more peripheral (Goodman et al., 1987; Steward et al., 1993). Second, children generally try to answer specific questions that we know they cannot possibly answer accurately (e.g., Poole & White, 1993), and adults and children alike often try to answer even bizarre questions (e.g., "Is a cup sadder than an orange?"; Pratt, 1990; Winer, Rasnake, & Smith, 1987). Although some studies have shown that children are more accurate when interviewers warn them that it is appropriate to say, "I don't know," they do not tend to use this option very frequently (for a brief review, see "The Ground Rules" section of chap. 4).

The implicit social rules of interviews (i.e., children may believe they are supposed to answer adults' questions) exacerbate memory deficiencies (i.e., the information requested may not be available), making specific questions problematic, especially when interviewers ask forced-choice and yes–no questions. For example, Walker, Lunning, and Eilts (1996) asked kindergartners, second graders, and fifth graders to watch a videotape and answer 36 forced-choice questions such as, "Did you see a little girl or a little boy on the video?". The placement of the correct answer was counterbalanced so that it appeared equally often in the first or second position in the question, or not at all. As predicted, the kindergartners were significantly less accurate than the older children, but children in all three age groups showed a response set favoring selection of the second option. Kindergartners answered correctly only 17.5% of the time when neither option was correct, whereas second and fifth graders more often provided a correct "neither" response (37.5% and 48.3% of the time, respectively). Thus even the older children answered correctly less than half of the time when the correct option was not embedded in the question.

Some researchers believe that yes–no questions (e.g., "Was his name John?") are more problematic than other types of specific questions (e.g., "What was his name?"). Conversational convention dictates that children should try to answer questions and be cooperative, so some children frequently say "yes" to yes–no questions. For example, when Poole and Lindsay (1995) asked preschoolers yes–no questions about science demonstrations they had actually experienced and completely novel demonstrations, the children erroneously responded "yes" to 62% of the questions about demonstrations they had never experienced.

A questioning strategy that is especially likely to produce errors involves a yes–no question followed by a request to describe. An example would be a sequence such as "Did Mr. Science put something yucky in your mouth? Tell me about that yucky thing." In one study (Poole & Lindsay, 1996), 26% of 3-year-olds and 32% of 4-year-olds falsely assented to questions such as this that dealt with touching experiences, even though the events never happened and the only time they had heard of the events was during one prior interview. (Assention rates were virtually zero for 5- to 8-year-olds on such questions.) Although some children (8% of the 3- to 4-year-olds in the first interview) responded "yes" the very first time they were presented with these questions, the later errors seemed to indicate that children had difficulty distinguishing between information that was familiar because it was mentioned in a prior interview and information that was familiar because the event had been experienced. As we shall see later in this chapter, the rates were even greater when children had heard their parents discussing the events outside the interview context. Furthermore, it is not the case that interviewers can screen out insincere responses by evaluating whether children can actually describe the events: The majority of children who falsely acquiesced to a question about touching also narrated that experience when interviewers asked them to do so, as did some of the children who initially said "No." Unfortunately, question pairs of the "Did he . . ." "Tell me about . . ." variety are extremely common in forensic interviews of children.

Peterson and Bell (1996) analyzed interviews with 2- to 13-year-olds who had been questioned about visits to a hospital emergency room where they had received treatment. These researchers compared responses to initial free-recall prompts, Wh-questions (i.e., who, what, and where questions, such as "Who else was there?"), and yes–no questions (e.g., "Was your dad there?"). Compared with other question forms, yes–no questions elicited very little information from the children, yet they were responsible for a disproportionate number of errors. In a second paper, Peterson and Biggs (1997) analyzed children's errors on specific questions. Responses to yes–no questions generally were accurate when the correct answer was "yes," with 81% and 96% accuracy for the 2- and 13-year-olds, respectively. The younger children in particular often were wrong when they said "no," however, with 2-, 3-, and 4-year-olds performing at chance levels. Because other researchers have found high error rates for "yes" responses as well (e.g., Poole & Lindsay, 1995), interviewers must avoid relying solely on children's answers to yes–no questions. Although accuracy on yes–no questions is worrisome, children are less likely to falsely assent to questions about unusual or unlikely events, however. For example, 5-year-olds who were interviewed about a visit to the pediatrician acquiesced to fewer suggestions about events that were unlikely to occur during a medical examination (7%) than about features that were typical of a medical exam but did not actually happen during the exam in question (20%; Baker-Ward et al., 1993).

In sum, performance is generally impaired when interviewers ask numerous specific questions. Children are better able to resist the implicit social pressure of specific questions when they are older, when the target event was extremely salient or memorable, and when the specific question implies something that violates expectations about what might reasonably have happened.

Repeating Questions/Retelling Stories

Child witnesses often are interviewed repeatedly, both forensically and informally, sometimes as often as 12 or even 30 times during the course of an investigation (Humphrey, 1985, cited in Ceci, Bruck, & Rosenthal, 1995; Whitcomb, 1992). What impact does repeated interviewing have on the quality of children's event reports? The answer to this deceptively simple question must be, "It depends," because there are many types of repeated questions (Fivush & Schwarzmueller, 1995; Poole & White, 1995). Questions can be repeated within an interview or in different interviews, and repeated questions can be nonsuggestive or highly suggestive. The impact of repeated questioning is not uniform, but varies depending on the timing of repetition and the type of questions that are repeated.

There are three reasons why it can be beneficial to repeat questions. First, because children (especially preschoolers) report different details in different interviews, repeating open-ended questions can elicit new information (Howe, Kelland, Bryant-Brown, & Clark, 1992). Second, repeating open-ended questions in successive interviews can delay the loss of information that naturally occurs over time, an especially important benefit if children might need to testify after a lengthy delay. The value of a "consolidating" interview sometimes is greater when the first interview occurs shortly after the witnessed event (e.g., Baker-Ward, Hess, & Flannagan, 1990; Tucker, Mertin, & Luszcz, 1990; but see Powell & Thomson, 1997b) rather than weeks afterward (Goodman, Bottoms, Schwartz-Kenney, & Rudy, 1991), and when the initial interview elicited a detailed narrative (e.g., Flin et al., 1992). Third, repeated interviewing may teach younger children to engage in "memory talk" so they will need fewer specific prompts later to relate events fully (Hudson, 1990; Rogoff & Mistry, 1990).

Although repetition can help preserve memories, it also can be risky to interview children numerous times. The risks fall into two general categories: the impact of implicit social demands and the impact of explicit suggestions. Regarding the former, adults do not usually repeat questions in normal conversation unless the listener failed to give the desired answer, and hence children sometimes change their answers when specific questions are repeated (Siegal, 1991; Siegal, Waters, & Dinwiddy, 1988). Poole and White (1991, 1993), for example, found that 4-year-olds were less likely than older children or adults to answer repeated yes–no questions consistently. Furthermore, subjects of all ages tended to use fewer uncertainty qualifiers (e.g., "I'm not sure but . . .") in their answers to repeated questions, making their later answers appear more confident than their original answers had been. Finally, when interviewers repeatedly asked for information that the children did not have, increasing numbers speculated anyway. Poole and White concluded that repeating open-ended questions within an interview is rather harmless, but that repeating closed or specific questions is risky because it tends to elicit inconsistency and speculation. Consistent with this conclusion is a finding by Memon and Vartoukian (1996) that children's accuracy increased slightly when interviewers repeated open-ended questions within a session but decreased slightly when interviewers repeated specific questions.

Regarding explicit suggestions, there is no doubt that accuracy declines quite seriously when misleading questions are repeated, especially with younger witnesses (e.g., Cassel, Roebers, & Bjorklund, 1996; Ceci, 1995; Ceci & Bruck, 1993). As we discuss in the following section, there are several reasons why children sometimes comply with repeated misleading questions, including a desire to be cooperative and genuine memory confusion.

There is no consensus on whether investigative interviewers should be restricted to only a single interview or allowed to gather evidence in a small number of nonsuggestive interviews. On the one hand, there is little evidence that testimony is affected adversely by repeated nonsuggestive interviews; in fact, multiple interviews can increase the amount of information obtained and afford interviewers a second chance to clarify children's accounts. On the other hand, repeated suggestive interviews can degrade accuracy, and multiple interviews provide opportunities for children to be interviewed suggestively between sessions during informal conversations with parents, grandparents, or other adults. Regardless of whether protocols favor a single interview or allow for a small number of nonsuggestive interviews, research on repeated interviewing provides the best argument for videotaping all interviews to record the consistency of reports and the methods used to obtain them. (For reviews of the literature on repeated interviewing, see Fivush & Schwarzmueller, 1995, and Poole & White, 1995).

Exposure to Misleading or Suggestive Information

Case studies and systematic research clearly demonstrate that adults sometimes elicit false allegations from children. For the most part, these demonstrations do not show that children are liars or generally unreliable witnesses. Rather, certain situations—when combined with children's immature abilities to conduct conversations, relate story narratives, and decode social expectations—create a volatile mixture that dramatically elevates the risk of errors. In this section, we review three major ways in which children's accounts can be influenced: by asking explicitly misleading questions, by using suggestive questions and instructions, and by exerting social pressures in other ways.

Explicitly Misleading Questions

In the classic early research on misinformation, adult participants witnessed an event and then answered a series of questions about that event. The variable of interest was the extent to which the wording of initial questions influenced the witnesses' accuracy on subsequent questions. For example, when initial questions include true presuppositions (i.e., the question mentions objects that did exist in the event) or false presuppositions (i.e., the question mentions objects that were not in the event), witnesses are more likely to later report having seen the mentioned objects (Loftus, 1975). Of interest is that errors occur even when the misinformation is implicit. For example, witnesses who were asked how fast two cars were going when they *smashed* into each other were more likely to report having seen broken glass than witnesses who were asked how fast the cars were going when they *hit* one another (Loftus & Palmer, 1974).

Many researchers have shown that misleading questions can influence children's answers to later questions that are not explicitly misleading. In an early study, Ceci, Ross, and Toglia (1987, Experiment 1) read short stories to children between the ages of 3 and 12 years and then conversed with them in a misleading way 1 day later. For example, an adult reminded the children, "Do you remember the story about Loren, who had a headache because she ate her cereal too fast? Then she felt better when she got to play with her friend Tricia's Pac Man Game?" whereas Lauren actually had a stomachache from eating her eggs too fast. The children were later shown four pictures—two of which had appeared in the story and two of which contained suggested information—and were asked to point to two pictures of scenes that had appeared in the story. Age differences emerged only when children had been given misleading information. Percentages correct in the unsuggested condition were 84%, 87%, 95%, and 95% for the groups ages 3–4, 5–6, 7–9, and 10–12 years, respectively. In contrast, percentages correct in the biased condition were 37%, 58%, 67%, and 84%.

Although authors frequently comment that preschool children make more errors than older children or adults, suggestibility to misleading questions declines gradually well into the school years. For example, Warren and Lane (1995) found that third and fourth graders who were exposed to misleading questions on two occasions included suggested details in their subsequent free-recall narratives more frequently than did adults. This finding is especially disturbing because children's free recall often is assumed to be highly accurate.

Not all studies reveal such age differences, however (Zaragoza, Dahlgren, & Muench, 1992).[4] Because suggestibility depends on available memories for both the original and the misleading information, the misinformation effect depends on the timing of the misleading information. Studies with both adults and children tend to find larger suggestibility effects when there is a delay between the original event and presentation of the misinformation (Reyna, 1995). Small delays reduce suggestibility, possibly because witnesses can detect discrepancies between the original and suggested information. For example, Goodman et al. (1991) interviewed children about a medical visit only once, after a 4-week delay, or twice, after 2-week and 4-week delays. Although the interviews included some misleading questions, children who were interviewed twice were more accurate on specific questions and, in the final interview, less likely to go along with misleading abuse-analogue questions.

It is unclear to what extent misinformation actually impairs memories of the original stimuli or simply leads to biased reporting. This distinction is forensically relevant: If biased questions merely influence responses, it is possible that memories of the original events could be recovered even after children have been exposed to misleading interviews. Cohen and Harnick (1980), for example, found that 9-year-olds were less accurate than 12-year-olds when responding to misleading questions (e.g., "The young woman was carrying a newspaper when she entered the bus, wasn't she?") but were just as accurate when subsequently tested using multiple-choice questions. Other researchers have also shown that children sometimes acquiesce to misleading questions despite accurate memories of the target events (e.g., Cassel et al., 1996; Poole & Lindsay, 1996; also see Marche & Howe, 1995).

Newcombe and Siegal (1996, 1997) pointed out that children might

---

[4]Most studies either find no age differences in the misinformation effect or find that younger children are more suggestible than older children. There are conditions, however, in which suggestibility *increases* with age. For reviews and a theoretical explanation of age trends in suggestibility, see Brainerd and Reyna (in press) and Brainerd, Stein, and Reyna (in press).

report misinformation even when they *know* that it conflicts with the original event, because they believe that the suggested response is acceptable or even preferred. To illustrate, Newcombe and Siegal (1996) read a story to 3- to 5-year-old children about a little girl, Karen, and her first day at school. The following day, an experimenter introduced either biased or unbiased information about two critical details of the story. One week later, interviewers asked the children about the original details of the story. During this interview, questions were asked either in an explicit format that focused on the time of the target information (e.g., "Do you remember how Karen was sick when you heard her story for the first time?") or a nonexplicit format (e.g., "Do you remember how Karen was sick when you heard her story?"). The preschoolers gave many suggested answers when questioned in the nonexplicit format but fewer when questions clearly marked which event was under discussion.

Can young children always distinguish between the target information and the misinformation? Lindsay et al. (1995) modified the story used by Ceci et al. (1987) to determine whether the effects of prior misinformation would be eliminated or reduced if children knew that the adult was an unreliable source of information. An assistant first read the Loren story to kindergartners and third graders, and either 1 day or 3 days later, another assistant reviewed the story with the children but provided some misleading information. A different assistant subsequently asked the children questions about the story. This assistant told half of the children that the other assistant had accidentally said some things that were wrong, and carefully explained that they should not base anything on what that experimenter had said. These instructions reduced suggestibility considerably, but there was still a reliable suggestibility effect at both ages. Lindsay et al. thus agreed with Ceci et al. that both cognitive and social factors contribute to developmental trends in suggestibility.

Other investigators have studied developmental trends in immediate responses to misleading questions (e.g., "And then he hit you, didn't he?"), and most have shown that children's responses to such questions are less accurate than those of adults. After showing a videotape to kindergartners, second- and fourth-grade children, and adults, for example, Cassel et al. (1996) asked participants 23 leading questions about the tape. Kindergartners responded incorrectly to 61% of the misleading questions, compared with error rates of 33% and 27% for second and fourth graders, respectively, and 10% for adults. Across these age groups, 43%, 36%, 26%, and 16% of the participants also answered *unbiased* questions (e.g., "Can you tell me who owned the bike?") erroneously, leading Cassel et al. to conclude, "These data clearly indicate the strong bias subjects of all ages have to produce some answer (even a wrong one) to a specific, though nonbiased request" (p. 129).

Although young children are more likely than older children to err in response to explicitly misleading or leading questions, false responses are not limited either to young children or to questions about minor details of nonstressful or observed events. Eisen, Goodman, Qin, and Davis (in press) studied 108 children who had been hospitalized for a 5-day inpatient stay for the assessment of abuse. During this stay each child received a complete physical exam and medical assessment, an anogenital exam, a forensic interview directed at assessing allegations of abuse or neglect, and a psychological consultation. On the final day of the stay, the children answered questions about the anogenital exam that included misleading questions that were unrelated to abusive or inappropriate behavior on the part of the doctor or nurse and misleading questions that implied abusive or inappropriate behavior. On nonabuse questions, the 3- to 5-year-olds erred 32% of the time, compared with 17% and 6% for the 6- to 10-year-olds and 11- to 15-year-olds, respectively. Performance was better on abuse-analogue questions (e.g., "The doctor did not have any clothes on, did he/she?"), but the 3- to 4-year-olds erred on 20% of these questions, compared with a 4% error rate for the 6- to 10-year-olds and completely accurate performance for the 11- to 15-year-olds. This study is especially compelling because it assessed acquiescence to misleading questions among a group of children who were being evaluated for suspicions of abuse and who had therefore experienced frequent questioning about whether they had been hurt or touched inappropriately. As Eisen, Goodman, and Qin (1995) concluded in an earlier presentation of this research, "Our data, along with past data collected in nonabused groups, indicates that young children are more susceptible to false suggestions, although they were more often resistant to such inquiries than not. It is clear that some children will respond affirmatively to many types of questions in an indiscriminate manner" (p. 12). Similar developmental trends in response to misleading questions were evident in another study involving children questioned about the VCUG procedure described earlier (Goodman, Quas, Batterman-Faunce, Riddlesberger, & Kuhn, 1994). Children ages 3 to 4 years assent to misleading abuse-analogue questions as much as 20% of the time in such studies, whereas older children do so much less often (e.g., Goodman, Bottoms, et al., 1991; Goodman, Rudy, Bottoms, & Aman, 1990).

Suggestive Questioning and Instructions

As with the terms *open-ended* and *specific*, the term *suggestive questioning* has varying meanings. Some authors have said that yes–no questions are not inherently suggestive, because although some children falsely acquiesce to such questions, they rarely elaborate by providing narratives that would mislead adults. As we discussed previously, however, Poole and Lindsay (1995, 1996) have documented that children will provide narratives about fictitious events they only heard their parents describe. Furthermore, recent evidence indicates that even *without* prior suggestions, a variety of instructions, when combined with specific questions, can prompt preschoolers to provide false information.

In a highly publicized set of studies, Ceci and his colleagues asked children to think about events that had happened to them and events that had not. In their first study (Ceci, Huffman, Smith, & Loftus, 1994, with additional data discussed in Ceci & Bruck, 1995), preschool children selected cards that contained various prompts, such as "Got finger caught in a mousetrap and had to go to the hospital to get the trap off." The interviewer then asked, "Think real hard, and tell me if this ever happened to you. Do you remember going to the hospital with a mousetrap on your finger?" More than half of the children produced false narratives for at least one fictitious event, and a quarter produced false accounts for the majority of the fictitious events. These narratives often were rich with details, and 27% of the children later refused to acknowledge that the events had not really happened.

Ceci, Loftus, Leichtman, and Bruck (1994) later told children that certain events had happened and asked them to "make a picture of it in your head, and think real hard about each thing for a minute." The percentage of fictitious events the children reported remembering increased over sessions (from 29% in the first session to 43% in the 12th session), and most of the children who falsely assented continued to believe that the events had occurred even when a new interviewer informed them that they had been told many things that did not really happen. Ceci and Bruck (1995) attributed these errors to source-monitoring deficiencies: Children and adults alike have difficulty distinguishing between events that happened and events they merely thought about or heard discussed, but young children are especially prone to such errors.

Interviewing Environment and Social Pressures

In addition to explicitly leading or suggestive questions, subtle and not-so-subtle social pressures may influence children's reports, leading some critics to chastise interviewers for offering encouragement that might be leading (e.g., "You are doing a really good job"). In fact, Goodman, Bottoms, et al. (1991) found that both 3- and 7-year-olds made fewer errors when describing an inoculation experience when interviewers were generally supportive (complimenting the children and serving juice and cookies) and that the supportive atmosphere eliminated age differences in acquiescence to misleading questions. On the other hand, children interviewed by a police officer who expressed concern about possible abuse ("I am very concerned that something bad might have happened the last time that you were here") were less accurate in free recall and made more additional comments to some misleading questions (Tobey & Goodman,

1992). It is important to note that both studies focused on *noncontingent* reinforcement, as the children were not reinforced for particular answers. Similarly, Ceci et al. (1987) found that children were more likely to be misled by an adult than by a 7-year-old, indicating that they are sensitive to the social pressure of being interviewed by an authority figure (also see Carter, Bottoms, & Levine, 1996).

Serious problems arise when evaluative comments are contingent on (i.e., paired with) explicitly misleading assertions. For example, when an interviewer asked 4- to 6-year-olds several misleading questions and followed the children's comments with accusatory statements ("He wasn't supposed to do that . . . that was bad"), the children made more errors and endorsed more biased interpretations of the events, leading Lepore and Sesco (1994) to conclude that "4- to 6-year-olds will produce misleading reports about their interactions with either familiar or unfamiliar adults when they are prompted to do so by an opinionated adult interviewer" (p. 108). Clearly, interviewers should avoid offering their own evaluations during forensic interviews.

Garven, Wood, Malpass, and Shaw (in press) recently evaluated the effects of combining suggestive questions such as "Did he touch you on your bottom?" with other social pressures. These researchers identified five "social incentive" techniques that interviewers had used to encourage abuse reports from children in the McMartin Preschool case: other people (saying that other children had already told), positive consequences (giving praise or approval), negative consequences (criticizing a child's statement), already answered (repeating a question that the child had already answered), and inviting speculation (comments such as "Let's figure out what happened"). To evaluate the impact of these techniques, they arranged for 66 children, ranging from 3 to 6 years of age, to attend a special story time led by a male graduate student, followed by an interview 1 week later. Each child was assigned to one of two interviewing conditions: suggestive questions designed to induce the child to make a variety of false allegations about the graduate student (e.g., that he broke a toy or threw a crayon at a child who was talking) or suggestive questions plus the social incentive manipulations. Children of all ages agreed with misleading questions at a substantially higher rate when suggestive questions were combined with social incentives: 58% of the children who experienced the full range of interviewing pressures made one or more false reports, compared with 17% of the children who experienced only suggestive questions.

Misleading Information Encountered Outside Formal Interviews

Children do not need to answer suggestive questions in order to absorb misinformation or respond to social expectations. Rather, information that children encounter *before* they become involved in formal interviews can influence the accuracy of their responses to later nonsuggestive and suggestive questions. For example, Bruck, Ceci, Francoeur, and Barr (1995) arranged for an experimenter to give evaluative feedback to children 4 to 18 months after they received a school-entry inoculation at their pediatrician's office. For three sessions, experimenters visited the children at home or in their preschool for 45 minutes of play. During these visits, the experimenters interspersed exchanges about common events with statements about the children's clinic visit. Children in the "positive feedback" condition were told that they had been brave when they got their shot with comments such as "Laurie and Dr. F . . . said that when you got your shot, you were really a brave kid. They said you didn't cry at all when you got your shot. It was like it didn't even hurt you at all." In contrast, children in the "neutral feedback" condition received comments such as "Laurie and Dr. F . . . said they remembered the day you went to get your shot. They said that first you came into the office and Maureen, the secretary, talked to your mom (or dad)." Some children also were misinformed about what the female research assistant and the male pediatrician actually did (e.g., some children were falsely told that the research assistant gave the inoculation). In a fourth session, interviewers asked the children about the clinic visit and then had them rate how much the shot had hurt and how much they had cried. Children in the positive feedback condition produced lower "hurt" and "cry" ratings than did children in the neutral feedback condition, and approximately one third of the children who had been misled about the gender of the person who administered the shot erred in identifying the correct professional. Moreover, errors occurred even in response to open-ended questions such as "Tell me everything that happened" and "Tell me everything he did." In fact, 48% of the "false allegations" by misled children were spontaneous, in contrast to nonmisled children who, with only one exception, erred only in response to direct questions (e.g., "Who . . . ?"). Clearly, it can be risky to interview children long after events have taken place, especially when there have been more recent discussions of the event that included misleading information.

Children's resistance to leading questions also is affected when expectations or stereotypes are implanted. In a creative study by Leichtman and Ceci (1995), younger (3 and 4 years) and older (5 and 6 years) preschoolers observed while a stranger, "Sam Stone," visited their classroom. Children assigned to the stereotype condition had previously been told on several occasions that Sam was clumsy and prone to breaking things, whereas children in the control condition received no specific information about Sam. After Sam's visit, the children were interviewed either suggestively or nonsuggestively on four occasions, followed by a fifth exit interview that was identical for all children. Data were therefore available on four conditions of information exposure: control (no stereotypes or suggestions), stereotype (but no suggestive interviews), suggestive interviews (but no stereotype), and stereotype plus suggestions.

No child in the control group made a false allegation during the free-narrative portion of the exit interview, and few children claimed that anything bad had happened in response to probe questions. Children who received misinformation only before Sam's visit also made no false allegations about transgressions during free recall, although their performance declined dramatically when specific questions were posed, with 37% of these children indicating that Sam had committed at least one offense. Some children in the suggestive interviewing condition made accusations even during free recall, and 45% made a false claim in response to probe questions. The number of errors increased markedly when stereotypes were followed by suggestive interviews: 46% of the younger children and 30% of the older children provided false accusations in their free narratives, and in response to probe questions an alarming 72% of the younger children accused Sam of one or more misdeeds. The ease with which stereotypes influenced children's accounts is noteworthy, because stereotypes could be involved whenever allegations develop during custody disputes in which children overhear negative comments about one or both of their parents. In addition, negative stereotypes could affect children's reports in complicated, multivictim cases. For example, when investigators told 15 of the 34 alleged victims of Kelly Michaels that Kelly was in jail for doing bad things (Ceci & Bruck, 1995), some children never "took the bait," but others did come to report that Kelly was "bad."

Developmental trends in susceptibility to misleading information encountered outside the interview environment also were apparent in Poole and Lindsay's studies of "Mr. Science" (Poole & Lindsay, 1995, 1996). These researchers documented that even 8-year-olds can be influenced to report complete mini-events that never occurred, that adults can influence children to produce false reports even when interview questions are not suggestive, and that false reports occur even when the misleading information involves touching.

In both studies, children individually participated in 16 minutes of science demonstrations with a research assistant called "Mr. Science" and were then asked a series of open-ended questions about the session. Approximately 3 months later, parents read a story to their children entitled "A Visit to Mr. Science." This story began with accurate contextual details about the visit (e.g., arriving at an ivy-covered building) and then described two demonstrations the child had experienced, two novel demonstrations, and a nonexperienced event that involved the child being touched by Mr. Science. After the parents read the story to their children three times, research assistants interviewed the children using the five open-ended questions from the previous interview, followed by leading question pairs. Leading question pairs began with a yes–no format question such as, "Did Mr. Science show you a pulley machine with ropes to pull?," followed by one prompt for a "yes" response ("Tell me about the pulley machine") and another for a "no" response ("Can you tell me about the pulley machine?"). Furthermore, each child in the pilot study answered one question about nonexperienced touching that was mentioned in the story (whether Mr. Science had put something "yucky" in their mouths); in the second study, each child answered one question about touching that was mentioned in the story and one question about a novel touch event (either the "yucky" question or a question about whether Mr. Science had hurt their "tummies").[5] Finally, in both studies interviewers ended interviews with a series of source-monitoring questions. During the source-monitoring procedure, the existence of the story was acknowledged and the child was asked which events had actually happened and which events were only mentioned in the story.

Results from the Mr. Science studies illustrate that children can be influenced by information their parents mention, even though the parents never said that the events had actually happened. In the first study, 41% of the 3- and 4-year-olds described a nonexperienced event from the story during initial free recall, although only one child spontaneously reported the touching experience. However, 53% of the children said "yes" to the leading question about nonexperienced touching, and 59% provided at least some descriptive information about that event when asked to do so.

The second study demonstrated that false reports are not confined to younger children. Participants were 3- to 8-year-old children who experienced three sessions: the initial demonstration session and interview, an interview immediately after hearing the misleading story, and a final interview 1 month later. These children reported numerous nonexperienced events in their free-recall narratives during the interview that took place right after the story reading (i.e., 114 children volunteered 41 descriptions of nonexperienced science demonstrations and 17 descriptions of nonexperienced touching), and rates of false reporting in free recall were constant from 3 to 8 years of age. In the same interview, between 33% and 42% of the children in each age group said "yes" to questions about touching experiences that were only mentioned in the story; 1 month later, this remained true of the 3- and 4-year-olds (53% and 58%) but not of the 5- to 8-year-olds (17%, 28%, 11%, and 14%, respectively). The children did not simply nod or say "yes" to these misleading questions: They often provided descriptions when asked to do so. Within a day of the final story-

---

[5]The implanted abuse-analogue questions were not worded to be traumatic events in the story. For the "yucky" event, the story said that Mr. Science washed the child's hands and face with a wet wipe that got too close to the child's mouth and tasted yucky. For the stomach event, the story said that Mr. Science tried to put a reward sticker on the child's shirt but that he had to push it a little hard to make it stick. These studies involved no overt deception; the children were merely read the stories but were never told that the fictitious events had actually happened.

reading session, for example, 73% of the 3- to 4-year-olds, 92% of the 5–6-year-olds, and 93% of the 7- and 8-year-olds who responded "yes" also provided descriptions of the event (as did some of the children who initially responded "no"). These errors clearly were attributable to the misinformation provided by the parents and not just to the use of specific questions: No 5- to 8-year-old falsely responded "yes" to a touch event that had not been mentioned in the story, and although children in all age groups sometimes answered "yes" regarding science demonstrations they had never observed or heard about, they more often reported having experienced science demonstrations that were mentioned in the story.

In Poole and Lindsay's studies, the most striking developmental trends were evident when interviewers asked the children to distinguish between events that had really happened and events that were only described in the story. In the second study, for example, all of the 3- and 4-year-olds who erroneously reported touching continued to report this fictitious event even after explicit source-monitoring instructions, whereas the percentage of older children who remained adamant was 29%, 83%, 33%, and 37% for the 5-, 6-, 7-, and 8-year-olds, respectively. Age trends also were pronounced a month later. In the final interview, the younger children continued to claim that they had experienced most of the events they had erroneously claimed earlier, with 90% of the 3-year-olds and 73% of the 4-year-olds maintaining erroneous "yes" responses. In contrast, 5- to 8-year-olds maintained erroneous "yes" responses to 67%, 40%, 0%, and 33%, respectively, of the touch events to which they had acquiesced in the earlier interview. Stated simply, the performance of 3- and 4-year-olds was not helped much by asking them specific questions about the source of their knowledge, whereas the older children were better able to reconstruct the source of their knowledge.

Overview

What can we conclude about children's suggestibility from these studies? First, younger children often are more vulnerable to suggestion than older children, and in many studies preschoolers are the least likely to reject misleading information even after adults tell them that they were misinformed. Second, children often resist suggestions about significant events that involve their own bodies better than they resist suggestions about other details or events (e.g., Goodman et al., 1990). Nonetheless, some preschoolers readily misreport inappropriate touching, and older children make errors as well (e.g., Eisen et al., in press; Poole & Lindsay, 1996). Third, misinformation is most likely to produce erroneous responses to specific or misleading questions (Leichtman & Ceci, 1995; Poole & Lindsay, 1995, 1996). Fourth, factors that impair memory—including delays between events and presentation of misinformation, delayed testing, and questions about less salient events—also increase suggestibility (Pezdek & Roe, 1995; Reyna, 1995). Although suggestibility varies as a function of witness age, the timing of misleading information, the salience of the event, and the types of questions asked, three conditions have especially damaging effects on the accuracy of children's testimonies.

First, interviewers who have a bias about what might have happened tend to elicit more false information from children. In a study by Ceci, Leitchman, and White (described by Ceci & Bruck, 1995), for example, 34% of the 3- to 4-year-olds and 18% of the 5- to 6-year-olds corroborated one or more false events that the interviewer erroneously believed had transpired. The children also became more credible and less inconsistent as interviewing proceeded. The effect of interviewer bias is likely determined by the tendency to use specific questions, which children tend to answer. As we reported earlier, specific questions, yes—no format questions followed by requests to describe, and misleading questions all elicit false information from some children, especially when children have heard misleading information outside the interview.

A "tone of accusation" is also important (Lepore & Sesco, 1994). For example, when Goodman, Wilson, Hazan, and Reed (1989, described by Goodman & Clarke-Stewart, 1991) interviewed fifteen 7- to 10-year-olds about a brief interaction with a research assistant that occurred 4 years earlier, they included misleading questions (e.g., "He gave you a hug and kissed you, didn't he?") and established an accusatory atmosphere with comments such as "You'll feel better once you've told" and "Are you afraid to tell?" Although the children did not acquiesce to questions about spanking or touching, some children did make errors that might lead to suspicions of abuse. For example, one child falsely reported that she had been given a bath, five agreed to having been hugged and kissed, and two said they had had their pictures taken in the bathtub.

Third, nonsuggestive, open-ended interviewing does not guarantee that children will provide accurate event narratives, especially when they have been exposed to misinformation in prior interviews or by other sources. Indeed, children sometimes report events that never occurred even during their initial narratives, before interviewers ask any specific questions (Poole & Lindsay, 1995, 1996; Warren & Lane, 1995). Errors induced by various misinformation procedures tend to drop out of children's testimonies at a faster rate than either accurate reports or spontaneous errors, but in certain contexts these errors nonetheless show disturbing stability over time and repeated interviews (Brainerd & Poole, 1997; Brainerd, Reyna, & Brandse, 1995; Poole, 1995).

Although there is not a great deal of research on the characteristics of children's false reports, can professionals reliably distinguish between true reports and fictitious reports developed after a series of misleading interactions with adults? When Ceci, Loftus, et al. (1994)

showed 10 videotapes of children from their study to 12 clinical and research psychologists who specialize in interviewing children, the professionals were unable to distinguish between the true and false descriptions.[6] It is difficult to distinguish between true and fictitious reports not because the children's true reports are so impoverished but rather because their false reports often contain characteristics that professionals associate with accurate testimony, such as idiosyncratic details and spontaneous corrections (Bruck, Hembrooke, & Ceci, 1997; Ceci, Loftus, et al., 1994).

Bruck et al. (1997) conducted an extensive content analysis of children's false narratives to illustrate how repeated misleading interviews both elicit false reports and obscure the differences between true and false narratives. These investigators asked 16 preschool children to describe a positive event that recently had happened (helping a visitor who tripped and hurt her ankle), a negative event in which the child had been punished, and fictitious positive and negative events (helping a lady find her lost monkey in the park and a food-stealing incident). They then traced the children's narratives about these events across five interviews: an initial baseline interview; two suggestive interviews that involved visualization techniques, repeated misinformation, and selective reinforcement; a fourth interview in which the children told events to a hand-held puppet; and a final interview by an unfamiliar research assistant.

Bruck et al. (1997) coded the children's narratives for variables that often are presumed to discriminate between true and false reports, including the number of details, spontaneous reminiscences and consistency, contradictions, and narrative cohesion. With repeated interviewing, subtle differences between true and false reports disappeared as the false narratives became more elaborate and convincing. For example, there were no significant differences by the third interview in the number of details children provided regarding true and false events, and the false stories actually contained *more* emotional terms and descriptives than the true events. By the fifth interview, there was no difference in the proportion of consistent (i.e., repeated) details reported regarding true and false events, and the number of contradictory details increased across repeated interviews for both true and false events. Bruck et al. concluded,

> To summarize, we examined the linguistic structure of the children's true and falsely suggested narratives; we examined changes in structure and content of these narratives as a function of repeated interviews. Replicating many of the results of a pilot project involving a different sample of children (Bruck, Ceci, & Hembrooke, 1995), our analyses

---

[6]In this study, professionals judged the credibility of children's reports by watching videotapes that they were allowed to replay as often as they chose.

revealed the following. First, it is the first narrative which was elicited by nonsuggestive techniques that allows the clearest differentiation between true and false stories. This is because children mainly deny the false stories and as a result these contain no details. However with repeated interviews, the false stories quickly come to resemble the true stories in terms of the number of details provided, the spontaneity of the utterances, the number of new details, [contradictions] across narratives, the elaborativeness of the details, and the cohesiveness of the narrative. It is only consistency across narratives that differentiates true from false events; it seems, however, that could become a less potent predictor when children are repeatedly interviewed. When false stories are told as a result of repeated suggestive interviewing, they take on additional qualities that make them seem more believable than true narratives: specifically, after a number of interviews, false narratives contain more descriptive, elaborative and emotional material than true narratives. (p. 211)

Similar findings were reported by Lamb et al. (1997) in a recent field study of investigative interviews (see "Criterion Based Content Analysis/Statement Validity Analysis" in chap. 6).

In conclusion, it is not the case that children's event reports are generally distorted and unreliable, nor is it the case that children cannot be prompted to falsely report events that might be considered abusive. Rather, the quality of children's testimony is a joint product of their cognitive and social maturity, their experiences outside formal interviews, and the interviewing context. The studies reviewed in this chapter have shifted the focus of discussion from whether children will or will not lie about abuse to discussions of reliability, or the extent to which their reports reflect their original experiences. In an interesting analogy to other types of evidence, Robert Rosenthal (personal communication, November 1, 1996) compared finding a knife at the scene of a crime to interviewing a child. In the former case, the prosecution would need to describe how the knife was placed in a bag, transported to storage, and secured. In other words, the prosecution would need to demonstrate that there were no gaps in the chain of custody of the knife that could introduce error. The issue in many child abuse investigations is similar; in this case, the "chain of custody" of the child's memory must be documented.

Eyewitness Research Confronts the Realities of Investigative Interviewing: Challenges for Future Research

When investigative interviews are concerned with sexual abuse allegations, interviewers know that children may avoid discussing abuse out of embarrassment, to avoid causing trouble for the perpetrator, or because they have been threatened to keep silent. Even when genital touching occurs as part of a socially sanctioned doctor's visit, many children who are interviewed about their experiences fail to mention genital touching until they are questioned directly (Saywitz, Goodman, et al., 1991). Reluctance to disclose abuse is used to justify a variety of interviewing techniques that are potentially error-producing, including commenting about the child's presumed emotional state, repeatedly asking direct questions about abuse, and prompting children with the assistance of props such as dolls or body drawings.

Forensic interviewers may justify these strategies by asking, "How can we get children to discuss abuse without asking about abuse?" Therefore one of the most pressing but unresolved issues in the field of interviewing is the extent to which interviewers should use direct questions about abuse or other prompts to encourage children to disclose. In many of the studies described in this chapter, children were asked numerous leading or misleading questions, but—especially for school-aged children—there may be little risk in asking a single specific question about abuse when the children know that they can correct the interviewer and say "No" or "I don't know." According to Ceci and Bruck (1995), "Although there is scientific evidence that the use of any one of these techniques may usurp the child's memory, we do not conclude that the presence of any one of these techniques in a single forensic or therapeutic interview necessarily renders all of the child's reports suspect *if these are used by a neutral interviewer in a single interview*" (p. 296, italics in the original).

The interviewer behavior that prompted criticism of child protection strategies (i.e., specific and repeated questioning about abuse) seems to have originated from the assumption that children are unlikely to disclose abuse without such scaffolding from interviewers. Recent evidence, however, indicates that repeated or highly suggestive procedures may not be necessary to protect children, because the majority of children who have previously disclosed also disclose during investigative interviews. Bradley and Wood (1996) evaluated more than 200 validated sexual abuse cases involving 3- to 18-year-olds, 72% of whom reportedly disclosed to someone prior to contact with the Department of Protective and Regulatory Services or police. During investigative interviews, only 6% of these victims initially denied abuse and only 4% recanted their accusations. Similarly, Sternberg et al. (1997) reported that two thirds of their sample of children referred for forensic interviews made a specific and detailed allegation in response to a single, nonleading prompt, and an additional 15% made vaguer illusions to the abuse. Although these data might be overly optimistic because they deal with a group of children whose abuse had been confirmed, Keary and Fitzpatrick (1994) also found that the majority of children referred because of an informal disclosure also disclosed during an evaluation (typically lasting two or three sessions) that followed recommendations to avoid overly suggestive or leading questions. Rates of disclosure by this "prior disclosure" group, broken down by age, were 59% (0–5 years), 93% (6–10 years), 95% (11–15 years), and 100% (16+ years). In contrast, children referred on the basis of emotional problems, sexual behavior, or physical signs "suggestive of child sexual abuse" (p. 546) were much less likely to disclose, with corresponding disclosure rates of 8%, 15%, 23%, and 0%.

Other data suggest that delayed and gradual disclosure in the face of specific abuse questions is characteristic of children who have not previously disclosed, but who *are* repeatedly interviewed by adults who suspect abuse. A frequently cited article is a retrospective analysis by Sorensen and Snow (1991) of case files concerning children referred for therapy. Sorensen and Snow reported that three fourths of these children denied abuse initially and that they often moved into tentative disclosure before making a full disclosure. A large proportion of these children were questioned about abuse on the basis of very weak evidence, however, such as time spent with an alleged abuser (28%) or sexual behavior that was believed to be inappropriate (14%), and it is unclear how many children disclosed accurate accounts of abuse under repeated questioning.

To determine when it is appropriate to confront abuse issues directly in an interview, researchers need to undertake further research on practical source-monitoring questions. This is because concerns about erroneous "yes" responses diminish if it can be shown that most children can subsequently clarify their answers. It also would be useful to have data on the degree of risk associated with direct questions in different types of cases. For example, the probability that false allegations will arise in response to direct questions about abuse should be dramatically less when there is clear physical or external evidence of abuse than in cases in which suspicions either stem from ambiguous evidence or it is known that the children received detailed information about possible abuse. (See Poole & Lindsay, 1998, for a discussion of how the risk of specific questions varies across settings with different base rates of abuse.) Until data are available on these issues, however, research can only inform interviewers about the least suggestive methods of interviewing; we cannot currently specify which techniques are in the best interests of particular children.

GUIDELINES FOR DEVELOPMENTALLY SENSITIVE INTERVIEWS

Although many questions about children's eyewitness testimonies remain unanswered, studies like those reviewed in this chapter have prompted psychologists, legal professionals, and child-protection specialists to draft general guidelines for developmentally appropriate interviews (e.g., American Professional Society on the Abuse of Children, 1990; Home

Office, 1992; Lamb, 1994; Lamb et al., 1994, 1995, in press; Steward et al., 1993; Yuille, Hunter, Joffe, & Zaparniuk, 1993). Although guidelines differ in some respects, they share two goals: to increase children's understanding of the interview process itself and to emphasize practices that maximize children's accuracy. Five basic principles are paramount:

- Children should be interviewed as soon as possible after the alleged events.
- Children learn to participate in interviews. Interviews should begin with a "settling-in period" that gives children a chance to acclimate to the interviewing environment, build rapport with the interviewer, receive instructions about the "rules" of the interview (e.g., their right to say "no" or to ask for clarification of a question), and practice being informative (e.g., Lamb et al., 1994, 1995, in press; McGough, 1996; Sternberg et al., 1997).
- Interviewers should structure conversations around open-ended questions. When focused questions are needed to clarify details or raise additional topics, interviewers should select questions that provide the most options for responding, and they should follow specific probes with more general or open-ended prompts.
- Interviewers should remain neutral, avoid offering their own reactions or perceptions, and be open to multiple interpretations of children's statements.
- Depending on the age of the child and the circumstances, interviewers should conclude with opportunities to review and clarify reported information, explanations of how interviewers could be contacted later, and discussions of neutral topics that close interviews with a supportive tone.

In the next chapter, we show how these general principles have guided the development of interview protocols by teams of investigators, task forces, and professional organizations. We then explain in chapter 4 how interviewers can implement these recommendations by describing each phase of an investigative interview. Because the protocol in chapter 4 reflects the findings described in this chapter, we will revisit the above ideas there, albeit with a focus on how to translate these general suggestions into concrete procedures and question sequences.

II

INTERVIEW PROTOCOLS

INTRODUCTION

INTERVIEW PROTOCOLS

The research reviewed in chapter 2 convincingly demonstrates that interviewers can influence children's accounts. Interviewers affect children by their choice of the physical environment for conducting interviews, their demeanor and behavior, and their selection of questioning strategies. These facts have created a sense of urgency about the need to develop and implement formal protocols for investigative interviews, and many jurisdictions are now attempting to develop uniform interview standards. Are these efforts an overreaction to the problems identified when interviewers used unusually suggestive techniques in laboratory studies? Do the studies reviewed in chapter 2 realistically represent the ways in which adults *actually* talk to children in nonforensic and forensic settings?

We can evaluate the need for formal protocols by comparing the circumstances associated with false reports in eyewitness studies against the data on how adults actually talk with children. Two classes of studies are especially relevant: analyses of adult–child conversations in everyday settings such as home or school and analyses of the questions interviewers ask children in legal settings. The startling finding is that in both types of studies, most of the things adults say to children are conveyed in ways that are known to dramatically elevate error rates. It thus appears that investigative interviewers must learn a linguistic style that differs from the one adults normally use when interacting with children if they are to elicit useful and accurate accounts.

Before describing the structure of interview protocols in the following chapters, it is helpful to describe how adults talk to children when they are *not* limited by formal guidelines. This information underscores the need for protocols and explains why mastering a protocol may require a considerable amount of practice and feedback.

THE STRUCTURE OF ADULT–CHILD CONVERSATIONS AT HOME AND SCHOOL

In everyday life, adults modify their speech patterns in numerous ways when speaking to children. Researchers use a variety of names to describe these adjustments, including "motherese," "parentese," "child-directed talk," "A-C speech," and "ACL" (for "adult-to-child language"). The characteristic features of ACL are evident in the language of mothers, fathers, unrelated adults, and even older children to young children, and such adjustments occur in individuals from diverse ethnic and social backgrounds (Reich, 1986). The extent of language adjustment varies, however, depending on the adult's experience with children and whether the task or situation allows children to give feedback to their conversational partners.

How does ACL differ from language directed to adults? First, ACL generally is simpler and seems to promote greater understanding. For example, utterances tend to be shorter but gradually increase in length as the child's age increases (Moerk, 1974; Phillips, 1973). ACL also tends to focus on objects that are currently visible and events that are currently happening or have recently happened (Phillips, 1973). ACL sentences have simplified structures, with fewer pronouns, modifiers, and function words. ACL often is spoken more slowly as well, with an extremely low rate of grammatical errors and more exaggerated enunciation (Reich, 1986).

Because ACL may have evolved to promote greater understanding by listeners with more limited linguistic abilities, it might seem logical to recommend that interviewers simply talk as they normally would speak to any child. This would be problematic, however, because daily conversations between adults and children are highly structured by the adults. As Gleason (1977) concluded from her research on language addressed to 4- to 8-year-olds, ACL is a "language of socialization" that teaches children "what to do, what to think, and how to feel" (p. 139). As such, ACL contains a high proportion of utterances that point out objects or direct children's behavior with imperatives (e.g., "Don't touch that") or implied imperatives (e.g., "You don't want to touch that"). ACL also includes numerous tutorial questions, or questions that ask for information the adult already knows. ACL is characterized by devices that maintain conversation and promote language development. For example, many researchers have reported that approximately one third of ACL samples involved self-repetitions by adults (e.g., "Put the red truck in the box now ... The red truck ... No, the RED truck ... In the box ... The red truck in the box"; Snow, 1972, reprinted in Reich, 1986, p. 95). In another common utterance type (expansion), the adult repeats the child's phrase in a more sophisticated form. As Reich summarized, "In conversations with children, parents typically supplied the entire context, leaving very little room for the child to deflect conversation. . . . The child hardly had to do more than say *yes* or *no*" (p. 94). Investigative interviewers would be criticized for leading the child or reinforcing particular types of statements if they spoke in this fashion during forensic interviews. One implication of ACL, however, is that children probably come to adult–child interactions expecting that adults will direct the conversation. Moreover, they frequently may assume that adults already know the answers and that the goal of conversation is to figure out which answers the adults would prefer.

Children's expectations about conversations with adults are undoubtedly refined by exposure to formal schooling as well. Critics have argued that school language is so discrepant from the conversational patterns of some cultures that it is a source of confusion and failure. In school language, a typical interaction involves a three-part sequence comprising a question, an answer, and an acknowledgment. Consider the following example from Blank and White (1986, p. 1):

Teacher: OK, current events, Glenn?

Student: Pablo Casals, the well-known cellist, died at ninety-six.

Teacher: OK, shush! Jim?

Student: The war over in the Middle East is still going on.

Teacher: Is it going on in the same way? Frank?

Student: Egypt asked for Syria to intervene. They want a security meeting or a quick meeting of the U.N. Security Council.

Teacher: OK, for what reason? Do you know? Anyone know why Egypt called a meeting of the Security Council of the U.N.? What has the Security Council just initiated?

Student: A cease-fire.

Blank and White summarized three criticisms of such exchanges: The questions do not allow a free exchange of ideas, they are phrased to elicit a predetermined set of responses, and basic pragmatic rules are violated because questions are asked by someone who already knows the answer. Although the skills needed to participate in this type of conversation are well-honed by elementary school, children begin early in life to expect these types of interactions from adults.

How might "tutorial" experiences change children's expectations about answering adults' questions? In one analysis of school transcripts, teachers asked increasingly specific questions until someone gave the desired answers or it became apparent that no one was going to, in which case the teachers provided the answers themselves (Whittaker & Robinson, 1987). Whittaker and Robinson argued that this type of interaction serves a useful purpose: It teaches children to attend to the distinction between a verbal message itself and the speaker's intended meaning. Simply stated, schools instruct children to provide the answers their teachers want.

In summary, adult speech to children in everyday contexts often is simplified, with adults structuring and controlling the conversations. Children may therefore enter interviews expecting a series of specific questions, and interviewers may naturally behave in accordance with these expectations. Research confirms that this is exactly what often happens in forensic settings.

THE LANGUAGE ADDRESSED TO CHILD WITNESSES

In an early study of interviewer behavior, Bartz, Legrand, Wakefield, and Underwager (reported in Underwager & Wakefield, 1990) analyzed 150 interviews with 99 children who were involved in allegations of sexual abuse. These cases spanned 20 states and a variety of alleged offenders (i.e., day care providers, divorced parents, friends, strangers, neighbors, and abuse in intact families). Six types of interviewer behaviors were defined as potential sources of error: Closed questions (which suggest the answer), modeling, pressure, rewards, aids, and paraphrase (which might reinforce the child's response). Overall, two thirds of the adults' behaviors were of one of these categories. Further analyses of nine interviews with young children (average age = 4.1 years) indicated that 35% of the important elements in the children's accusations were first stated by the interviewer.

Although Bartz et al. used a very broad definition of "error-producing" behavior, other researchers have confirmed that interviewers frequently direct conversations with children. One recent study involved detailed analyses of 42 interviews with boys and girls ranging from 2 to 13 years of age, all conducted by CPS workers from a single state (Warren, Perry, et al., 1995; Warren, Woodall, Hunt, & Perry, 1996). Interviewers generally controlled these conversations, and adult speech filled the majority of time even during the initial rapport-building interactions. Many interviewers (29%) did not establish rapport beyond asking a few fixed questions (e.g., child's name, age), and only 29% commented at all on the ground rules for the interview (such as the child's right to say "don't know" or to correct the interviewer). In only one of the 42 interviews did an interviewer ask for a free narrative and then allow a child to provide one without interruption (Hulse, 1994), and only 11% of the questions asked during abuse-related portions of the interview were general questions that could be answered with multiword narratives. Instead, 89% were specific questions, and

63% were yes–no questions. Furthermore, 94% of the interviewers introduced information that the child had not previously volunteered, averaging more than seven pieces of new information per interview, and interviewers frequently repeated that new information—up to 60 *times* during the course of a single interview.

Similarly, analyses of "front-line" forensic interviews in Israel, Florida, and Tennessee (conducted by specially trained "youth investigators," police officials, and CPS workers, respectively) indicated that fewer than 5% of the interviewers' utterances in the substantive portions of the interviews involved open-ended invitations designed to elicit free narratives (Lamb, Hershkowitz, Sternberg, Boat, & Everson, 1996; Lamb, Hershkowitz, Sternberg, Esplin, et al., 1996; Sternberg, Lamb, Hershkowitz, Esplin, et al., 1996). Other studies of investigative interviews concur that these communication patterns are not atypical (Davies, Wilson, Mitchell, & Milsom, 1996). For example, Bull and Cherryman (1995) reported that many interviews of suspects in the United Kingdom were characterized by failures to use pauses and silences, lack of rapport, lack of empathy/compassion, inflexibility, and the use of leading questions.

In summary, there is little evidence that most interviewers spontaneously follow the general guidelines reviewed in chapter 2. On the contrary, interviewers often direct conversations by using a high proportion of yes–no questions, filling in pauses with conversation of their own, and fielding guesses to keep the conversation going. When these strategies monopolize an interview, it becomes impossible to separate the child's testimony from the adult's influence, and the information gathered can easily be discredited by claiming that the child was simply following the interviewer's lead. It has been proposed that protocols might provide interviewers with alternative ways of structuring conversations with children without dramatically reducing the amount of legally relevant information that children volunteer. Chapters 3 and 4 review recent efforts to achieve this goal.

3

THE DEVELOPMENT OF
INTERVIEW PROTOCOLS

Standards of practice must guide how people actually practice—not how they are trained, not how they think about practice, not how they discuss practice, but what they actually do. Standards provide bounds for practice. . . . Practitioners in psychology would not wish to engage in psychotherapy, or present themselves as experts in forensic and other critical settings, and then practice in ways inconsistent with our best knowledge of psychological principles.

Robyn M. Dawes
"Standards of Practice"
Scientific Standards of Psychological Practice:
Issues and Recommendations

The field of investigative interviewing is still in its infancy. In the future, interviewers might have empirically based "decision trees" to help them decide how to interview, depending on such factors as the child's age, the circumstances that necessitated the interview, and the potential uses of the resulting information. Instead, what we currently have is a set of protocols designed to increase the quality and quantity of information that interviewers elicit from children, but no information about how the choice of protocol affects the decisions professionals make on behalf of children. Despite the fact that systematic research is only in its early stages, however, remarkable similarities exist in the recommendations that have been offered by professionals throughout the world. The goal of this chapter is to describe the central features of the most widely publicized and respected guidelines in investigative interviewing. We highlight the similarities among these guidelines in this chapter, then devote the whole of chapter 4 to presenting a generic, flexible protocol that reflects areas of consensus.

Efforts to construct interview protocols involve two basic strategies. The first and easiest task is to eliminate techniques that are explicitly suggestive or that impair accuracy for other reasons. Relying heavily on the types of studies reported in chapter 2, early recommendations to interviewers were primarily lists of "don'ts" rather than lists of "dos," with advice to avoid leading questions, developmentally inappropriate language, and suggestive feedback. Because risky interviewing practices have been discussed quite extensively, there is a high degree of consensus concerning the items on these "don't" lists. Practitioners often throw up their hands in dismay at such recommendations, however. Devoid of practical advice on how to encourage conversation and interview effectively, discussions that focus on interviewing mistakes often leave practitioners feeling paralyzed in their efforts to help children.

A parallel strategy is necessary when developing practical interview protocols: Investigators must adopt better procedures to replace the risky practices they have been urged to avoid. As the following examples demonstrate, protocols vary somewhat with respect to the strategies suggested to encourage elaborate narratives from children. Familiarity with a variety of protocols therefore provides interviewers with a larger repertoire of communicative and investigative tools.

The literature on evaluating child sexual abuse allegations is the richest source of opinion on how to interview children, with hundreds of books and articles that collectively suggest a wide variety of practices. Ultimately, however, policymakers must sift through this forest of advice and confront two questions. First, does empirical evidence document the value of these techniques? Second, is there sufficient consensus in the professional community regarding recommended practices? In this chapter, we address these questions by reviewing selected guidelines from two types of sources: interview protocols developed to support ongoing research on investigative interviewing, and summary statements published by professional organizations or expert teams. In the first section, we describe protocols developed by research groups that were interested in specific issues or concerns. The Cognitive Interview was originally formulated in the United States as a technique to elicit information from adult eyewitnesses, with modifications for children representing a later development that is still being studied. The Structured Interview, developed by a group of psychologists in Germany and the United Kingdom, was designed to determine which components of the Cognitive Interview contributed to its success. In the second section we describe two other protocols that also advocate "phased" approaches to interviewing: the Step-Wise Interview from Canada and the National Institute of Child Health and Human Development (NICHD) interview protocol. We then (in the third section) discuss consensus statements from professional organizations and expert teams. The most elaborate of these is the Memorandum of Good Practice, a government protocol assembled by a team of professionals in England and Wales in response to legislation that allowed videotapes of initial investigative interviews to be admitted as evidence in criminal proceedings. Areas of consensus and disagreement are summarized in our concluding section.

THE COGNITIVE INTERVIEW

The procedure for interviewing eyewitnesses that has attracted the most systematic research is the Cognitive Interview, developed in the early 1980s by Ron Fisher, from Florida International University, and Edward Geiselman, from the University of California, Los Angeles. The Cognitive Interview was designed to increase the completeness and accuracy of eyewitness accounts by deriving interview instructions and procedures from "generally accepted scientific principles of memory" (Fisher, Geiselman, & Amador, 1989, p. 722). Because the Cognitive Interview guidelines are frequently updated to accommodate new findings, the Cognitive Interview is best viewed as an approach to interviewing, or a set of flexible tools, rather than a static set of instructions. This approach includes three components: (a) principles of memory and cognition that describe the conditions associated with the accurate retrieval of event memories; (b) principles of communication and social interaction that guide the verbal and nonverbal behaviors of interviewers; and (c) the sequence of the Cognitive Interview. Because descriptions of these components have had a far-reaching impact on protocols that were developed after the initial version of the Cognitive Interview, we briefly summarize each of these principles after discussing the purposes and limitations of the technique.

Purposes and Limitations

The original goal of the Cognitive Interview was to improve the quality of police interviews with adult eyewitnesses. As noted by R. Fisher, Geiselman, and their colleagues (e.g., R. Fisher, 1995; Fisher, McCauley, & Geiselman, 1994), the completeness of eyewitness testimony often is a decisive factor in determining whether or not cases are solved, yet police officers receive less than adequate training in how to conduct effective interviews. For example, more than half of the police departments polled by the Rand Corporation (1975) provided no formal training in interviewing for new investigators. Instead, police officers in many jurisdictions learn to conduct interviews by observing other officers or by trial and error. Moreover, police officers conduct interviews for a variety of reasons, and the techniques used in these situations (such as interviews with suspects) often influence their behavior when interviewing young victims and eyewitnesses. It is not surprising, then, that many police interviews mirror the style found when adults talk to children: a brief introduction and request for a description, after which officers initiate a series of "staccato" style interactions consisting of closed, short-answer questions that elicit only brief answers before posing a final question such as "Is there anything else you can remember about the event?" (Fisher et al., 1994; Fisher, Geiselman, & Raymond, 1987; Sternberg, Lamb, Herskowitz, Esplin, et al.,

1996). Because the Cognitive Interview breaks this pattern of conversational control and encourages witnesses to report longer narratives, there has been considerable interest in testing whether children also respond favorably to Cognitive Interview instructions.

A few caveats are necessary before describing this interview technique. First, the Cognitive Interview was developed for interviews with adult witnesses when the crime was known to have occurred, and modifications may be needed when interviewing children about alleged crimes. Second, Cognitive Interview procedures were designed for use when questioning cooperative witnesses. As Fisher and Geiselman (1992) pointed out, "Witnesses who intentionally wish to withhold information will not be 'broken' by the Cognitive Interview" (pp. 6–7). For example, the Cognitive Interview does not advise investigators on how to encourage adolescents to retract inconsistent stories or how to deal with children who have been threatened into silence. Nevertheless, many researchers have found that interviewers who have been trained to use the Cognitive Interview procedures generally elicit more complete information from eyewitnesses than interviewers who use their standard procedures (Köhnken, 1995; Köhnken, Milne, Memon, & Bull, 1994), although the same amount of information is often obtained using other systematic or structured approaches that embody many Cognitive Interview components (e.g., Memon, Wark, Holley, Bull, & Koehnken,[1] 1997).

The principles underlying the Cognitive Interview provide a useful outline of the basic issues interviewers face when they set out to obtain narrative accounts of experienced events. Early versions of the instructions focused predominately on promoting memory retrieval, whereas the revised instructions also address the dynamics of interviewer–eyewitness interactions and expectations or emotional states that might interfere with complete recall. In the following paragraphs, we summarize the principles discussed by Fisher and his colleagues (e.g., Fisher & Geiselman, 1992; Fisher et al., 1994); research on the Cognitive Interview and adaptations for children are described after the general principles are explained.

Principles of Memory and General Cognition

Limited Mental Resources

Cognitive psychologists agree that witnesses have limited mental resources to apply to any given task. Proponents of the Cognitive Interview therefore recommend that interviewers attempt to eliminate distractions that could interfere with retrieving relevant memories. Specific recommen-

---

[1]This is a variant spelling of *Köhnken*. The name appears herein according to the form published in the original source.

dations include explicitly asking the eyewitness to concentrate, conducting interviews in quiet locations, and avoiding interruptions.

Context Re-creation

Mental representations of events include information about the target events as well as information about the contexts in which the events occurred (i.e., internal contexts such as emotional states and external contexts, including the surrounding environment). Consequently, context re-creation should improve the recollection of experienced events. Techniques include asking the eyewitness to think about the context of the events, asking specific questions to re-create these contexts, sketching the location of the events, or asking witnesses or victims to visit the scene of the alleged crime.

Extensive and Varied Retrieval

In memory studies, the total amount of information recalled often increases when individuals recall events more than once, because different details may be retrieved each time. Proponents of the Cognitive Interview assume that repeated memory searches are useful, but also that conducting searches in varied ways is more fruitful than simply repeating the same search process twice. There are many techniques that encourage witnesses to search their memories in different ways, such as varying the way questions are worded; asking witnesses to use various sensory modalities (e.g., sight, sound, smell) as cues or to recall events in different temporal sequences (forward and then backward); and asking for recall from another perspective (e.g., from the perspective of someone else who was at the crime scene). These last two techniques received only brief mention in Fisher and Geiselman's (1992) handbook because they were more difficult to implement and were rarely adopted by professionals who were trained to use the Cognitive Interview (Ron Fisher, personal communication, June 13, 1997).

Multiple Coding and Guided Imagery

Psychologists have long proposed that two types of representations are established in memory whenever we experience an event. The first type of code contains detailed information that is closely linked to the perceptual properties of the information (e.g., visual details, sounds, smells, etc.), whereas the second type of code is more abstract and represents meaning or relationships among units of information. This latter code will be heavily dependent on reporters' interpretations of events and their prior knowledge of specific details or relationships involved in the events (Paivio, 1971; Reyna & Brainerd, 1995).

Proponents of the Cognitive Interview assume that different codes might be activated, depending on the retrieval context, which in interview situations includes the general instructions and types of questions. This idea is strongly supported by laboratory studies of basic memory processes (e.g., Brainerd & Reyna, 1993). Eyewitnesses may be biased to report only the overall meaning or "gist" of an event, but interviewers can encourage them to report perceptual details by instructing them to close their eyes, create a mental image of the event, and report informative details about those images (Fisher & Geiselman, 1992).

Witness-Compatible Questioning

Many psychologists also assume that eyewitnesses can access only one mental representation at any particular time. Interview questions therefore should be compatible with the mental representation the eyewitness is currently using. This can be accomplished by having a checklist of topics that need to be covered rather than a predetermined set of questions, so that interviewers do not interrupt the speaker's train of thought by interposing unrelated questions.

Principles of Communication and Social Interaction

Transfer of Control to Witnesses

Along with many other experts, proponents of the Cognitive Interview emphasize that witnesses are the authorities on the topic, and therefore they should be the primary participants in the interview. Interviewers need to communicate this fact and avoid behaviors that transfer control back to themselves. A common but mistaken belief is that "interviewing requires asking many good questions" (Ron Fisher, personal communication, January 29, 1996). A better approach is for interviewers to encourage active participation, ask open-ended questions, avoid interrupting the witness, and be tolerant if the witness strays from responding to the immediate question.

Developing Rapport

Fisher and Geiselman underscored the importance of developing rapport with witnesses who have been physically or psychologically affected, and they suggest specific techniques for personalizing the interview and communicating empathy. Some of these techniques, such as using the child's name and repeating the child's last comment when expanding for a follow-up question, are appropriate during interviews with alleged child abuse victims. Other techniques, including statements of empathy that might be construed as telling the child that the event occurred (e.g., "I know you are afraid you might be hurt again"), could be harmless when the crime is a documented fact but should be avoided during investigative interviews of alleged abuse victims.

Converting Conscious Recollections Into Detailed Descriptions

Papers on the Cognitive Interview discuss a variety of techniques for encouraging detailed responses. Suggestions that generalize to child interviews include using feedback (e.g., "OK," "continue," "mm-hmm") and allowing witnesses to use nonverbal means of communicating (acting out a movement or drawing a picture, but see chap. 6 for further discussion of this issue).

The Sequence of the Cognitive Interview

The structure of the Cognitive Interview is a sequence of five stages: (a) the introduction; (b) open-ended narration; (c) the probing stage, during which the interviewer guides the witness to exhaust the contents of memory; (d) a review stage, during which the interviewer checks the accuracy of notes about the interview and provides additional opportunities to recall; and (e) the closing. Fisher and Geiselman's handbook (1992) includes descriptions and suggested wording for each of these stages, as well as analyses of sample interviews that illustrate appropriate practices and errors (e.g., questions that shift topics abruptly, complex wording, negative wording). Although the examples came from interviews with adults, these errors also occur when professionals interview children (Köhnken, 1993).

The section of the Cognitive Interview that requires the most extensive training is the probing stage. The purpose of this stage is to use repeated and varied retrieval probes to elicit as much information as possible, using nonleading questions. One approach to the probing stage would be to select, from the open-ended narration, the mental image that contains the most pertinent information (from the investigator's perspective) or the clearest image (from the witness's perspective; Ron Fisher, personal communication, January 29, 1996). The interviewer directs the witness to report everything possible about this image and then asks questions about aspects of the image that were not mentioned. The interviewer then selects another image and requests open-ended narration before asking nonleading questions about that. The interviewer should warn the witness not to fabricate, and at no time offer instructions that suggest imagination or fantasy. Rather, the series of questions in the probing state should build on the witness' prior responses, as in the following example:

Interviewer: When did you see him best?

Witness: When he was sitting on the bed.

Interviewer: OK, try to think about when he was sitting on the bed. Now, close your eyes and try to see the same picture of the man when he was sitting on the bed. Do you have a clear picture of him, or is it difficult?

Witness: I can see him really good.

Interviewer: Okay, now tell me as much as you can about what he looks like.

Professionals who interview children need to be sure that they do not ask questions during the probing stage merely for the sake of asking questions, however. It is important to emphasize that the Cognitive Interview was designed for cases in which detailed information was critical to solving cases. In sexual abuse cases, however, the alleged abusers are typically known to children, so there often is no reason to ask for detailed descriptions of an offender's appearance. The probing stage *is* essential, however, to flesh out sketchy descriptions or accounts that lack clear information about locations, time, or the sequence of events. Fisher and Geiselman's (1992) recommendation to choose questions on the basis of the witness' prior narrative is extremely useful even when interviewing young children.

Efficacy of the Cognitive Interview

Over time, both the Cognitive Interview and the research designed to evaluate it have become more sophisticated. Although the original Cognitive Interview addressed fewer issues than the revised version, many researchers have documented its effectiveness with adults (Köhnken, 1995). Four studies met Fisher and McCauley's (1995) criteria for proper tests of the revised instructions: two laboratory and two field investigations. Laboratory studies are important because investigators know what the target events were, and therefore they can compare the amount of accurate and inaccurate information that witnesses recall under varying interview procedures. Field studies, which rely on real crimes or traumatic events, have the advantage of generalizing techniques to actual victims and professional interviewers, but these types of studies do not permit researchers to evaluate accuracy unless the actual events were recorded.

In one laboratory study (Fisher, Geiselman, Raymond, Jurkevich, & Warhaftig, 1987), the revised Cognitive Interview procedure yielded 45% more correct information than the original version and almost twice as much information as a standard police interview—without significantly increasing the number of incorrect or false details the adult witnesses mentioned. In a second laboratory study, George (1991, cited in Fisher & Geiselman, 1992) found that the average Cognitive Interview yielded 36% more information than standard British police interviews. The value of the Cognitive Interview also has been confirmed in field studies (Fisher et al., 1989; George, 1991, as cited in Fisher & Geiselman, 1992). Although accuracy rates could not be computed in these field investigations, corroboration rates were similar for information elicited from Cognitive and standard interviews.

In a meta-analysis of 32 experimental comparisons from 25 reports that included laboratory and field studies, the Cognitive Interview yielded approximately 36% more correct information than comparison interviews (e.g., standard police interviews or interviews conducted by research assistants who received training that did not involve specific techniques used in the Cognitive Interview) without a notable increase in the proportion of the information that was incorrect (i.e., 82% correct information in standard interviews compared with 84% in Cognitive Interviews; Köhnken et al., 1994; also summarized in Köhnken, 1995).

Modifications of the Cognitive Interview for Children

Despite its apparent strengths, many psychologists have wondered whether the Cognitive Interview is developmentally appropriate for children under the age of 7 or 8 years (Cronin, Memon, Eaves, Küpper, & Bull, 1992). Three techniques in particular might be problematic for young children: General requests for repeated recall, requests to recall in varied temporal orders, and requests to recall from a variety of physical perspectives.

The overriding concern about repeated recall is that children might feel pressured to change their answers because they interpret repeated requests to mean that their first answers were somehow inadequate (Poole & White, 1991; Siegal, 1991). Even without such complicated inferences, children may simply be puzzled by repeated requests. The following dialogue from a study by Cronin et al. (1992) illustrates this concern:

Q: OK, what about the day the nurse came, can you tell me about that? I know you've told me already but I need to find out again.

A: Yes, just in case I'm saying the right things.

Q: The best thing to do is to start again and tell me everything you can remember.

A: Well, I can't tell you the same things. (p. 4)

Cronin et al. also expressed concern about the use of "change-order" and "change-perspective" instructions, because the ability to recall in correct temporal order or from varying perspectives increases with age. The following response illustrates how children might fail to understand these directions:

Q: What I'd like you to try and do now is imagine that you are the nurse and that you can see the room from where she was standing, by the wall chart. Try and tell me what she could have seen from where she was.

A: Umm. Did you see the letters, can you see the letters good, and I said yes and that's all she said to me. (p. 5)

Because children have more difficulty than adults in understanding specific memory instructions (e.g., Memon, Cronin, Eaves, & Bull, 1996), it is not surprising that the Cognitive Interview does not enhance memory quite as much when used with child witnesses as when used with adults (Memon & Bull, 1991). For example, Geiselman and Padilla (1988) and Saywitz, Geiselman, and Bornstein (1992) found that 7- to 12-year-olds reported between 18% and 26% more accurate information with the Cognitive Interview, without an increase in errors. In contrast, other researchers either failed to find that specific Cognitive Interview instructions helped children recall information (e.g., Memon, Cronin, et al., 1996) or found an increase in the number of errors along with an increase in the amount of correct information (Köhnken, Finger, Nitschke, Höfer, & Aschermann, 1992; McCauley & Fisher, 1995; Memon, Wark, Bull, & Koehnken, 1997; Milne, Bull, Koehnken, & Memon, 1995).

It may be that children need special training in order to fully understand some of the Cognitive Interview procedures (Geiselman, Saywitz, & Bornstein, 1993). To address this possibility, investigators have modified the Cognitive Interview to give children practice by first having them describe a familiar action (such as brushing their teeth or playing a popular computer game). In one experiment, 7-year-old children interviewed using the modified Cognitive Interview procedures recalled almost twice as many actions from a witnessed event as those who experienced a standard interview. In a second experiment, the Cognitive Interview was superior even though the comparison interview was developed by professional social workers and was administered by professional interviewers (Fisher et al., 1994).

In a recent study of the modified Cognitive Interview, 86 second graders either watched or participated in a "Simon Says" game with an unfamiliar adult (McCauley & Fisher, 1995). Seventy of the children were later interviewed twice, once several hours after the event and again 2 weeks later, whereas the remaining children were interviewed only after a 2-week delay. The investigators compared three interview procedures: the Cognitive Interview, a Standard Interview, and an interview by one of two professional social workers who interviewed children in the criminal justice system (the Professional Interview). Standard Interviews included the following items in sequence: rapport building with focused questions about familiar topics (e.g., "How many brothers and sisters do you have?"); instructions to tell everything remembered about the target events, even if the details did not seem important; probes about any statements that were vague (e.g., "You said you played a game. . . . Can you tell me more about it?"); and final requests for information about anything else the children could report.

The Cognitive Interview differed from the Standard Interview during the rapport-building and probing stages. Cognitive interviewers built rapport by asking children to describe a favorite game in detail, with the interviewers feigning ignorance as an excuse to request more information. This strategy reverses the usual social roles and conveys that the child, not the adult, is the authority in the interaction. After initial free recall, Cognitive interviewers asked participants to visualize the room in which the event had occurred by closing their eyes and picturing who else was in the room and how the room looked and felt. When children indicated that they had a good mental image, interviewers asked them to describe it, instructed them to describe actions, and then asked specific probes to elicit clarifications. Interviewers also encouraged the children to demonstrate actions they could not describe verbally. This sequence of visualization instructions and questions was repeated to elicit information about the woman who played the games.

In this study, even second graders benefited from Cognitive Interview instructions. McCauley and Fisher (1995) focused on comparisons between the Standard and Cognitive Interviews, both of which used trained research assistants as interviewers. The modified Cognitive Interview resulted in 64% more correct information than did the Standard Interview in the first interview and 46% more correct information in the second interview. Furthermore, accuracy rates were comparable across the two conditions.

Although these results are encouraging, it is important to emphasize that these studies involved interviews about events that actually had occurred. This reflects the origin of the Cognitive Interview as a tool for interviewing adult bystander/participant witnesses. In child sexual abuse cases, however, interviews also are conducted with some children who have not been abused but who *have* been exposed to previous conversations about abuse. The value of the Cognitive Interview in these circumstances remains unknown. On the one hand, practice recall (i.e., describing a favorite game in detail) is an effective and nonsuggestive rapport-building procedure, so this component of the Cognitive Interview probably is appropriate regardless of a child's age or abuse status. On the other hand, visualization of context might be helpful or problematic, depending on the child's age and the validity of the allegations. Children who are not victims should have difficulty visualizing alleged crimes, and the Cognitive Interview might reveal this and encourage retractions or inconsistent testimony that could help identify false allegations. In contrast, the act of visualization might also consolidate a false memory or lead children to expand allegations because of source-monitoring problems, particularly when they are young or are interviewed repeatedly. There currently is insufficient evidence on the impact of visualization techniques, but available studies have not found that visualization consistently helps children (cf. Dietze, 1994; Dietze & Thomson, 1993).

For the time being, interviewers should be cautious about using visualization techniques with children under the age of 10 years, particularly prior to disclosures about the target events, because doing so could provide fodder for legal challenges. Visualization techniques and instructions to repeatedly think about nonexperienced events feature prominently in discussions of adults' and children's false memories (e.g., Ceci, Huffman, et al., 1994; Lindsay & Read, 1994), and therefore it probably is best to avoid these instructions until the relevant research has been conducted. Instead, interviewers can benefit from other components of the Cognitive Interview that are less controversial. But which aspects of the Cognitive Interview are essential for producing detailed narratives? The Structured Interview was developed to answer this question.

Testing Selected Cognitive Interview Techniques With Adults and Children: The Structured Interview

Cognitive Interview procedures include several techniques or strategies that might account for its superiority over standard police interviews. For example, training alone could improve interviewers' motivation and enhance the effort they make to elicit detailed accounts. Similarly, a few general behaviors, such as using open-ended questions and not interrupting witnesses, could account for why witnesses generally recount more information with the Cognitive Interview. Researchers in Germany and the United Kingdom have worked together on a series of studies designed to determine whether specific techniques described in early versions of the Cognitive Interview actually elicit more information than is obtained when interviewers follow only the motivational, social, and conversational guidelines. To this end, they developed an interview protocol, called the Structured Interview, that mimics the Cognitive Interview in all but a few specific respects. In one study, for example, the Structured Interview followed the general form of the Cognitive Interview but without context reinstatement, "report everything" instructions, probing of images related to various parts of the event, and recalling in reverse order (Memon, Wark, Bull, & Koehnken, 1997). These researchers reasoned that if the Structured Interview produces as much accurate information as the full Cognitive Interview, then obviously it is unnecessary to press witnesses for information using the specific techniques that they excluded from the Structured Interview.

Günter Köhnken—in collaboration with Ray Bull, Angela Holley, Amina Memon, Rebecca Milne, and Linsey Wark—developed a training manual for research with the Structured Interview (Köhnken, 1993). The manual includes an introduction to the Structured Interview and the role of the interviewer, a list of good interviewer behaviors (e.g., "express attention and interest frequently by nodding, "mhm" etc., but do not give qualitative feedback ['good', 'right']"), a description of the overall structure of the interview, and detailed instructions for each portion of the interview as well as practice exercises. The protocol includes the following eight phases:

1. Greeting the child
2. Establishing rapport
3. Explaining the purpose of the interview and reminding the child not to guess or fabricate
4. Asking the child to give a free report
5. Asking the child if he or she can remember more
6. Questioning
7. Making a third retrieval attempt
8. Closing (e.g., thanking the child for cooperation)

The Structured Interview thus parallels the Cognitive Interview by emphasizing rapport, allowing witnesses to guide interactions, recommending open-ended rather than specific or leading questions, and encouraging multiple recall attempts.

How does the Structured Interview perform when compared with the Cognitive Interview? Although results vary from study to study, discrepancies are easily resolved by considering known memory phenomena. In an article by Memon, Wark, Bull, and Koehnken (1997), for example, 109 children between the ages of 8 and 9 years watched a brief magic show and then were interviewed either once (10–13 days after the event) or twice (1–2 days and 10–13 days after the event). In the early interview, half of the children received a Cognitive Interview and the other half received a Structured Interview designed to replicate all the features of the Cognitive Interview except for specific mnemonic procedures such as mental context reinstatement and "reverse order" recall. The children were similarly assigned to either the Cognitive or Structured Interview for the delayed interview.

Even though the Cognitive Interview was compared with another structured protocol, children interviewed using the Cognitive Interview recalled more information after the short delay than did children who received the Structured Interview. The Cognitive Interview also was associated with more errors, but at a rate of only about 1 additional error for every 6 additional correct details (yielding similar error rates across the two interviewing conditions). After the longer delay, the advantage of the Cognitive Interview was no longer evident, however. The authors speculated that the Cognitive Interview might be most effective in eliciting details from images, which generally are less available as time passes.

The Cognitive Interview also may produce the same information as a Structured Interview when witnessed events are not particularly salient or memorable. For example, Memon, Wark, Holley, et al. (1997) showed a brief videotape of a crime to 66 college students and assigned each to one of three interviewing conditions: Cognitive Interview, Structured Interview, or untrained interviewer. There was the typical advantage of the Cognitive Interview when the authors eliminated data from the second retrieval attempt (reported in Memon, Wark, Holley, Bull, & Köhnken, 1995); however, the second retrieval attempt eliminated the advantage of the Cognitive Interview relative to the Structured Interview. In this study, interviewers asked witnesses to describe a very brief videotaped event (1.5 min long) that certainly was not as meaningful as participating in a live event, and consequently there may have been little information available to report. Similarly, the Cognitive Interview failed to elicit more information than the Structured Interview from 8- to 9-year-olds who had watched a brief videotaped event, although children who received the Cognitive Interview were less suggestible when later asked misleading questions (Memon, Holley, Wark, Bull, & Koehnken, 1996).

In sum, several tentative conclusions can be drawn about interview strategies. A commonsense conclusion is that the advantage of the Cognitive Interview over comparison interviews becomes smaller as the similarities between the interview protocols increase. Consequently, the advantage of the Cognitive Interview over the Structured Interview (which includes numerous Cognitive Interview components) generally is less than the advantage of the Cognitive Interview over interviews by investigators who do not follow structured protocols or recommendations about optimal question types, question orders, pacing, or demeanor. Also, the benefit of the Cognitive Interview is less whenever witnesses have less elaborated memories and, hence, fewer details available to report. The advantage of a full range of Cognitive Interview techniques or strategies therefore tends to be lost when the witnessed event is not particularly salient (i.e., watching a brief film or event as a bystander), when there is an extended delay between the event and the interview, or when comparison interviews encourage multiple retrieval attempts (as does the Cognitive Interview). The superiority of the Cognitive Interview will be most obvious when available memory representations are rich in perceptual details and the interviewer probes for this information.

The Cognitive Interview and the evaluative research associated with it have had wide-ranging influences on attitudes about interviewing. Most other interview protocols also recommend that phases of the interview follow a similar sequence: rapport building, providing clear instructions about the purpose and rules of the interview, focusing on eliciting a free narrative without interruptions from the interviewer, clarification, and clos-ing.[2]

OTHER PHASED APPROACHES

The Step-Wise Interview

The sequence of stages followed in the Cognitive and Structured In-terviews also is represented in a protocol that is aptly named the Step-Wise Interview. This interviewing approach is associated with the writings of John Yuille, from the University of British Columbia, and his coauthors (Marxsen, Yuille, & Nisbet, 1995; Raskin & Yuille, 1989; Yuille, 1988, 1991; Yuille & Farr, 1987; Yuille et al., 1993). According to Yuille et al. (1993), the protocol serves four major goals: (a) minimizing trauma to the child by increasing the skill of the interviewer and decreasing the need for multiple interviews; (b) minimizing contamination of the child's statement by directing the interviewer to use nonsuggestive probes; (c) maximizing recall by drawing on Cognitive Interview techniques when appropriate; and (d) maintaining the investigative integrity of the inter-view by promoting a flexible protocol that can be modified to meet the different needs of child protection, treatment, and criminal prosecution (Marxsen et al., 1995; Yuille et al., 1993). For example, question formats that have a higher risk of eliciting errors might be deemed inappropriate for most cases that could result in criminal charges but appropriate for some cases with prior documented disclosure, unambiguous physical evidence, or no possibility of criminal conviction (e.g., child protection procedures). The Step-Wise Interview has been adopted for use by police and child protection workers in many parts of Canada and the United States, and the sequential format was adopted for published guidelines in England and Wales (see Home Office, 1992) as well as in many U.S. jurisdictions (e.g., Cook County Task Force on Intake and Interviewing, 1996).

The core of the Step-Wise Interview is a funnel approach that begins with the most open-ended questions and progresses down to more specific questions as necessary. The overall format, described by Yuille et al. (1993), involves nine basic steps:

1. Rapport building
2. Requesting recall of two specific events
3. Explaining the need to tell the truth

---

[2]There have been debates about what it means to use the Structured Interview as a comparison against which to test the Cognitive Interview. An article by Memon and Stevenage (1996), with replies by Fisher (1996) and others, provides a good introduction to this debate.

4. Introducing the topic of concern
5. Encouraging a free narrative
6. Asking general questions
7. Asking specific questions (if necessary)
8. Using interview aids (if necessary)
9. Concluding the interview

Although the Step-Wise, Structured, and Cognitive Interviews are similar in many respects, descriptions of the Step-Wise and Structured Interviews emphasize discrete stages, each characterized by specific types of questions. In contrast, phases of the Cognitive Interview that deal with the target event are characterized less by the type of question interviewers ask and more by the need to explore various images from witnesses' initial free recall, with a sequence that involves visualization, description, and clarification of each image. There are potential tradeoffs between these techniques: It can be more difficult to train interviewers in the Cognitive Interview, because they are encouraged to be more interactive and make more spontaneous decisions, but Cognitive Interview trainers typically provide considerable practice with witness-based questioning.

At the beginning of a Step-Wise Interview, the interviewer begins to establish rapport by discussing neutral topics that are appropriate for the child's age. After this preliminary interaction, the interviewer asks the child to describe two specific past experiences, such as a birthday party or a recent outing. This part of rapport building provides baseline data on the child's verbal skills, allows the interviewer to reinforce the child for talking, and gives the child practice responding to open-ended and nonleading questions that will set the stage for the remainder of the interview.

After rapport has been established, the interviewer explains the need to tell the truth and underscores the serious nature of the interview in a nonthreatening way. The topic is introduced in a step-wise fashion by first attempting the least suggestive opening remarks. For example, the interviewer might begin with "Do you know why you are talking with me today?" Discussion of people the child likes and dislikes could follow if more neutral remarks do not begin a conversation. At no time are the suspect or the alleged acts specifically mentioned by the interviewer.

As with the other protocols described in this chapter, the substantive part of the interview begins when the interviewer asks the child to describe events from beginning to end, without leaving out any details. For children who have experienced repeated abuse, Yuille et al. (1993) recommended probing with script-based questions first—such as "Can you tell me how it usually happens?"—followed by questions about specific episodes. Because departures from a script are often well remembered, specific episodes can be explored by asking the child if the actions ever happened in a different place or in a different manner. Yuille et al. also recommended labeling multiple incidents for future reference; for example, by saying, "You said it happened in the kitchen. Let's call it the kitchen time" (p. 107).

Following the child's initial narrative, the interviewer probes for additional information, first with general and then with specific questions. General questions are open-ended and take the form, "You mentioned _____, do you remember anything more about that?" Topics that produce distress can be handled in various ways; one recommendation is to shift to a more neutral topic, then back again. The interviewer uses specific questions to fill in details and follow up inconsistencies. Whenever possible, multiple-choice format questions are avoided. When they are used, Yuille and his colleagues recommended including more than two alternatives and repeating the question later in the interview with the options offered in a different order. As in the Cognitive Interview, a second attempt to elicit a narrative can be made after specific questioning is completed, provided the interviewer clarifies that the original testimony is not being questioned (e.g., "I think I understand most of what you told me, but my memory's not so hot. Will you help me by telling me once more everything you remember about the time in the kitchen?"; Yuille et al., 1993, p. 109). In laboratory studies, children as young as 4 years answered similar nonsuggestive questions three times in a row without an increase in errors, although occasionally with mild annoyance (Poole & White, 1991, 1993).

The Step-Wise protocol permits interviewers to use drawings and dolls for clarification *after* children have disclosed an event. This cautious use of ancillary aids ensures that interviewers do not use props to suggest sexual themes before a child acknowledges participation in sexual events. The interviewer concludes by thanking the child, answering any questions the child has, and telling the child how to contact the interviewer if he or she has additional information to discuss.

The Canadian Ministry of Social Services, in consultation with John Yuille, has compiled videotapes of actual interviews for training purposes. These tapes provide valuable lessons that are impossible to glean from the written protocol alone. A striking feature of the interviews is the relaxed yet uncluttered environment that centers around a table and chairs. Each interviewer's demeanor is calm, unhurried, and accepting, with pauses to permit spontaneous additions by the child and opportunities for the interviewer to develop thoughtful questions. A field test of the protocol generated positive responses, with interviewers reporting that the protocol was especially helpful for organizing their interviews. Comparisons of standard and Step-Wise Interviews found that 30% of the standard interviews produced information that was judged to be deficient, whereas only 5% of the

Step-Wise Interviews contained information that was deemed contaminated or inadequate (Yuille et al., 1993). As with the Cognitive and Structured Interviews, however, few attempts have been made to examine the structure and yield of investigative interviews conducted with children using the Step-Wise procedures. As a result, the strengths and weaknesses of these approaches are poorly understood.

The NICHD Protocol

An interview protocol developed by researchers at the National Institute of Child Health and Human Development (NICHD) is similar in many ways to the Cognitive, Structured, and Step-Wise Interview procedures, by which its developers were influenced (Lamb, Sternberg, & Esplin, in press). As in the Cognitive Interview, for example, the NICHD interview protocol is designed to give children practice providing detailed accounts of experienced events before interviewers ask them about the issues under investigation. Both protocols also require interviewers to admonish children to tell the truth and encourage them to correct the interviewer or say "I don't know" when relevant. Experimental versions of the NICHD protocol also have included context reinstatement techniques inspired by the developers of the Cognitive Interview, including visits to the scene of the alleged events (Hershkowitz et al., in press). The NICHD interview protocol includes the following phases or stages, in sequence:

1. Introduction of parties and their roles
2. The "truth and lie ceremony"
3. Rapport building and language sampling
4. Description of a recent salient event
5. First narrative account of the allegation
6. Narrative accounts of the last incident (if the child reports multiple incidents)
7. Cue questions (e.g., "You said something about a barn. Tell me about that.")
8. Paired direct-open questions about the last incident
9. Narrative account of the first incident
10. Cue questions
11. Paired direct-open questions about the first incident
12. Narrative accounts of another incident that the child remembers well
13. Cue questions
14. Paired direct-open questions about this incident
15. If necessary, leading questions about forensically important details not mentioned by the child

16. Invitation for any other information the child wants to mention
17. Return to a neutral topic

Because detailed analyses of forensic interviews have documented that interviewers seldom used the open-ended invitations that are widely recommended by experts on investigative interviewing (Lamb, Hershkowitz, Sternberg, Boat, & Everson, 1996; Lamb, Hershkowitz, Sternberg, Esplin, et al., 1996; Sternberg, Lamb, Hershkowitz, Esplin, et al., 1996; Warren et al., 1996), and because their own initial efforts to change interviewer behavior proved frustrating, Lamb and his colleagues decided to supplement their general guidelines with specific interview scripts that interviewers were asked to follow verbatim. In their first experimental study of Israeli children who had previously disclosed sexual abuse, Sternberg et al. (1997) reported that children whose interviewers followed either of two scripted protocols provided more than six times the number of details in response to the first substantive prompt (i.e., "Now that we know each other a little better I want to talk about the reason that you are here today. I understand that something may have happened to you. Please tell me everything that happened, every detail, from the very beginning to the very end."; p. 1145) than did children whose interviewers simply followed general guidelines. Furthermore, the interviewers elicited more than twice as much information, using the same prompt, when the children had been trained during the rapport-building phase to provide narrative responses to open-ended prompts rather than responses to more specific questions.

Sternberg et al. (1997) scripted only through the beginning of Phase 5 on the above list; that is, through the first question about the substantive issue under investigation. Close examination of the interview transcripts showed that the investigators quickly reverted to reliance on focused and specific questions as soon as they finished the scripted portions of the interview. As a result, these researchers developed more elaborated interview scripts that covered all 17 of the phases listed above, and initiated field studies in Israel and the United States to evaluate the effectiveness of these more explicit scripts. Although this research is still in its early stages, preliminary analyses have revealed that these scripts are extremely useful in forensic contexts. A version developed for interviews of preschoolers has yet to be evaluated, and it is not known to what extent the additional details elicited using these scripted protocols are accurate or forensically valuable. Furthermore, because the interviews were developed for and field tested on children who had already disclosed abuse, we also do not know how effective these procedures would be when abuse has been only suspected by third parties but has not been acknowledged previously by the children.

SUMMARY STATEMENTS BY PROFESSIONAL ORGANIZATIONS AND EXPERT TEAMS

Memorandum of Good Practice

In 1992, the Home Office and the Department of Health in England and Wales published the *Memorandum of Good Practice*. This document outlines procedures for conducting and recording interviews with children who are involved or might be involved in criminal proceedings.[3] The *Memorandum* was a response to the Criminal Justice Act of 1991 that permitted a recorded interview to substitute for the first stage of a child's evidence in chief, provided the child was available for cross- and reexamination (or met one of several reasons for nonavailability specified by the Criminal Justice Act of 1988).

The *Memorandum* is an impressive model of protocol development. Early drafts were rich with research citations that documented the evidence underlying specific recommendations. Although these citations were deleted to produce a more readable final version, the protocol was an informed summary of best-practice standards (see Bull, 1992, for a summary of the procedures and agencies involved in producing the *Memorandum*). Equally impressive is the scope of topics covered by the *Memorandum*: explanations of relevant criminal law for practitioners in England and Wales, detailed explanations of the pragmatics of video recording (e.g., what equipment to use, how to store tapes and deal with eventual destruction of tapes), the interview protocol, and special topics such as recommendations regarding interviews with children who have special needs and the use of dolls and other props. The organization of the *Memorandum*—including left-column summaries, numbered paragraphs, and a quick-reference summary table— resulted in a document that is both accessible for training purposes and efficient as a reference for experienced interviewers.[4]

The *Memorandum* specifies a phased approach in which interviewers proceed from the most general to the most specific questioning. The overall format involves rapport building, free narrative account, open-ended questions, specific yet nonleading questions, closed questions, leading questions (which are rarely used), and closure. The *Memorandum* permits the use of "facilitative" styles of questioning (e.g., open-ended discussions of good and bad people or secrets) for reticent children, provided that (a) there is prior discussion and agreement with "senior managers," (b) the interviewer avoids suggestive questioning, and (c) the child is encouraged to give a spontaneous account.

---

[3]Copies of the *Memorandum* are available from Her Majesty's Stationery Office, P.O. Box 276, London, SW8 5DT; telephone (U.K.) 171–873–9090.
[4]The *Memorandum* currently is being revised by a team under the direction of Graham Davies for a project sponsored by the Home Office.

Davies, Wilson, Mitchell, and Milsom (1996) reported the results of a 27-month evaluation conducted under the auspices of the Home Office to assess the impact of the 1991 Criminal Justice Act and the *Memorandum*. Evaluation involved two surveys: an initial survey distributed in 1993 to document concerns and expectations before most workers had practical experience with the Act, and a second survey, completed in 1994, of professionals who had actually been involved in legal proceedings brought under the Act. There was initial enthusiasm for the *Memorandum* that was maintained in the follow-up data: 98% of social workers and 100% of police officers agreed in principle with the introduction of the *Memorandum*. Respondents did voice several concerns, however. One sore point was that police officers often led joint interviewing, which led social workers to feel "divorced from the investigative process" (p. 8). Social workers complained that the *Memorandum* was rigid in some areas and vague in others, and that it provided insufficient examples. Both social workers and police officers felt that the *Memorandum* was too rigid when interviewing young children or children with special needs, and both groups felt that there was not enough time for planning the interviews. Regarding compliance with the protocol, a review of 40 tapes revealed that interviewers generally followed the stepwise approach outlined in the *Memorandum*, although they frequently omitted the free-narrative phase and used an excessive number of closed rather than open-ended questions. Despite these difficulties, there was a clear account of the event in three quarters of the tapes.

Because the *Memorandum* requires interviewers to videotape investigative interviews, it was possible to examine conviction and acquittal rates for trials that admitted videotaped interviews versus those that relied on live examination[5]: There was no association between verdicts and the type of examination-in-chief submitted, leading Davies et al. to conclude that "videotapes do not have less impact on a jury than a live account" (p. 35). This finding is especially important in light of concerns that videotaping interviews might provide opportunities for defense attorneys to challenge interview techniques. In fact, defense attorneys were more likely than prosecuting attorneys to request exclusion of the videotapes, suggesting that they feared the impact of the videotape more than they relished the opportunity to challenge interviewing practices.

American Professional Society on the Abuse of Children Guidelines

In 1990, the American Professional Society on the Abuse of Children (APSAC)[6] produced a statement entitled *Guidelines for Psychosocial Evaluation of Suspected Sexual Abuse in Young Children*. In the Statement of Pur-

---

[5]"Live" testimony includes testifying via closed circuit television.
[6]Copies of the *Guidelines* are available from APSAC at 407 South Dearborn, Suite 1300, Chicago, Illinois 60605. Telephone (312) 554–0166.

pose, APSAC distinguished between investigative interviews, which focus on eliciting statements about alleged sexual abuse and are normally limited to a single session, and the goals of the *Guidelines*, which were to provide guidance to mental health professionals who are retained to explore a broader range of issues (including the child's general adjustment and functioning). However, APSAC pointed out that the general principles contained in the *Guidelines* would apply to investigative interviews as well.

The *Guidelines* were constructed by a task force under the direction of Lucy Berliner. The group first compiled specific recommendations from the results of an open-ended survey that they had mailed to selected professionals, then revised this draft to respond to written and verbal comments from a large group of practitioners. The resulting version was published in APSAC's newsletter and was subsequently revised following further feedback.

The *Guidelines* recommend that interviewers prepare by interviewing the primary caretaker to obtain background information and by collecting collateral information as necessary. The preferred practice is to see the child alone whenever possible. Reflecting concerns about suggestibility, the *Guidelines* advocate starting with open-ended questions and proceeding to specific questions only as necessary, with interviewers resorting to highly specific questioning only when "other methods of questioning have failed, when previous information warrants substantial concern, or when the child's developmental level precludes more non-directive approaches. However, responses to these questions should be carefully evaluated and weighed accordingly" (p. 5). Finally, the *Guidelines* recommend cautious use of interview aids such as anatomical dolls and drawings.

The major differences between the *Guidelines* and most investigative protocols are discussions of the number of sessions and the type of questions that are recommended. The *Guidelines* note that two to six sessions might be involved, although not all of these would include specific questions about sexual abuse. Moreover, the *Guidelines* recommend that children be questioned directly about possible sexual abuse at some point in the interview. Although these recommendations provide more leeway for repeated interviewing and directive questioning, the *Guidelines* warn evaluators not to engage in repeated directed questioning when the child does not report abuse, and they instruct evaluators to consider and rule out alternative explanations for suspicions of abuse.[7]

---

[7]Many professional organizations in addition to APSAC have published interviewing guidelines. For example, the National Center for Prosecution of Child Abuse, with the American Prosecutors Research Institute and the National District Attorneys Association (1993), produced an interviewing protocol that focuses more on eliciting detailed information about alleged events, and therefore their guidelines are more tolerant about asking numerous specific questions than are most current guidelines. Because we could not review every published protocol, we did not select protocols for this discussion if it was unclear how the specific guidelines had been developed, if the guidelines lacked sufficient research citations to justify the various recommendations, or if the protocol raised issues already discussed in this chapter.

Other Summary Statements

Numerous summary statements have cropped up in the past few years that represent a growing consensus about the format, contents, and importance of investigative interviews. One statement resulted from a conference in 1993 sponsored by the U.S. National Institute of Child Health and Human Development and two Swedish organizations (Lamb, 1994). Written by Michael Lamb with input from 19 other cosigners,[8] this document underscored the need to emphasize open-ended questions, ask direct questions as nonsuggestively as possible, and attempt to follow direct questions with questions that elicit free narratives.

Other recent articles also have outlined the characteristics of forensic interviewing that enjoy the most widespread acceptance (e.g., Lamb et al., 1994, 1995, in press; McGough & Warren, 1994; Walker & Hunt, 1998; Warren & McGough, 1996). Two features of these summary statements are noteworthy. First is the diversity of professionals represented among them, including mental health practitioners, specialists in language and cognitive development, and legal professionals. Second is the extent of agreement on the basic structure of investigative interviews: a "funnel" approach in which interviewers begin with open-ended questions and proceed to more direct questions with caution, always attempting to push the interview back to open-ended probes that elicit narrative information from the child (e.g., Lamb et al., 1994, 1995, in press). Although these core recommendations have become so commonplace that they now appear commonsensical, in fact they represent a dramatic departure from the way adults generally talk to children.

CONCLUSION

Research on improvements in interviewing practice paints an optimistic, albeit a preliminary, picture of directions for policy making and future research. The results of laboratory and field studies provide assurance that interviewers can reduce the number of specific and leading questions they ask without compromising the amount of information they elicit from children. Furthermore, interviewers who prepare children to relate events with clear instructions or opportunities for practice recall actually elicit more usable information with fewer specific questions than do interviewers who simply follow their default procedures. In a comparison of expert recommendations, interviewer practices, and state statutes, Walker and Hunt

---

[8]Cosigners of the interdisciplinary consensus statement were A. Bentovim, D. Besharov, B. Boat, R. Bull, A. Cederström, S.-Å. Christiansson, P. Esplin, L. Feuk, W. Friedrich, G. Goodman, I. Hershkowitz, P. Hwang, C. Jamieson, M. Lamb, J. McCann, W. Mollerstrom, E. Normann, H. Sariola, K. Sternberg, and U. Undeutsch.

(1998) also were struck with the high degree of consensus regarding the core structure of an investigative interview:

> Although this sample from North America and Europe represents various perspectives and interests, the recommendations for sound interviewing practices are quite consistent. For example, every professional recommended building rapport with children before incident-related questioning begins. Each one also recommended requesting a free narrative before engaging in direct questioning and asking direct questions only if free narrative reports are inadequate. Nearly all of the publications specifically recommended obtaining official information and discussing the "ground rules" for the interview, and several suggested asking developmentally appropriate questions, formally closing the interview when questioning has been completed, and using demonstration aids only if necessary. Some recommended explaining the interview purpose and conducting a practice interview before forensically relevant questioning begins. No one in our sample recommended asking children to differentiate "good" or "bad" touches. (p. 57)

Available data are limited in some important respects, however. Two basic research designs have been used to compare specific protocols: laboratory studies of children who were interviewed about events that actually occurred, and field studies in which the true state of affairs was unknown or cases were selected because the alleged abuse seemed likely to have occurred. Ultimately, however, the goal should be to determine whether any given protocol leads to more accurate determinations when interviewers question children who have been abused *and* children who have not been abused but who are the focus of suspicions (Bruck & Ceci, 1996). Obviously, the methodological challenges of conducting "diagnostic accuracy" research are far greater than the challenges of conducting "eyewitness accuracy" research. Until there is a sufficient body of such studies, however, experts will continue to debate when it is appropriate to ask direct questions about abuse and whether there is a place in investigative interviews for interview aids such as dolls or drawings. Because these issues are complex, chapter 6 focuses exclusively on ancillary techniques and chapter 7 shows how the accuracy of decisions is affected by variables such as the proportion of nonabused children in particular samples and the diagnostic sensitivity and specificity of the assessment techniques. In the chapter that follows, we build on the material presented in the present chapter, articulating in more detail the structure of model investigative interviews.

4

A FLEXIBLE INTERVIEW PROTOCOL

English-speaking children delight in the rhyme and riddle of Humpty-Dumpty: "Humpty-Dumpty sat on a wall./ Humpty-Dumpty had a great fall./ All the King's horses and all the King's men/ Couldn't put Humpty-Dumpty together again." The answer to this riddle is that Humpty was "an egg." The answer to the riddle of legal proceedings involving child witnesses is that if the initial interview is improperly conducted, like Humpty-Dumpty, the child's account can never be put together again. Without exaggeration, the investigative interview is the single most important component of any trial involving a child witness. The skill of the interviewer is more important than the sophistication of the judge or jury assigned to decide the case, more important than any of the other players—the lawyers and their experts. A skilled interviewer can empower the child to capture his or her experiences while memory of them is most fresh and vibrant. When the child's memories are carefully and neutrally extracted, both the needs of the legal system and the child are well served. In contrast, when the interview is inartfully conducted, the "Humpty-Dumpty Effect" is set in motion.

Lucy S. McGough
"Commentary: Achieving Real Reform:
The Case for American Interviewing Protocols"
In *Monographs of the Society for Research in Child Development*

Developmental psychology has a long history of measuring children's knowledge through conversation and an equally long history of questioning the accuracy of the results. Although the rise in sexual abuse allegations prompted the current wave of research on interviewing, some of the problems faced by interviewers were recognized years ago by students of cognitive development. When Piaget described his "clinical" method for assessing children's understanding of their physical and social worlds, for example, he remarked on how difficult it was to distinguish "from among the results of the examination the point to be regarded as the child's original contribution and that due to previous adult influences" (1929, pp. 27–28). Dissatisfied with Piaget's lack of attention to this problem, and his pessimistic view of children's abilities, many psychologists delighted readers in the 1970s by demonstrating how children sometimes answered maturely when creative assessment methods shifted attention away from adult authority (e.g., McGarrigle & Donaldson, 1974) or reduced violations of conversational rules (Siegal, 1991). When psychologists and linguists began to develop investigative interview protocols, they benefited from a rich tradition of inquiry into how environmental context and conversational style affect the accuracy of children's answers to adults' questions.

The principles summarized in this chapter emerged from research on a variety of topics, including cognitive and language development, children's eyewitness testimony, and of course, evaluations of investigative interview protocols such as those we described briefly in chapter 3. Investigative interviewing principles should be helpful to all professionals who interview children about their lives, including mental health practitioners who are primarily concerned with prevention and treatment, educators aiming to improve their students' narrative skills, and parents or researchers who want information that is influenced as little as possible by the social dynamics of adult-to-child questioning. Throughout our discussion, we frequently refer to "forensic" rather than "investigative" interviewing to underscore principles and assumptions that are recommended whenever the information gathered might have legal implications, whether or not the interviews are conducted as part of a formal investigation.

This chapter is divided into three major sections. In the first, we contrast forensic versus nonforensic interviewing and explain why information collected for some purposes (e.g., planning a treatment program) may have limited value for forensic decisions (i.e., making determinations of guilt or innocence). In the second section, we discuss factors that are especially relevant when planning investigative interviews (including interview preparation, the physical setting, videotaping, the presence of support persons, and the number of interviewers). Finally, we describe the overall structure of an investigative interview and elaborate on each of the phases common to all of the sample protocols discussed in chapter 3. We postpone two additional topics—the implications of language development for phrasing questions and research on ancillary techniques—for fuller discussions in chapters 5 and 6.

FORENSIC AND NONFORENSIC INTERVIEWING

Many professionals who work with children were trained primarily to provide services after a need for intervention had already been identified. Unfortunately, procedures and terminology in mental health, medical, and educational settings developed somewhat independently of the literatures on cognitive development and forensic issues, creating communication difficulties that continue to foster controversy. For example, research shows that procedures that might make sense in therapeutic settings (e.g., playroom environments, props for reenactment, or directive questioning about pain or harm) are not always appropriate for forensic purposes. Furthermore, the underlying assumptions of therapeutic interviews often undermine or contradict those that guide investigative interviewers, and thus most authors warn against professionals assuming dual roles with individual clients. As Ceci and Bruck (1995) summarized, therapists

> should not attempt to "crack" the case or to discover other aspects of abuse that may be helpful to the courts. In general, they should stay out of the legal arena when the case concerns someone with whom they have a pre-existing therapeutic relationship; in such cases, they should leave forensic activities to another. (p. 290)

C. B. Fisher (1995) echoed this sentiment in her review of ethical problems that arise when helping professionals confuse abuse validation with child advocacy. Consequently, the first task in understanding current interview protocols is to distinguish investigative approaches from therapeutic or clinical approaches.

In their training sessions for interviewers of alleged and actual sexual abuse victims, Steller, Raskin, and Esplin (e.g., 1989; Raskin & Esplin, 1991) emphasized the distinction between "clinical" and "forensic" interviewing. According to these psychologists, clinicians generally assume that their clients are telling the truth and that both sexual abuse and subsequent discussions about victimization are traumatic. Moreover, because information collected in clinical settings is not intended specifically for legal purposes, clinical interviewing often is aided by techniques that lack scientific validation (e.g., free play, drawings, good touch/bad touch) and that require subjective interpretation. In contrast, forensic interviewing is characterized by skeptical neutrality on the part of the interviewer, techniques that are grounded in research on the development of memory and language, concern about the possibility of interviewer influence, and the collection of data that require minimal interpretation.

Using the term *clinical interviewing* to capture the diverse ideologies of practitioners is irksome to some professionals, because many therapists align themselves with the assumptions and standards of proof in the forensic arena. Furthermore, many of the guidelines for conducting forensic interviews are good interviewing practices regardless of how the resulting information will be used. Nevertheless, Steller et al.'s (1989) dichotomy does capture important differences in emphasis between forensic and nonforensic approaches and thus serves as a useful starting point for our discussion.

1. *The assumption of honesty.* Nonforensic interviewing often is concerned with narrative truth rather than historical truth. *Narrative truth* is a term used to describe a social consensus about truth that evolves in the context of a specific relationship. For example, some therapists concern

themselves primarily with the client's reality and operate on the assumption that clients are telling the truth, at least as they currently perceive it. Indeed, some authors have argued that therapists help to "invent" narrative truth by organizing information from their clients into consistent themes by way of their interpretations and summaries (Spence, 1984). As Campbell (1992) noted,

> Over the course of treatment, clients and therapists continually revise their constructions of narrative truth until it is fine-tuned in a manner they find mutually acceptable. . . . Narrative revisions encourage clients and therapists to store information that appears consistent with their initial impressions of narrative truth—and reject information that is not. (p. 475)

In contrast, forensic interviewing should be characterized by fact finding and the assumption of neutrality. A forensic interviewer should serve as a neutral conversational guide who provides as little feedback as possible for fear that it may direct the witness.

2. *The role of intuition.* Nonforensic interviewing often involves interpretation of the child's behavior, statements, and emotional reactions, whereas forensic interviewing involves the search for information that does not require interpretation. When information is ambiguous, forensic interviewers should strive to disambiguate that information.

3. *Scientific validation.* Nonforensic interviewing sometimes involves techniques that lack scientific validation (e.g., interpretations of drawings) or that are derived from practitioners' experiences. Forensic interviewing should be characterized by techniques that have survived empirical scrutiny in laboratory or field research.

4. *Physical environment and materials.* Nonforensic interviewing often takes place in environments that represent extremes on the continuum from "child-centered" to "adult-centered." Therapeutic or educational environments are often playrooms that provide numerous toys and props for children to explore (and be distracted by); in contrast, questioning during medical examinations can occur in sterile and threatening settings. Forensic interviewing should take place in environments that discourage fantasy play but that maximize children's ability to converse without distraction or intimidation.

5. *Interviewer demeanor.* Nonforensic interviewing may involve explicit verbal reinforcement and expressions of empathy, often because interviewers are concerned with the impact of events on children rather than with accurate recall of the events themselves (Lamb et al., 1994). Forensic interviewers, in contrast, should adopt a neutral but relaxed tone and avoid communicating expectations or emotional reactions. Expressions such as "I know this may be hard for you to talk about" or "I know this is embarrassing" should thus be avoided in forensic interviewing. Forensic

interviewers may collect data that are relevant to making decisions about treatment, but their interviews should not be part of the treatment process.

6. *Concern about suggestibility.* Forensic interviewers are especially concerned about issues of suggestibility and children's desire to please adults. Consequently, forensic interviewers should withhold potentially suggestive techniques, such as directive questioning, until less suggestive procedures already have been exploited. Concern about suggestibility also drives the recommendation that all primary investigative interviews should be videotaped to provide a record of children's disclosures in relation to the prior behavior and comments of their interviewers.

Summary: Forensic Interviewing Is Hypothesis-Testing and Child Centered

Overall, two general principles characterize forensic interviewing. First, forensic interviews are characterized by a *hypothesis-testing* rather than a hypothesis-confirming approach. Interviewers prepare by gathering information about the alleged incident and generating a set of alternative hypotheses about the sources and meaning of the allegations. When children use terms that suggest sexual touching, for example, interviewers test the children's understanding and use of those terms. Similarly, when children report information that could be inconsistent (e.g., that the assailant never took his pants off although the victim saw his penis), interviewers try to determine whether these events could have occurred as described.

Second, forensic interviews are *child centered.* Although interviewers direct the flow of conversation, children should determine the vocabulary and specific content of the conversation as much as possible. In contrast, many nonforensic interviews, such as conversations between parents and their children or between teachers and students, are adult directed, with adults suggesting events through directive questioning or offering their own interpretations of children's behavior or reactions (e.g., "That must have been frightening").

Implications of Forensic and Nonforensic Assumptions: A Hypothetical Case

Let us now consider a hypothetical example[1] to illustrate why information collected in nonforensic interviews may have limited value for legal proceedings. Sandra, the single mother of 5-year-old Bradley, contacted a

---

[1]We constructed this example with feedback from two clinical psychologists who represented cognitive–behavioral and psychodynamic orientations. The goal was to illustrate a variety of concerns that frequently crop up when sexual abuse allegations are made in the context of a therapeutic relationship. Any similarity between this case and an actual case is merely coincidental.

local counseling service and voiced concern that her ex-husband was too rough in disciplining her son. Although she did not believe that his disciplinary practices were abusive, Sandra thought that harsh discipline was causing Bradley to play aggressively, and she worried that it was contributing to academic problems that included a delayed interest in reading. Sandra went on to describe how Bradley had regressed developmentally as evidenced by bed-wetting and fussy eating habits. Because Sandra's financial means were limited, Bradley was accepted into counseling on a sliding-fee basis. At an initial meeting, Sandra told the counselor that she needed assistance in helping Bradley cope with the differences between the two households. This presenting complaint, together with a brief developmental and family history and behavioral checklist completed by the mother, was the only information available to Pat, the counselor, before she met Bradley.

Pat developed rapport with Bradley by watching him play with a sandbox, plastic toys, a dollhouse with family dolls, and an assortment of art supplies. She recorded in her notes that Bradley soiled his pants during an early visit, confirming his mother's complaint. She also noted that Bradley placed the boy and father doll in bed together in the doll house, prompting Pat to ask, "Do you always sleep with your daddy?" to which Bradley responded, "Yes."

Sandra arrived extremely upset for the third session. A teacher had complained about Bradley's inappropriate references to "penises and butts" during bathroom breaks and that he was unresponsive to feedback when told that such talk was unacceptable. Sandra confided the suspicion that Bradley might have been sexually abused by his father. During a subsequent session, the counselor asked Bradley if his father touched his penis or butt, which Bradley confirmed. Because Bradley's reported problems were typical of the boys she had treated for sexual abuse, and he acquiesced to questions about touching, the counselor filed a report of suspected sexual abuse in compliance with her interpretation of the state's mandatory reporting law.

In the ensuing investigation, how useful is Pat's testimony about Bradley's reports of genital touch? Note the following problems. First, Pat did not look beyond the mother's comments to consider whether her perceptions might be in error and whether Bradley's behavior might be situation specific. Discussions with other informants, for example, would have revealed that Bradley had no academic problems and that other adults did not believe that his play was unusually aggressive. Furthermore, conversations with other family members, including the maternal grandmother, would have revealed that Bradley had not regressed in his toileting behavior. Rather, he had never used the bathroom reliably, and this problem was complicated by recent constipation. Second, note that the counselor assumed that Bradley's behavior with dolls represented actual behavior with his father, but she never asked Bradley to explain his play. Third, in the absence of audiotapes, it was unclear whether Bradley's disclosures were influenced by directive questioning or whether the counselor made any attempt to distinguish sexualized touching from touching done in the context of caretaking (e.g., medical treatment and cleanup related to his constipation). Fourth, although Bradley's school behavior was troublesome, Pat never considered the possibility that Bradley's rude comments might have emanated from interactions with schoolmates or the two teenage half-brothers with whom he was often left when visiting his father, rather than from sexual abuse.

In summary, the counselor adopted a *confirmatory* strategy in response to the possibility of sexual abuse. She interpreted the behavior reported by Sandra as responses to abuse when, in fact, neither Bradley's behaviors nor their etiologies were sufficiently understood. Her approach illustrates a number of concepts that are discussed in chapter 7 ("Improving Judgment and Decision Making"). "Potty" talk, for example, is actually quite common among preschoolers and is not diagnostic of abuse. Similarly, negative behaviors, toileting problems, and school problems are frequently reported by parents (Mesibov, Schroeder, & Wesson, 1977) and can have various etiologies. Because examples of sexually abused boys with these problems sprung readily to mind, the counselor assumed that these factors were functionally related. In addition, she appeared to reason from reversed conditional probabilities, assuming that "potty" talk in school identifies abuse because abused children often make inappropriate sexual comments. The counselor asked Bradley specific leading questions designed to confirm abuse but consistently failed to ask questions that would explore alternative explanations for his behavior. One therapist who reacted to the above case concluded that this was an example of a "theme played out at the therapist's initiation rather than the child's."

Professionals do not necessarily need training in forensic interviewing to adopt a fact-finding approach to Bradley's difficulties. For example, Pat could have considered each of Sandra's complaints individually at the beginning of therapy, seeking permission to obtain information from collateral sources to determine whether Bradley's behaviors were consistent across situations. She also could have avoided a single interpretation of Bradley's problematic behavior or comments when multiple meanings were possible. Finally, Pat could easily have used open-ended questions that allowed Bradley to describe his play and school behavior. If concerns developed about Bradley's sexual knowledge, such strategies would have helped Pat to learn that Sandra's complaints about Bradley's school performance and behavior were not shared by other adults and that Bradley was often left unsupervised with young teenage boys. This information would have simplified the task of investigating the sources of Bradley's knowledge.

Unfortunately, experience and training outside forensic contexts often do not prepare professionals for the complexities of conducting investigative interviews. Although specialists are in good agreement about the overall goal of adopting a hypothesis-testing and child-centered approach, there are still many areas of disagreement about how these goals should actually be pursued in interview preparation and practice.

PLANNING THE INTERVIEW

Preinterview Preparation

There are no uniform guidelines about how much information interviewers should gather before meeting with the child. When sexual abuse is suspected, some experts believe that interviewers should know only children's names and ages, a procedure referred to as a *blind interview* (Morgan, 1995). Because details of complaints are not given to interviewers, this procedure reduces the possibility that interviewers can direct children's statements to confirm allegations (or at least reduces later criticism about such influence).

Although blind interviews are sometimes recommended or required (as in Idaho's response to the Supreme Court ruling in the famous 1989 *Idaho v. Wright* case; Cantlon, Payne, & Erbaugh, 1996), they have some significant drawbacks as a general policy. First, it may be more difficult to develop rapport when interviewers know little or nothing about a child's family structure or past activities. Interviewers should avoid giving the impression that they already know a great deal about a child, because this might discourage the child from volunteering information (Warren, 1997), but basic information about recent holiday or birthday celebrations can be useful when building rapport. Second, an uninformed interviewer has no specific information to draw on when introducing the topic of abuse. If a child fails to respond to general probes (i.e., "Do you know why you are here today?"), the interviewer cannot use knowledge about the location or time of the abuse to frame other prompts. As Morgan (1995) acknowledged, blind interviews require more highly trained interviewers and may not work well with young children, who often ignore general prompts. Most important, blind interviewing may reduce the interviewer's ability to consider alternative hypotheses about the meaning of a child's statements. This consideration is especially critical when the child is young, the original allegations were based on ambiguous information, or the allegations arose in the context of complicated and hostile relationships between significant adults in the child's life. For example, an interviewer would have difficulty narrowing down the location of abusive incidents if he or she was unfamiliar with a preschooler's caretaking environments and the child's names for those environments. Similarly, consider abuse reports filed by day care workers who had observed sexualized play and conducted the initial interviews. In such cases, it would be very helpful to know exactly what the children said to the day care workers, names of frequent playmates, and any relationships between surface features of the game and other recent events in the children's lives. For these reasons, the National Center for Prosecution of Child Abuse, the American Prosecutors Research Institute, and the National District Attorneys Association (1993) advise interviewers to "resist pressure for a 'blind' interview. Interviewing a child without knowing any of the details revealed to others is analogous to performing a medical examination without knowing the patient's history or looking for an unfamiliar destination without a road map" (p. 59).

Currently, most authors recommend that interviewers prepare to talk with children by gathering information about the allegations, familiarizing themselves with topics that can help build rapport (e.g., friends, pets, and favorite or recent activities), and collecting information that might be helpful for clarifying details during the interviews themselves (e.g., caretaking and custody arrangements, unusual names for significant family members and friends). Some information may be obtained from CPS files, police reports, or by interviewing family members or the reporting parties. These contacts also provide an opportunity to warn adults not to discuss the allegations with the children. Because current interview protocols discourage interviewers from leading children and recommend that interviews be videotaped, there is little concern that background information will direct interviewers' questions in ways that might contaminate children's reports.

The amount and nature of preinterview preparation varies, depending on the circumstances and the available resources. It is not in the child's best interests to delay an interview unnecessarily. For example, suppose an 11-year-old child spontaneously but casually disclosed sexual abuse during a unit on sexuality in school by saying, "I can make Daddy's penis salute me." Preliminary discussion with the mother could precipitate family discussions (including threats) that might contaminate the child's report. Similarly, a preschool child who reported abuse by a trusted babysitter immediately after it occurred will produce the most accurate statement if interviewed as soon as possible. Because neither the alleged perpetrator nor the timing or location of the incident is ambiguous in this case, a brief discussion with the parent prior to the interview may be all that is necessary. Generally speaking, it is most important to collect background information when circumstances increase suspicions that the allegations might be false; for example, when the reports are based on ambiguous information (e.g., unclear statements by the child or inferences from the child's behavior), the investigator suspects exposure to sexualized information, the relationship between the reporting adult and the accused was hostile before the allegation was made, or the reporting adults have an atypical concern about their own victimization or the victimization of other children.

Although it is not desirable or possible to list specific information that should be collected in all cases, the following list of topics illustrates the types of information that might be useful to forensic interviewers investigating allegations of child sexual abuse. (Pence & Wilson, 1994, discuss topics that might be addressed when interviewing nonoffending parents and conducting other collateral interviews.)

- Child's name, age, sex, and relevant developmental or cultural considerations (e.g., developmental delay, hearing or speech impairment, bilingualism)
- Nature of the allegation and circumstances surrounding the allegation
- Family composition/custody arrangements
- Family members' and relevant friends' or caretakers' names (especially how the child refers to significant others, with special attention to nicknames and duplicate names)
- Caretaking schedules and environments as well as the child's names for these environments
- Relevant medical treatment or conditions (e.g., genital rashes, assistance with toileting, suppositories or recent experiences with rectal thermometers)
- Family habits or events related to allegation issues (e.g., showering or bathing with the child, a mother who allows children in the bathroom while she changes tampons, physical play or tickling)
- The content of recent sex education or abuse prevention programs (especially when the allegation stemmed from sexual acting out rather than a direct report of abuse)
- Family names for body parts
- Possible motivations for false allegations (e.g., family or neighborhood hostilities that predate suspicions of inappropriate behavior)

Consideration of the preceding topics will help interviewers identify misunderstandings and, at a later time, refute defense claims that the child initially implicated an individual other than the accused (e.g., because of ambiguous kinship terms); described objects that raise doubts about the alleged location (e.g., the child actually was talking about something that happened at day care); initially described only routine caretaking; or was mimicking behaviors learned outside an abusive encounter.

The Physical Setting

The optimal environment for interviewing is a center specifically equipped for this purpose (e.g., Child Victim Witness Investigative Pilot Projects, 1994; Home Office, 1992). When such facilities are not available, attempts should be made to duplicate their most important characteristics.

At a minimum, interview locations should have a comfortable waiting room with neutral toys and games, refreshments and bathroom facilities, and an interview room. When constructing new centers, it is desirable to have an observation room adjoining the interview room that is equipped with a one-way mirror, seating for several adults, and sound connection between the two rooms. To reduce distractions, it also is helpful if children can use a bathroom or get a drink without having to pass through the waiting room. Efforts should be made to reduce children's fears that they are in a medical facility or have been taken to a police station because they are in trouble. Special efforts to decorate the waiting room to look less like a pediatrician's office will be particularly helpful for younger children.

Interview rooms should be child friendly but uncluttered. Children take time to adapt to novel environments, and they attend better when rooms are free of distracting items. Rooms with sofas or overly large facilities may encourage small children to bounce about or roam. The room should be simple, with a table and chairs, a cupboard for supplies, and sufficient space to place audio and video recording equipment at an acceptable distance from the child. A single videocamera with a wide-angle lens, or a two-camera setup, can monitor the entire room. The stark appearance of an interview room can be broken with a colorful but repetitive-patterned wall covering that does not encourage inspection by the child. When interviews take place in public facilities such as schools, unnecessary equipment such as toys, computers, or typewriters should be removed from the interview area.

Videotaping

Few topics are as controversial as the issue of videotaping interviews. Eyewitness researchers generally favor videotaping all interviews (e.g., Ceci & Bruck, 1995; Lamb, 1994), a policy that has been in practice in some locations for years. In contrast, many prosecuting attorneys are vehemently opposed to videotaping because the videotape may focus attention on the skill and practices of the interviewer. Defense attorneys also have reservations about the evidentiary use of videotapes, because tapes give victims another chance to influence juries or triers of fact. (In England and Wales, motions to suppress videotaped interviews are made by the defense more often than by the prosecution; Davies & Wilson, 1996.) Videotaping or audiotaping also requires well-maintained equipment; protocols to regulate access to the tapes, storage, and eventual destruction of the tapes; and interviewing practices that do not allow defense counsel to focus opportunistically on questionable interviewer techniques or errors.

The pros and cons of interviewing have been extensively summarized and debated (e.g., Child Victim Witness Investigative Pilot Projects, 1994;

McGough, 1994, 1995; Morgan, 1995; Pence & Wilson, 1994). In addition to the practical difficulties of managing equipment and the resulting tapes, six major concerns have been mentioned by opponents of videotaping:

1. Videotaping shifts focus to the skill of the interviewer and allows defense counsel to exaggerate the impact of interviewer procedures or errors.
2. In-court use of videotaped interviews is misleading because greater weight is given to these statements than to other statements, and tapes effectively allow alleged victims to testify twice (e.g., Stern, 1992).
3. Videotaping focuses attention on inconsistencies in children's reports and other behaviors that reduce credibility (e.g., topic drifts, silly behavior, inappropriate affect).
4. Videotaping may make children uncomfortable and reticent.
5. Poor-quality tapes may cast doubt on the integrity of the interview. More serious, technical errors that result in destruction of evidence may lead to dismissal of charges.
6. Singling out children who report sexual assault for videotaping will "reify in the law that children per se are more suspect and potentially dangerous witnesses" than are adults. There is no rational basis, however, for drawing the line either with children or with investigative interviews; that is, the arguments supporting videotaping of children apply equally well to other vulnerable classes of witnesses (e.g., the developmentally disabled, the elderly) and to noninvestigative interviews (e.g., therapy sessions, taking medical history; Lucy Berliner, personal communication, September 4, 1996).

In contrast, a number of advantages have also been mentioned:

1. In theory, videotaping should reduce the number of times witnesses are questioned.
2. Videotaping encourages interviewers to use proper techniques and allows them to review their performance. Consequently, the videotape documents that suggestive or leading questions were *not* used to elicit the allegations.
3. Videotapes are a compelling tool for the prosecution because they preserve evidence of emotional reactions and spontaneous corrections or additions.
4. Videotaping may discourage recantation.
5. Videotapes can be used to refresh children's memory before they testify.
6. Videotapes can be used to convince nonoffending parents that the abuse occurred or to elicit confessions from the perpetrator.

The Child Victim Witness Investigative Pilot Projects' final report (1994) includes an excellent empirical evaluation of these arguments. In this field study, videotaping was associated with a reduction in the number of formal interviews, although other factors may have accounted for this result (such as the reliance on trained interview specialists). In a survey, many professionals emphasized that the availability of the videotapes permitted them to defend the quality of their interviews and allowed them to capture the children's initial emotional responses before these could be blunted by repeated interviews and hearings. The researchers did not obtain much evidence regarding recantation, but many professionals commented that the tapes helped induce confessions. Furthermore, they believed that tapes were useful for making decisions about the strengths and weaknesses of the child as a witness. Most important, the tapes did not appear to provide defense counsel with evidence to impeach children or opportunities to focus unduly on interviewer errors.

Perhaps the most revealing data on the impact of videotaping were the final evaluation comments. Only 5% of respondents in Sacramento and Orange counties wrote that interviews should not be videotaped in the future and, surprisingly, the deputy district attorneys most strongly favored videotaping. Concluding their extensive analysis, the project advisory panel wrote the following:

> Should investigative interviews of children be videotaped? The pilot projects answer this question, and the answer is "Yes." The pilot projects provide clear support for videotaping interviews that occur at well run multidisciplinary interview centers. Moreover, most professionals involved in the pilots believe videotaping should be routine. In Sacramento and Orange counties, the specter of injustice that is feared by opponents of videotaping did not materialize. What emerged instead is a clear consensus that videotaping helps lower trauma for children and contributes to the search for truth. (p. 79)

Support Persons

Adults often believe that children will be more relaxed and cooperative if a support person sits with them during the interview. In sexual abuse cases, trauma and embarrassment are often mentioned as reasons for providing emotional support. However, intuitions about children's behavior are not always accurate. The presence of mothers during inoculations, for example, increases the intensity and duration of crying (Gross, Stern, Levin, Dale, & Wojnilower, 1983), and many social workers report little trouble in getting children to separate or in encouraging them to talk alone. In one analysis of 55 videotaped interviews of high-risk sex abuse cases, the children were rated as relaxed, attentive, and displaying few emotional behaviors during the interview (Wood, Orsak, Murphy, & Cross, 1996).

The desire to put children at ease is not either a pro-prosecution or a pro-defense goal. As Montoya (1995) pointed out, the defense may perceive the most benefit from procedures that relax a child, because they can argue that the child's demeanor is inconsistent with abuse. The effectiveness of this strategy is poorly understood, however. For example, Haskett, Wayland, Hutcheson, and Tavana (1995) found that some protective service workers justified decisions to substantiate on the grounds that the child readily disclosed abuse and was matter of fact, whereas others used hesitancy and embarrassment to justify substantiation. Haskett et al. concluded,

> Given the wide range of affective and behavioral responses of abused children and the difficulty in separating the child's reactions to the alleged abuse from their responses to the interview process, the use of affect as evidence of the validity of allegations ... seems highly problematic. (pp. 41–42)

In Wood, Orsak, et al.'s (1996) study, emotionality had no impact on judgments of credibility by experienced child protection and law enforcement professionals. Thus it is unclear how children's credibility is influenced by attempts to comfort them during interviews. In any event, researchers have shown that the presence of others during a stressful event is associated with a variety of beneficial and inhibitory effects, and that any generalizations about the impact of others on children's reports are likely to be wrong under some circumstances.

The primary purpose of a support person is to provide an environment in which the child will feel secure enough to discuss abuse issues. Unfortunately, it is difficult to predict when support may be helpful or necessary. One problem is that many professionals overemphasize children's fears and underestimate their ability to discuss stressful events. Following extensive interviews about sexual activities and assault experiences, for example, most of the 13- to 17-year-olds in one study reported being substantially or markedly comfortable with most aspects of the interviews, and a surprising 95% indicated that they were willing to participate in other similar interviews (Jones, Gruber, & Freeman, 1983). Moreover, adults are not very accurate at predicting how younger children will perform in specific stressful situations such as testifying in court (see Montoya, 1995, for an excellent discussion). Second, the presence of familiar adults could be comforting early in an interview but could also inhibit children from using sexually explicit language during phases of the interview designed to elicit details. Third, there is no conclusive evidence that social support actually improves the quality of children's testimonies. Investigators have studied how the presence of a peer influences children's descriptions of events, but the results have been inconsistent (e.g., Cornah & Memon, 1996; Greenstock & Pipe, 1996; Moston, reported by Moston & Engelberg, 1992). Although social support might encourage abused children to report more information under some circumstances, we need information about the impact of social support on the testimonies of nonabused children, who probably have been exposed to conversations about abuse, before concluding whether or not social support helps investigators to distinguish between abused and nonabused children. Some support individuals, such as the child's mother, could distract the child, interrupt conversation, prompt the child, or encourage later defense claims that the child merely complied with prior instructions from the parent.

Because there is no conclusive evidence that the presence of others is generally beneficial during investigative interviews, and there is concern that additional participants may interfere with the interview, most authors recommend that children be interviewed alone. If the investigative team approves a support person for a very young or distressed child, it still makes sense to attempt an initial interview with the child alone. If it appears that the child would benefit from a companion, the companion and the child should be warned that only the child is allowed to answer questions (e.g., "Mrs. Larsen can't talk now—this is your special time to talk"), and it is better to have the companion positioned out of the child's sight (but on videotape) to avoid criticisms that the child was responding to nonverbal feedback or reactions from a trusted adult.

The Number of Interviewers

Local customs and requirements generally dictate how many professionals will be involved in conducting investigative interviews. Although we know of no systematic data on how individual versus team interviewing affects the quality of information obtained from child witnesses, the interviewing literature nonetheless identifies numerous potential advantages and disadvantages of both strategies (Pence & Wilson, 1994). For example, it may be easier for a child to develop rapport with a single interviewer, leading to less stress and facilitating disclosures. On the other hand, a team approach involving both CPS and law enforcement may reduce the number of interviews by ensuring that a wider variety of topics is covered initially, may facilitate accurate notetaking, and may allow interviewers to share their perceptions and participate in joint decision making. When two professionals are present, however, it is generally recommended that only one conduct the interview, with the second taking notes and suggesting additional questions at the end of the interview. An alternative strategy for team investigation is to appoint a single interviewer but allow the team to plan which topics should be covered. If specially equipped interviewing rooms are available, other team members can view the interview through a one-way mirror and submit additional questions to the interviewer before the interview is closed. (A break may help an interviewer pull his or her thoughts together and formulate better follow-up questions even when another professional is not watching. Bug-in-the-ear devices also are used at some sites to permit suggestions from those watching the interview without having the interviewer leave the room.)[2]

THE INTERVIEW PROTOCOL

We now turn to the structure and content of the investigative interview itself. As we showed in chapter 3, there is remarkable overlap in the interview guidelines from various research groups and professional panels. After briefly recapping the areas of consensus we identified in chapter 3, our goal in this chapter is to provide detailed recommendations for interviewers to follow.

As discussed in chapter 3, experts agree that

1. the nature of the interaction and the goals of the interview should be explained clearly to the child at the outset, using opening remarks that introduce the interviewer and the interviewing environment;
2. initial rapport building should motivate the child to be informative;
3. the interviewer should clearly explain such ground rules as the child's right to ask for clarification, say "I don't know," and correct the interviewer's false assumptions or inaccurate summaries;
4. the interview should proceed from open-ended to specific questions, with the interviewer avoiding reference to details of the allegations until the child volunteers them;
5. the interviewer should attempt to clarify the child's comments and elicit legally relevant information about actions and persons;
6. the interviewer should close the interview without making promises that might not be kept (e.g., "You won't have to talk about this again") and without reinforcing the child for having made specific types of comments.

Authors use a variety of terms to describe this progression through distinct interview stages, including Step-Wise (Yuille et al., 1993), structured (Köhnken, 1993), funnel (Fallon & Pucci, 1994), or phased approaches (Bull, 1995; Lamb et al., 1994, 1995). We use the term *phases* to describe progression through the interview from preparation and topic-identification to open-ended questioning, specific questioning, and closing.

---

[2]For additional information on interviewing in a center that is specifically designed for this purpose, including discussions of agency considerations, intake issues, and preinterview recommendations, see Sorenson et al. (1997).

An outline of the interview phases appears in QuickGuide 4.1 (see the end of this chapter); the empirical justification for each of these components and examples of the principles underlying each phase follow. Although some of the issues we discuss are relevant only to interviews concerned with allegations of sexual abuse, others are relevant to all conversations concerned with eliciting autobiographical narratives.

Interviewer Behavior and Demeanor

Throughout the interview, the interviewer should

- appear relaxed and not react with surprise to disclosures of abuse.
- avoid touching the child during the interview.
- not ask the child to demonstrate events that require the child to remove clothing.
- not make comments such as "Good girl" that might be interpreted as selective reinforcement of specific types of answers.
- avoid questions that ask why the perpetrator or child behaved in a particular way (e.g., "Why didn't you tell your mother that night?"). Such questions are difficult for children to answer and may communicate a belief that the child is at least partially responsible for what happened.
- not use the words *pretend, imagine,* or other phrases that suggest a fantasy or play mode.
- ask the child to repeat inaudible comments by saying "What did you say?" or "I couldn't hear that, can you say that again?" instead of guessing (e.g., "Did you say 'pee pee'?").
- defuse the situation by focusing on less stressful topics when a child becomes visibly upset and emotional until the child regains composure. Avoid extensive comments about the child's feelings; such comments project adult expectations onto the child and may provide an excuse for the child to avoid talking.
- not use bathroom breaks or drinks as reinforcements for talking. For example, never say, "Let's just finish up these questions and then I'll get you a drink." When interviewers make such comments, the child's answers may be considered less credible because the child could have answered merely to end the conversation.

Introductions and Initial Rapport Building

The goal of introductory comments is to "set the stage" for the interview by orienting the child to the context of the interview and the interviewer's job. Children have expectations that could interfere with attending to or trusting the interviewer, and they sometimes give bizarre and illogical answers when they are questioned by adults in novel situations (Siegal, 1991). Left to their own interpretation of an interview situation, children are likely to assume that adults already know the relevant information and are therefore asking for confirmatory information. For example, children learn that the question, "Can you please pass the salt?" is best answered by passing the salt—not by answering "yes." Similarly, they might assume that they should answer the question "What did he look like?" even if they didn't see a male. As Siegal explained,

> If knowledge creates power, a situation of confrontation may develop in which the children can feel obligated by using extraneous information provided by adults to give a response. The result may be an answer to a question different from the one that the experimenter had intended. (p. 122)

Just as children might believe that they are supposed to talk even when they have no information about the topic at hand, they might also believe that they do not *need* to talk if they have already been interviewed, because it is obvious to them that adults should already know what was previously described. One purpose of introductory comments, therefore, is to begin acclimating the child to the physical environment and the interviewer, with subsequent truth/lies and ground rules phases further clarifying the goals of the interview.

Several common mistakes that can distort the interview process are jumping into questioning without suitable introductions or a chance to glance about the room, and wearing formal clothing or uniforms that suggest specific roles to the child (e.g., police uniforms) or that invite distracting questions (e.g., guns). In daily conversation, adults frequently interrupt children or tolerate only short lapses before jumping in with specific questions. Therefore, the introduction should model a relaxed and patient atmosphere, setting a tone that will be carried throughout the interview. A useful training practice for novice interviewers is to require a 10-second pause between the child's response and the interviewer's next comment or question.

For taped interviews, the session begins with the placement of identifying information on the audiotapes or videotapes. Optimally, the interviewer should record the date, time, place, and name of the interviewer and child on the tapes prior to the interview, playing back this information for an equipment check. When the child and interviewer enter the room, the interviewer should provide a brief explanation of the interviewer's job and the purpose of the recording equipment. For example, guidelines from the Child Victim Witness Investigative Pilot Projects (1994) specify that children older than 8 should be asked if they have any questions about the room, and they should be allowed to inspect the room and the recording equipment if they choose to do so. Younger children may be more distracted by such offers, although it is wise to give them a few moments to look about the room while the interviewer casually discusses any items that seem to attract their attention. In a simple but effective example, Sternberg et al. (1997) included instructions like the following in the protocol for a study of sexual abuse interviews conducted in Israel:

Tape label: My name is _____. The date is _____. I am interviewing (child's name) at (time).

Introduction: Hello, my name is _____. I am a police officer/detective/social worker and part of my job is to talk to children about things that have happened to them.

Explain taping: As you can see, I have a videocamera/tape recorder here. It will record what we say so that I can remember *everything* that you tell me. Sometimes I forget things, and the tape lets me listen to you without having to write everything down.

Although some interviewers are concerned that the presence of recording equipment will inhibit children from talking, even young children generally are nonchalant about equipment once their initial questions are answered (e.g., "It's not working, I can't hear anything!"). For example, Poole and Lindsay (1995, 1996) successfully taped dozens of 3- and 4-year-old children by positioning them next to inexpensive "boom boxes." Whereas less cooperative children tended to finger clip-on microphones and stroll away from remote microphones placed on a table, instructions such as "You need to stay right here so my tape recorder can pick up what you say" anchored the children and provided a rationale for repositioning them without appearing to chastise (e.g., "Oh, this tape recorder doesn't work very well, so you need to sit right here").

Because children may have expectations about police officers or other professionals that impede their performance as informants, interviewers are free to go into more detail during initial introductions. For example, they might ask the child what he or she knows about the interviewer's job and elaborate on the child's answer (e.g., "Do you know what a social worker does? Well, part of my job is to talk with children and their parents and to help them with problems. I talk to a lot of children in [name of town]").

As part of initial introductions, interviewers often begin to build rapport by asking children a few questions about interests or family. As we explain under "Practice Interview," however, asking children a long list of questions that can be answered either by single words (e.g., "What grade are you in? What is your teacher's name?") or by reciting lists (e.g., "What games do you like to play?") might teach children that the interviewer will do most of the talking and that all the children need to do is provide short answers. Although some interviewers might prefer to ask a few warm-up questions early in the interview, we suggest that interviewers rely predominately on the practice interview phase to build rapport. After a few minutes to settle into the room and complete introductions, therefore, interviewers can transition into the truth/lies ceremony.

The Truth/Lies Ceremony

Statutes requiring children under the age of 10 to demonstrate their competency to testify have gradually disappeared. Due to continuities in custom and practice, however, many children who testify in court still participate in a *voir dire*, or a preliminary examination that explores their ability to answer simple questions about home and family, to recall past events, and to demonstrate that they understand the difference between the truth and a lie and have some understanding of the moral obligation to tell the truth. This latter requirement is usually met by the child's reporting that punishment is a likely consequence of lying (e.g., "What would your mommy do if you told a lie?"; see Walker, 1994, for prototype competency examinations for children of various ages).[3]

There are no uniform guidelines about the need to discuss truth and lies during forensic interviews. Some articles on interviewing make no mention whatsoever of this issue; most suggest a short discussion in case the recording is used in court. Interviewers should check with their super-

---

[3] Ambivalence about dropping the competency requirement is illustrated by a discussion of Indiana Rule 601 that appeared in Volume 13 (*Indiana Evidence*) of *Indiana Practice* (Miller, 1995). Until 1990, children in Indiana under the age of 10 years could testify only if they could be shown to understand the nature and obligation of the oath. According to U.S. District Judge Robert Lowell Miller, Jr., Indiana courts continued to conduct hearings to determine competency even after the repeal of that statutory provision. Miller began his summary by stating

> A literal reading of Rule 601 leaves no room for judicial evaluation of whether a tendered witness has the mental capacity to perceive, remember, narrate, and honor the oath. . . . Nevertheless, several courts have continued to engage in competency evaluations under the federal and state counterparts of Indiana Rule 601. (p. 8)

Miller concluded that none of the four theories that were offered to justify such evaluations seemed sound. These included the assumption that a witness without mental capacity sufficient to "perceive, remember, and narrate is so bereft of probative value that Rule 403 may warrant exclusion on grounds of waste of time, jury confusion, or unfair prejudice" (p. 8). Another strategy was to allow the witness's opponent to rebut by showing "an absence of the qualities that formerly rendered persons competent to testify" (p. 9). Yet another was to show that the witness was so impaired as to be unable to meet the requirement that testimony be based on personal knowledge, or met criteria for being considered insane. Finally, Miller noted that an unofficial commentary on Rule 603 suggested that a witness might be excluded on the grounds that he or she was unable to comprehend the oath. As Miller explained, "If Rule 601 is viewed as containing some latent exception, [competency evaluations] may continue to be justified in some cases" (p. 11).

visors and district attorneys for guidelines in their region of practice. Lamb et al. (1994) included the following example of simply warning a child of the need to tell the truth:

> I'm the kind of doctor who helps moms and dads and kids, and I understand that your family needs some help. In order to help you, though, I need to find out the truth about what happened. Your job is to help me learn the truth about what happened. (p. 268)

Sternberg and her colleagues (1997) later added a longer discussion in a study with actual youth investigators in Israel:

> I meet with a lot of children and during our discussions they tell me the truth about things that have happened to them. I want to make sure that you understand the difference between the truth and a lie: If I were to say, for example, that my shoes were purple (or red or green), is that the truth or a lie?
> [Wait for the answer]
> If, for example, I was to say that my hair is purple, would that be the truth or a lie?
> [Wait for the answer]
> I see that you understand the difference between telling the truth and telling a lie, and that's very important. During our discussion, I want you to tell me only the truth, only things that really happened to you. (p. 1144)

As we discussed in chapter 2 ("Understanding Truth and Lies"), these types of instructions are subject to criticism because (a) there is little evidence that children who pass such questions report witnessed events more accurately than same-age peers who do not (e.g., Goodman, Aman, & Hirschman, 1987; Pipe & Wilson, 1994); (b) there is no evidence that providing simple instructions encourages children to filter out misinformation they have heard (e.g., Huffman, Warren, & Frazier, 1997); and (c) such questions only test children's understanding of lying, but they do not measure other cognitive milestones, such as memory-source monitoring, that might be related to testimony accuracy. Nevertheless, such conversations are currently considered satisfactory demonstrations in jurisdictions that require explicit discussions of the truth.

Although interviewers often feel pressured to complete conversations before children become restless, orienting comments and a brief discussion of the truth need not be lengthy. To avert subsequent criticism, it is preferable to alternate mention of "the truth" and "a lie" in multiple-choice questions to prove that the child was not simply selecting the last item stated by the interviewer, and to get a verbal acknowledgment of the child's intention to tell the truth (e.g., "So I want you to tell me only about true things today, OK?"). Be sure to modify instructions to accommodate children's level of cognitive development. Young children might not know color terms such as "purple" or "white," so it is best to ask young children to label colors or, better yet, common objects during the truth/lie ceremony, as illustrated by the following example (in which *I* stands for "interviewer" and *C* for "child"):

I: I meet with lots of children so that they can tell me the truth about things that have happened to them. So before we begin, I want to make sure that you understand the difference between the truth and a lie. What is this?

C: A pen.

I: All right. If I said, "I have a ball in my hand," would that be the truth or a lie?

C: A lie.

I: Yes, that would be a lie because . . . ?

C: Because you have a pen in your hand.

I: What is this?

C: A crayon.

I: If I said, "There is a crayon on the table," would that be the truth or a lie?

C: The truth, because there is a crayon on the table.

I: I see that you understand the difference between the truth and a lie. It's very important that you tell me only the truth today. You should only tell me about things that *really* happened to you. Will you do that?

C: OK.

It is important not to ask children to define lies or the truth. Like adults, they are likely to have difficulty with such questions, leaving the interviewer in an awkward situation. For example, only 8% of 6-year-olds and 31% of 10-year-olds studied by Pipe and Wilson (1994) offered a definition when asked, "Do you know the difference between the truth and a lie?" whereas all of the 10-year-olds and 78% of the 6-year-olds responded accurately to the question, "If I said that you are 12 years old, would that be the truth or a lie?"

The Ground Rules

Children have a tendency to answer any questions an adult asks and are often reluctant to say "I don't know" (Hughes & Grieve, 1980). Consequently, it is often recommended that the interview begin with a brief explanation of the ground rules, including the child's rights to ask for clarification and to say "I don't know" (e.g., Warren & McGough, 1996). Extensive training to resist confusing questions is more important when the child will be interviewed by more than one adult or by adults who are not expert interviewers.

How well do children heed warnings about their right to refuse questions? Although children are often responsive to warnings, warnings have neither large nor uniformly positive results. For example, Moston (1987) found that instructions to say "I don't know" increased the number of times 6- to 10-year-old children provided such responses but did not significantly affect the number of accurate or inaccurate answers they volunteered. Moston's findings might have reflected the willingness of the children in his study to say "I don't know" even without explicit instructions, but the disappointing results also could have stemmed from the fact that explicit instructions tend to increase "I don't know" answers to questions that the children might otherwise have answered correctly. Saywitz, Moan, and Lamphear (1991) reported that warnings helped 7-year-olds resist misleading questions but also led them to provide fewer correct responses. In general, warnings are more effective with older children. Memon and Vartoukian (1996), for example, found that 5- to 7-year-old children were largely unaffected by a warning that questions would be repeated, whereas Warren, Hulse-Trotter, and Tubbs (1991) found that warning 7-year-olds, 12-year-olds, and adults that questions would be "tricky" reduced compliance with suggestive questions.

Even young children are less likely to answer misleading questions if interviewers begin with a discussion of the ground rules (Mulder & Vrij, 1996). Mulder and Vrij arranged for 4- to 5-year-olds and 8- to 10-year-olds to witness a staged event, after which each child was interviewed by an assistant who asked one open-ended question and three misleading questions that contained false presuppositions (e.g., "Who threw the book across the classroom?" when the book was not thrown). Each child received one of four introductory comments: (a) no ground rule instructions, (b) instructions that the interviewer did not see the event and therefore could not help the child answer the questions, (c) instructions to say "I don't know" when necessary, or (d) both "cannot help" and "I don't know" instructions. Ground rule discussions dramatically reduced the number of incorrect answers from children in both age groups: The younger children who heard both instructions incorrectly answered only 17% of the misleading questions, compared with 59% for children who received no ground rule discussion, and rates of inaccurate answers were similar for the older children as well (20% vs. 59%, respectively). It is possible that ground rule instructions were highly effective in this study because the interviews were short and the target questions contained explicitly false information. In contrast, the researchers who obtained less impressive results generally asked children numerous specific questions, many of which were not explicitly misleading.

Because we really do not know how to warn children that they should take time to think, ask for clarification, or say "I don't know" without reducing the effort they make to recall details that might not pop readily to mind, it clearly is better to avoid misleading or difficult questions than to rely on children to cope with these interview pressures. Unfortunately, there is no controlled research in forensic settings to guide us in selecting one set of instructions over another. Instructions can be as simple as the following:

> If I ask you about something that you don't remember, I want you to say, "I don't know." If I ask a question that you don't understand, I want you to tell me that you don't understand, OK? For example, suppose I asked you to tell me my dog's name. Can you tell me my dog's name? That's right, you don't know my dog's name, so "I don't know" is the right answer. Sometimes you might have to think about a question for a little bit. You don't have to answer right away.

The following example, from Pence and Wilson (1994), illustrates an expanded introduction for older children:

> Lead: Alex, we are going to be asking you a lot of questions today. I want you to try and answer the ones you know the answer to. But this is not a test. If I ask you something and you don't know what the answer is, you can just tell me, "I don't know" and that is the right answer. When we're talking, I want us to talk about stuff that really happened. We don't talk about make believe or pretend. Please don't guess or, if you do, tell me it's a guess. Do you understand?
>
> Child: Yeah.
>
> Lead: OK. Let's say I ask you what your mother's favorite color is. You don't know because she's never told you. But you see that she wears a lot of yellow and she wants to paint your room yellow. So what would you tell me her favorite color is?
>
> Child: I don't know ... but it might be yellow?
>
> Lead: That's the right answer! Very good. Now sometimes I might use a word that you don't know what it means. If I do that, it's okay for you to say, "I don't know what that word is." I'll try to explain it or find an easier word. OK?
>
> Child: [Nods]
>
> Lead: I might ask you a question that you know the answer to but have trouble talking about. If that happens, you just tell me and we'll try and figure out a way to make it easier for you.

It may also be important to communicate the need to correct interviewers who incorrectly reformulate children's statements or who verbalize inaccurate hypotheses. Sternberg et al. (1997) thus included the following in their experimental protocols: "If I ask you a question that you do not understand, or that you do not know the answer to, simply tell me, 'I don't know.' If I say things that are not correct, you may correct me, OK?" (p. 1144).

Interviewers must be sensitive to the child's age when attempting such instructions, because some of the above dialogue might be confusing for preschoolers. Regardless of the child's age or the use of warnings, it is always best to use simple, open-ended questions during the substantive portion of the interview and to avoid specific questions as much as possible. Interviewers can ask children to demonstrate their understanding of the ground rules by role-playing corrections, as in the following example of interviewing a seventh-grade girl:

I: For example, what if I said, "How do you like being in the sixth grade this year?"

C: I'm not in the sixth grade, I'm in the seventh grade.

I: That's right—you understand that you can correct me?

C: Yes.

As we mentioned earlier, researchers have not studied whether the truth/lie ceremony and the explanation of ground rules should take place before or after rapport building, so interviewers should let their own judgment and style dictate the order of these phases. Early placement of these phases provides interviewers with opportunities to reinforce the principles during rapport building. However, young children might not carry the lessons from these phases throughout rapport building and into the substantive portions of the interview, making it preferable to discuss the ground rules immediately before introducing the target topic. Of course, interviewers are free to conduct an early discussion of the ground rules but then briefly remind children of these rules at other appropriate places, such as after the free-narrative phase but immediately before specific questioning begins. Interviewers thus might want to organize these preliminary phases in accordance with their individual styles and the varied personalities of the children they interview. When children know the purpose of the interview and disclose very early, perhaps before the interviewers have had a chance to complete initial introductions, interviewers should allow children to tell their stories in their own words without interruption, thereby skipping to the free-narrative phase. Before asking specific questions, the interviewers can backtrack and deliver truth/lie and ground rule instructions before prompting the children to elaborate or clarify with focused requests. Interviewers should use brief but explicit transition comments to orient these children to the shift in focus, as in the following example:

> Sally, I need to ask you some questions about the touching at Allen's house, so I will understand everything about that. I need you to tell me just the truth, though, so before I ask you these questions I want to see if you understand the difference between the truth and a lie. Sally, what do I have in my hand? . . . [complete truth/lies ceremony and the ground rules]. Okay, you understand that I need you to answer with the truth and not to guess or make anything up. Now I'm going to ask some questions about that time with Allen. You said that your mom was at the grocery store but then you said that she talked with Allen. Can you help me understand that?

Whenever a child spontaneously discloses and is having no difficulty narrating the event, interviewers probably would delete the practice interview phase to avoid shifting the focus of the interview to an irrelevant topic. For children who do not sponanteously discuss the target event, the following phase completes the rapport-building process.

Rapport Building With a Practice Interview

Although most authors emphasize the need to build rapport with child witnesses, few researchers actually have documented the value of rapport building or compared alternative procedures. It is not surprising, then, that experts have recommended a variety of practices ranging from brief discussion of the child's school, family, or favorite activities to developmental assessments and free-play that may take 30 minutes or more. On the basis of recent findings from field research, we suggest that interviewers use a practice interview to complete the rapport-building process and to communicate that the children are expected to provide detailed information.

A recent study by Sternberg et al. (1997) provides a basis for selecting rapport-building strategies and helps identify a potential problem with conducting formal developmental assessments during forensic interviews. This study involved 51 interviews conducted in Hebrew by 14 Israel "youth investigators" who are statutorily mandated to conduct investigative interviews of alleged child abuse victims (see Sternberg, Lamb, & Hershkowitz, 1996, for details of the Israeli system for investigating child sex crimes). The children, ranging in age from 4 to 12 years, were interviewed using one of two protocols that differed only with respect to the rapport-building phase. The children were of comparable age in the two interview conditions, and there were no differences between groups in the severity, repetitiveness, or types of reported abuse.

The two protocols focused on similar topics during rapport building: the child's family, school, and celebration of a recent holiday. The interviews varied in style, however. Interviewers in the open-ended introduction condition elicited information with open-ended utterances like "Tell me everything you did on the first night of Hanukkah," whereas interviewers in the direct introduction condition used focused utterances like "Did you light candles on the first night of Hanukkah?" Both styles of introduction took approximately 7 minutes to complete, following which the youth investigators switched to substantive issues using the same open-ended invitation before completing the interview as they saw fit. The two conditions thus represent two major styles that often appear in published discussions of interviewing: rapport designed to empower the child as an informant and encourage elaborated narratives (i.e., open-ended questions), or reliance on specific questions (e.g., "What is your favorite TV show?").

The results confirmed that open-ended rapport building greatly improves the quality of children's responses to subsequent target questions. The number of details contained in the children's responses to the first substantive question ranged from 10 to 357 (M = 91) in the open-ended condition, compared with between 0 and 133 (M = 38) in the direct condition. Open-ended rapport building thereby yielded 2½ times as many details and words on average than did direct rapport building. Children in the open-ended condition continued to provide longer and richer responses to subsequent invitations during the substantive portion of the interview.

The results of other studies in which children were trained to provide elaborated narratives (e.g., Saywitz & Snyder, 1993) likewise show us that children develop expectations and tune their verbal behavior during the early minutes of an interview. Unfortunately, interviewers often dominate this portion of the conversation (e.g., Warren, Woodall, et al., 1996), thereby necessitating more specific and leading questions than might otherwise be necessary. One solution, of course, is to have interviewers follow protocols that require child-centered discussion of neutral events early in the interview.

Before describing several rapport-building techniques that accomplish this goal, a brief discussion of developmental assessments is warranted. Authors frequently suggest using the initial portion of interviews to conduct formal or informal developmental assessments, particularly when witnesses are young. The goal of these assessments—to gauge the cognitive and linguistic level of the child—makes perfect sense. As Morgan (1995) summarized, assessment serves two purposes. First, it establishes a reference point against which to compare the child's subsequent verbal behavior. For example, children might regress to baby talk when the topic of sexual abuse comes up or discuss abuse in an inappropriately mature manner, prompting the interviewer to ask questions about issues such as emotional states or the source of the child's vocabulary about sexual issues. Second, assessments help the interviewer phrase questions at the appropriate developmental level. For example, interviewers sometimes assess children's knowledge of colors, telling time, or dates by asking specific questions ("Do you know when your birthday is?") or asking children to perform various actions ("Can you give me five crayons?"). Pence and Wilson (1994), for example, described using animal flash cards to test children's comprehension of concepts such as "on" or "off" that are useful for later questions such as "Did he have his pants on or off?"

Two potential problems arise when such techniques are used without planning, however. As Sternberg et al. illustrated, they bombard children with specific questions that could inhibit later productiveness (e.g., "What color is the bird? What is the bird sitting on? What is the nest on?"). Furthermore, they might give interviewers false confidence in children's abilities, because such questions generally can be answered from rehearsed knowledge or contextual cues which are not available when comparable questions are asked about abusive events. Finally, if the assessment drags on past a few minutes, performance on substantive portions of the interview can be compromised. In practice, the majority of questions asked during these assessments probably do not help adults evaluate children's responses to abuse questions. At best, the presence of lengthy assessments only imparts specious authenticity to the interview process.

Although it is not necessary to eliminate developmental assessments, it is desirable to adapt them to the goals of the interview. Rapport building with a practice interview does just that. By asking children to discuss non-threatening, significant events in narrative form, interviewers can quickly assess children's verbal fluency and their ability to relate prior experiences. When there is serious doubt about a young child's ability to provide evidence, judges or prosecuting attorneys can arrange separate competency evaluations, during which the target events are not discussed, to provide interviewers with more detailed information about the ability to recall past events and answer focused questions.

The general purpose of the practice interview is to minimize the use of specific questions and encourage the child to volunteer elaborated narratives. This can be accomplished by asking the child to relate one or two events, perhaps by beginning with preliminary chit-chat about school or personal interests before asking the child to recall significant events such as a recent holiday or birthday party. During this portion of the conversation, interviewers convey in a relaxed tone that they are utterly fascinated by everything the child has to say. The following example is from a protocol used by M. Lamb and his colleagues in an ongoing study:

1. **A few days ago** [or "a few weeks ago"] **was Easter** [your birthday, your brother's birthday, July 4th, Christmas, etc.]. **Tell me all about your Easter** [or whatever]. [Note: This sec-

tion changes, depending on the time of year. During interview preparation, the interviewer should identify a recent event the child experienced and then ask these questions about that. If possible, interviewers choose incidents that took place at about the same time as the alleged abuse.]
[*Wait* for the child's response.]

2. **I want you to tell me all about Easter** [or whatever]. **Think hard and tell me what happened from the time you got up that morning until** [some incident or event mentioned by the child].
[*Wait* for the child to answer.]

3. **Then what happened?**
[*Wait* for the child to answer.]

4. **Tell me everything that happened after** [another incident/event mentioned by child] **until you went to bed that night.**
[*Wait* for the child to answer.]

5. **Tell me more about** [something just mentioned by child].
[*Wait* for the child to answer.]

6. **It's really important that you tell me everything you remember about things that have happened to you.**

In practice, small children often have difficulty giving narrative answers to questions about specific events. In such cases, a useful alternative is to ask the child to recall a scripted (i.e., recurring) event. Suggestions include asking what the child does to get ready for school or day care in the morning (e.g., "Let's talk a little now about things that you do every day. First you get out of bed in the morning, right? And then, what do you do? What happens at your house/apartment in the morning?"; from Walker, 1994); relating what happens during a trip to the child's favorite fast-food restaurant; or asking about going to the grocery store (Morgan, 1995). Of course, preliminary discussions with a parent or guardian are necessary to identify the most appropriate topic. Other "training to talk" topics include the detailed actions involved in brushing one's teeth, or a favorite activity or television show about which the interviewer feigns complete ignorance (e.g., "I don't have any children your age, and I've never seen the Power Rangers. Tell me everything about them ... like how many there are, what they do ... I'm really interested in this."). Of course, because accounts of everyday rituals may draw on script rather than episodic memory (Lamb et al., 1994), they may not provide the sort of training or practice that optimizes the child's informativeness about recent incidents of abuse.

Introducing the Topic

After the child has been "trained to talk" with a practice interview, the substantive portion of the interview begins when the interviewer prompts a transition to the target topics, perhaps in one of the following ways:

> Now that I know you a little better, it's time to talk about something else. Do you know why you are here today?

> Now that we know each other a little better, I want to talk about the reason that you are here today. Tell me the reason you came to talk with me today.

> Now it's time to talk about something else. I understand some things have been happening in your family (or, "I understand that some things have been happening at camp"). Tell me about them.

> I know that you had to move to Mrs. Leidel's house, and she is taking care of you now. Tell me about that.

It is important to avoid mentioning a particular individual or action during this phase of the interview and to avoid words such as *hurt, bad, abuse,* or other terms that project adult judgments onto the situation or imply harm (Pence & Wilson, 1994; Yuille et al., 1993). If the child does not respond to the initial open-ended prompt, the interviewer may need to try progressively more directive utterances in an attempt to initiate discussion of the substantive issues. Experts agree that it is always preferable to attempt more open-ended prompts before jumping to more specific ones; for example, "I understand someone has been bothering you" is preferable to "Your mom said that JayJay tried to touch your privates yesterday." (Also note that investigative interviewers in some jurisdictions are not allowed to disclose the source of a report without permission.) Interviewers also may remind children that their job is to help children who have problems as a way of introducing the topic shift. If the allegation was prompted by reports of the child's sexual behavior, the interviewer can be more direct without having to mention the alleged abuse (e.g., "I understand you were playing a game yesterday that your teacher wanted you to stop playing. Tell me how you play that game.").

Authors recommend a variety of strategies for raising the topic without asking a direct question about abuse. For example, Yuille et al. (1993) suggested asking children, "Who are the people you like to be with?" and "Who are the people you don't like to be with?" A related technique described by Morgan (1995) is to create a "favorite thing/least favorite thing" list for various people in the child's life. Morgan also described how to use the topics of "privacy" and "safety" to pave the way for the child to raise abuse issues. Other investigative guidelines have recommended discussions of safety, problems in the home, touching, or secrets, using a "hypothetical" approach ("What might happen if you had a yucky secret and you told me?" (e.g., MacFarlane, 1986). These techniques all avoid mentioning a specific suspect or type of event, and they use the least directive question that is necessary to raise the issue of abuse. These approaches may be rather opaque to a young child, however, especially if the child was not particularly distressed by the events in question. In addition, many of these techniques will elicit discussions of nonabusive experiences that could mushroom into abuse allegations in the hands of unskilled interviewers. (All parents touch their children's bodies during routine caretaking, first aid, and medical treatment, for example.) Unfortunately, the benefits and pitfalls of these techniques have not yet been evaluated systematically.

A somewhat less opaque introduction produced disclosures from 96% of the alleged victims interviewed in a study by Sternberg and her colleagues (1997): "Now that we know each other a little better I want to talk about the reason that you are here today. I understand that something may have happened to you. Please tell me everything that happened, every detail, from the very beginning to the very end" (p. 1146). Of course, all of these children had already made informal disclosures to someone else (their parents, for example), and different prompts might be necessary for children who are referred because of suspicions rather than disclosures by the alleged victims.

In summary, the general principle is to raise the question of abuse without having the interviewer state the allegation to the child. Interviewers therefore start with the most general, open-ended introduction and progress toward more specific topic introductions only if necessary. Boat and Everson (1986, also described in Kuehnle, 1996), for example, described four levels of escalation toward increasingly directive questions, beginning with questions about critical times or events when the abuse might have occurred, then questions about particular individuals who are suspected of being perpetrators (but without mentioning sexual abuse), then questions about different types of abuse (but without mentioning specific individuals). Kuehnle warned that the fourth level—direct questions about allegations—could potentially contaminate the memories of young children, should be used with caution, and should always be followed by prompts for children to elaborate in their own words. As we discussed in chapter 2, research has shown that a percentage of young children falsely respond "yes" to direct questions about events, even when those events involve bodily touch. The risk of error from using such questions is a function of several factors, including the age of the child (preschool-aged children are more likely to falsely respond "yes"), the base rate of abuse in the population interviewed (more errors will be made when there is a lower probability of abuse, such as when children are asked sexual abuse questions as part of routine investigations of neglect), and the extent to which interviewers can filter out false "yes" responses with subsequent questioning (school-aged children are better able than preschool-aged children to retract false "yes" responses that were due to mere acquiescence). Ultimately, each interviewer must decide whether the risk to a particular child warrants raising the topic with a question that specifically mentions some or all of the allegation. When interviewers choose to use specific questions, it is helpful to reiterate the child's right to say "no," and ask questions about nonexperienced events to demonstrate that the child actually says "no" when appropriate.

The Free Narrative

Once the target topic is raised, interviewers should encourage children to provide narrative descriptions in their own words. Unconstrained narratives have long been recognized as the best source of information about children's lives (e.g., Pear & Wyath, 1914), and recent research has provided a number of supportive reasons. Information volunteered in response to open-ended questions is more accurate than information elicited with specific questions (see chap. 2), and responses to open-ended invitations are longer and richer than responses to focused questions (Lamb, Hershkowitz, Sternberg, Boat, & Everson, 1996; Lamb, Hershkowitz, Sternberg, Esplin, et al., 1996; Sternberg, Lamb, Hershkowitz, Esplin, et al., 1996; Sternberg et al., 1997). Unfortunately, interviewers often fail to use open-ended invitations early in the interview, and even when they do, they often jump unnecessarily to specific questions after the child's first response (Davies et al., 1996; Warren et al., 1996).

When both the child and the interviewer have been primed by the earlier practice interview, it is easy to tack on an open invitation after raising the topic:

Topic Introduction: Now that I know you a little better, it's time to talk about the reason you are here today. Tell me why you came to talk to me today.

Free Narrative: [Wait for a response; if the child mentions an event, prompt for a free narrative.] It is important for me to understand everything about ... [e.g., what John did]. Tell me everything you can about that.

School-aged children may benefit from longer invitations modeled after instructions from the Cognitive Interview (see chap. 3) that emphasize reporting details: "I want to understand everything about that [e.g., touching]. Start with the first thing that happened and tell me everything you can, even things you don't think are very important."

While children are speaking, interviewers should be relaxed and avoid continuous eye contact or staring (Home Office, 1992). Provided interviewers do not reinforce particular types of utterances, they can encourage children by repeating phrases after a pause (e.g., Child: "And I was watching TV and he came and sat next to me." Interviewer: "He sat down next to you"), or by neutral acknowledgment that they are listening (e.g., "Mmm"). Interviewers also can ask for repetitions (e.g., "I couldn't hear that name ....) or give neutral permission to discuss difficult topics (e.g., Child: "And then he touched my [pause]," Interviewer: "It's okay to say it."). Breaks in the conversation can be repaired with open-ended comments such as the following: "Then what?" "Tell me more about that." "And then what happened?"

A common interviewing error is to shift to specific questioning prematurely without attempting to keep children in the free-narrative phase (Davies et al., 1996; Lamb, Hershkowitz, Sternberg, Esplin, et al., 1996; Sternberg et al., 1997). Interviewers should be patient when children pause, and allow time for them to interject new information. Only when it is clear that children are not going to volunteer additional information should interviewers shift into the questioning and clarification phase.

Questioning and Clarification

The questioning phase is a time to get additional details about the event or events; to pursue issues that have special legal relevance (e.g., identifying a specific incident if the child only talked in general terms); and to clarify comments the child made (e.g., to identify the perpetrator unambiguously). There are two general rules for the questioning phase: (a) the interviewer should continue to use the child's terms and avoid volunteering details the child has not mentioned and (b) the interviewer should select open-ended questions rather than more directive questions whenever possible. When interviewers use a focused question, they should attempt to return to more open-ended prompts. Lamb et al. (1994, 1995), for example, suggested that direct questions (e.g., "Were your clothes off or on?") always be followed by open-ended questions (e.g., "Tell me more about that.") to switch the burden as soon as possible from recognition to recall memory processes.

The general principles for phrasing questions that are outlined in chapter 5 should be followed throughout questioning and clarification: (a) ask only one question at a time, (b) use the noun–verb–noun order whenever possible, and (c) avoid words or terms that are not appropriate for the child's age. In our discussion, we describe the progression of questions using the terms adopted by the *Memorandum of Good Practice*: open-ended, specific yet nonleading, closed, and leading (which generally are avoided). There is no consensus in the interviewing literature about how to define these terms on a question-by-question basis, but they still are useful for conveying a progression from least suggestive to most suggestive questioning.

Following the child's initial response, the interviewer should prompt for additional information using general, or open-ended, invitations for more detail. An open-ended question allows the child latitude to select particular details and generally requires a multiple-word response. Because children often say little in response to generic invitations to report "more," questions that provide some direction without leading the child often result in the most information. Once the child answers a particular question, however, it is best to use different words for follow-up probes: Repeated questions often yield little additional information and may be perceived as coercive or suggestive. In one study with 3- to 8-year-olds, the following open-ended questions about visual details and sounds or conversation resulted in information that was just as accurate as children's initial free recall (Poole & Lindsay, 1996):

> Sometimes we can remember a lot about how things looked. Think about all of the things that were in [location]. Tell me how everything **looked**.

> Sometimes we remember a lot about sounds, or things that people said. Tell me about all of the things you **heard** [in the . . . or when . . .].

During open-ended questioning, interviewers should use the information the child has already provided as the basis for asking for more information, as illustrated by the following prompts:

> Expansion: Earlier you said something about a cream. Tell me everything about that.

> Clarification: You said you were alone, but you said your mom heard you talking. I'm confused about that. Can you tell me about that again?

Interviewers may need to clarify details or ask for additional information with *specific but nonleading* questions. Note that whether a question is leading or not depends on the child's prior responses: A question is not leading if it reiterates what the child said; however, even a question with the word *he* is leading if the gender of the individual is not yet specified. Specific but nonleading questions ask about specific details and generally can be answered with a word or brief comment, but they do not suggest particular answers. The following specific but nonleading questions build on information the child has already provided:

> Context: Do you remember what you were doing when . . .?

> Clarification: You said he put his mark on you. Tell me what that is.

Interviewers will use a variety of question types to explore required information. For example, a question about *when* an event occurred might be specific, such as "Do you remember what day of the week that was?" for an adolescent (if the event occurred very recently), or closed, such as "Do you remember when that happened? Was it on a school day or a weekend?" for a school-aged child. The term *closed questions* refers to questions that provide a limited number of options, such as multiple-choice and yes–no questions. These are more problematic than specific questions because children may feel they should always respond by choosing one of the alternatives. As a result, Raskin and Yuille (1989) recommended deleting the presumed answer in multiple-choice questions. For example, if the reporting party indicated that he or she had witnessed abuse in the child's bedroom, the interviewer might ask, "Did that happen in the kitchen, the bathroom, or another place?" Note that for this example, however, the interviewer simply could have asked the open question, "Where did that happen?" If the child responded, "In my house," the interviewer could have proceeded with another open question, "Where in your house?" or the specific question, "In what room?" Closed questions should be avoided, but closed questions that permit a variety of responses —such as "Did that happen at your house or some other place?"—are preferable to questions that limit the range of suggested responses, such as "Did that happen at your mom's house or your dad's house?" Yes–no questions should be used with caution, because studies have shown that young children sometimes err by saying "yes" to questions about events that did not happen (e.g., Poole & Lindsay, 1995, 1996; Steward & Steward, 1996).

When an interviewer goes down the hierarchy of question types to a specific or closed question, an effort should be made to return to open-ended questions. An interviewer can raise an issue with a closed question, then explore it with more general questions. The following sequence of questions, used in ongoing research by M. Lamb et al., may explore repeated incidents of sexual abuse:

> Did it happen one time or more than one time?
> [If child says "lots of times"]:
> Tell me about *the last time* something happened. I want to understand what happened that time from the very beginning to the very end.
> [Wait for the child's response.]
> And then what happened?
> [Wait for the child's response.]
> Tell me more about [an event or something the child mentioned].

The interviewer can ask the same questions about "the first time" or "another time you remember well."

Interviewers also can remind children of their right to say "I don't know" during the questioning phase of the interview. One way is to phrase questions "Do you know what color the towel was?" or "What color was the towel, or can't you remember?" Remember that children might offer answers to specific questions even when they have no basis for doing so, and therefore insisting on details might lead to statements that can be used to discredit children. Interviewers need to exercise caution and not demand a level of detail that is unnecessary. There is no need to ask about the color of clothes or towels, for example, unless that information is important (e.g., because it will identify items that have been retrieved from the scene of the alleged crime). Likewise, it is inappropriate to ask how deep the penetration was or how many times something happened as children often lack the capacity to answer these questions accurately.

Leading questions either imply an answer or assume facts that might be in dispute. In court, leading questions unmistakably suggest the desired answer, as in "Then he pushed you, didn't he?" In forensic interviewing, even yes–no questions can be considered leading, especially if there is evidence that a child almost always answers "yes."[4] The danger of leading questions is illustrated by the following case. During a criminal trial, a defense attorney consulted an interviewing expert to generate a list of possible topics for leading a 7-year-old witness. During cross examination, he asked about "Sis," a friend of the child's. He proceeded to ask questions about "Sis," but converted the name into "Sister." The suggestible witness engaged in a conversation about a sister who did not exist, acquiesced to a direct question about having a sister, and was discredited in front of the jury (Roger Wotila, personal communication, August 30, 1996).

QuickGuide 4.2 summarizes the types of questions and their preferred order. Less suggestive questions always are preferable to more suggestive questions. It is extremely difficult to select the optimal questions or respond quickly to surprising information from a child, however, and interviewers need to reassure themselves that most children are not highly suggestible and that many excellent interviews contain several unfortunate, even laughable, questions. Two strategies are helpful for minimizing mistakes. The first is careful preinterview preparation, which should include planning developmentally appropriate questions about aspects of the event that might be in doubt (e.g., when the events occurred). A second strategy is to be familiar with a list of question "frames" that can be quickly adapted (e.g.,

---

[4] A handbook for interviewing workshops in Wisconsin (Fallon & Pucci, 1994) illustrates the difficulty of defining what constitutes a "leading" question. The authors began by commenting that "Defining a leading question, especially in the context of a child abuse investigation, is often very difficult." They noted that the Wisconsin Supreme Court defined a leading question as one that unmistakenly suggests the desired answer. However, determination of what is leading "depends upon a host of tangible and intangible variables" including the age, maturity, and intelligence of the child, the setting, the tone of voice used by the questioner, whether the child is alone or accompanied by someone who might influence the child, and the extent to which the question provides a "reasonable opportunity to be answered in a number of ways." The notion of a leading question is not one that is amenable to simple definition, and Fallon and Pucci accurately warned inteviewers that, ultimately, "determination will be made by the judges or juries if and when your case is presented in court" (p. 52).

"You said _____. Tell me more about that."). QuickGuide 4.3 provides a brief list of such generic prompts or frames that might assist interviewers. Finally, all interviewers should be comfortable with the fact that they can take a minute and reflect on their notes without feeling pressured. Children generally respond patiently to comments such as, "Let me think for a minute, I want to be sure I understand exactly what happened."

The questioning and clarification phase is often the most difficult part of the interview. Interviewers must listen to the child, mentally review the information provided thus far, make decisions about further questioning, and decide when to close the interview. Two overriding considerations guide interviewers during this phase: Interviewers must attempt to obtain legally relevant information, and interviewers must continually work to clarify potentially ambiguous or conflicting information.

For sexual abuse interviews, legally relevant information includes whether the event was a single incident or repeated, whether there were other witnesses or victims, and whether the child can describe a specific incident that is oriented in time and space. Other issues may be important, particularly if physical evidence (e.g., a photograph) has been found.

Interviewers should decide which topics are important for each specific case while preparing for the interview, keeping in mind that unnecessary questions might elicit inconsistent answers or otherwise lead children to discredit themselves. For example, young children have difficulty specifying the date or time of events, but it may be unnecessary to narrow down the time frame beyond specifying a period of several months (e.g., "in the fall," or "between Christmas and summer"). In Michigan, for example, time is not an element in criminal cases involving child sexual abuse. In *People v. Naugle* (1986), the Michigan Court of Appeals set forth four factors to consider when determining how specific the time of assault must be in sexual conduct cases: the nature of the crime charged, the victim's ability to specify a date, the prosecutor's efforts to pinpoint a date, and the prejudice to the defendant in preparing a defense. Expectations about producing a specific week or date are relaxed when the child is young or the alleged victimization was ongoing (because it is difficult to remember specific instances of repeated events). In *People v. Miller* (1987), the court affirmed a 3-month variance as sufficiently specific where "the facts demonstrate that the prosecutor has stated the date and time of the offense to the best of his or her knowledge after undertaking a reasonably thorough investigation," and the Naugle court cited *State v. DBS* (1985), which rejected a defendant's attempt to invoke an alibi defense against charges of incest when the time variance was 10 months.[5] Interviewers therefore

---

[5] We thank Nancy Diehl (personal communication, November 18, 1996), Office of the Wayne County Prosecuting Attorney, and Michelle Fisher, fall 1996 intern, Wayne State University Law School, for providing this summary of case law regarding the time element in child criminal sexual conduct cases in Michigan.

need to exercise considerable discretion in deciding how much to probe children for information that is difficult for them to remember, and rely on their district attorneys and supervisors for guidelines pertinent to their jurisdictions. A general rule about time is that children have less difficulty answering questions about concrete activities, such as whether it was a school day or not a school day, or what show they had just finished watching on television, and answers to these questions can be used to reconstruct the timing of an event without having to ask children about dates or clock times (see chap. 5 for additional information about wording such questions).

Fisher and Geiselman (1992) suggested that interviewers should cover various topics in a flexible manner and sequence, using the child's narrative as a guide. If the child briefly mentions an event, for example, it is best to probe for information about that event before asking about related events. Similarly, the interviewer might work for a clear picture of one event, including unambiguous information about the identity of the perpetrator, before asking whether other individuals were present.

In addition to covering such required topics, interviewers must continually monitor whether the child's reports are clear and unambiguous. The questioning and clarification phase is the time to focus on *testing alternative hypotheses* about the allegation. Asking questions about the context of a touching event, for example, might determine that a father was treating a medical condition or responding to a request to help the child in the bathroom (e.g., "What were you and Daddy doing in the bathroom when he touched you? And then what happened?"). Similarly, imagine that a child acted out sexually with a friend at day care and subsequently responded to the question, "Where did you learn to do that?" by saying "From Mommy and Daddy." The request, "Tell me about the time you learned to do that" could elicit the fact that the child recently had walked in on his parents having sex, which precipitated family conversations about sexuality, or that the parents had recently introduced the child to a sex education book.

Whenever there is acrimony between the alleged perpetrator and the individual who reported the allegation, interviewers should consider the hypothesis that the child was told about abuse that never actually occurred. As discussed in chapter 2, research currently is in progress to determine how accurately children respond to questions that require them to distinguish between events they experienced and events they only heard their parents mention. As we noted earlier, asking children if an event "really" happened may not be successful, because information from parents is assumed to be accurate and "real." It also is problematic to ask children questions such as "Did someone tell you to say that Johnny touched you?" because caretakers often instruct abused children to cooperate and tell the interviewer everything that happened. Children might therefore report that someone told them to tell although no one coached them about abuse that never occurred. Finally, children may not master concepts such as "know," "remember," and "guess" until after 7 years of age, making it difficult to phrase questions about the source of information in a way that all children will understand (Abbeduto & Rosenberg, 1985). Until there is empirical support for specific instructions, interviewers who need to explore the possibility that adults have suggested events can attempt to determine whether individual children can accurately answer questions about the source of information before asking similar questions about the reported abuse (e.g., Kuehnle, 1996). The following example illustrates this process:

I: I need to ask you a question, but first I need to make sure that you will understand. So I'm going to tell you about my dog. He is this big, and he is black. What color is my dog?

C: Black.

I: How do you know that my dog is black?

C: Because you told me.

I: Okay. You told me that Sam took his thing out and tried to rub it against you. Do you know that because you saw it with your own eyes and you remember, or did someone tell you that Sam took his thing out?

C: I remember.

Be cautioned that preschool children might not follow this line of questioning and that answering the preliminary question accurately does not ensure that children always will answer the target question accurately.

In addition to testing alternative hypotheses about the source of the allegation, interviewers need to test alternative hypotheses about specific comments that children make during the interview. For example, the comment "He touched my hot dog" should be followed by a request for clarification (e.g., "Tell me what a hot dog is"), keeping in mind that it is preferable to let the child complete his or her narrative before interrupting with specific questions such as this one. Similarly, ambiguous names such as "teacher," "grandpa," or even "Uncle Bill" require follow-up questions to ensure that adults will agree on the individual's identity. If the child reports conflicting information about an event, the interviewer should explore whether the child actually is describing more than one event; if the child's use of language is creating an apparent contradiction (e.g., the child says that Grandpa kept his clothes on but took his pajamas off); or if the child has strayed off topic.

Although the wording of some protocols implies that interviewers should be directed by the type of question (asking only open-ended questions first, followed by specific questions, etc.), the goal is to ask the least suggestive question possible to obtain the necessary information. Interviewers will use a variety of question types during questioning and clarification, always building on the child's prior answers to minimize the number of times the interviewer shifts topics abruptly. Before proceeding to the closure phase, interviewers should check their notes to determine that they have covered the required topics and have elicited an unambiguous description of the events.

Closure

Interviewers can initiate the closure phase by asking children if they have anything else to say (e.g., "Is there something else you'd like to tell me today?") and if they have any questions (e.g., "Are there any questions you would like to ask me?"). The conversation can revert to neutral topics to defuse tension, and children can be thanked for coming. It is important that children not be reinforced for reporting specific information and that interviewers not make promises that they might not be able to keep (e.g., that the child will not be interviewed again). Finally, it is helpful to give school-aged children or accompanying adults a contact name and telephone number in case they want to discuss something further.

CONCLUDING COMMENTS

The protocol sketched above was designed to reduce the frequency of interviewing errors that researchers have identified in transcripts of actual investigative interviews. Specifically, we mentioned in the introduction to Part 2 that the interviewers studied by Warren, Woodall, et al., (1996) often did an inadequate job of building rapport, failed to mention ground rules, progressed prematurely to specific questions without letting children tell their stories in their own words, and relied heavily on specific and yes–no questions. Clearly, interviewers who follow the phased approach in this chapter should be less likely to rely on the adult-directed style that so often characterizes conversations between adults and children. This protocol, however, still gives interviewers considerable flexibility: It does not dictate how much information should be collected before conducting an interview, which topics should be chosen for initial rapport building or the practice interview, or which questions interviewers should ask before they close an interview. As such, it may take considerable practice and experience before most interviewers will be able to implement this protocol in a manner that is appropriate for children of different ages and circumstances. The second half of this book deals with advanced topics— such as language development, ancillary aids, and decision-making concepts—that will help interviewers convert the guidelines in this chapter into productive conversations with children.

This guide is a brief summary of information discussed in chapter 4. Individual circumstances and regional variations in practice may require modifications of the phases in this QuickGuide.

The Introduction
- Repeat identifying information on tape.
- Introduce yourself to the child by name and occupation.
- Explain the taping equipment and permit the child to glance about the room.
- Answer spontaneous questions from the child.

The Truth/Lies Ceremony
- Ask the child to label statements as "truths" or "lies."
- Get a verbal agreement from the child to tell the truth.

The Ground Rules
- Explain the child's right to say "I don't know."
- Explain the child's responsibility to correct the interviewer when he or she is incorrect.
- Allow the child to demonstrate an understanding of the rules with a practice question (e.g., I: "What is my dog's name?" C: "I don't know.").

The Practice Interview
- Ask the child to recall a recent significant event (e.g., a birthday celebration) or describe a scripted event (e.g., what he or she does to get ready for school each morning).
- Tell the child to report everything about the event from beginning to end, even things that might not seem very important.
- Reinforce the child for talking by displaying interest both nonverbally and verbally (e.g., "Really?" "Ohhh").

Introducing the Topic
- Introduce the topic with the least suggestive prompt.
- Avoid words such as *hurt, bad,* or *abuse.*

The Free Narrative
- Prompt the child for a free narrative with general probes such as, "Tell me everything you can about that."
- Encourage the child to continue with open-ended comments such as, "Then what?" or "Tell me more about that."

Questioning and Clarification
- Cover topics in an order that builds on the child's prior answers, to avoid shifting topics during the interview.
- Select less directive question forms over more directive questions as much as possible (see QuickGuide 4.2).
- Do not assume that the child's use of terms (e.g., "Uncle," "pee pee") is the same as an adult's.
- Clarify important terms and descriptions of events that appear inconsistent or improbable.

Closure
- Revert to neutral topics.
- Thank the child for coming.
- Provide a contact name and telephone number.

QUICKGUIDE 4.2
The Hierarchy of Interview Questions

This is a hierarchy of question types from least suggestive to most suggestive. Whenever possible, select questions from the top of the hierarchy.

Free Narrative and Other Open-Ended Questions

Free-narrative questions are used at the beginning of the interview, after the topic has been introduced, to encourage children to describe events in their own words.

Examples: "Tell me everything you can about that."
"Start with the first thing that happened and tell me everything you can, even things you don't think are very important."

Open-ended questions allow children to select the specific details they will discuss. Open-ended questions encourage multiple-word responses.

Examples: "You said he took you into a room. Tell me about all of the things that were in that room."
"You said, 'That other time.' Tell me about that other time."

Specific but Nonleading Questions

Specific but nonleading questions ask for details about topics that children have already mentioned. Use these questions only when the details are important, because children often try to answer specific questions even when they do not know the relevant information.

Examples: "Do you remember what you were doing when he came over?"
"What was he wearing when that happened?"

Closed Questions

Closed questions provide only a limited number of options. Multiple-choice and yes–no questions are closed questions. Multiple-choice questions—particularly when they have more than two options—are preferable to yes–no questions because they permit a wider range of responses.

Example of a multiple-choice question:
"Did that happen in the kitchen, the bathroom, or some other place?"
Example of a yes–no question:
"Was your mom home when that happened?"

Explicitly Leading Questions

Explicitly leading questions suggest the desired answer or contain information that the child has not yet volunteered. Even yes−no questions are considered leading by many psychologists, particularly if the child is young or the interviewer does not reiterate the child's right to say "no." Leading questions should be avoided during forensic interviews.

Examples: "You told your mom you were scared of him, didn't you?"
"Did he have his pants on or off when he lay next to you?"
(when the child did not mention that he lay down).

QUICKGUIDE 4.3
Sample Question Frames

Familiarity with a list of flexible question frames can help interviewers ask follow-up questions that are not leading.

Elaboration
   "You said _____, tell me more about that."
   "And then what happened?"
   "Sometimes we remember a lot about sounds or things that people said. Tell me all the things you heard _____ (when that happened, in that room, etc.)."
   "Sometimes we remember a lot about how things looked. Tell me how everything looked _____ (when that happened, in that room, etc.)."
Clarification
   Object or action: "You said _____, tell me what that is."
   Ambiguous person: "You said _____ (Grandpa, teacher, Uncle Bill, etc.). Do you have one _____ or more than one _____?"
                        "Which _____?"
                        "Does your _____ have another name?" (or "What does your _____ [mom, dad, etc.] call _____?")
Inconsistency
   "You said _____, but then you said _____. I'm confused about that. Tell me again how that happened."
   "You said _____, but then you said _____. Was that the same time or different times?"
Repairing Conversational Breaks
   "Tell me more about that."
   "And then what happened?"
Embarrassed Pause
   "It's OK to say it."
   "It's OK to talk about this."
Inaudible Comment
   "I couldn't hear that. What did you say?"
Single or Repeated Event
   "Did it happen one time or more than one time?"
   (if child says, "Lots of times"):
      "Tell me about the last time something happened. I want to understand everything from the very beginning to the very end."
      "Tell me about another time you remember."

III

CUSTOMIZING INTERVIEWS

INTRODUCTION

CUSTOMIZING INTERVIEWS

One of us recently enjoyed a long layover in Orly airport outside Paris. With a Fodor's guidebook in hand, Deb chatted with a 3-year-old girl who was delightfully oblivious to "*Je ne comprends pas*." In the course of their exchange, Deb handed the girl a notepad and pen, gesturing for her to draw a picture, and the toddler set to work drawing five standing people plus an extra head. Each person was a small circle attached to a single, elongated worm, with a dotted eye or two gracing some of the forms. And there they stood, perfectly typical toddler people, parading like five large penises across the page!

The toddler people illustrate a major controversy that bedevils discussions of forensic interviewing: Because young children often provide so little information in response to general, open-ended prompts, interviewers sometimes resort to specific questions or ancillary techniques, such as dolls and drawings, to prompt fuller descriptions. Interviewers discovered that these techniques elicited information from children long before research was able to determine whether that information actually improved the accuracy of professionals' decisions, compared with the decisions that would have been made on the basis of children's original, albeit impoverished, descriptions. Systematic data have since cast doubt on some of these practices. For example, there is a long clinical tradition of inferring sexual abuse from phallic-looking shapes in children's drawings (e.g., Riordan & Verdel, 1991), although we now know that such shapes appear frequently in children's drawings and have no forensic value whatsoever.

As described in chapters 3 and 4, there is general agreement among professionals about the ideal structure of investigative interviews. There is much less consensus about the advanced topics described in the next two chapters, however. Regarding language development (chap. 5), we know which types of questions are easy or difficult for children to answer, but this knowledge does not tell us when the forensic value of potential information warrants posing a difficult question. For example, children are more likely to answer "no" or give an uninterpretable answer when asked "Can you tell me what he was wearing?" rather than the direct question, "What was he wearing?" (because "Can you . . ." questions make it easy to opt out of answering by saying "no"), but they are more likely to merely speculate in response to the direct question (because they assume the adult wants them to respond). Deciding which (if any) of these questions to ask is a complex issue that involves judgment about the likelihood that the event actually happened, the importance of detailed information about someone's clothing, and the probability that this particular child will answer any question asked. In fact, researchers have criticized both the tentative "Can you . . ." question form (e.g., Walker & Hunt, 1998) and the direct question form (e.g., Poole & White, 1991). Overall, reviews of language development provide a wealth of useful information, but this information does not always specify the ideal practice to adopt in specific interviews.

Meanwhile, recent research has demoted most ancillary techniques involving props from routine, child-oriented practices to largely experimental techniques whose role in investigative interviews should be limited. In chapter 6 we explain why inappropriate use of ancillary techniques in educational or therapeutic contexts could interfere with subsequent or ongoing investigations and why they should be used in primary investigative interviews only as directed by supervisors. Much remains to be learned, however, and developmentally sensitive questioning, with or without interview aids, remains the greatest challenge facing investigative interviewers.

5

TALKING TO CHILDREN

What is said is slippery stuff.

Paul Ziff
Understanding Understanding

Two communication styles are inappropriate when interviewing children for forensic purposes: talking as if they were adults, and talking as if they were children. It is obvious that interviewers will confuse children if they use difficult words, ask complex questions, or shift topics abruptly. It is less obvious that the way adults normally talk to children also is problematic. This is because daily conversations at home and school generally do not empower children to inform adults. Instead, adults often use conversations to tell children how to behave or to test their knowledge of facts that adults already know. As described in Part II, adults tend to dominate conversations with children, and they encourage children to talk by expanding their comments, correcting them, and asking many specific questions. As a result, children sometimes say whatever they think adults want to hear. In contrast, skilled interviewers adopt a linguistic style that differs from their casual conversations with either adults or children. This style is conceptually simple, but it is structured to make social and linguistic sense to children.

In this chapter, we review language development and suggest some general guidelines for asking developmentally sensitive questions. We begin by discussing the types of questions that professionals actually ask children in legal settings, and then review children's developing language system and offer suggestions for improving communication between interviewers and children. Although many of our examples include "specific" questions (because they ask about particular details of an event), readers should remember that these questions are not appropriate early in an interview (see chap. 4). We end the chapter with a quick reference guide for planning interview questions.

THE QUESTIONS ADDRESSED TO CHILD WITNESSES

There often are startling mismatches between children's developing language systems and the questions that adults ask them in legal settings. Brennan and Brennan (1988) described a simple yet telling example in their book *Strange Language: Child Victims under Cross Examination*. These investigators obtained 26 transcripts of evidence given in court by children in Australia and focused on a set of 5,654 individual questions asked during cross-examination. They selected two groups of questions: randomly selected questions (called "random lawyer" questions) and questions with linguistic features that might be difficult for children to understand (called "selective lawyer" questions). They compared these with questions that counselors had asked alleged victims of sexual abuse and questions from teachers in typical classroom situations.

Brennan and Brennan (1988) used a simple yet straightforward technique to judge the difficulty level of these questions: They asked child volunteers (ages 6–15 years) to repeat questions that originally had been directed to other children of the same age. Although children might be able to repeat questions they do not understand, they often incorrectly repeat questions that exceed their memory capacity or that include unfamiliar words or question forms, thereby signaling potential problems.

When the children repeated selective lawyer questions, the percentage of repetitions that preserved the original sense of the questions ranged from 0% for the group of 11-year-olds to a maximum of only 50% for the group of 6-year-olds. (The average across all age groups was 17.6%.) The 6-year-olds probably performed better than the older children because adults asked them simpler questions, indicating that the legal professionals had adjusted the complexity of their speech for younger witnesses. More than 90% of these questions were repeated erroneously by 14- and 15-year-olds, however—suggesting that the lawyers had seriously overestimated the linguistic abilities of children in this age group. For random lawyer questions, meaning-preserving repetition rates ranged between 50% for the 10-year-olds to 90% for the 6-year-olds (average = 64.0%). In comparison, the children successfully repeated 85.7% of the teachers' questions and 99.4% of the counselors' questions.

Evidently, even school-aged children frequently misconstrue questions. For example, one target question was "All right, so between his patting you and his attempt or his trying to put his squash racquet in your bag there was nothing else, is that right?" (Brennan & Brennan, 1988, p. 34), which 11-year-old James repeated as, "As you attempt trying to put his squash racquet in your bag there nothing else was there?" (p. 34). Brennan and Brennan (1988) noted that this reconstruction, which failed to preserve the meaning of the original question, included four omissions, one addition, and two substitutions. In such cases, we cannot assume that the question the child "heard" was the one the adult asked. Consequently, if the child later answered a similar question differently, we could not assume that the event had not really happened or that the child was an unreliable witness. Other studies on "lawyerese" have demonstrated that children and adults alike are confused by questions that include negatives (e.g., "Did Sam not knock over Katie's blocks?"); double negatives (e.g., "Did Sam not say he was not having a good day?"); difficult vocabulary (e.g., "In the incident depicted, was the perpetrator in chartreuse apparel?"); multiple-part questions (e.g., "At the end of the video, was Sam mad or was Katie happy?); and embedded propositions (e.g., "At any time before or after she cried did the blocks fall down?"; Perry & Teply, 1984–1985; Perry & Wrightsman, 1991; examples are from a study by Perry et al., 1995). Unfortunately, children do not always realize when they fail to comprehend a question, and they rarely ask for clarification. For example, Perry et al. (1995) asked children to push a green button if a question was easy to answer and a red button if a question was hard to answer. Kindergartners gave wrong answers to 45% of the questions they had indicated were easy, and fourth graders, ninth graders, and college students on average responded incorrectly to 25% of the questions that they thought were easy.

The data from Brennan and Brennan (1988) show that professionals frequently question children inappropriately, but their study may have overestimated the complexity of the questions adults typically pose to child witnesses. After all, children are interviewed in court by attorneys whose interests are served by showing that these witnesses are confused or unable to provide consistent testimony, and thus attorneys' questions do not illustrate the way other professional interviewers talk when they *want* to be understood. Furthermore, most children who are involved in sexual abuse allegations never testify in court, so studies of courtroom dialogues might misrepresent interviews with alleged victims. Unfortunately, the bizarre questions found in courtroom transcripts cannot be dismissed as mere anomalies of our adversarial criminal justice system, because studies of investigative interviews raise similar concerns about the language addressed to children.

By content analyzing 42 sexual abuse interviews undertaken by CPS personnel, Warren et al. (1996) conducted an intriguing study of interviewer–child dialogues. Try to identify the communication breakdown in each of the following excerpts from their sample:

Example 1

> Interviewer: Is it good or bad to tell a lie?
>
> Child: G. A. touched me.
>
> Interviewer: Jesus loves me? Is that what you said?
>
> Child: Yeah. (p. 235)

Example 2

> Interviewer: What is this? Wait a minute, I'll get the rest of them up here in a minute. Is that what you want to see, the rest of them? Okay, I'll tell you what, we'll put the rest of them up there. There's, there's a big doll, how about that one? And then I got this doll, kinda like a mamma doll. She's a she. Then I got a little girl doll. See those are my friends right there. Okay. Now can you help me name these parts on them? Can you tell me what this is? What is this?
>
> Child: Huh? (pp. 240–241)

Example 3

> Child: Well, he licked his finger and rubbed me down there.
>
> Interviewer: He licked his finger and rubbed you down there? Tell me about that baby oil.
>
> Child: Well he rubbed me in the place I showed you.
>
> Interviewer: Okay. What did he do with the baby oil? (p. 241)

Example 1 illustrates how adults try to cope when they cannot understand children. Children are often unintelligible, and adults frequently offer a guess before moving on. Example 2 is a multiple question, one of 520 that Warren and her colleagues (1996) found in a subset of only 20 investigative interviews. These question series included the juxtaposition of unrelated questions in rapid sequence (e.g., "Did he say anything, like you better not tell? Or did he try to scare you, or threaten you, or anything? Or did he give you anything?"; p. 240) and "mixed series" multiple questions, such as Example 2, in which interviewers interspersed questions with comments. Mixed series generated uninterpretable responses or no responses at all 22% of the time—almost twice as often as multiple questions as a whole. Equally distressing was the fact that multiple questions generated yes–no responses 42% of the time, although, of course, it was not clear which question the children were answering! In Example 3, the interviewer mentioned an object (baby oil) *before* the child revealed it during the interview. Warren et al. (1996) observed mistakes such as this one in 94% of the interviews sampled.

Other problematic questions can be appreciated only by looking at blocks of utterances. For example, "anaphoric reference" involves linking pronouns or articles back to their prior referents in the conversation. Consider the sentences, "A girl was riding her bike in the countryside. *The* girl got lost." Most adults assume that the girl who got lost was the same girl who rode her bike in the countryside—a linguistic consequence of linking *the girl* with a referent in the prior sentence (example from Warren & McCloskey, 1997, p. 232). Anaphoric pronominal reference occurs when pronouns such as *he, she, they,* or *it* refer to previously mentioned people or things (e.g., "Mother came home and she took a nap"). Unfortunately, children may not always link pronouns to the referents that adults have in mind, and this problem is exacerbated when there is a large linguistic distance between the referents and the pronouns. In a detailed study of interviewer language, Hulse (1994) counted the number of utterances (turns taken by the interviewer or the child) that transpired between the original referents and the subsequent anaphoric pronouns. In a sample of 20 investigative interviews, the mean distance (i.e., number of intervening utterances) was 6.8 when interviewers questioned children 2–6 years of age and 32.0 when interviewers questioned older children (7–13 years). This startling number illustrates the enormous linguistic burden children often face when they are interviewed.

In summary, adults frequently pose questions that children have difficulty understanding. Communication breaks down for a variety of reasons: Adults may misunderstand children's speech, interject new information into the conversation, use words that children do not understand, present multiple questions without waiting for a response, or use linguistic forms that are hard even for adults to comprehend. Clearly, skilled investigative interviewing requires a working knowledge of language development.

LANGUAGE DEVELOPMENT

The study of language generally is divided into four major topics: (a) phonology (language sounds and the rules for combining sounds); (b) semantics (the acquisition of meaning, including the meaning of individual words in sentences or, in everyday terminology, vocabulary development); (c) syntax (the rules for combining words or their equivalents, e.g., adding "s" for plurals); and (d) pragmatics and conversational competence (the social functions of language). Rudimentary knowledge in each of these areas is extremely useful for professionals who interview children.

Phonology

Because adults misunderstand children so frequently, it is surprising that discussions of language in legal settings rarely consider phonology.

Interviewers sometimes respond to unclear speech by simply ignoring it. Communication also breaks down when interviewers take children's productions literally instead of testing their intended meaning (e.g., assuming that a child who said "pee pee" and "bee bee" at two different points in time is producing two distinct words with distinct meanings).

To understand phonology, we have to begin with the smallest unit of language that signals a change in meaning: the phoneme. Phonemes are categories of sound that signal differences among words, and these categories vary from language to language. For example, /r/ and /l/ are two phonemes in English because we perceive "rice" and "lice" as two different words. Japanese speakers produce sounds that are similar to our /r/ and /l/, but substituting these sounds would not be semantically meaningful. In every language, children learn that some variations in sound mark changes in meaning whereas other variations are nonfunctional. Once sounds have been categorized into phonemes during development, it can be extremely difficult to learn to recognize other phonemes. For example, aspirated (e.g., *pit*) and unaspirated (e.g., *spit*) *p*s are contrastive in Arabic but not in English, and therefore English speakers have great difficulty learning to hear and produce these phonemes in appropriate contexts when they learn Arabic (deVilliers & deVilliers, 1978).

Although even infants can discriminate differences between various speech sounds such as /p/ and /b/, children do not immediately use these differences to signal differences among words. For example, the distinctions between [/b/ and /p/], [/d/ and /t/], [/g/ and /k/], [/z/ and /s/], and [/v/ and /f/] are based on a feature called *voicing*, with the first member of each pair being the voiced consonant. (Voicing is easy to feel by alternating between /z/ and /s/ while holding your hand on the front of your throat.) In an object-naming task, Garnica (1973) found that children could not distinguish between words that differed only in voicing until 2 years of age, and other researchers have discovered errors in the phonological perception of some sounds at 3 years of age (e.g., Edwards, 1974).

The ability to produce phonemes correctly lags considerably behind the ability to perceive them. Many sounds have not been mastered by age 4, and 10% of children do not master all sounds until approximately 8½ years of age (Reich, 1986). As a result, it is helpful to keep three developmental phenomena in mind. First, children's pronunciations are not consistent, and they do not use contrasts correctly 100% of the time even after particular contrasts have been learned. Second, children may avoid saying words that contain a sound they cannot pronounce. (If a child seems to be avoiding a particular word for this reason, it is helpful to find an alternate name for the target object, action, or person.) Finally, children's mispronunciations are not entirely random but follow certain general, if not universal, rules (deVilliers & deVilliers, 1978; Reich, 1986). Knowing the most common errors can help interviewers interpret the speech of small children and those whose speech is unclear.

The first type of production error involves the *deletion of sounds*. This includes a tendency to drop consonants from consonant clusters (e.g., *tring* for *string*) and to drop final consonants (e.g., *ee* for *eat*). (Consonants are often pronounced correctly in initial positions before they are pronounced correctly in final positions.) In the early stages of development, children may also drop unstressed syllables in words; for example, saying *way* for *away*.

A second type of production error involves the *addition of sounds*. Children may avoid a final consonant or consonant cluster by adding a vowel, as in *piga* for *pig*, or *pulay* for *play*. According to Reich (1986), this is rather uncommon for native speakers, but occurs when speakers attempt a sound combination that is not in their native phonology.

Third, sounds may be *substituted*. These errors may involve substituting voiced for unvoiced consonants, consonants that are pronounced in the front of the mouth (e.g., /b/,/p/,/d/) for the more difficult back consonants (e.g., /g/,/k/), or glides (/w/,/y/) for liquids (/l/,/r/). The prevalence of these mistakes testifies to the fact that some sounds are easier to produce in certain syllabic positions than are others.

Fourth, sounds may be *assimilated*. Sounds are made in various parts of the mouth, and it is easier to articulate a word when the sounds at the beginning and end are produced in the same location. Assimilation occurs when children alter the place of articulation for one sound to match the place of articulation of an adjacent sound (*goggy* for *doggy*).

A fifth type of error involves the *reversal of sounds*. This unusual error occurs, for example, when *puc* is substituted for *cup*.

Finally, some mispronunciations involve multiple processes, making it difficult to associate the intended and produced words. For example, Reich (1986) cited an example from Ingram (1976) of a child who produced *bap* for *lamb*, a substitution that requires seven rules to unpack!

Unless interviewers have extensive training in language development, they may not recognize the most likely referents for children's mispronounced words. This is one reason why audiotaping and videotaping are extremely helpful, because interviewers can review tapes and adjust their interpretation of children's intent.

What should interviewers do when they cannot understand a child or they suspect that mispronunciation is causing confusion? The first rule is to avoid suggesting a specific interpretation, because children often go along with interviewers' hunches. Second, it may be useless to repeat the utterance and ask the child for verification (e.g., by saying "Did you say 'pulay'?"). Phonological perception develops more rapidly than production, so children generally recognize the discrepancy between their pronunciation and the adult version and sometimes reject the adult's imitation in frustration (e.g., "No, I said 'PULLLAYYY' "). It is better to ask the child to repeat the word or phrase, write it down phonetically, and follow up with a series of questions that might clarify what the phrase means. If the child has garbled the name of a person, for example, an interviewer might ask, "I didn't hear that . . . what did you say?" followed by "Who is that?" If the child was stating a verb, as in "He [garble] me," the interviewer might ask, "Tell me how he did that," or "I don't know that word. Tell me what that is." When a child's articulation is a major issue in the investigation, it is helpful to design initial rapport-building questions to elicit information about systematic mispronunciations (e.g., by asking the child to identify a few pictures that illustrate problematic sounds). Finally, interviewers should speak clearly throughout the interview, because children's comprehension may suffer when adults attempt to imitate baby talk. (See Bernthal & Bankson, 1993, for an elaborated discussion of phonological development that includes useful information about dialectal variations sometimes used by children from African American or Hispanic backgrounds.)

Vocabulary

One way to simplify speech for children is to avoid using words they do not know. This is easier said than done. Children and adults often use the same word to mean different things, and it is not uncommon for children to use words that they do not really understand (Walker & Warren, 1995). One of our children, for example, told impressed guests that her parents "studied child abuse" for several months before asking her father, "What's child abuse?" Interviewers must therefore learn which types of words and concepts are generally difficult for children to understand at various ages. Before describing some of these difficult words and concepts, however, we first review several features of vocabulary development that have special relevance for investigative interviewing.

General Principles of Vocabulary Development

Anomalous use of words. Children interpret specific words and sentences quite idiosyncratically. For example, children do not necessarily share adults' definitions of superordinate labels such as *clothes* or *furniture* (Rosner & Poole, 1978, 1981). As a result, a child who wore a bathing suit during the target event might report that she was not wearing any clothes, or respond "no" to the question, "Did he take off your clothes?"

Children who lack an appropriate word may use words that sound similar or erroneously map unfamiliar words onto familiar words. For example, when Rosner and Poole (1978, 1981) asked children to judge whether words were "furniture" or "not furniture," some children interpreted *chest* to mean the game *chess*. Similarly, Warren-Leubecker, Tate,

Hinton, and Ozbeck (1989) reported that children interpreted *jury* to mean *jewelry* (see also Saywitz, 1989). Interviewers can minimize confusions by using concrete, basic-level words such as *dog* instead of superordinate words (e.g., *animal*) or subordinate words (e.g., *beagle*). With young children, interviewers also need to ensure that the topic of conversation does not suddenly shift because of a sound-alike substitution. Finally, interviewers need to ask follow-up questions to ensure that adults' interpretation of a word matches the child's intended meaning (for example, by saying "What does that look like?").

Cultural lists. As Walker noted in her *Handbook on Questioning Children: A Linguistic Perspective* (1994), some interviewers assess developmental level by asking children to recite cultural lists, such as the days of the week, the numbers from 1 to 10, or other lists that children routinely memorize before they start school. There are two problems with this practice. First, because teachers ask these sorts of questions in school, children might infer that the goal of the interview is to provide short, focused answers to whatever questions the adult asks. Second, the ability to recite lists cannot be taken as evidence that children understand the concepts contained in those lists. As Walker pointed out,

> Children are routinely asked questions like, "You know the days of the week, don't you? So what day did this take place?". . . As a measure of competency, then, these cultural lists merely indicate that the child has acquired the *vocabulary*. They should not be given any other significance at all. (p. 16, italics in the original)

In other words, reciting the days of the week during rapport building does not mean that the child will be able to answer a question such as "What day of the week did that happen?" accurately; similarly, being able to recite numbers does not mean that the child can answer the question "How many times did that happen?" accurately.[1]

Interviews as language lessons. The acquisition of language is undoubtedly the "greatest intellectual feat any of us is ever required to perform" (Bloomfield, 1933, cited in Medin & Ross, 1992, p. 311). Most notable is the speed with which children learn their language simply by being exposed to it. By age 6, the average child has a working vocabulary of between 8,000 and 14,000 words (Carey, 1978). This means that children learn approximately five to eight new words per day between the ages of 1 and 6 years (deVilliers & deVilliers, 1978; Medin & Ross, 1992), often learning a word from a single exposure to it in a process known as *fast mapping* (Wilkinson, Dube, & McIlvane, 1996). Therefore, interviewers must be

---

[1]One of us (DP), at age 7, routinely disclosed to priests during required confessions that she lied and disobeyed her mother 300 to 400 times per week. She recalls being proud of knowing the large numbers and deciding that these numbers would cover her bases. More than 30 years later, there was a twinge of familiarity when she read a transcript of an interview with a preschooler who reported hundreds of undetected murders and other unlikely events.

extremely careful not to inadvertently teach abuse or abuse-related words to children by embedding new words in their conversation. In general, interviewers should not use terms that children have not already volunteered; whenever possible, interviewers should use children's own words for objects, body parts, and actions.

"Simple" words. Intuitions about which words are easy or difficult are often wrong. For example, developmental linguists such as Anne Graffam Walker and Amye Warren have been interested in children's reactions to questions with the word *any*, as in "Did anything else happen?" because children often respond "no." There are several possible reasons for this. First, *any* words are nonspecific and require the listener to search through all possibilities. Second, even adults use *any* words in a peculiar way (e.g., "I didn't have anything for breakfast . . . just a roll"), indicating that the meaning of *any* may in fact be quite different than the meaning of *some* (example from Walker, 1995). Finally, some children may interpret *anyone* as a specific name, thereby rejecting questions such as "Did anyone touch you there?" (Walker, 1994).[2] Preliminary research suggests that simply saying *some* rather than *any* does not always improve children's accuracy, however (Woodall, 1996). Clearly, even frequently used words may be opaque to children.

Adults have difficulty estimating children's vocabularies not only because apparently simple words can be difficult but because vocabulary acquisition is context dependent. For example, children may accurately use temporal terms (e.g., *before*, *after*) to describe scripted events (i.e., repeated events such as what one does to get ready for school in the morning) before they use these words to describe unique occurrences of unfamiliar events (French & Nelson, 1985). Because many words are initially understood only in certain contexts, it is wise to avoid using words that are known to be difficult even if a particular child occasionally uses those words.

Problem Words and Concepts

There are many reasons why children misunderstand words. A word may be difficult because it is rarely used around children, because it taps a cognitive concept that has not yet been acquired, or because it appears in a sentence that is too advanced grammatically. There is considerable variability from child to child in the ages at which particular words are understood, of course, and thus the ages mentioned in this brief review should be taken as broad generalizations rather than as rigid rules about devel-

---

[2]Reich (1986) repeated a delightful story from Philip Dale regarding names. When Dale's daughter was 2 years old, she looked at him in his bathing suit and said something unintelligible. Dale responded, "Yes, my tummy is hairy," to which she remarked, "My tummy doesn't have a name" (pp. 158–159).

opment. With this caveat in mind, the following categories of words are especially problematic for children.

Words describing touch. Probably no single question is as common in investigative interviews with children as "Did he touch you here [or 'there']?" Unfortunately, even 6-year-olds may believe that only hands can touch, and so children may deny that an individual touched them yet proceed to describe penetration (Warren, 1992; Woodall, 1996). Similarly, some 7-year-olds do not seem to understand the word *move* when it is used in reference to a penis (Walker, 1994). With a young child or one who has provided inconsistent descriptions of abuse, Walker recommends asking whether someone "put" something on the child or using more familiar terms such as *wiggle* or *poke*.

Although children often use words more restrictively than adults, the reverse also holds. For example, a child may say that someone put his penis "in my pee pee" or "in my butt" when there is no evidence of penetration. Most children do not conceptualize their interior anatomy, and thus they consider any contact with their bodies, such as ejaculation between the thighs, to be "in" them. (Young children also erroneously use *in* to mean *between.*) Interviewers therefore need to ask follow-up questions to discover exactly what happened. For example, penetration could not have occurred if the child did not remove his or her pants, so questions about clothing constitute indirect sources of information.

In a widely cited example first recounted by Berliner and Barbieri (1984), the following interchange took place between an interviewer and a 5-year-old girl whose literal interpretation of questions was problematic:

Defense Attorney: And then you said you put your mouth on his penis?

Child: No.

Defense Attorney: You didn't say that?

Child: No.

Defense Attorney: Did you ever put your mouth on his penis?

Child: No.

Defense Attorney: Well, why did you tell your mother that your dad put his penis in your mouth?

Child: My brother told me to.

At this point, it looked as if the child had completely recanted her earlier testimony about the sexual abuse and had only fabricated the story because her brother told her to. However, the experienced prosecuting attorney recognized the problem and clarified the situation:

Prosecuting Attorney: Jennie, you said that you didn't put your mouth on daddy's penis. Is that right?

Child: Yes.

Prosecuting Attorney: Did daddy put his penis in your mouth?

Child: Yes.

Prosecuting Attorney: Did you tell your mom?

Child: Yes.

Prosecuting Attorney: What made you decide to tell?

Child: My brother and I talked about it, and he said I better tell or dad would just keep doing it. (p. 132)

Adults often recognize ambiguity in other people's messages and can look beyond a literal question to understand another person's intent. Children are less skilled at accurately inferring someone else's perspective. Consequently, interviewers must constantly monitor whether children are being overly restrictive, overly general, or overly literal in their use of language.

Temporal terms. It is sometimes necessary for legal purposes to specify when an event took place (although the degree of specificity required depends on a variety of factors, including the specifics of the case and the jurisdiction or local laws). Languages mark temporal relations in two ways: grammatically (e.g., "Dad hits" vs. "Dad hit") and lexically (with terms such as *yesterday, tomorrow*, etc.; Nelson, 1991). In the course of language development, lexical terms for temporal concepts generally are learned after the acquisition of tense. In one study, for example, 2-year-olds could not distinguish between *yesterday, today*, and *tomorrow*; 3-year-olds generally used *yesterday* to mean *not today*; and 4-year-olds understood *yesterday* and *tomorrow* equally well (Harner, 1975).

Five-year-olds usually understand *yesterday* and *tomorrow*, as well as *always, never*, and *sometimes* (Siegal, 1991). Nonetheless, children's understanding of time and dates is very limited before the age of 8 to 10 years, as Friedman (1991) illustrated. Friedman staged two target events for 4-, 6-, and 8-year-olds, one 7 weeks before testing and the other 1 week before testing. During the testing, children indicated which event was "a long time ago" as opposed to "a short time ago" and then answered questions about the time of day, day of the week, month, and season when the first event occurred. Children in all age groups were able to identify which of two events had occurred more recently, and they could specify the general time of day (i.e., waking, eating lunch, etc.), but only the 6- and 8-year-olds were above chance on day of the week, month, or season. The performance of the older children was still poor, however: Only 39% of the 6-year-olds and 63% of the 8-year-olds recalled the exact or adjacent day of the week (Experiment 3). Perhaps this is why defense attorneys sometimes badger children for specific information about days and times: Young children often answer inconsistently, which casts doubt on their credibility.

(See Friedman, Gardner, & Zubin, 1995, for an extended discussion of limitations in children's judgments of the order of past events.)

Interviewers also must be careful about the terms *before* and *after*, because children use these terms long before they have a firm grasp of their meanings in various contexts. Remember that children may use these words at an early age to describe familiar events but flounder when using the same words to describe one-time events. Children also have more difficulty when events are mentioned in a sequence that does not match their actual order, as in "Before you ate dinner, did you tell your mom?" (Walker, 1994). *Before* and *after* can be used in a variety of ways (e.g., "when you came before the court"), as prepositions or conjunctions, and in a variety of sentence contexts. For all of these reasons, Walker advises using *first* instead of *before* to improve accuracy (although even 5-year-olds sometimes misunderstand both of these terms; Richards, 1982). *At the same time* appears to be understood earlier than *before* or *after* (Munro & Wales, 1982), but *while* may be more difficult than either (Feagans, 1980), indicating that words that mark simultaneity are not necessarily easier for young children to understand than words that denote sequence.

How can interviewers help children identify the time of an event? Children's errors in identifying time of day or day of the week are not random. In one study, for example, most first- and third-grade children ruled out the morning as a possible time when asked to report about an event that had occurred on a school day during the afternoon, and even nursery-school children rarely identified Saturday or Sunday as the day of the event (Friedman, 1991). Young children therefore may find it easier to express time in terms of meaningful markers, such as which television show they were watching when the event occurred or whether or not it occurred on a school day. Some jurisdictions do not require young children to specify timing except in a general way (e.g., it may be sufficient to say that the event happened in the fall), whereas in others the degree of detail expected may be a function of case characteristics. For example, it may be more important to specify the time when the child reported a single event that took place 6 months ago rather than repeated abuse by an individual who had routine access to the child (Nancy Diehl, personal communication, September 18, 1996). Investigative interviewers should obtain guidelines for their regions of practice regarding the degree of detail required and avoid asking children under the age of 8 to provide unnecessary information.

Because even older children and adults do not immediately or accurately remember the exact timing of events, it is best to identify the time frame by asking broader questions about the context first, hoping that the witness will volunteer relevant details about time. Asking children whether they remember what they were doing when a particular event occurred, for example, often leads them to mention whether or not it happened on a school day and may elicit references to significant events that can be used to specify the date (e.g., that the child had a special friend sleep over). Because children have difficulty identifying the time of specific instances of repeated events, especially when the initial interview is delayed, reducing the delay before an interview is one way to improve children's accuracy (e.g., Powell & Thomson, 1996, 1997b).

"More/less" and "some/all." Although children frequently ask for *more*, children under age 6 typically do not understand the contrastive use of the term, and therefore questions such as "Did you go to Bill's house more than one time?" can be problematic with preschoolers (Walker, 1994). A better way to ask about frequency is to choose a multiple-choice question such as, "Did that happen one time or more than one time?"

Children also may not realize that *some* is subsumed by *all* until age 6 or 7 years, so they may deny that they have some of a thing when, in fact, they have all of it (Rosner & Poole, 1985). For example, "Did he take off some of your clothes?" is a poor question because (a) it is leading, (b) it uses the superordinate word *clothes* (which can lead to an incorrect "no"), and (c) it includes the word *some*. A child might respond "no" because he took off *all* of her clothes.

Remember. It is not until 8 or 9 years of age that children use the word *remember* the way adults do. For example, a child might believe that something must have been forgotten before it can be remembered (Walker, 1995), and thus he may respond "no" when asked whether he remembers certain events—including those he has recently described.

In addition, "Do you remember . . ." questions tend to string several ideas together. A child may therefore answer "no" when asked "Do you remember telling your mother that John poked you in the bottom?" because she does not remember telling her mother, she did not literally say that he "poked" her bottom, *or* because she is confused. Although "do you remember" questions can be straightforward (e.g., "Do you remember me?"; Walker, 1994), it obviously is best to avoid complicated "do you remember . . ." questions.

"The" versus "a." The distinction between these articles is so difficult that one Korean psycholinguist failed to master the difference despite living in an English-speaking environment for many years (Reich, 1986), and some English speakers as old as 9 years (and even adults) occasionally make errors. Adults may be confused when children use *a* when *the* is more appropriate given the prior conversation or the situation. For example, the difference between "I don't like a dog" and "I don't like the dog" is subtle, but whereas a child appears off topic with the first statement, the second statement implies that a dog was involved in the event.

Referring to persons. Clear identification of people is a crucial component of testimony. We expect children to discuss people by referring to their names or their kinship relationship (e.g., Daddy, Mommy), but several problems muddy our ability to interpret children's statements. First, many children know more than one person with a particular name, so interviewers should avoid confusion by exploring the possibility of duplicate names during preinterview preparation. Second, multiple names or nicknames are not uncommon and may confuse interviewers. Finally, kinship terms are difficult for children to understand, and their use varies considerably across cultural groups.

Kinship terms are part of a class of words called *shifters*: words that change their referent according to the identity of the speaker and his or her temporal or spatial location. Although children often use kinship terms such as *uncle*, they do not begin to understand them until age 4 or so, and complete understanding comes as late as age 10 or older (Reich, 1986). *Mother*, *father*, *sister*, and *brother* are learned earliest, whereas a complete understanding of *aunt*, *uncle*, *cousin*, *niece*, and *nephew* are learned rather late. To compound the confusion, some families apply kinship terms to family friends, and interviewers must therefore be careful to identify specific individuals clearly, exploring the possibility that the child knows more than one individual who has a particular name.

"This/that," "here/there," "come/go," "bring/take." Although one of the words *this, that, here,* or *there* usually appears among the first 50 words learned, full acquisition of these contrasts is quite delayed because these terms, like kinship terms, are shifters (i.e., their meaning depends on the location of the speaker or who is speaking). When 7-year-old children were asked to "Make the dog over here/there hop" by a speaker who was either beside or across from the child, for example, only 30% appeared to have mastered the contrasts in all situations (Wales, 1979). It is interesting that the children used different strategies when answering these questions: Some always selected the object nearest themselves, some chose at random, and some chose correctly when the speaker was beside them but inconsistently when the speaker was across from them. Likewise, the meaning of *come/go* and *bring/take* depends on the location of the speaker and listener. Although these words appear by 2 years of age in spontaneous speech, in some situations it is not until 7 years that more than 90% of children's responses are correct (Richards, 1976). On the basis of such data, Reich (1986) concluded that "what appears to an adult to be a single consistent distinction is acquired by children quite slowly, word by word and case by case" (p. 157).

Legal terms. It is obvious that young children do not have a legal vocabulary, but it is worth mentioning how little even older children know about terms that are common in courtroom proceedings. Warren-Leubecker et al. (1989) reported that many children under 7 years did not know what a lawyer was or had mistaken notions (e.g., "loans money," "write down everybody who's bad"), and 30% of 12-year-olds could not define *jury*. Saywitz (1989) obtained similar results when she asked 4- to 14-year-olds about words such as *court, jury,* and *judge.* Many legal words also have double meanings that can confuse children, such as *court* (*tennis*), *charges* (*credit card*), *swear* (*bad words*), and *case* (*beer, suitcase*). Adults must monitor their speech carefully to avoid using legal terms or jargon.

Summary

Children learn the meaning of words over a period of many years, and specific words appear in their speech long before they have grasped the full adult meaning of those words. They are likely to understand common prepositions (*in, on, up, down, in front of*) by 5 years or earlier, although their knowledge of other subjects (e.g., their own body) can lead them to use these words in ways that confuse adults. Temporal terms are notoriously difficult for children. Even *before* versus *after* causes problems well up to 7 years of age, and children are very limited in their ability to identify days or times accurately before at least 10 years of age. Shifters are found in many parts of speech, including nouns (kinship terms), verbs (*come* vs. *go*), adverbs (*here* vs. *there*), and articles (*a* vs. *the*), and these words also are acquired late in development. Although some of these contrasts are learned earlier than others, interviewers should not assume an understanding of relational words until approximately 10 years of age. Children, especially teenagers, often seem surprisingly mature and sophisticated in an interview, but this can lead adults to overestimate their knowledge base. Even throughout the teenage years, interviewers should test children's understanding of difficult words such as legal terms before using those words freely during questioning.

The Development of Syntax

A full understanding of syntactic development requires a background in linguistics. Still, it is easier to adjust syntax to accommodate children than it is to simplify vocabulary. This is because many words that are conceptually difficult, such as shifters, are difficult to avoid, but interviewers can avoid complicated question formats by following a few general rules.

There are two ways to train interviewers to simplify the grammatical structure of their questions. On the one hand, interviewers can study developmental "norms," which are tables that list the ages at which most children comprehend specific types of questions. There are two problems with this approach. First, it is difficult to remember such details in the heat of an interview, so interviewers tend not to use this information very effectively. Second, wide individual differences ensure that the norms will not describe all children equally well. On the other hand, it is not really necessary to adopt different types of questions for different ages, because questions that are difficult to process often can be reworded. Instead of memorizing a complicated list of developmental norms, interviewers simply can learn to phrase questions to *all* ages of interviewees in a way that makes fewer cognitive demands on listeners.

Word Order and Passive Voice

The most common word order in English is the order that children across the world use most often in their early speech: subject–verb–object. Questions that reflect this word order are processed more accurately by young children than questions that violate the so-called noun–verb–noun (NVN) strategy (i.e., the noun before the verb is the agent).

In adult speech, the most common violation of the NVN pattern is the passive construction. There are a variety of passive constructions, and these appear in children's speech at different ages (Gordon & Chafetz, 1990). Short passives, such as "the doll was broken," are commonly used when the speaker does not know who performed the action or does not want the listener to know. Full passives, such as "The doll was broken by my brother," generally do not appear in the speech of children or in adult speech directed to children (i.e., "He broke the doll" is much easier to say). Some passives are reversible (i.e., they make sense even if the nouns are reversed, as in "John was touched by Mary") and others are nonreversible (such as "John was burned by the stove"; Reich, 1986). Full command of the passive voice in spoken language does not emerge until age 10 to 13 years (Walker, 1994), and even college students struggle to fully comprehend the difference between active and passive voices (Romaine, 1984).

Interviewers generally worry about children's ability to understand passives rather than their ability to produce them. Children around 3 to 3½ years of age sometimes perform worse than chance in comprehending passives, probably because they interpret the sentences as if the subject–verb–object order applied (e.g., Bever, 1970; deVilliers & deVilliers, 1973). As a result, "Were you hit by John?" might be interpreted by a child as "you," "hit," "John," resulting in a cry of denial ("no!"). Even 5-year-olds sometimes misinterpret 20% of the full passives that adults address to them (Lempert, 1978), with error rates varying according to whether the first or second noun, or both, are animate or inanimate. It is thus best to avoid passives completely and conduct all conversation in the active voice, with the subject of the sentence specified first.

Word Order: Embedding

Adults often pack information into an utterance by using complex sentences or questions (i.e., utterances with more than one verb). For example, adults frequently use relative clauses to modify a noun, as in the question, "Did the woman who was watching talk to you?" A variety of syntactic devices are used to compress additional information into a sentence, as in these two examples from transcripts analyzed by Brennan and Brennan (1988): "At or after you finished seeing Mum at the hospital, were you walking home?" (asked to a 9-year-old), and "Would it be incorrect to suggest that it was not so much a tripping but because of the state of inebriation of yourself, that you fell over?" (asked to a 15-year-old, p. 76). Both examples illustrate *left-branching,* or the placement of clarifying information *before* the primary focus of the question. In contrast, right-branching places qualifications or expansions *after* the primary question (e.g., "Were you walking home after you finished seeing Mum at the hospital?"). Left-branching, particularly when there are numerous embeddings in a single statement, interrupts the NVN order and is difficult for adults as well as children to understand. It is better to keep the subject and main verbs together at the beginning of the question (e.g., "Did you run home when he hit you?" rather than "Did you, when he hit you, run home?).

Multiple Questions

Another way of compressing speech is to ask several questions at once. Even short questions can still be difficult to answer if they contain more than one concept, as in this example from an investigative interview analyzed by Warren et al. (1996, p. 240): "You don't remember? Did anyone ever wake and see this happening?" A frequent type of multiple question begins with "Do you remember..." as in "Do you remember telling Mommy that Daddy hurt your pee pee in the shower?" A child may respond "no" because he does not remember telling, because Daddy did not hurt his "pee pee," or because he did not use the word *shower* when he told his mother. Examples such as the following were common in transcripts analyzed by Warren et al.:

> Interviewer: He never kissed you? Did he ask you to kiss him? Have you touched him?
>
> Child: No. (p. 240)

To avoid multiple questions, interviewers should (a) ask children to provide only one piece of information at a time, (b) be tolerant of pauses in the conversation so that children have time to reply, and (c) take time to formulate questions carefully.

Negation and Tag Questions

Children and adults find it more difficult to understand questions that include a negative (e.g., "Did he not tell you to sit on the floor?") or a double negative (e.g., "Did he not say he was not going to hurt you?") than more direct questions (Perry et al., 1995). A type of question that frequently includes a negative is tag questions, or questions that transform declarative sentences into questions by tagging on a request for confirmation (e.g., "You were crying then, weren't [i.e., were not] you," or "He had a knife, didn't he?"). Although tag questions appear in the speech of 4-year-olds, many 12- to 14-year-olds in one study still could not restate a declarative sentence into a tag question without error (Dennis, Sugar, & Whitaker, 1982). Adults might think that the problem with negatives and tag questions is simply that children have not learned the obvious. Actually, the correct answer to these questions is arbitrary and varies from language to language. In Japanese, for example, if you held up the pepper and said "This is salt, isn't it?" the correct answer would be "yes" (i.e., it is not salt; Harker, 1986). Negative tag questions, like negatives in general, are linguistically complex and should not be used. Positive tag questions (e.g., "And then you told your mom, right?") avoid the problem of negative wording but, like negative tags, are extremely suggestive because they imply that the speaker would prefer a particular answer.

Pointing Words

Some words have no meaning apart from the specific context in which they occur, including the pronouns *I* and *you*, words like *that*, and contrasts such as *come/go*. Although children master pronouns earlier than pointing words like *this/that* and *here/there*, they may still have difficulty with them in certain questions. For example, "When she came home, did your mom take a nap?" implies that *she* refers to *mom*. Depending on how many other parties were being discussed, however, children might interpret this question differently. The ability to match pronouns with prior or subsequent nouns may not be fully developed until about age 10, and preschoolers are particularly bad at "carrying forward" pronouns (Walker, 1995).

Anaphora involves linking words or phrases to prior referents (e.g., "Did he poke you with *it*?"). An example of unclear anaphora, from Brennan and Brennan (1988, p. 70) is "Well you are not sure whether you said those things to the police which are wrong?" (a question that elicited the response, "Mmm" from an 11-year-old; p. 70). Even in relatively non-stressful situations, children often will process each question independently of prior utterances (see chap. 2), and thus interviewers cannot trust that children will keep track of these types of pointing references.

Pointing words, which are also called *deictic* words or *indexicals* (Walker, 1994), are problematic because they require children to monitor what has already been stated, link words to prior referents, and take the role of the speaker into consideration (Hulse, 1994). To simplify the child's task, interviewers should try to increase the redundancy of their speech by repeating critical information instead of using pointers such as *he*, *she*, *that*, or *it*. For example, the question, "Did he do that one time or more than one time?" can be made more redundant by saying, "Did he use that cream one time or more than one time?"

Wh- Questions

Wh- questions (who, whose, what, where, when, why, how, how much, or how many) are frequently used when more than a yes or no answer is desired. Children appear to answer what, who, or where questions earlier than when, how, and why questions, perhaps because the concepts underlying the later questions are acquired more slowly (deVilliers & deVilliers, 1978). The following examples of preschool children who were making food with play putty underscores the need for caution on the part of interviewers (deVilliers & deVilliers, p. 98):

Child: Look, a meal.

Adult: Oh, but what are you going to eat it with?

Child: With my bib on.

* * *

Adult: Oh, but what are you going to eat with it?

Child: A fork.

Specialists in language development love to pore over interview transcripts, because adults' interpretations of children's utterances, and the subsequent direction of the interview, can be as amusing as the children's responses themselves. Interviewers need to avoid literal interpretations of children's responses to difficult questions lest they conclude, for example, that children had been forced to eat forks. Such processes can easily contribute to ever-escalating claims of bizarre abuse.

Professionals with an interest in investigative interviewing have voiced special concern about questions that ask children "why" something did or did not occur. There are two problems with questions regarding motivation, such as "Why did you go inside the house if your friends were all playing in the yard?" First, the ability to reflect on one's own mental state is a sophisticated cognitive achievement. Generally, children under the age of 7 to 10 years cannot describe their motives very well, and the ability to describe other people's motives may not emerge before 10 to 13 years of age. Second, children may believe they have done something wrong when adults ask questions such as "Why didn't you tell anyone?" (Walker, 1994). Interviewers should thus avoid unnecessary "why" questions.

Another problematic Wh- question involves "how many," as in "How many times did she do that?" Even children who understand the purpose of such questions may have difficulty reflecting on past experiences and accurately reporting number, as in this example from Hulse's (1994) transcript of an interview between a CPS worker (W) and a child (C) age 7 years 9 months:

W: Okay. Can you remember how many times Tom did this to you?

C: No.

W: Would you say it's a like a lot, like a hundred?

C: (nods head yes)

W: Has it been just a few times, just a few times?

C: Just a few times.

W: Just a few. If you were saying a few, would that be like ten times or less than ten or more than ten?

C: A little but more than ten.

W: A little more than ten? (p. 61)

Interviewers can avoid such interchanges, yet still address whether or not abuse was repeated, by first asking whether an event happened one time or more than one time and then asking the child to describe another event (e.g., "Tell me about the time you remember best").

Nominalization

Nominalization involves changing a verb into a noun. As Brennan and Brennan (1988) summarized, "Nominalization refers to the language process where an action is objectified so that neither the agent nor the recipient are mentioned. There is a great deal lost in the translation" (p. 65). Examples from their transcripts (p. 66) included "the actual taking down of the pants" and "You were not troubled by that were you . . . the massage of the breast?" Statements containing nominalizations are poorly understood by adults and should be avoided completely with children.

Summary

Interviewers can help children understand by asking about one concept at a time, using only the active voice, and maintaining a subject–verb–object format that places the main ideas early in the question. It is best to avoid the passive voice, embedding or left-branching, tag questions, and pointing words that require children to identify meaning by linking the words to referents earlier or later in the question or conversation.

Pragmatics and Conversational Competence

Pragmatics is the study of language in social contexts: the practical uses of language and its effects on other individuals. The development of pragmatics involves (a) adopting social conventions for participating in conversation; (b) learning to use language for various purposes such as requesting, persuading, or promising; and (c) adjusting one's speech according to the social context (such as one's relationship to a conversational partner, a partner's knowledge, etc.). While children are developing *linguistic competence* by mastering phonology, semantics, and syntax, they also are mastering *communicative competence* by learning to adapt their language to the demands of the situation (Warren & McCloskey, 1997).

Participating in Conversation

In an introduction to the development of communicative competence, Warren and McCloskey (1997) reviewed a variety of developmental phenomena that have practical implications for investigative interviews. Because interviewers must be aware of these phenomena to interpret children's comments, we introduced these concepts earlier by discussing children's answers to interview questions during eyewitness studies (see chap. 2).

One interesting line of research has investigated when children learn to participate in dialogue with others and how they attempt to maintain coherent conversations. As Warren and McCloskey (1997) pointed out, even 1-year-olds have a well-developed sense of taking turns in conversation, but strategies for maintaining discussion about a single topic are acquired only gradually. As these authors summarized:

> Younger children's conversations are typically loosely organized, involving unrelated topics and abrupt topic shifts, and they do not always abide by Grice's (1975) principle of relevance, which states that conversational participants should make their contributions relevant to their partner's immediately prior utterances or to the overall topic. Older, school aged children show greater topic coherence (Hobbs, 1990; Reichmen, 1990) and more gradual topic shifts (Wanska & Bedrosian, 1985). By adolescence, children's conversations with peers may involve hierarchically organized superordinate and subordinate topics, and speakers may "topic hop" between levels with ease. (p. 221)

Children's lack of attention to an overall topic was apparent in the Mr. Science study (Poole & Lindsay, 1996) that we summarized in chapter 2. Recall that some children who answered four open-ended questions about a science experience did not assume that a final prompt to describe "something else" also referred to the science experience. Instead, even 8-year-old children sometimes responded by providing additional information about their families or other activities. In general, older children are more likely to indicate when they are shifting topics (Warren & McCloskey, 1997), so that younger children's off-topic comments may not always be apparent to investigative interviewers. Clearly, the gradual development of topic coherence implies that investigative interviewers should redundantly restate the topic when they question children, and that they should seek clarification whenever they think that children may have strayed off topic.

Young children use a variety of strategies for maintaining turn-taking and relating their utterances to those of their conversational partners. An early strategy discussed by Warren and McCloskey (1997) involves repeating their partner's prior utterance. As Keenan (1977) summarized, "One of the most commonplace observations in the psycholinguistic literature is that many young children often repeat utterances addressed to them" (p. 125). In a workshop on children and language in legal settings, Walker (1995) also pointed out that repetition is one of several strategies children use to maintain conversation when there is a breakdown in understanding, as in this example from Saywitz (1988):

Attorney: When you were at your grandma's house with your daddy, whose mamma is your grandma?

Jenny: Grandma Ann. (gives grandma's name)

Attorney: Is she your daddy's mamma?

Jenny: Huh? (doesn't understand the question)

Attorney: Is she your daddy's mamma? (leading question requiring only a nod)

Jenny: Daddy's mamma. (repeated the end of the sentence) (pp. 38–39)

Because repetition serves a wide variety of purposes in adult conversation, Keenan (1977) interpreted this behavior as a hallmark of emerging competence rather than a sign of incompetence. She explained,

We can say that in repeating, the child is learning to communicate. He is learning not to construct sentences at random, but to construct them to meet specific communicative needs. He is learning to query, comment, confirm, match a claim and counterclaim, answer a question, respond to a demand, and so on. In short, he is learning the human uses of language. (p. 133)

When children repeat questions or parts of questions, however, interviewers should not treat these as affirmations, because it is possible that the children simply are confused.

Another interesting phenomenon is how children respond to indirect requests. Research shows that even young children generally respond to indirect requests from their mothers, despite the fact that the literal meaning of their mothers' utterances does not demand a response. For example, mothers might say "What are you doing?" or "That's no good" rather than "Don't do that" (Warren & McCloskey, 1997). Because children do not consistently distinguish between literal and intended meaning until 6 years of age or later,

Warren and McCloskey agreed with Shatz (1978; Shatz & McCloskey, 1984) and others that young children sometimes respond to adult utterances on the basis of objects or actions mentioned in the utterance. Similarly, in eyewitness studies (e.g., Poole & Lindsay, 1995, 1996), children sometimes responded to questions such as, "Can you tell me about the tops" by generating responses related to the object mentioned in the question, even though they did not see or play with those objects during the event under discussion. In these cases, children failed to respond literally by answering "no" and instead assumed that the adult expected them to provide descriptive information. In these studies, many children who provided false answers subsequently said that the events did not actually happen, however—demonstrating that their responses resulted from misunderstanding about their role in the interview rather than from memory failure. Expecting that adults want answers, together with learning that one should be cooperative with individuals in a position of authority, undoubtedly contributes to the fact that children's answers to specific questions are less accurate than their answers to questions that do not contain embedded objects or actions that can form the basis of a false narrative. Furthermore, children are sensitive to the social context in which specific or misleading questions are asked, fielding fewer false responses to warm, supportive adults than to adults who act cold and intimidating (Carter et al., 1996).

Warren and McCloskey (1997) also reviewed the research on signaling comprehension failures. It is well known that young children often fail to detect when a speaker's message is ambiguous, and even when they detect ambiguity they generally do not tell the speaker that they are confused. Simple conversational skills, such as asking for clarification when one is uncertain about the meaning of an utterance and changing one's utterance when the listener is confused, are sophisticated strategies that develop gradually during early and middle childhood. (Indeed, there is substantial variability in adults' ability to navigate these interpersonal waters.) Although experienced interviewers tell children that they can ask for clarification, it is still necessary to minimize the ambiguity in questions—for example, by avoiding potentially confusing words such as pronouns.

Sociolinguistics: The Impact of Culture on Conversational Conventions

Adults who are exposed primarily to a single culture may fail to realize how many aspects of conversation are culturally prescribed. One professor who trained TESL teachers (for "teaching English as a second language"), for example, complained that teachers often misinterpret the conversational behavior of Hispanic children and their parents (Sharon Russell, personal communication, February 1987). Some Hispanic adults consider it confrontative and disrespectful to look authority figures in the eye while speaking (particularly about a misdeed), whereas Anglo teachers often interpret averted gaze as a sign of disrespect. Requiring children to make eye contact by demanding, "Look at me when I ask you a question," therefore is not productive.[3] Anglo teachers also have expressed discomfort when Hispanic mothers make comments that authority figures view as personal or intrusive (e.g., referring to a teacher's pregnancy), although such comments may simply reflect a tradition of establishing one's social connection and similarity before discussing important or sensitive issues (particularly those regarding family). The tradition of obligatory chitchat before a business transaction also has surprised visitors to parts of Africa (Steve Collarelli, personal communication, February 5, 1996).

Interviewers also may misinterpret conversational guardedness, as when they fail to recognize that some Native Americans are reluctant to comment on another person's intentions or thoughts. Consider the following quote from Downs (1972) about the Navajo's concept of individualism:

> Among adults this emphasis on individualism manifests itself in an unwillingness to make a statement that could be considered a commitment of another person. One learns quickly to phrase questions about other people so that an answer can be given by the informant without violating this rule. Brothers and sisters politely refuse to discuss the others' likes and dislikes, or husbands profess complete ignorance of whether or not their wives want to attend a Squaw Dance. This gives an outsider a first impression that the Navajo know very little about one another, an impression that later is seen to be manifestly false. It is simply a violation of Navajo mores to express an opinion for someone else. (pp. 24–25)

In general, interviewers should avoid interpreting the body language or "appropriateness" of conversation unless they are familiar with the cultural norms of the people with whom they are interacting.

Another area of diversity that surprises students of language is the degree to which various cultural groups structure conversations differently. Mainstream academic discourse has been described as having a "topic-centered" structure, with dialogue organized hierarchically under a superordinate topic. Another style that has been studied among African American children has been called *topic associating* (Michaels, 1981). Such discourse consists of "im-

---

[3]Correcting children's behavior can be disruptive for a number of reasons. Consider the following example from Warren et al. (1996) of an interviewer who stopped a child's free narrative:

Interviewer: Can you tell me what happened to you?

    Child: Yeah.

Interviewer: What happened to you?

    Child: We was in Alton Park. He took Jo's keys somewhere and then he told me to//

Interviewer: Sit up and sit right. Big girls supposed to talk real loud for me. (p. 239)

plicitly associated personal anecdotes," a style that is perceived by some teachers as having "no beginning, middle, or end, and hence, no point at all" (p. 429). In reality, linguistic analyses of these narratives have revealed that topic shifts are signaled by shifts in intonation and tempo, shifts that many teachers are not trained to detect. As a result, teachers sometimes misinterpret African American children and ask them thematically inappropriate questions that interrupt their train of thought. As one child lamented about "Sharing Time," "She was always stoppin' me sayin,' 'That's not *important* enough,' and I hadn't hardly started talking!" (p. 439).

Appreciation of the differences between Asian cultures and American English has been aided by increased business dealings abroad. Discussing a course on the pragmatics of Japanese, for example, Harker (1986) noted that vagueness is regarded by Japanese speakers as "a virtue" that doesn't put anyone on the spot, particularly if the answer is 'no' " (p. 19). A telling illustration of such vagueness is the ubiquitous use of the word *hai* or *yes*, a word that can mean, literally, "yes," or "yes, your thoughts on this topic are different from mine," or "yes, I heard what you are saying." It is interesting that the Japanese habit of leaving things unspecified, such as the subject of a sentence, along with using *yes* to be polite, are conversational habits shared by many American preschoolers. What seems odd to speakers in the United States is a norm to maintain social harmony, a norm that might be more widespread than the abrupt, direct style of academic English.

Clearly, interviewers must be attuned to the social aspects of a conversation and appreciate that children are trying to comply with the perceived demands of the situation. Adults snicker when children interpret language too literally, yet adults routinely take children's language at face value and ignore the social or cultural contexts in which that language is produced. Whenever possible, practitioners should have some familiarity with the conversational conventions of the children they interview.

SUMMARY

Interviewers need to inhibit a number of habits that are common when adults talk to children. These include using baby talk, guessing what a child probably said, using words that might be beyond the child's scope of knowledge, and using words that require the child to infer links between various parts of a conversation (such as pronouns or other pointing words). Skilled investigative interviewers ask about one concept at a time and use simple subject–verb–object constructions in their sentences. Although we have discussed only a small portion of what language specialists have discovered about children's language, children of all ages would be well served if interviewers adopted the simple guidelines that are summarized in QuickGuide 5.1.

QUICKGUIDE 5.1
Guidelines for Talking With Children

Phonology
- Speak to the child using proper pronunciation. Do not use baby talk.
- Do not guess what a child might have said. If a comment is uninterpretable, ask the child to repeat the comment.
- Remember that the child may pronounce words differently than an adult would. If there might be another interpretation of what the child said (e.g., *body* or *potty*), clarify the meaning of the target word by asking a follow-up question (e.g., "I'm not sure I understand where he peed. Tell me more about where he peed.").

Vocabulary
- A word might not mean the same thing to the child and the interviewer. Instead, the child's usage may be more restrictive (bathing suits, shoes, or pajamas may not be *clothes* to the child; only hands may be capable of *touching*); more inclusive (*in* might mean *in* or *between*); or idiosyncratic (i.e., having no counterpart in typical adult speech).
- Avoid introducing new words, such as the names of specific persons or body parts, until the child first uses those words.
- The ability to answer questions about the time of an event is very limited before 8 to 10 years of age. Try to narrow down the time of an event by asking about activities or events that children understand, such as whether it was a school day or what the child was doing that day. Even the words *before* and *after* might produce inconsistent answers from children under the age of 7 (e.g., "Did it happen before Christmas?").
- When the child mentions a specific person, ask follow-up questions to make sure that the identification is unambiguous.
- Beware of *shifters*, words whose meaning depends on the speaker's context, location, or relationship (e.g., *come/go*, *here/there*, *a/the*, kinship terms).
- Avoid complicated legal terms or other adult jargon.

Syntax
- Use sentences with subject–verb–object word orders. Avoid the passive voice.
- Avoid embedding clauses. Place the primary question *before* qualifications. For example, say "What did you do when he hit you?" rather than "When he hit you, what did you do?"
- Ask about only one concept per question.
- Avoid negatives, as in "Did you *not* see who it was?"
- Do not use tag questions, such as "This is a daddy doll, *isn't it*?"
- Be redundant. Words such as *she, he, that*, or *it* may be ambiguous. When possible, use the referent rather than a pointing word that refers back to a referent.
- Children learn to answer *what, who*, and *where* questions earlier than *when, how*, and *why* questions.
- Avoid nominalization. That is, do not convert verbs into nouns (e.g., "the poking").

Quickguide 5.1 continues on next page

Pragmatics
- Different cultural groups have different norms for conversing with authority figures or strangers. Avoid correcting a child's nonverbal behavior unless it is interfering with your ability to hear the child or otherwise impeding the interview.
- Language diversity includes diversity in the way conversations are structured. Be tolerant of talk that seems off topic and avoiding interrupting children while they are speaking.
- Children may believe that it is polite to agree with a stranger. It is especially important to avoid leading or yes–no format questions with children who might always be expected to comply even when adults are wrong.

6

ANCILLARY TECHNIQUES

> In today's increasingly circuslike atmosphere in which fears of widespread but undiscovered child abuse compete for attention with fears of false allegations of abuse, there is no more crucial agenda than the development of better techniques for interviewing children. The goal is to avoid tragedy on either side—either by failing to detect real instances of abuse or by mistakenly identifying abuse where none exists. As is becoming all too apparent, it is dismayingly easy to err in either direction.
>
> Judy DeLoache
> "The Use of Dolls in Interviewing Young Children"
> *Memory and Testimony in the Child Witness*

Investigative interviewers use many creative methods to encourage discussions of abuse. Techniques range from popular aids, such as anatomical dolls, to lesser-known strategies, such as drawing time lines to help children identify the approximate dates of events. Unfortunately, it is difficult for practitioners to evaluate many of these ancillary techniques. Most interview aids came into practice when practitioners were responding to rapid changes in the number and complexity of abuse allegations, and front-line workers in educational, criminal justice, and social service settings could not wait for research results before interviewing the increasing numbers of children with special communication needs. As a result, news of innovative techniques for interviewing preschoolers, reticent children, and children with language impairments were passed on by word of mouth, workshops, and publications, generally in the form of personal testimonials. Because research on interviewing was just beginning, however, practitioners were often advised to adopt techniques even when no systematic evaluations had been attempted.

In this chapter, we review the evidence for using a diverse array of popular ancillary techniques for conducting interviews and interpreting children's responses. Although numerous interesting techniques are currently in use, we discuss only the small number that have attracted the attention of researchers: drawing/drawings, dolls, other cues and props, special techniques for interviewing children with disabilities, and criterion-based content analysis/statement validity analysis.

DRAWING/DRAWINGS

Professionals have used drawings in at least four ways during interviews with children. First, drawings of people, such as family members performing activities (kinetic family drawing: Burns & Kaufman, 1970; Hackbarth, Murphy, & McQuary, 1991); specific themes (e.g., a worry); and free drawings have been content-analyzed for clues regarding the possibility of abuse (e.g., Miller, Veltkamp, & Janson, 1987; Riordan & Verdel, 1991; Yates, Beutler, & Crago, 1985). Because explicit depictions of abuse are uncommon in young children's drawings, helping professionals have attempted to base judgments on subtle features such as the size of body parts or the colors used (Wakefield & Underwager, 1994b). Unfortunately, such uses of drawings as projective tests have no proven validity (Buros, 1989; pp. 422–425), and studies designed to identify differences between the drawings of abused and nonabused children have suffered from a variety of methodological shortcomings.

One methodological problem is that many studies concerned with the interpretation of drawings have lacked appropriate comparison groups. When researchers compare abused children who were identified because of behavioral problems or overt family conflicts with children who have no similar problems, for example, they might mistakenly conclude that certain features of drawings are associated with abuse when, in fact, these features are only associated with variables that increase the chances of referral (e.g., family disharmony, socioeconomic status). For example, Hackbarth et al. (1991) compared the kinetic family drawings of sexually abused and "non-identified" comparison children. Comparison children were selected to match sexually abused children on age, sex, and ethnicity, but the authors mentioned no attempt to match children on other demographic characteristics that might influence family drawings (e.g., children's academic achievement or parental education). Instead, comparison children were selected from a list of children with "normal" adjustment (good relationships with other people, participation in play, management of emotions, and ability to work), and the drawings of these children suggested more positive adjustment than did those of sexually abused children. This finding is unsurprising in light of the way the abused and nonabused children were selected and does not address the value of drawings for distinguishing between sexually abused and nonabused children.

Another methodological challenge is that allegations of abuse often prompt questions about sexuality that could influence children's drawings whether or not they have been abused. Thus, researchers who wish to evaluate the use of drawings in forensic interviews should include a comparison group of children who were not abused but who were nonetheless involved in abuse investigations.

Of course, drawings are not used only as projective tools. Many professionals recommend having paper and crayons on hand to put children at ease and facilitate rapport building. Although this appears to be an innocuous and developmentally appropriate practice, some interviewers allow children to continue drawing during the substantive portions of the interview, without explicit instructions to draw the events in question. This practice could distract small children, however, and increase the likelihood that interviewers will resort to specific or leading questions to direct children's attention back to the desired topic. Another possible problem is that children might be preoccupied with drawing and answer the interviewer's questions haphazardly. Until firm data are available, it would be prudent to remove drawing materials and encourage children to devote their full attention to the interviewer.

In the course of investigative interviews, children also may be asked to draw the events under discussion in the hope that drawing will prompt them to disclose more information (e.g., National Center for Prosecution of Child Abuse, 1993). Drawing could facilitate reporting by easing stress, by extending the length of the interview and providing more opportunity for details to surface, or by introducing topics that can be explored verbally while the picture is being completed. Conversely, drawing could reduce the quality of narratives by distracting children or by encouraging creativity and fantasy.

Butler, Gross, and Hayne (1995) explored whether drawing would influence the completeness and accuracy of children's event reports. In the first experiment, 5- to 6-year-olds were interviewed 1 day after a visit to a fire station, either verbally or with explicit instructions to "draw what happened." The interviewers asked no specific questions during free recall, but children who did not spontaneously narrate their drawings were asked to do so. After free recall, the interviewers asked four direct questions, such as "Draw [or tell me] how you got there." In the second experiment, 5- to 6-year-olds and 3- to 4-year-olds participated in the same procedure but were interviewed 1 month after the target events. In both studies, data were based only on the children's verbal comments; the children were not credited with information depicted in the drawings unless that information also was described.

The results were encouraging. Regardless of the delay, children who drew while narrating the events provided more information than did children who responded only verbally, and both groups of children were equally accurate. This "drawing advantage" was especially evident among the 5- and 6-year-olds: Older children who drew reported almost twice as much information during direct questioning as did nondrawers. In contrast, the advantage of drawing was smaller for the 3- and 4-year-olds and was not statistically significant for any specific phase of the interview. It is interesting that there was no significant difference between drawers and nondrawers during free recall, suggesting that young children may need verbal structuring by adults even with supporting activities. Although Butler et al. did not present systematic data on the children's demeanor, they noted that drawing extended the interview time without awkward pauses or an atmosphere of adult pressure to respond. Likewise, Brennan and Fisher (1998) recently found that 9- to 10-year-old children who drew the events in question recalled 20% more facts about a first-aid lecture than did children who were interviewed without drawing, and error rates were comparable in the two interview conditions.

Although these data suggest that drawing may be a helpful interview aid, there are three important caveats. First, the events in these studies actually occurred, so we do not know whether drawings would help distinguish between children who had and had not experienced an event. Second, the drawings were taken at face value and were not interpreted symbolically; indeed, the researchers only coded the information provided verbally. An anecdote from Brennan and Fisher (personal communication, July 3, 1997) demonstrates how important it is that interviewers ask children for verbal clarification. One child in their drawing study drew hair on a picture of a doll, but when the interviewer asked the child to describe the hair this child responded, "The doll didn't have any hair, I just drew it like that." In other words, children might not take a literal approach to the task of drawing. Third, the results obtained by Butler and her colleagues (1995) and Brennan and Fisher (1998) were not replicated in another study of 5- to 6-year-old children (Salmon & Pipe, 1998).

Salmon and Pipe (1996) assessed the memories of 5-year-old children for a routine health assessment conducted at their school. Half of the children were interviewed 3 days after the assessment and again after 1 year, whereas the other half were interviewed only after the 1-year delay. The children were assigned to one of three interview conditions: verbal prompts only, interviewing with props (i.e., prototypical medical items and a doll), or interviewing with drawings. In the drawing condition, interviewers gave the children line drawings of items used in the event and asked them to draw the target event and describe their drawings. In all conditions, interviewers first asked children to recount the events, then prompted them (i.e., "I heard that she used some things like doctors use when you got the checkup—like I heard she used a little light") and asked specific questions (i.e., about who was present, where the child was touched, and which items were present and used).

Drawing did not help the children retrieve information. Children in all three groups reported similar amounts of information, but the children who drew provided significantly more inaccurate information during prompted recall. Like the results reported by Butler and her colleagues (1995), these data suggest that drawing has no apparent benefits over non-suggestive questioning for younger children and that the benefits of drawing during directive questioning must be weighed against the risk of inaccuracy.

Interviewers who use anatomical body drawings must also weigh benefits against risks. Line drawings of male and female bodies (both front and back views) are sometimes used to prompt the labeling of body parts and to communicate the appropriateness of discussing genital areas during the interview. There is no evidence that children label body parts less accurately on line drawings than when they point to dolls or to themselves, and no serious concerns have been raised about this practice being suggestive when it is used for clarification *after* children have made a disclosure. Interviewers who ask for genital labels early in an interview can be criticized for suggesting that sexual themes are expected, however—even when interviewers ask children to label nonsexual as well as sexual body parts. Because sexual themes typically do not occur in conversations with young children, the use of sexual words may attract children's attention and direct the conversation. Similarly, children who are interviewed more than once could be influenced by previous exposure to explicit body drawings.

The risks of using anatomical props are evident in a study by Steward and Steward (1996) of 3- to 6-year-old children who were asked to describe a pediatric clinic visit. Steward and Steward compared accuracy across four interview conditions: verbal questions alone (1), plus verbal questions facilitated using anatomical dolls (2), line drawings of nude male and female bodies (3), or line drawings presented using a computer (4). For the enhanced conditions (i.e., Conditions 2–4), Steward and Steward reported the percentages of inaccurate assertions about body touch before direct yes–no questions (i.e., when the props were merely present) and after direct questions that double-checked whether the children were touched in locations that they had not spontaneously mentioned. Although all the props yielded dramatic increases in the number of children who correctly reported that they had been touched, especially when responses were double-checked using direct yes–no questions, the props also were associated with increased rates of error. In an interview conducted immediately after the visit, for example, no child erroneously reported touching of the genitals, buttocks, or anus in the verbal condition and no child falsely reported touching to the buttocks when simply shown a body outline, but 12% of the children falsely reported touching of their buttocks when interviewers asked specifically about such touching while pointing to the body outline. Similarly, 7.5% of the children who were interviewed with anatomical body outlines falsely reported genital touch. (One pointed spontaneously and two erroneously nodded after direct questioning by the interviewer.)

Thus, although props such as anatomical drawings can cue children to report touching events that they actually experienced, a minority of younger children who have *not* experienced touching may be encouraged by props to report that they have been touched. Furthermore, we do not yet know how risky anatomical props might be when children have been exposed to misinformation prior to formal interviews (Bruck & Ceci, 1996). Clearly, interviewers are less open to criticism when they do not show anatomical drawings until after children have already disclosed touching and when they use open-ended questions such as "Show me where he touched you" rather than direct yes–no questions such as "Did he touch you here?"

ANATOMICALLY DETAILED DOLLS

The history of anatomically detailed (AD) dolls illustrates the different pressures that have confronted practitioners as opposed to researchers. As with many interviewing techniques, AD dolls were widely adopted in the 1980s even though there were no standardized protocols regarding their use and no systematic data regarding their value for determining whether or not children had been abused. As a result, doll use sparked considerable criticism and a flurry of research. Researchers have since documented how widely practitioners use AD dolls, the various functions dolls serve in investigative interviews, and the problems that arise when children's behavior with the dolls is overinterpreted or the dolls are combined with risky interviewing practices. Although many topics remain unexplored, six conclusions frequently surface in reviews of AD dolls:

1. **Despite the lack of standardized procedures, AD dolls are frequently used in investigative interviews.** In one nationwide survey of more than 200 professionals, 92% reported using AD dolls (Conte, Sorenson, Fogarty, & Rosa, 1991), and a survey in the Boston area (Kendall-Tackett & Watson, 1992) documented doll use by 62% of law enforcement professionals and 80% of mental health professionals. Sixty-eight percent of the child protection workers in North Carolina also reported using dolls, although fewer than half of these workers had received even minimal training and few had access to a manual or set of guidelines (Boat & Everson, 1988).

2. **AD dolls are not a psychological test for "diagnosing" abuse.** There are no uniform guidelines for using AD dolls and no evidence that the dolls should be viewed as a psychological or diagnostic test (Everson & Boat, 1994; Koocher et al., 1995; Lamb, 1994). As Koocher et al. concluded, "To elevate AD dolls to the status of a psychological test grants implications of utility and benefit that are undeserved and without basic foundation" (p. 201). Although many professionals believe that AD dolls

have a number of important uses, there is no evidence that the way children play with dolls or demonstrate during interviews reveals whether or not they have been abused. As Boat and Everson (1993) summarized, "explicit sexualized play with anatomical dolls, including enactment of sexual intercourse, cannot be considered a *definitive* marker of sexual abuse in the absence of a clear verbal account of abuse by the child" (p. 64, italics in the original).

Concern about the misinterpretation of children's behavior with dolls began with studies of how abused and nonabused children respond to AD dolls. In almost every study, some nonabused children inspected and touched sexual body parts (Koocher et al., 1995). In one study, for example, 71% of the 2- to 6-year-olds touched the male doll's penis (Glaser & Collins, 1989). Furthermore, even mildly suggestive instructions may increase the likelihood of sexualized behavior. For example, Everson and Boat (1990) videotaped more than 200 children, first with an interviewer who allowed free play before asking the children to identify body parts and show "what the dolls can do together" and finally when the children played alone with the dolls. None of the 2-year-old children displayed intercourse positions, but many older children positioned the dolls suggestively while the interviewer was present (rates for the 3-, 4-, and 5-year-olds were 10%, 9%, and 18%, respectively). Fewer children displayed suggestive intercourse positioning when they were left alone (3%, 5%, and 7%, respectively), but more demonstrated obvious intercourse positioning (percentages for 3-, 4-, and 5-year olds playing alone were 3%, 7%, and 12%, respectively).

Specific or leading questions may lead young, nonabused children to manifest dramatically more sexualized behavior with AD dolls. After a pediatric examination during which half of the children experienced a genital exam and half did not, Bruck, Ceci, Francoeur, and Renick (1995) asked 3-year-old children direct questions with the aid of an AD doll about whether Dr. F. had touched their buttocks and genitals (e.g., "Did Dr. F. touch you here?"); had the children demonstrate with the doll (e.g., "Show me on the doll how Dr. F. touched your [child's word for buttocks]"); and asked them to demonstrate on their own bodies. The children's reports were highly inaccurate (e.g., 50% of the children who had not experienced a genital exam nonetheless reported genital touching when asked specific questions), and the dolls did not help the children provide additional accurate information beyond what they provided verbally or with their own bodies. In addition, the dolls elicited behavior that could have alarmed investigative interviewers, such as inserting fingers into the genital and anal cavities when asked to show how the doctor had touched them. Unfortunately, there is no evidence that practitioners can distinguish the difference between depictions of abuse and curious or playful behavior: In one survey of 295 child protection workers, law enforcement officers, mental health practitioners, and physicians, there was no behavior that all groups unanimously viewed as normal play behavior (Boat & Everson, 1988).

Because children's behavior with AD dolls is highly variable, researchers have not found consistent differences between the behavior of abused and nonabused (i.e., not known to be abused) children (e.g., Cohn, 1991; Kenyon-Juma, Burnette, & Robertson, 1991; see Ceci & Bruck, 1995, for a review). When there were differences in the frequency of sexual depictions, the relatively high rate of occurrence among nonabused children still precluded using doll play as a sole indicator of abuse (e.g., 20% of nonabused children in Jampole & Weber's 1987 study displayed sexual acts; but see Koocher et al., 1995, for possible limitations in the samples). Thus when one child psychiatrist used AD dolls in a structured interview and noted spontaneous behavior and comments, she was able to classify only 53% of the children correctly (Realmuto, Jensen, & Wescoe, 1990), and 14 professionals (3 each of pediatricians, child psychiatrists, social workers, attorneys, and psychologists) who observed the tapes misjudged the actual abuse status one third of the time (Realmuto & Wescoe, 1992). It is interesting that the highest rate of agreement—86%—was between the observers and the child psychiatrist who had conducted the interview, leading Realmuto and Wescoe to speculate that

> either the professional in the interview situation and the observers of the interview situation synthesize the child's comments, affects, and behaviors in a similar but inexplicable manner, or the observers are more influenced by the interviewer's behavior, which in some way revealed her own determination. (p. 723)

Methodological concerns also limit the conclusiveness of research on anatomically detailed dolls. Whether or not they have been abused, children who are being interviewed about abuse often have been exposed to explicit questions about abuse or, in many cases, prior interviews using AD dolls (Ceci & Bruck, 1995). Even when there are differences between abused and nonabused groups in the degree of explicit sexual behavior with dolls, it is not known whether those differences reflect abuse status per se, family circumstances that prompted the abuse allegations in the first place, or exposure to sexual questions and information during the investigations. This concern is illustrated by the results of a study by Boat, Everson, and Holland (1990): After just a single interview with AD dolls, 37% of the mothers of 3- and 4-year-old children reported that their children showed more interest in sexual issues and 50% believed that their children were more sexually focused. As Ceci and Bruck (1995) concluded,

> This last conclusion brings us full circle to our earlier caution about the effects of prior interviews: In those studies that have compared abused children's doll play with the doll play of nonabused children, any differences could be due to the former group's prior exposure to

the dolls (during actual investigations) rather than to the dolls' diagnostic validity. Even nonabused children exhibit heightened sexual interest following a single doll experience. (p. 169)

3. AD dolls currently serve a variety of functions during interviews. As Everson and Boat (1994) noted in their review of 20 AD doll protocols, dolls sometimes are introduced as comforters, icebreakers, memory stimuli, anatomical models, and demonstration aids. We will consider each of these functions in turn.

Two of the 20 protocols reviewed by Everson and Boat (1994) mentioned allowing children to hold the dolls as play objects or sources of comfort, although obviously this function can be served without using AD dolls. The icebreaker function, mentioned in five of the protocols, involves using dolls to raise the issue of sexuality by focusing children's attention on sexual issues and body parts. A related function involves using the dolls as a memory stimulus in the hope that one or more features of the dolls will trigger spontaneous comments about abuse. The introduction of AD dolls as icebreakers or memory stimuli early in the interview could be considered overly suggestive, particularly when the dolls are presented unclothed, because they communicate that the interviewer is expecting conversation about sexual issues. Sixteen of the 20 protocols also mentioned using AD dolls as anatomical models to assess children's labels for body parts. Once again, labeling early in the interview could be viewed as leading or suggestive, whereas labeling for clarification purposes is less open to criticism.

The protocols reviewed by Everson and Boat (1994) most frequently recommended using dolls as a demonstration aid (i.e., to allow children to reenact events with the dolls instead of, or as a supplement to, verbal accounts). This use of the dolls has been criticized for two reasons. First, as discussed below, preschoolers may not yet be cognitively capable of using dolls to represent themselves, and it may therefore be incorrect to assume that their actions are reenactments of experienced events. Second, the availability of dolls may lead interviewers to rely on them too heavily and ignore good interviewing practices. For example, Boat and Everson (1996) analyzed videotaped interviews of 2- to 12-year-old children conducted by CPS staff in a southern state. The most frequent interviewer error was premature introduction of the dolls as a demonstration aid, a problem that occurred in 41% of the interviews with younger children (2–5 years) and 28% of the interviews with older children (6–12 years). Some interviewers failed to ask for any verbal description (e.g., saying, "You don't need to tell me; just show me"), whereas others introduced the dolls before the children had finished their verbal accounts. In addition, the words *play* or *pretend* were found in 28% of the interviews with younger children and 9% of the interviews with older children. Boat and Everson concluded that

EXHIBIT 6.1
Four Major Uses of Anatomically Detailed Dolls and Concerning
Practices Associated With Each Use

Comforter: The dolls function as "play" objects for a child to hold and cuddle for comfort.
- Presenting the dolls unclothed.
- Naming the dolls with no input from child.

Icebreaker: The dolls aid in focusing a child's attention on sexual issues and body parts. The presence of dolls with genitals may convey tacit permission for a child to talk about or demonstrate sexual knowledge or experience and also may convey that the interviewer is comfortable with the subject of sex.
- Using the name of a possible perpetrator when introducing the dolls (e.g., "This doll is your daddy and he has private parts.").
- Modeling sexual behaviors (e.g., "These dolls can kiss and hug like real people. See?").
- Introducing the dolls with phrases that might encourage fantasy (e.g., "Let's pretend." or "Let's play.").
- Probing or manipulating dolls' genitals or breasts.

Anatomical Model: The dolls are used to assess a child's labels for body parts and understanding of body functions, or assess a child's knowledge of the mechanics of sexual intercourse or personal sexual exposure.
- Naming dolls before child's disclosure or naming.
- Using the word *play* in introducing the dolls (e.g., "Do you want to play with these dolls?").
- Naming sexual parts before asking child for a name.
- Introducing fantasy or conjecture (e.g., "Let's pretend you've seen one of these before. What would you call it?").
- Probing or manipulating dolls' genitals or breasts.
- Failing to use child's labels for sexual body parts.
- Being insensitive to child's distress at exposure to doll genitalia (e.g., forcing a reluctant child to undress the doll).
- Modeling sexual behaviors (e.g., "See, this is good touch and this is bad touch.").

Exhibit continues on opposite page

interviewers overrelied on the dolls in 35% of the cases sampled, although egregious errors (e.g., interviewer placing the dolls in a sexual position) were rare.

In sum, each of the functions identified by Everson and Boat (1994) could be innocuous, but all also could be suggestive if the dolls were introduced repeatedly, prematurely, or in combination with inappropriate questions. Exhibit 6.1 summarizes each of the functions and "concerning interviewer practices" discussed by Everson and Boat (from Boat & Everson, 1996).

4. It may not be appropriate to use AD dolls with either preschoolers or children who have the cognitive capacities of typical 2- to 4-year-olds. AD dolls were created to serve as communication aids for children who were likely to have difficulty describing abuse. The cognitive abilities required to use the dolls representationally typically are lacking in children

EXHIBIT 6.1 *(Continued)*

Demonstration Aid. The dolls serve as props to help a child with limited verbal skills show, rather than tell, what happened to him or her, or to enable a child to demonstrate what happened after the child has given a verbal description (to enhance the interviewer's understanding or to function as a separate modality for assessing consistency of a child's disclosure).

- Failing to first elicit a verbal description or using the dolls prematurely (e.g., "You don't need to tell me—just show me"; child is giving adequate verbal description—not confused or stuck).
- Using "play" language that might encourage fantasy (e.g., "We can play like this is you.").
- Making an assumption of nudity.
- Modeling sexual behavior or behaviors with dolls (e.g., "Did he move his finger around or just let it lay there?").
- Requesting a demonstration before a verbal disclosure (e.g., "Can you show me with the dolls how Daddy touched you on your bottom?" when the child has not disclosed this information).
- Failing to follow up on sexual demonstration by using clarifying questions (e.g., child places dolls in front-to-rear contact and interviewer fails to acknowledge or clarify this behavior).
- Inaccurately describing what child demonstrated (e.g., child demonstrates inserting finger in anus and interviewer asks, "Did he rub your bottom?").
- Introducing fantasy or conjecture (e.g., "If someone has hurt a little girl's bottom, show me how he would do it.").
- Overinterpreting child's behaviors with dolls in absence of clarifying questions (e.g., child avoids looking at doll's penis; "That penis reminds you of what your uncle did, doesn't it?").
- Failure to notice child describing doll, not self or alleged perpetrator (e.g., child says, "He had a mustache and a blue shirt"; doll has the same features but interviewer does not clarify).

Note. From B. W. Boat & M. D. Everson, "Concerning Practices of Interviewers When Using Anatomical Dolls in Child Protective Services Investigations," *Child Maltreatment, 1,* 96–104, Copyright 1996 by Sage Publications, Inc. Adapted by permission of Sage Publications, Inc.

under 5 years of age, however, and may also be lacking in older children whose communication difficulties are related to general cognitive delays.

Several studies conducted by Judy DeLoache have shown how commonsense notions about children's abilities, and especially about the value of cues and props, can be wrong. In several early studies, preschoolers watched an experimenter hide a small toy somewhere in a scale model of a room (e.g., behind the sofa). The experimenter then asked the children to retrieve a larger version of the toy from the comparable location in a full-sized room. Although the 2½-year-olds enjoyed playing the game and searching for the toy, they seemed totally unaware that the scale model and the room were related, and few of them retrieved the toy without error. In contrast, the 3-year-olds efficiently retrieved the toy most of the time (DeLoache, 1990).

The problem, according to DeLoache (1990), is that young children have difficulty achieving a "dual representation" of a single object: Because the scale model is a salient object itself, young children cannot recognize that it also is a representation of the room. To test this notion, she conducted several clever studies designed to modify the salience of the scale model (DeLoache, 1990, 1995a; DeLoache, Miller, & Rosengren, 1997). As she predicted, the youngest children were more accurate when they were shown a photograph or line drawing of the scale model rather than the model itself, presumably because this reduced the salience of the model *as an object* and increased its salience *as a representation* of another object. The children also performed well when they were tricked into thinking that the scale model *was* the room—shrunk by a magic shrinking machine. In contrast, the children were *less* accurate when they were allowed to play with the model for 5 to 10 minutes, an experience designed to increase the salience of the model as an object. This later finding is strikingly counterintuitive, because children generally perform better when they are familiar with the materials involved in solving a problem, but it is fully in accord with DeLoache's interpretation of children's difficulty with dual representation.

The results of DeLoache's studies raise an interesting and important question about AD dolls: If young children have difficulty understanding the symbolic function of models, how can they accurately reenact events with AD dolls? Often, it seems, they cannot. In one study (DeLoache & Marzolf, 1995), 2½-year-olds who had stickers placed on their bodies by a research assistant were accurate less than half of the time when asked to place miniature stickers on the same parts of a doll, even though the stickers were still visible on their bodies! Even 3-year-olds made frequent errors, with only 63% of these children placing more than half of their stickers correctly. Furthermore, when asked to indicate where they had been touched, 2½- to 4-year-olds were *more* accurate without the dolls than with the dolls. In a brief summary of her research program, DeLoache (1995b) concluded:

> To my mind, the most important research finding about the use of dolls with very young children is that there is no good evidence that the dolls help. In three recent, carefully designed, and well-controlled studies of nonabused children . . . interviews using dolls elicited no more or better information than interviews done without them. My study . . . suggested that the presence of the doll might even interfere with the memory reports of the youngest children, a possibility that Melton and Limber (1989) have raised. The idea that very young children might actually provide less information in the presence of dolls is consistent with my prior research demonstrating the great fragility of symbolic understanding and use in this age group. (p. 178)

5. AD dolls may not increase the amount of information that children report. In a recent study of front-line forensic interviewers, Lamb, Hershkowitz, Sternberg, Boat, and Everson (1996) found that the average number of relevant details provided by children (ages 2–12 years) was no greater when interviewers used AD dolls, and the average responses of children interviewed with dolls were briefer and less detailed. Interviewers used few open-ended invitations either with or without dolls, but the interviewers had to "work harder" to elicit information when dolls were present. At the very least, these findings suggest that anatomical dolls did not enhance, and may have diminished, the informativeness of the alleged victims.

It also is problematic to elicit disclosures from children using dolls and direct abuse questions, because some young children who have not been touched erroneously respond "yes" when interviewers ask direct questions about abuse (e.g., "Did he touch you here?") while pointing to an anatomical doll. In Steward and Steward's (1996) study of 3- to 6-year-olds, for example, 18% of the children who had not previously disclosed anal touching made a commission error to a direct question immediately after a pediatric visit; the percentage of errors increased to 30% 1 month after the visit and 36% at the final 6-month follow-up.

6. Fewer interviewers might find the dolls necessary if they encouraged verbal reports more effectively. Lamb, Hershkowitz, Sternberg, Boat, and Everson's (1996) findings contradict the impression of many clinicians that dolls are necessary to help children overcome the embarrassment and fear of disclosing abuse. How could there be such a discrepancy between clinical impressions and the results of recent studies? One possibility is that AD dolls became popular during a time when there was little systematic research on how to interview children effectively. As long as interviewers used rapport-building techniques that did little to encourage verbal reports or relied on specific, closed questions, dolls may well have provided significant relief from the frustration of children's short, uninformative answers. If so, the perceived value of dolls might decline sharply as interviewers develop more effective means of eliciting verbal reports. In the interim, however, the availability of dolls may delay the adoption of more effective interviewing strategies. For example, Boat and Everson (1996) reported that interviewers sometimes relied on the dolls so much that they failed to obtain verbal descriptions at all.

What, then, is the consensus about AD dolls? There is none. Recommendations range from enthusiastic endorsement through cautious tolerance to adamant censorship. Because practitioners should be aware of both the published literature and the evolution of positions from major professional organizations, we end this discussion of AD dolls by contrasting earlier guidelines from professional organizations with more recent conclusions from other authors who have reviewed the literature on AD dolls.

Because AD dolls have been widely accepted by practitioners, professional organizations have avoided taking a strong negative stance regarding this class of techniques. In 1991, for example, the American Psychological Association's (APA's) Council of Representatives adopted a

"Statement on the Use of Anatomically Detailed Dolls in Forensic Evaluations," which recognized the absence of norms to guide practitioners and the need for additional research on AD doll use. Two of the recommendations remain timely: Practitioners should videotape or otherwise document their procedures, and they should be prepared to justify their procedures and interpretations using clinical and empirical evidence. The Statement concluded:

> Anatomically detailed dolls are widely used in conducting assessments in cases of alleged child sexual abuse. In general, such dolls may be useful in helping children to communicate when their language skills or emotional concerns preclude direct verbal responses. These dolls may also be useful communication props to help older children who may have difficulty expressing themselves verbally on sexual topics.
>
> These dolls are available from a variety of vendors and are readily sold to anyone who wishes to purchase them. The design, detail, and nature of the dolls vary considerably across manufacturers. Neither the dolls, nor their use, are standardized or accompanied by normative data. There are currently no uniform standards for conducting interviews with the dolls.
>
> We urge continued research in quest of more and better data regarding the stimulus properties of such dolls and normative behavior of abused and nonabused children. Nevertheless, doll-centered assessment of children when used as part of a psychological evaluation and interpreted by experienced and competent examiners, may be the best available practical solution for a pressing and frequent clinical problem (i.e., investigation of the possible presence of sexual abuse of a child).
>
> Therefore, in conformity with the *Ethical Principles of Psychologists*, psychologists who undertake the doll-centered assessment of sexual abuse should be competent to use these techniques. We recommend that psychologists document by videotape (whenever possible), audiotape, or in writing the procedures they use for each administration. Psychologists should be prepared to provide clinical and empirical rationale (i.e., published studies, clinical experience, etc.) for procedures employed and for interpretation of results derived from using anatomically detailed dolls. (American Psychological Association, 1991, p. 722)

Similarly, a consensus statement published by the American Professional Society on the Abuse of Children (APSAC) in 1990 encouraged the clinical tradition of using symbolic props, but with selective caution about AD dolls:

1. A variety of non-verbal tools should be available to assist the child in communication, including drawings, toys, doll-houses, dolls, puppets, etc.
2. Anatomically detailed dolls should be used with care and discretion. Preferred practice is to have them available for identification of

body parts, clarification of previous statements, or demonstration by non- or low-verbal children after there is indication of abuse activity.

3. The anatomically detailed dolls should not be considered a diagnostic test. Unusual behavior with the dolls may suggest further lines of inquiry and should be noted in the evaluation report, but is not generally considered conclusive of a history of sexual abuse. (p. 5)

Problems that arose while the APA statement was being formulated led several psychologists to launch the Anatomical Doll Working Group, whose task was to review the AD doll research comprehensively. Published in 1995 by Koocher et al., this report added several caveats to the APA statement that reflected increasing concerns about doll use, including the admonition that (a) use of AD dolls does not constitute a test with predictive or postdictive validity, (b) decisions should not be made on the basis of spontaneous or guided doll play alone, (c) caution is needed when interpreting the doll play of children ages 4 years and under, and (d) training should emphasize normative differences among children from different racial and socioeconomic backgrounds.

Although the APA and APSAC statements condoned careful use of dolls, others have strongly opposed the use of dolls or any other props that are associated with play as diagnostic tools in forensic evaluation. Ceci and Bruck (1995) ended their analysis of dolls as follows:

> Simply put, we conclude that there is no available scientific evidence that supports the clinical or forensic diagnosis of abuse made primarily on the basis of a very young child's interaction with anatomical dolls. . . . In part, this position is based on the grounds that an assessment tool should only be used if it provides reliable additional information. There is no evidence that the dolls do this; in fact, in some cases, the dolls seem to impede children's reporting, and in some cases, the dolls appear to lead to false judgments about the status of abused and nonabused children. (pp. 184–185)

Gardner (1996) went even further, arguing that "interviews in which suggestive materials are used—specifically anatomically detailed dolls, body charts, and materials depicting explicit sexual organs—should not be admissible in a court of law" (p. 508). Such conclusions reflected the growing number of literature reviews that revealed a lack of information on the reliability and validity of AD doll techniques (e.g., Elliott, O'Donohue, & Nickerson, 1993; Wolfner, Faust, & Dawes, 1993). Consequently, interviewers need to realize that the benefits they expect from using dolls can easily be outweighed by questions regarding the reliability of the children's reports (Mason, 1991; White, 1988).

CUES OR PROPS

Professionals are always searching for nonsuggestive ways to facilitate children's recall. Even infants are more likely to remember events when environmental cues are reinstated (Rovee-Collier & Hayne, 1987), and thus the impact of cues or props on children's events reports has received considerable attention. The term *cues* refers to a range of retrieval aids, including reinstatement of the environmental context (e.g., by bringing children back to the scene of a crime), suggesting items verbally (i.e., verbal cues), and displaying objects (e.g., a stethoscope), whereas the term *props* generally is reserved for object cues. There are two primary concerns about using cues and props for investigative interviews. First, the presence of relevant cues might lead some children to elaborate from general knowledge or fantasy, thereby increasing the amount of inaccurate information they report. Second, the presence of irrelevant cues could be inherently suggestive, leading the investigators who selected the cues in the first place to confirm their a priori beliefs.

Mel Pipe and her collaborators (e.g., Gee & Pipe, 1995; Pipe, Gee, & Wilson, 1993; Pipe & Wilson, 1994; Priestley & Pipe, 1997; Salmon, Bidrose, & Pipe, 1995; Salmon & Pipe, 1997) have been especially interested in the use of cues and props. Four general conclusions emerge from their studies: (a) cues often, but not always, help children report additional information; (b) some of this additional information is erroneous; (c) real objects facilitate accurate recall more effectively than do toys; and (d) the use of cues magnifies age differences in the completeness of recall during the preschool years but decreases age differences during the school years.

Regarding variability in the effectiveness of cues, specific object cues seem to enhance recall more reliably than cues that merely reinstate environmental context. Pipe and Wilson (1994), for example, failed to find that context reinstatement was helpful when they arranged for 6- and 10-year-old children to watch magic tricks and interviewed them about these events approximately 2 weeks and 2 months later. Children in a "no-cues" condition answered questions in an unfamiliar room, whereas children in the "contextual-cues" condition answered questions in the same room, complete with pink velvet curtains, table and coverings, and several items that were not related to specific actions (e.g., the magician's hat and cloak). Despite these distinctive features, recall was the same regardless of where the children were interviewed. Pipe and Wilson speculated that this was because the target actions were not integrated with the context in any meaningful way or perhaps the interviewing environments were too similar to detect a benefit from context reinstatement. Another possibility is that most children remembered the gist of the events anyway, so that context reinstatement was not necessary to remind children of the general themes. It is possible that revisiting a scene might be helpful when children are having difficulty identifying target events, especially when those events took place a long time ago. Context reinstatement also may be more effective when children are asked to recall events in which they participated rather than events they merely observed.

In contrast, Wilkinson (1988) found that context reinstatement did help 4-year-olds recall a walk through a park. The day after watching a series of activities (e.g., finding a ball), children who described what had happened while walking along the path recalled more information than did children who recalled the events in a school room. Was context reinstatement per se responsible for these results? Not necessarily. Any procedure that extends the duration of an interview in a relaxing and non-threatening way might improve recall. In fact, police investigators informally report that "walking" witnesses can encourage disclosures of sensitive or embarrassing information. Still, because the target actions were closely linked to environmental cues in Wilkinson's study, revisiting the park might indeed have been more effective than merely strolling.

Although context reinstatement did not affect children's performance in Pipe and Wilson's (1994) study, object cues related to specific activities that had occurred during the magic show were helpful. Children who were interviewed in the "relevant-cues" condition, with items used in the magic show displayed on the table, or in the "irrelevant-cues" condition, with relevant and irrelevant items, reported more information than did children interviewed without these cues. Like the results of other studies (e.g., Priestley & Pipe, in 1997; Salmon & Pipe, 1997), these data indicate that specific object cues can ameliorate children's tendency to volunteer only a few broad ideas.

The benefits of cues must be weighed against the risk that the presence of cues may lead children to report more inaccurate information. In a study by Gee and Pipe (1995), children who were interviewed in relevant-cues and irrelevant-cues conditions reported comparable amounts of inaccurate information, but slightly more than children in the context-cues or no-cues conditions. Interviews after long delays and repeated interviews involving props sometimes—but not always—predispose children to report more inaccurate information than do interviews without props (compare Gee & Pipe, 1995, and Pipe et al., 1993, with Salmon & Pipe, 1997), especially when interviewers offer certain instructions. Gee and Pipe reported that object cues did not disrupt accuracy rates when the cues were merely present, but the prompt "What can you tell me about these things?" did increase the error rate, perhaps because children thought that the interviewer expected them to discuss both the relevant and irrelevant items. Priestley and Pipe (1997, Experiment 3) found that children who sorted props into relevant and irrelevant groups were less accurate in reporting what they had seen than were children who merely viewed the props during the interview, which indicated that explicit questioning about the relevance of props might not ameliorate the suggestiveness associated with items that are unrelated to the target event.

As noted earlier, real items (e.g., an actual stethoscope) are better object cues than toy items (e.g., a reduced-sized plastic stethoscope). Salmon et al. (1995) reported that real items and toys both elicited more information than did no cues at all, but toys elicited more than twice as many errors from 5-year-olds as did real items in prompted recall, and the same was true when these children were reinterviewed 1 year later (Salmon & Pipe, 1997). Similarity between the props and the items involved in the alleged event might be important as well. Priestley and Pipe (1997) found that scale-model replicas of items led children to recall more actions than did toy props, but scale models also increased the children's error rate. In contrast, presenting toy props in a spatial layout comparable to that in the original event yielded better recall than did presentation without the spatial cues, without compromising accuracy.

Finally, although data are limited, the presence of cues appears to increase age differences in completeness of recall during the preschool years but reduce age differences among school-age children. This occurs because older preschoolers benefit from cues much more than 3-year-olds do (Salmon et al., 1995), and hence the presence of cues exaggerates age differences among younger children. In contrast, props elevate the performance of younger school-aged children closer to that of older children, thereby reducing age differences among this group (Gee & Pipe, 1995; Pipe et al., 1993).

Because props, especially those that are not highly similar to the original objects, can lead children to report information from general knowledge rather than from memories of specific events, Priestley and Pipe (1997) emphasized that this type of prompted recall has some important limitations:

> In conclusion, if props such as models and toys are to be used in clinical and other interviews, consideration needs to be given to their intended function. If the purpose is to facilitate children's reporting of a past event, the more similar the items are to actual items from the event, the more likely they are to facilitate retrieval. In addition, however, it may be necessary to consider the event itself, whether it is relatively distinctive, or involves more familiar routines, and whether providing props is likely to access gist memory rather than specific information relating to a particular episode (cf. Reyna & Titcombe, 1995). Interviewers need to take into account not only the nature of the event, but also the length of delay between the event and the interview, the type of props used, and their manner of presentation. The use of props when interviewing young children should be treated with caution. (p. 85)

As with all techniques that are designed to facilitate memory retrieval, interviewers should use cues in therapeutic and forensic settings with great caution. To date, researchers have studied only children recalling events that *actually occurred*, and thus it is unknown whether or not cues would increase errors in children who have not experienced the target event but who may have been exposed to false information. To avoid being suggestive, interviewers should use cues only to encourage children to expand on information that has been mentioned already. For example, interviewers can label events the child describes to facilitate returning to those topics or to prepare the child for providing testimony in open court (e.g., "Okay, let's call that the kitchen time"; Yuille et al., 1993).

INTERVIEWING CHILDREN WITH DISABILITIES

Children with disabilities are especially vulnerable to abuse (Westcott, 1991), yet they also are the least likely to be heard and believed (Westcott, 1994). The challenges of interviewing children with disabilities are similar to, and sometimes more severe than, the challenges of interviewing preschoolers. Like preschoolers, children with disabilities often have difficulty providing free narrative accounts and may need support in the form of specific questions or interview aids, but they also are especially susceptible to subtle forms of suggestion. For example, mentally handicapped children are particularly likely to acquiesce to yes–no questions (Sigelman, Budd, Spanhel, & Schoenrock, 1981) and to provide erroneous information to specific questions (Dent, 1986; see Milne & Bull, 1996, for a review of research on interviewing children who have mild learning disabilities). Children with physical limitations may have come to expect that adults will structure interactions and may therefore be especially likely to comply with implicit social demands. As Westcott (1994) summarized,

> Children with disabilities are used to being given little choice or control over their everyday lives and may find it particularly difficult both to tell *on* and *to* a non disabled adult. . . . Thus they may view themselves as particularly discredible, and may be especially sensitive to the social pressures existing in the interview. (p. 25)

Clearly, some special concerns apply to interviews of disabled children (e.g., Bull, 1995), and thus preliminary assessments or special interview preparations often may be necessary to ensure that disabled children will be interviewed effectively. Specific procedures and recommendations have not been compiled, but we summarize some of the pertinent issues and concerns in the following paragraphs.

Visual Impairments

Children with visual impairments may understand some concepts later than their peers. Language difficulties are especially evident in children who lost their vision before age 5. Without the benefit of visual memories, these children sometimes understand words incompletely, and this leads them to use words inconsistently across contexts (Higgins, 1973). Interviewers should be especially aware of the need to elicit information in a variety of ways and to avoid taking single answers at face value. Well into the school years, children with visual impairments may have special difficulty with language concepts such as personal and possessive pronouns (e.g., *her* vs. *their*). In addition, these children sometimes show immediate or delayed echolalia (Bradley-Johnson, 1994), so interviewers should avoid questions that can be answered by partial repetition when preliminary conversations reveal a tendency to repeat phrases.

Many children who are blind or visually impaired have additional handicaps, such as hearing loss, that could raise questions about their ability to fully comprehend questions addressed to them during investigative interviews. Consequently, language assessments could be useful for establishing competence or planning special accommodations. According to Bradley-Johnson (1994), the results of verbal tests must be regarded with caution, however, because visually impaired children often are reinforced for rote memory and thus verbal tests can overestimate their ability to understand language in natural contexts. Bradley-Johnson therefore recommends that performance in the classroom or at home be observed as part of the language assessment. Her book *Psychoeducational Assessment of Students Who Are Visually Impaired or Blind* (1994) summarizes assessment issues and norm-referenced tests.

Hearing Impairments

Children with hearing impairment are a diverse group and differ along many dimensions, including the degree of loss, the age at onset of loss, the value of amplification, the primary mode of communication, and the presence of coexisting handicaps (Bradley-Johnson & Evans, 1991). Children with conductive hearing losses benefit from amplification and can be assessed for language skills as would hearing children. Those with sensorineural losses often use amplification as well, but the result is a distorted input that may be poorly understood. Children with hearing impairments also receive communications (e.g., reading speech, sign, gesture) and express themselves (e.g., sign, gesture, voice) in a variety of ways. As a general rule, language specialists should interpret individual children's profiles, determine their primary mode of communication, and make decisions about special accommodations. Ethical standards require interpreters to sign all speech that would be available to a hearing individual, and thus interviewers should not make side comments (e.g., "I really don't think he is paying attention") to an interpreter in the child's presence.[1]

Many authors report that children with hearing impairments tend to respond impulsively and that a relaxed, unpressured atmosphere is especially important with these children. Moreover, interviewers should emphasize that the child is free to say "I don't know" and ask for clarification, perhaps during a short training session to illustrate these options. (See chap. 4 on ground rules for the interview.)

Augmentative and Alternative Communication (AAC)

In addition to signs and gestures, nonspeaking children may communicate using eye movements, picture boards, and a variety of computer-based technologies. AAC includes any system, tool, or approach—technology or nontechnology based—that supplements or replaces traditional communication modes. Two issues are involved when communication requires AAC: competency in the traditional sense (i.e., whether the child has the cognitive skills needed to respond accurately to questions about life events) and the degree to which the child's communication is free from suggestion or adult influence.

Adult influence in AAC can range from obvious to extremely subtle. At one extreme is facilitated communication, a group of methods in which a child responds by typing while an adult supports the child's arm or provides other physical contact. There is compelling evidence that facilitated communication often is influenced mainly by the ideas of the facilitator rather than those of the child (Burgess et al., 1988; Jacobson, Mulick, & Schwartz, 1995), and thus the technique is problematic for investigative procedures. Subtle forms of suggestion also are possible when a child interacts independently with technological devices. For example, many forms of AAC require that a professional make initial programming or training decisions that determine the range of possible messages that the child can communicate.

No guidelines exist regarding the evaluation of children who rely on AAC. Lynn Sweeney (personal communication, January 15, 1997), a consultant in Michigan on legal issues related to AAC, suggests that at least two individuals be involved in making recommendations about individual cases: the professional who has had the most contact with the child or the

---

[1]Contact the Registry of Interpreters for the Deaf for a list of certified interpreters in your area, 8630 Fenton Street, Suite 324, Silver Spring, Maryland 20910, or http://www.rid.org/about.html/. For an online pamphlet on attorneys', courts', and government agencies' responsibilities to deaf and hearing-impaired persons under the Americans with Disabilities Act, with helpful suggestions for working with an interpreter, visit http://www.captions.com/legal.html/.

development of the child's communication system, and an independent specialist. The latter specialist should be a certified speech/language pathologist with augmentative communication expertise.[2]

CRITERION-BASED CONTENT ANALYSIS/STATEMENT VALIDITY ANALYSIS

Over the past decade, there has been considerable interest in statement validity analysis (SVA), a procedure developed by a German forensic psychologist named Udo Undeutsch (1982, 1989). Undeutsch proposed that reports of experienced events differ in quality and content from reports of events that have not been experienced, and he introduced SVA as a comprehensive procedure for evaluating the credibility of victims and witnesses. SVA has three components: an investigative interview of high quality, evaluation of the alleged victim's statement using criterion-based content analysis (CBCA), and an evaluation of the circumstances of the allegation and the child's behavior and demeanor. Most attention has been focused on the CBCA procedure, in which trained coders look for utterances that reflect one of several criteria believed by Undeutsch to indicate that the report is based on memory of an experienced event as opposed to one that was imagined, fabricated, or learned about from someone else (Lamb, Sternberg, Esplin, Hershkowitz, & Orbach, 1997).

Independent coders are highly reliable in coding interview transcripts, agreeing with one another regarding the presence of the CBCA criteria almost all of the time (Horowitz, Lamb, Esplin, Boychuk, & Reiter-Lavery, 1997). The validity of the technique is less clear, however. Initial studies of highly selected samples found that CBCA scores discriminated extremely well between "likely" and "doubtful" allegations (Boychuk, 1991; Raskin & Esplin, 1991). A later study of a more representative sample, however, revealed less optimistic results. Starting with 1,187 interviews of alleged victims of sexual abuse, Lamb, Sternberg, Esplin, Hershkowitz, Orbach, and Hovav (1997) selected 98 cases (involving children ages 4–13 years) in which sufficient evidence independent of the children's narratives enabled them to classify the allegations as plausible or implausible. The interviews were scored for the presence or absence of 14 criteria, such as logical structure and contextual embedding, that are believed to be characteristic of true narratives (Undeutsch, 1982, 1989). Narratives from plausible cases did contain more criteria overall than did narratives from implausible cases, but the differences were too small to justify using CBCA to assess the

---

[2]Lynn Sweeney is available to answer questions about interviewing children who use AAC; contact her at 517-775-8082.

validity of allegations in forensic contexts. Lamb, Sternberg, Esplin, Hershkowitz, Orbach, and Hovav (1997) concluded,

> The surprisingly small differences between the plausible and implausible accounts occurred not because the plausible cases obtained particularly low scores but because some of the implausible cases obtained unexpectedly high scores. [The findings] underscore that CBCA scores should not yet—and perhaps should never—be used in forensic contexts to evaluate individual statements. (pp. 262–263)

Results from a study by Huffman and Ceci (1997) bolster this conclusion. Huffman and Ceci sent transcripts of videotapes from Ceci, Loftus, et al.'s (1994) suggestibility study to psychologists who were experienced with CBCA. These videotapes contained narratives from preschoolers about events that had actually happened to them and false narratives that interviewers elicited from the children by mentioning fictitious events, asking the children to picture the events in their heads, and asking them to describe the events if they could remember. Huffman and Ceci reported that CBCA ratings by psychologists identified true stories 74% of the time and false stories 46% of the time (chance is 50%), whereas the undergraduate students were accurate 67% and 71% of the time, respectively.[3]

Because the CBCA technique focuses on statements derived from free-recall memory, the quality of the interviews is critical: Interviews in which most information was obtained in response to focused questions do not contain many utterances that should be scored. As a result, further investigation of the CBCA technique using interviews of uniformly high quality is still needed. Until such studies are conducted, however, the CBCA technique cannot be viewed as a valid technique or aid.

FINAL COMMENTS

As frustrating as the current state of affairs is for practitioners, the available evidence does not allow us to recommend a variety of ancillary techniques that interviewers can use for special circumstances. As with most forensic and investigative protocols, we take a conservative approach and recommend that interviewers focus on strategies that encourage verbal reports, using interview aids sparingly and cautiously, if at all.

Controversy about the value of ancillary techniques stems partially from the different goals of various parties involved in child protection. A

---

[3]CBCA scores have been shown to discriminate between children who are telling the truth and children who are asked to fabricate a story (e.g., Honts, 1994), but lying is not equivalent to the types of mechanisms described in chapter 2, in which many children actually come to believe misinformation suggested by adults. Furthermore, analyses of children's lies have not traced the evolution of fictitious narratives across a large number of interview questions or separate interviews, as has been the case in studies of testimony implanted by other means.

good example is the use of time lines, one of many topics that was not reviewed in this chapter because it has not yet attracted the attention of researchers. In some jurisdictions, prosecuting attorneys recommend seeking information about the timing of events by drawing a line that is anchored by significant events in the child's life (e.g., the start of school, Christmas, and the end of school). The interviewer then asks the child to mark on the line approximately when the alleged abuse occurred. The resulting response may be useful to prosecutors regardless of whether or not it is accurate, because it provides the information needed to pursue the case (although it may complicate prosecution if the child indicates a general time during which contact with the alleged perpetrator was impossible). There is no evidence, however, that children, particularly preschool children, actually can provide accurate information using a time line. Professionals who are reluctant to stop using the technique nonetheless can maximize its potential value by judicious planning. For example, it may be possible during preinterview preparations to identify a small number of significant events that occurred recently in the child's life. During the investigative interview, the interviewer could first ask the child to place these events on the time line to demonstrate the ability to represent temporal relationships in this way, before asking about the target event. Although it still is risky to generalize from significant events identified by parents to alleged events reported by the child, the interviewer at least would have made an attempt to determine whether the child understood the concept of the time line and, in the process, have helped avoid criticism of his or her reliance on an unresearched technique.

Because interviewers are under increasing pressure to justify their practices, it is crucial that they be aware of discrepancies between widely held beliefs and the scientific literature. "Good touch–bad touch" discussions, for example, were not recommended in any of the protocols reviewed by Walker and Hunt (1998), although they remain popular. Furthermore, although most interviewers in one agency evaluated by Wood, McClure, and Birch (1996) questioned children about good and bad touches, Wood et al. did not find a single child who ever disclosed abuse during this portion of the interview. They concluded, "There seemed to be no reason for the discussion of good touch/bad touch, except that it had become agency practice at some time in the past" (p. 224).

Interviewers need to have two skills when selecting techniques. First, because interviews are part of a diagnostic process, practitioners need a basic understanding of decision-making processes and concepts, and these issues therefore are discussed in the next chapter. Second, practitioners need efficient ways to keep abreast of new data—a daunting task when so much information is published outside their immediate area of expertise. To this end, in chapter 8 we discuss interviewer training and how to locate resource materials.

IV

PROFESSIONAL
DEVELOPMENT ISSUES

INTRODUCTION

PROFESSIONAL DEVELOPMENT ISSUES

Criteria for qualifying courtroom "experts" generally are lax, specifying only that professionals have had relevant training or experience (Myers, 1993). Critics have argued, however, that professionals who offer opinions or explain research findings in child abuse cases should be required to demonstrate knowledge of key concepts related to the "diagnosis" of abuse.[1] For example, attorneys have suggested to us that experts must be familiar with specific high-profile research articles and be able to answer basic questions about diagnostic decision making. Such attempts to define competence in terms of relevant knowledge, rather than in terms of time spent in training or practice, place increased responsibility on professionals. Cur-

---

[1]There is no consensus on the best way to label the process of judging whether abuse occurred. As Myers pointed out (1993), the term *diagnosis* is somewhat misleading because abuse is an event, not a disease or disorder. To some extent, the (mis)use of medical terminology may have contributed in the past to the rapid acceptance of syndrome evidence and overgeneralizations about the consistency and continuity of abuse sequelae. We agree with Myers et al. (1989), however, that

> It would be a mistake to make too much of disagreement over applications of diagnostic terminology to child abuse. The concept of diagnosis is sufficiently broad to embrace clinical determinations regarding sexual abuse. By way of analogy, battered child syndrome is an accepted medical diagnosis despite the fact that an abuse assault is an event rather than a disorder. (pp. 72–73)

Analogies between the reliability of medical diagnoses and the reliability of clinical judgments about sexual abuse are very useful for developing understanding about the factors that contribute to accurate versus inaccurate decisions, and therefore the term *diagnosis* will probably continue until another analytical paradigm emerges that is more useful for discussing the veracity of event reports. (See Kihlstrom, in press, for a discussion of the term *syndrome*.)

rently, there is enormous pressure on all professionals who interact with children to be well-informed on a wide variety of topics related to diagnostic decision making and child protection, whether they testify in court or not.

How are helping professionals affected by these changing expectations? Teachers, therapists, and other mandated reporters are legally required to decide when evidence crosses the unspecified threshold that defines a reasonable suspicion (Kalichman, 1993), but experience conducting interviews does not prepare them to make those decisions. Similarly, professionals who conduct investigative interviews must make numerous decisions when they prepare for and conduct these interviews: They must prepare by collecting relevant information and developing alternative hypotheses about the origins of the allegations they are investigating, decide when to probe for clarifying information during the interview, and integrate information in the form of written summaries or opinions.

Our final two chapters address topics that are crucial to the continued professional development of adults who interview children. In chapter 7, "Improving Judgment and Decision Making," we describe concepts that have appeared with increased frequency in the child abuse literature and in workshops for judges and attorneys. Although we do not discuss the correlates and sequelae of abuse, the concepts discussed in chapter 7 can help professionals avoid common mistakes that crop up when they try to interpret and combine evidence. In chapter 8, "Keeping Pace With Changing Standards," we then discuss interviewer training and techniques for locating current resource materials on child development, advances in interviewing techniques, and child protection. This final chapter is designed especially for overworked practitioners who do not have convenient access to a research library. It offers tips for navigating unfamiliar libraries with maximum efficiency and discusses how to "shop at home" for resource materials, using abstracting services and the Internet.

7

IMPROVING JUDGMENT AND
DECISION MAKING

Never try to discourage thinking for you are sure to succeed.[1]
Bertrand Russell
"A Liberal Decalogue"
The Autobiography of Bertrand Russell: 1944–1969

Consider what the following two cases have in common[2]:

Case 1

In January of 1996, 7-year-old Jenny Lee was returned to her mother and stepfather after a year in foster care. Although Jenny Lee continued to act out sexually, and periodically talked about adults "peeping" her, her CPS case was formally closed.

---

[1]This is the third of 10 principles set forth by Bertrand Russell, philosopher and mathematician, in "A Liberal Decalogue" (first appearance in "The Best Answer to Fanaticism —Liberalism" in the *New York Times* Magazine, December 16, 1951, and reprinted in *The Autobiography of Bertrand Russell*, Vol. 3, 1969, pp. 71–72). The list describes two convictions: the (a) primacy of evidence over authority and (b) awareness of the fallibility of humans. The list in its entirety is as follows:

1. Do not feel absolutely certain of anything. 2. Do not think it worthwhile to proceed by concealing evidence, for the evidence is sure to come to light. 3. Never try to discourage thinking for you are sure to succeed. 4. When you meet with opposition, even if it should be from your husband or your children, endeavor to overcome it by argument and not by authority, for a victory dependent upon authority is unreal and illusory. 5. Have no respect for the authority of others, for there are always contrary authorities to be found. 6. Do not use power to suppress opinions you think pernicious, for if you do the opinions will suppress you. 7. Do not fear to be eccentric in opinion, for every opinion now accepted was once eccentric. 8. Find more pleasure in intelligent dissent than in passive agreement, for, if you value intelligence as you should, the

Jenny Lee's case began 2 years earlier when her teacher reported bizarre behavior and repeated masturbation at school. A school staff member who interviewed Jenny Lee reported that she talked about her stepfather coming into her room and making her "pee-pee hurt." Jenny Lee was initially interviewed twice by CPS workers in the presence of a police officer. These interviews demonstrated that she was highly suggestible and prone to change answers when questions were repeated or rephrased. During these interviews, which included reenactments with anatomical dolls, she identified four adults and several children as possible perpetrators, including her mother, stepfather, an uncle, a babysitter, and several children in the neighborhood. Questioning was leading, however, and the interviewers were somewhat bewildered by Jenny Lee's behavior while she was being questioned.

A conversation with her mother revealed that Jenny Lee was developmentally delayed as an infant, and her school file included assessments indicating that her cognitive functioning was about $1\frac{1}{2}$ years behind schedule. Over the next 2 years, Jenny Lee received therapy and was referred to numerous additional professionals. Among other documents, Jenny Lee's file contained evaluations from school psychologists, a psychiatrist, three psychologists employed at three different clinics, and a physician who had conducted two medical evaluations while seeking evidence of sexual abuse. One medical exam, conducted 6 months after Jenny Lee's case was opened, revealed evidence "consistent with abuse." Following criticisms stemming from the large number of suggestive interviews, conversations, and assessments that Jenny Lee had experienced, however, efforts to terminate parental rights were unsuccessful.

Case 2

In March of 1995, Jim Westbury was denied joint custody of his 5-year-old son Kyle after a protracted and acrimonious custody battle. Jim's story began 2 years earlier when his former wife, Jill, refused to let him spend time with Kyle. Jim filed several petitions for orders to show cause, alleging violation of court-ordered visitation, and subsequently requested an independent court-ordered evaluation of Kyle and his parents. The custody evaluator indicated that Jill was generally uncooperative during the evaluation and judged that Jim was the more stable parent. Two months later, Jill accused Jim of sexually abusing Kyle.

---

former implies a deeper agreement than the latter. 9. Be scrupulously truthful, even if the truth is inconvenient, for it is more inconvenient when you try to conceal it. 10. Do not feel envious of the happiness of those who live in a fool's paradise, for only a fool will think that it is happiness.

[2] These are fictional cases we constructed from recurring features of cases directed to us by professionals who were seeking advice or sharing experiences. Any similarity with actual cases is coincidental.

Jill claimed that when she was tucking Kyle into bed one night, he pointed to his genital area and said, "Kiss me here like Daddy does." The next day, she contacted an investigator from CPS, who helped her find Kyle therapy focused on sexual abuse. Kyle made no accusations of abuse to his therapist, and the CPS investigator could not substantiate abuse. Kyle's mother terminated therapy shortly after the court recommended visitation and counseling for both parents but resumed therapy with another agency more than a year later. Shortly afterward, she began denying Jim visitation, again charging sexual abuse.

An evaluator at a sexual abuse survivors clinic judged that Kyle was sexually abused because some of his behaviors were similar to most of the children she had seen who had been sexually abused. Jim and his attorney filed a petition for an evidentiary hearing into the latest of Jill's accusations. At the hearing it was determined that Jill had taken Kyle to three child sexual abuse clinics before settling on the survivors clinic. It also was determined that at each new evaluation, Jill helped Kyle explain what his father had done. Jill testified that this aided the evaluator in getting a clearer understanding of what Kyle had been through with his father.

During the evidentiary hearing, Jim's attorney made numerous "hearsay" objections, explaining that the United States Supreme Court had ruled that social workers and evaluators may not testify about what children say in sex abuse evaluations unless specific criteria were met. The judge overruled the hearsay objections, reasoning that because there was no jury present, he could properly weigh the evidence. When the evaluator from the clinic finished testifying, the court ruled that, to be on the safe side, Jim's visits must be supervised until further notice.

What do Jenny Lee's return home and Jim's custody decision have in common with one another, and with thousands of other cases involving accusations of sexual abuse? In both examples, investigations relied heavily on the clinical judgments of professionals rather than on the alleged victims' testimonies. In many probate and circuit court matters, interviews with children take a distant back seat to the conclusions of professionals —conclusions drawn from impressions of children's behavior, their performance on various tests, and the personality profiles of their alleged offenders. For the numerous cases in which interviews and assessments are not taped, decisions are based on scanty notes and memories of what children had or had not said, with little information available about the specific questions to which they were responding or the overall context in which they made their reports. These memories, together with theories about the correlates and sequelae of abuse, blend to produce the clinical impressions that determine the outcome of many abuse investigations. In Jenny Lee's case, frequent interviews and assessments cast doubt on her initial report of sexual abuse by her stepfather. In Kyle's case, professional opinions were allowed to override his initial denials of abuse. In both cases, clinical impressions and judgments spoke louder than the children themselves. How accurate are these impressions and judgments?

Unfortunately, clinical judgments can be surprisingly inaccurate. Studies have shown that mental health professionals often assign diagnoses when behavior does not meet published criteria (Morey & Ochoa, 1989); fail to discriminate the test results of actual clients from subjects who are asked to fake disability (Faust, Hart, & Guilmette, 1988; Faust, Hart, Guilmette, & Arkes, 1988); and overlook pathology in clients who are not typical examples, or good "prototypes," of a disorder (Garb, 1996). In fact, some researchers have shown that trained professionals often do no better than simple formulas at diagnosing or predicting clients' behavior, and no better than lay persons in treating behavior disorders (see Dawes, 1994b, and Grove & Meehl, 1996, for reviews, and Garb, 1989, 1992, for exceptions).

There is no reason to believe that the judgments made in child abuse evaluations deviate from these general trends. In one study, for example, clinical psychologists, social workers, and other relevant specialists heard a detailed, 2-hour-long case presentation during which they were allowed to ask for clarifying information (Horner, Guyer, & Kalter, 1993a). The participants then estimated how likely it was that the 3-year-old child had been sexually molested. Within all professional groups, the range of probability estimates was extreme (e.g., 3–75% for clinical psychologists and 1–70% for social workers). Moreover, written comments indicated that some professionals went beyond the information specified in the case presentation and were quite certain about extreme interpretations at either end of the range. Some respondents thus speculated about the exact nature of the sexual abuse, when they presumed it had occurred, whereas others speculated about the mother's motivations to falsify charges, when they presumed it had not.

There is no evidence that helping professionals as a group have characteristics or limitations that make them especially likely to disagree or to develop unfounded theories. Rather, studies of decision making in contexts ranging from parole board decisions to graduate school admissions provide converging evidence for three principles of human judgment and decision making. First, researchers have shown in numerous studies that clinical decision making generally is inferior to statistical decision making (i.e., decisions made by combining information mechanically; Dawes, Faust, & Meehl, 1989; Grove & Meehl, 1996). Second, some professionals become increasingly confident over time in the validity of their methods and judgments, even when neither experience nor confidence correlate well with accuracy (Dawes, 1994b). Finally, although we do not understand all of the reasons why humans often reach conclusions that are illogical or inaccurate, psychologists have identified a set of systematic cognitive biases that permeate human reasoning both in clinical and nonclinical settings (for a brief review, see Garb, 1994a). By understanding these biases, helping professionals can avoid some common impediments to effective problem solving.

Our discussion of judgment and decision making begins with a brief example to illustrate the limitations of expert opinion. We then describe some common cognitive biases that help create such faulty opinions. Our final section describes some simple strategies to help professionals gather and combine information appropriately when making decisions that affect children's lives.

AN EXAMPLE OF FAULTY EXPERT OPINION

Although philosophers and social critics never tire of arguing about the extent to which scientific findings are "contaminated" by values, there is no disagreement that conceptual frameworks are influenced by economic, political, and social circumstances. In short, ideas—like clothing—are subject to fads that reflect society's material circumstances, its social structures and activities, and the challenges posed by rapid social change.

The history of medical practice contains some of the most interesting examples of the interplay between complex social variables and the concepts we embrace to make sense of our lives. Brumberg (1982) described an engaging example in her article, "Chlorotic Girls, 1870–1920: A Historical Perspective on Female Adolescence." As Brumberg explained, chlorosis was a name given at the turn of the century to a blood disease, believed to afflict adolescent girls, that supposedly resolved itself with increasing age or marriage. Chlorosis was widely diagnosed, familiar to both physicians and the lay public, and identified in females from all social classes and in both urban and rural environments. Diagnosis and treatment of the disease continued in the absence of a clear set of symptoms, and with no consensus about its cause, until its virtual disappearance by the 1930s. Quoting a contributor to the *Annals of Medical History*, Brumberg asked, "What disease can compare with chlorosis in having occupied such a prominent place in medical practice only to disappear spontaneously while we are still speculating as to its etiology?" (p. 1475).

In Brumberg's analysis, understanding the mysterious disappearance of chlorosis requires more than just a discussion of medical advances such as improved nutrition. There were other important changes in the early 1900s, including an increased understanding of menstruation, the changing activity patterns of young women, and the home economics movement— a movement that defined mothers as the guardians of their children's health and vigor. As Brumberg noted, "By 1920, a girl with chlorosis was not only a social 'drag' but a liability with respect to her own mother's perception of herself as a competent domestic manager and nurturer" (p. 1476).

The history of ideas about women and children is rich with similar concepts that are amusing by today's standards, such as the consequences of a wandering uterus (Veith, 1965), or horrific, such as the medieval treatment of presumed witches (Barstow, 1994). But all of these ideas were widely accepted, consistent with existing knowledge, and powerful in their ability to color interpretations of behavior. All of us undoubtedly wonder whether we would have questioned these assumptions had we lived in the same time period. A powerful message from these examples is that neither widespread acceptance nor the published opinions of experts guarantees the enduring value of an idea.

It is no leap of the imagination to ask which of today's concepts might be the "chloroses" of tomorrow. For example, developmental psychologists have asked whether the concept of "adolescence" is just a social construction, borne out of a changing relationship between families and the means of production (Santrock, 1993). Other scholars have asked whether by using the label "IQ" we have created a concept that has no tangible counterpart in nature (Gould, 1996). Do similar concepts influence investigations involving child witnesses?

Although it is impossible to know which of today's popular concepts will disappear with time, it is clear that some ideas about abuse victims are not yet based on solid evidence. An example is the belief that sexual abuse history can be diagnosed accurately by nonsexual features of children's drawings (e.g., the absence of a chimney on a house). Similarly, high base-rate behaviors, such as sleep disorders or wetting among preschoolers, frequently have been cited as "evidence" of sexual abuse. (In one study on adults' memories of childhood sexual abuse, therapists generated 85 indicators of sexual abuse, including virtually all of the most frequent presenting problems of female clients; Poole et al., 1995.) Theories abound about the narrative and emotional content of "true" claims of sexual abuse, although the ability of these features to discriminate between true and false allegations is largely unknown (Poole & Lindsay, 1998). Just as chlorosis rose in popularity and then disappeared, helping professionals have, in the past decade, witnessed the emergence of a variety of "syndromes" designed to describe characteristics of abused children, seen these syndromes inappropriately used to diagnose abuse, and watched as the courts dismissed such evidence on the grounds that such syndromes "lack a firm scientific foundation" (*State v. Michaels*, 1993, described in Mason, 1995). As summarized in the San Diego County Grand Jury report (1994), "Child Sexual Abuse Syndrome (CSAS), or Child Sexual Abuse Accommodation Syndrome (CSAAS), or Post-Traumatic Stress Disorder (PTSD) or other theories utilizing behavior as a basis for proof of child sexual abuse is discredited and unacceptable" (p. 31).

There are two problems with beliefs that lack scientific support. First, as in Jenny Lee's case, these beliefs can be attacked in court and impede successful prosecution of actual abuse. Second, as in Kyle's case, beliefs can lead to strong suspicions of abuse where none occurred, an error that has devastating consequences for both children and adults.

How do such beliefs become established? One common mechanism is reliance on, or overgeneralization from, case studies. Case studies are extremely useful for taking a preliminary look at a phenomenon, but they have limitations when taken out of context. For example, when Faller (1988) analyzed 103 interviews with children whose offenders had confessed to some level of abuse, she identified three characteristics that frequently appear in the narratives of child victims: information about the context of the abuse (including idiosyncratic details); descriptions or demonstrations of the sexual victimization; and emotional features (embarrassment, disgust, anger, anxiety, and fear). Her study provided valuable normative data on children's narratives, including age differences in the frequency of these criteria in victims' testimonies, but because the study involved no comparison group, or interviews of children making allegations that later were deemed false, we cannot determine whether the features identified by Faller discriminate between true and false reports. In fact, contextual details and emotional reactions have been found in the narratives of children with implanted memories (e.g., Bruck et al., 1997; Ceci, Huffman, et al., 1994) and have been surprisingly absent from the narratives of some children who probably were abused (e.g., Wood, Orsak, et al., 1996). Additional information thus is necessary before we will know whether accurate judgments can be based on these criteria or features.

Applied settings also provide little opportunity for corrective feedback (Dawes, 1994b; Garb, 1989). In child abuse evaluations, for example, the truth rarely is established with certainty (Horowitz et al., 1995), and it is unusual for disconfirming evidence to appear *after* a judgment has been made so that individuals can identify case features that do not discriminate between true and false allegations. Lack of systematic feedback is characteristic of many professional settings. Whether the task is abuse evaluation, medical diagnosis, or graduate school admissions, professionals often develop unfounded theories in response to the natural limitations of their working environments, relying on cognitive strategies that, for most daily problems, serve humans rather well.

SYSTEMATIC ERRORS IN HUMAN JUDGMENT AND DECISION MAKING

To a large extent, therapists and child protection workers diagnose conditions just as physicians diagnose illness. In deciding whether to rule that physical or sexual abuse was probable, individuals or agencies must combine information about various "symptoms," including the possible motivations of the adult who reported abuse, the child's statements, physical evidence, and whether other information indicates that the abuse could have occurred as reported. Decision accuracy involves knowing (a) the strength of the relationship between symptoms and conditions and (b) the base rate of the condition in the population being evaluated. Relationships between symptoms and conditions can be expressed as conditional probabilities (e.g., the probability of sexual abuse given an explicit demonstration of intercourse, compared with the probability of no sexual abuse given an explicit demonstration of sexual intercourse), whereas the base rate can be expressed as a percentage (e.g., the percentage of children in the population who actually have been abused sexually). Misconstruing conditional probabilities and ignoring base rates are among the most common errors in studies of medical decision making (Schwartz, 1994), and they are a major concern in the child-abuse literature as well (e.g., Lindsay & Read, 1994). Other phenomena reviewed below are the confirmation bias, illusory correlations, the availability heuristic, anchoring and adjustment problems, ignoring regression to the mean, the conjunction fallacy, problem framing, and the imperfect relationship between confidence, accuracy, and experience.

Reversing Conditional Probabilities

To assign clients to diagnostic groups (e.g., depressed, physically abusive, etc.), professionals must attend to the indicators or characteristics of those diagnostic entities. Single indicators are rarely diagnostic. Rather, professionals often combine information from multiple indicators that have varying degrees of relationship to the target condition. These relationships often are represented as conditional probabilities in the form, "If A is present, there is an x% chance of B," as in, "If a woman has a positive mammogram, then there is a 7% chance that she has breast cancer" (example from Schwartz, 1994).[3]

Unfortunately, there is a widespread tendency to reverse conditional probabilities. For example, some readers might have thought that the 7% figure in the previous example was wrong, because they were thinking about the rate of positive mammograms among women with cancer rather than the rate of cancer among women with positive mammograms. (In addition, many people are not aware that in order to minimize the risk of overlooking disease, mammograms are designed to yield false positive rather than false negative warnings.)

---

[3] The concept of *incremental validity* refers to the degree to which an indicator improves decision accuracy once other information is already known (see Garb, 1984, for a general discussion). We do not discuss incremental validity because there is so little useful information about combining multiple indicators in applied settings with children. In child abuse studies, it is still not clear which single indicators discriminate abuse status (see Poole & Lindsay, 1998).

Reversing conditional probabilities is an especially common problem in fields that rely on follow-back studies—studies that begin with a group of adults and then examine the prevalence of predisposing factors or predictors in their childhoods. (Follow-back studies are often called "retrospective" when adults report about their childhood experiences. Other follow-back techniques involve searching school files, clinic files, or other permanent records such as diaries or family movies.) The major disadvantage of follow-back studies has been known to developmentalists for at least 20 years. For example, Robins (1966) pointed out that 75% of all alcoholics were truant as juveniles, compared with 26% of psychiatrically normal individuals, which suggests that truancy in high school might be a useful predictor of alcoholism. Follow-up studies, however, show that only 11% of truants become alcoholics, compared with 8% of nontruants. Because conditional probabilities cannot be reversed, Kohlberg, LaCrosse, and Ricks (1972) concluded that "follow-back studies are almost useless for prognostic-prediction purposes" (p. 1220).

As with many errors in reasoning, one can readily understand the problem of conditional probabilities by evaluating a familiar phenomenon, such as the consequences of sexual intercourse. Most of us know that the probability of a women being pregnant given that she has had sexual intercourse is not the same as the probability that she has had intercourse given that she is pregnant. "The latter probability is, of course, 1.00 (ignoring artificial insemination) while the former probability is, fortunately for many, much lower" (Schwartz, 1994, p. 55).

To evaluate conditional probabilities more accurately, it is helpful to picture them graphically, as in Figure 7.1. The smaller circle shows that among mothers who neglect their children in a hypothetical town called Cityville, most are hostile to questioning by child protection workers (95%). This could lead us to assume that a hostile reaction is pathognomonic (i.e., indicative) of neglect. If an investigator interviews a hostile mother, however, what is the probability that the mother neglects her children? In Figure 7.1, a hostile reaction is not particularly diagnostic of neglect, because 71% of all mothers (the larger circle) react with hostility to this line of questioning. In fact, the probability of being a neglectful mother given a hostile reaction is only 5% in this hypothetical example, compared with 4% for all mothers in Cityville.

Erroneous claims based on reversing conditional probabilities occasionally pop up in the child abuse literature. As mentioned by Dawes (1986), for example, the finding that 50% of child abusers have themselves been abused as children does not justify the claim by a self-help group that "about half the people who were physically abused as children end up mistreating their own children" (p. 430). Of course, retrospective findings do not help us predict the probability that a parent is an abuser given that they were themselves abused. Reconsider an example that appeared in

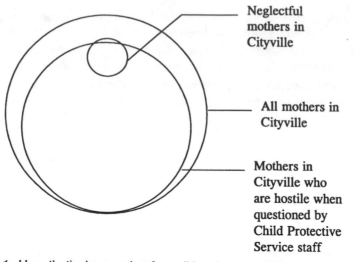

Neglectful
mothers in
Cityville

All mothers in
Cityville

Mothers in
Cityville who
are hostile when
questioned by
Child Protective
Service staff

Figure 7.1. Hypothetical example of conditional probabilities. Most neglectful mothers in Cityville are hostile to questioning by Child Protective Service staff. However, reacting with hostility to questioning is not a good indicator that the mother is neglectful, because 71% of nonneglectful mothers also react with hostility to questioning. In this example, the probability (*P*) of reacting with hostility (*H*) given a neglectful (*N*) mother is 95% [$P(H|N) = .95$], but the probability of being neglectful given a hostile reaction is only 5% [$P(N|H) = .05$].

chapter 1, in which an evaluator mentioned that the alleged offender had experienced an incident of same-sex fondling as an adolescent. Because same-sex contact is not unusual during childhood and adolescence, this information had little diagnostic value (cf. Kinsey et al., 1948; Laumann et al., 1994). The professional who emphasized the association between experiencing abuse and abusive behavior probably confused the proportion of child abusers who were themselves abused as children with the proportion of abused children who grow up to become child abusers.

Difficulties processing conditional probabilities can have serious consequences, as in a famous child abuse scandal in Britain (Schwartz, 1994). In this case, a physical sign found in some sexually abused children (a change in rectal muscle tone) was detected by doctors and used to justify removing nonabused children from their homes, illustrating confusion about the probability of the sign given abuse and the probability of abuse given the sign.

The Representativeness Heuristic

The representativeness heuristic also leads to the misuse of conditional probabilities. As described by Tversky and Kahneman (1974), the representativeness heuristic is the tendency to assess the probability that

A is associated with B on the basis of the perceived similarity between A and B. In a survey of doctoral-level therapists, for example, the only indicator of childhood sexual abuse that was mentioned by more than 14% of the respondents in all samples was adult sexual dysfunction (Poole et al., 1995). Clinical studies *have* found higher rates of sexual problems among abuse victims than among participants in control groups (Briere & Elliott, 1992), but sexual dysfunction is associated with many other background variables (Sutker & Adams, 1993). Nevertheless, the surface similarity between these events may lead clinicians to exaggerate the strength of the relationship.

An interesting historical example of confusing surface similarity and predictive accuracy was discussed by Kohlberg et al. (1972). When Wilkinson compared teachers' and clinicians' judgments of maladaptation during the 1920s, he found that the teachers viewed aggressive behavior as "sicker" than shyness, whereas the reverse was true for the clinicians. The clinicians' focus on shyness probably resulted from the association between that behavior pattern and withdrawal in adult schizophrenia. Kohlberg et al. noted that as time passed and teachers became more aware of clinicians' theoretical biases, their judgments became more similar to those of trained psychologists. This change of heart was misguided, however, because subsequent longitudinal research has clearly demonstrated a relationship between childhood aggression and later maladjustment, whereas associations between childhood shyness and later pathology are weak or nonexistent (Kohlberg et al., 1972; Quinton, Rutter, & Gulliver, 1990).

Even when professionals accurately assess conditional probabilities, a concern with representativeness can make it difficult to determine which evidence is diagnostically relevant. For example, people often focus on the probability of an indicator given the target condition but fail to compare that to the probability of the indicator when the target condition is *not* present. Indicators are useful only when they discriminate between two hypotheses. When they do not discriminate, but people nonetheless use the indicator to "prove" the presence of the condition, we have a phenomenon called *pseudodiagnosticity*. Consider the following example of pseudodiagnostic thinking from Dawes (1998):

> After the William Kennedy Smith rape trial, a number of "experts" on a talk show expressed the opinion that they wish they could have testified in order to inform the judge and jury of "what a rape victim was like." These experts who work in such places as women's shelters in fact had a great deal of experience with rape victims. What none had, however, was experience with women who claimed they were raped when they were not. But the whole point of the trial was to make a judgment about whether the person claiming was actually raped or not. Thus, all the experience in the world with actual rape victims can simply yield some estimate of the probability of particular types of

evidence given that person was a rape victim. But using that probability alone yields a "pseudodiagnostic" inference, because no comparison is made. (p. 532)

Representative thinking has been used to explain many types of erroneous reasoning, including pseudodiagnostic judgments and errors arising from disregarding base rates. (See Dawes, in press, and Schwartz, 1994, for more elaborated discussions of the representativeness heuristic.)

Ignoring Base Rates

Diagnostic accuracy obviously depends on conditional probabilities, or the strength of the association between indicators and conditions. It is less obvious that diagnostic accuracy also varies according to the base rate—the percentage of individuals in the target population who have the condition.

Consider a hypothetical example. Assume that physicians discover a new procedure for determining that a facial bruise resulted from a human hand rather than from a fall. This test produces a positive reading in 95% of the children who were bruised as a result of slapping. (In other words, the test sensitivity is 95%.) Further assume that the test also produces a false positive reading in 5% of accidental fall victims. To compute the predictive value of this test, we also must know what proportion of the children tested have been abused. For the first computation, assume that 10% of all children admitted to a particular hospital with facial wounds have been abused. Figure 7.2 summarizes the test results for a sample of 1,000 children; note that this test would produce 140 positive readings. But given a positive reading, the probability that the child had been slapped is only 95/140, or 68%.

Realistically, however, the test would not be conducted unless there were other reasons to assume that a child had been abused, such as an

	Abused	Non-abused
	100	900
Positive Test Result	95	45
Negative Test Result	5	855

Figure 7.2. Accuracy of a diagnostic test for abuse with a 95% detection rate and a 5% false positive rate. If the base rate of abuse is 10%, the probability of abuse given a positive test result is 95/140, or 68%.

implausible explanation for the bruise. Assume, therefore, that of all children admitted to this particular hospital with an *inadequately explained* facial bruise, 40% are in fact abused. The resulting calculations (Figure 7.3) show that the probability of being abused given a positive result jumps from 68% when the base rate is 10% to 93% when the base rate is adjusted to 40%. In other words, the predictive value of a positive result increases sharply as the base rate of the condition increases, despite unchanged test sensitivity.

The notion that base rates influence the accuracy of predictions that are made on the basis of the presence or absence of certain indicators is relevant for judgments about the validity of abuse allegations under varying circumstances. Ignoring for purposes of this discussion the problems of distinguishing between true and false allegations of abuse (see chap. 1), first assume that only 5% of sexual abuse claims are false. When 95% of the allegations are true, false positives will be infrequent even when predictors are not highly related to abuse. An indicator that appears in 80% of abuse cases and 20% of nonabuse cases, for example, would correctly substantiate abuse in 76 out of 77 cases in which the indicator was present. But if only 70% of the allegations were true, as suggested by some experts (Ceci & Bruck, 1995), 1 out of 10 substantiations of abuse would be erroneous. Simply stated, professionals need to adjust their confidence in the value of diagnostic tests or indicators according to the underlying base rates of abuse.

Information about base rates also can improve decisions in other ways. In one study, for example, medical personnel accurately estimated the proportion of male patients who would become violent in the next 6 months, but they underestimated that proportion for women, presumably because we associate violent behavior with men (Lidz, Mulvey, & Gardner, 1993). Knowing base rates for various groups can ameliorate biases due to factors such as gender and race (Garb, 1994a). Similarly, a large discrepancy from population base rates should alert investigators to consider possible reasons

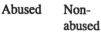

	Abused	Non-abused
	400	600
Positive Test Result	380	30
Negative Test Result	20	570

Figure 7.3. Accuracy of a diagnostic test for abuse with a 95% detection rate and a 5% false positive rate. If the base rate of abuse is 40%, the probability of abuse given a positive reading is 380/410, or 93%.

for the anomaly. For example, sexual abuse involving penile penetration by a biological father is a relatively uncommon form of sexual abuse (see Lindsay & Read, 1994, for a discussion). A sudden rash of such claims by younger children in a particular community should lead investigators to consider alternative explanations, such as exposure of the alleged victims to a particular adult (who might be coaching the children to hide his own abusive behavior) or to some other source of information.

Thinking About Indicators of Abuse: Combining Conditional Probabilities and Base Rates in the Odds Form of Bayes's Theorem

A convenient tool for thinking about the value of evidence in diagnostic decisions is the odds form of Bayes's theorem. Bayes's theorem is a consequence of simple principles of probability that are universally accepted. To understand the theorem, consider that *before* one gathers any evidence, one's best estimate of the probability of a condition is the base rate of that condition in the population under consideration. For investigative interviewers, this probability is the proportion of cases that are valid among all allegations made, which can be represented as prior odds (e.g., 7 valid cases for every 3 invalid cases, or 7:3). Professionals then seek information to indicate whether a particular child is more or less likely than average to be sexually abused. Indicators are useful only if they appear with more or less frequency among abused than among nonabused children, and they can be presented as conditional probabilities (the probability of the indicator given sexual abuse vs. the probability of the indicator given no abuse). Alternatively, they can be presented in a form that directly compares the frequency of the indicator in the two groups in the form of a likelihood ratio (the indicator is 10 times more frequent in abused than in nonabused children, or has a likelihood ratio of 10:1).

The odds form of Bayes's theorem states that the posterior odds of a condition are equal to the prior odds multiplied by the likelihood ratio. In other words, the final (posterior) odds are a function of the prior odds, based on preexisting knowledge, and the evidentiary value of the new information (the likelihood ratio).

Consider a simple example from Wood's (1996) introduction to Bayes's theorem in sexual abuse evaluations. Prior odds reflect the base rate of a condition in a relevant population. For example, assume that 70% of sexual abuse allegations made to CPS are reliable and 30% are not. If an allegation has been made, the prior odds of abuse (before any information is gathered) are therefore .70:.30, or 7:3. Now add a piece of information: imitation of sexual intercourse. Wood proposed (from data presented by Friedrich et al., 1992) that this behavior is 14 times more likely in abused than in nonabused children, and thus it has a likelihood ratio of 14:1. Without any additional information, the posterior odds that a child who imitated sexual intercourse had been abused are 7:3 × 14:1 (98.3, for a probability estimate of 97%).

Wood (1996) used a simple example involving two hypothetical school districts to demonstrate how intuitions about posterior odds often are inaccurate. In one school district, the "Dismal School District," the base rate of sexual abuse is 20%, whereas in the "Protective School District" the base rate is 5%. Assume that, in both schools, imitation of sexual intercourse is 14 times more common among abused than among nonabused children. Now suppose that two children, one from the Dismal School District and one from the Protective School District, were observed by their teachers imitating sexual intercourse. Wood asks, "What is the probability that these children have been sexually abused?" Applying Bayes's theorem, the probability is 78% for the child from the Dismal School District (1:4 × 14:1 = 14:4 = 78%) but only 42% for the child from the Protective School District (1:19 × 14:1 = 14:19 = 42%). Counter to many people's intuition, the child from the Dismal School District is more likely to have been abused. The formula merely reiterates a point made in our earlier section on base rates: As the base rate of a condition goes down, the significance of a positive indicator also goes down when the indicator has a fixed degree of association with the index condition.

Wood's (1996) tutorial reminds us that conclusions about the presence of a condition are drawn from two types of evidence: the base rate of abuse in the group to which the child belongs and the degree to which the evidence discriminates between abused and nonabused children. Wood outlined four criteria that must be met before an indicator should be used in sexual abuse evaluations (LR = likelihood ratio):

1. The indicator must be valid, with an LR greater than 1 (i.e., the indicator behavior must be significantly more frequent among abused than nonabused children).[4]
2. The strength of the indicator (the LR) must be known, at least approximately. If numerical estimates of the LR are unavailable, then common language equivalents (e.g., weak, very strong) may be used, although with some loss of precision.
3. The prior odds of abuse must be known, at least approximately. If precise figures are unavailable (National Resource Center on Child Sexual Abuse, 1993), then reasonable estimates or a range of estimates may be used.
4. The prior odds must be taken into account when conclusions are drawn from the evidence. (p. 32)

Many authors have underscored the limitations of using lists of in

---

[4]The indicator behavior also can be valid if it occurs significantly less frequently among abused than nonabused children.

dicators (e.g., Berliner & Conte, 1993). Wood summarized three reasons why this is the case: many indicators identified on the basis of clinical impressions have not been scientifically validated (i.e., it is not known whether the indicator is more often present among abused than among nonabused children); information regarding the strength of the indicator is lacking; and published lists rarely acknowledge that the indicators are not useful without consideration of prior odds.

Are professionals generally capable of taking these types of information into account when they make decisions about sexual abuse? The answer is yes and no. In an interesting study conducted by Wood and Wright (1995), 97 college students and 161 professionals who were attending training seminars on child interviewing sponsored by their states' CPS estimated the probability of abuse in a single case involving a child who displayed sexual behavior. Wood and Wright tested how judgments varied as a function of the information provided to the participants. Results showed that the professionals were able to adjust their estimates on the basis of the indicators mentioned, even when they were not presented with the actual likelihood ratios for those indicators, and they were more accurate on this task than were students. These professionals therefore distinguished between stronger and weaker evidence on the basis of prior knowledge that went beyond what would be expected from an untrained individual. The accuracy of both the professionals and the students improved when they were told how frequently the target behaviors occurred in clinical and nonclinical populations, although the professionals continued to outperform the students. Neither the students nor the professionals were influenced significantly by base rate information, however, suggesting that special training is necessary to learn how to incorporate base rates into decisions. Two additional findings were especially intriguing. First, although professionals outperformed students, level of experience did not correlate with professionals' judgments: Professionals with less experience did just as well overall as professionals with many years of experience. Second, the professionals consistently tended to make more conservative judgments about sexual abuse than did the students. As Wood and Wright pointed out, this finding runs counter to "the picture of 'reckless' child protection workers that is sometimes presented to the public" (p. 1269).

Understanding the importance of evidence strength and base rates is critical to understanding the limitations of many so-called "indicators" of sexual abuse. By itself, however, the odds form of Bayes's theorem does not resolve all the complexities involved in sexual abuse assessment. One still must have accurate information about likelihood ratios and base rates, and there is considerable room for debate even about the little information that currently is available. For example, consider a study by Friedrich et al. (1992) in which the rates of specific sexual behaviors were obtained for two groups: A group of children believed to have been sexually abused and a nonclinical control group. Some behaviors were much more frequent in one of the groups; for example, inserting objects into vagina or anus was 12 times more likely in abused than in nonabused children. The abused children had been involved in investigations, however, and many came from treatment settings. Evidence about the frequency with which anatomically detailed dolls and specific questioning strategies are used in such investigations makes it reasonable to assume that many of the abused children were exposed to these experiences—experiences that could increase sexual interest or disinhibit sexual behavior (e.g., Boat et al., 1990). Thus the groups studied by Friedrich et al. might be those that are *most* likely to differ in terms of rates of sexual behavior. Even so, Friedrich et al. concluded that the specificity of their sexual behavior inventory—or its ability to discriminate between abused and nonabused children—was "less than satisfactory," and too low to "be relied on in isolation as the primary indicator of sexual abuse" (p. 311). In real investigations, of course, professionals need to differentiate between children involved in allegations who were in fact abused as opposed to those who were not, rather than between children identified as sexually abused and children who have never been suspected of being abused. Sexual behavior inventories may do an even poorer job of discriminating between these two groups. (See Poole & Lindsay, 1998, for a discussion of approaches to assessing the credibility of reports of child sexual abuse.)

Mandated reporters must be especially cautious about claims that observed sexual behavior, or any other single indicator, is highly indicative of abuse. For example, the base rate of abuse for children who are not involved in sexual abuse allegations is the rate of abuse for the target age group in the population as a whole. Consider a preschool in which there is only 1 sexually abused preschooler for every 49 nonabused children. If a child is seen imitating sexual intercourse, and we accept the likelihood ratio of 14:1 for this indicator, it is still much more likely that the child is nonabused (78%) than abused (22%; i.e., 1:49 × 14:1 = 14:49).

Confirmation Bias

When a symptom is indicative of a particular disease, physicians seek information about other symptoms to confirm that the disease is present and to rule out other diseases. Thus medical diagnosis involves confirming one disease while disconfirming others. Similarly, helping professionals must decide which indicators or issues to explore. The process of collecting relevant information is more difficult than most people realize, however, because humans have a marked tendency to seek information that would confirm their hypotheses while ignoring disconfirming information.

The most famous example of this so-called confirmation bias is a game called the *four-card task*, described by Wason and Johnson-Laird (1972).

One version of this task is illustrated in Figure 7.4. Imagine a set of four cards, each with a letter on one side and a number on the other. (Adults often think this is a trick of some sort, but it is not. Assume that you know in advance that every card has a letter on one side and a number on the other.) The cards are placed on a table as shown in Figure 7.4. Now read the hypothesis printed below the cards: "If there is a *D* on one side of any card, there is a *3* on the other." The question is this: Which cards would you need to turn over to determine whether that statement is true for this set of four cards?

Any sizable group of adults typically generates a variety of answers, often including "only the *D*," "only the *3*," "the *D* and *3*," "the *D*, *3*, and *7*," and "all of the cards." In fact, all of these answers are false. The correct solution is to turn over the *D* and the *7*. Why? Most adults realize that we need to turn over the *D* to confirm that there is a *3* on the other side. We do not need to turn over the *3*, because it is irrelevant what is on the other side. (Suppose there is an *F*. This would not affect the truth of the hypothesis "If *D*, then *3*.") It is fairly obvious that we do not need to turn over the *H*, because this also is irrelevant. However, we *do* need to turn over the *7* to verify that there is not a *D* on the other side. *D-7* would disconfirm the hypothesis, proving it false. The fact that adults tend to overlook the *7* shows how we tend to choose information that will confirm our hypothesis but ignore information that might disconfirm it. This task is difficult because it requires us to imagine all possible combinations of letters and numbers and to conduct systematic "experiments" to test our hypothesis. Although adults have less difficulty with deductive or scientific reasoning when the tasks are phrased in terms of socially relevant problems (e.g., when the task deals with detecting cheaters, Cosmides, 1989), it generally requires specific training before these skills are mastered in professional settings.

Adults often seek confirming information preferentially even when the task describes meaningful events. Consider a medical example. Gruppen, Wolf, and Billi (1991) presented physicians with a clinical problem involving a patient who suffered from fever and a rash. The physicians were told that clinical information reduced the number of possible diag-

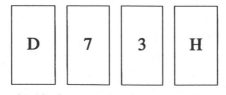

Figure 7.4. The 4-card task. Assume that every card has a number on one side and a letter on the other side. Which cards would you have to turn over to determine the truth or falseness of the following rule: "If there is a *D* on one side of any card, there is a *3* on the other"?

noses to only two diseases: Disease 1 and Disease 2. They also were told that 66% of patients with Disease 1 have fever whereas 34% do not. Because the patient was in crisis, there was time to collect only one additional piece of information. The physicians had three choices: They could find out (a) the incidence of fever among patients with Disease 2, (b) the probability of rash in Disease 1, or (c) the probability of rash in Disease 2. Which piece of information would best help the physicians make an accurate diagnosis?

Most commonly, the physicians asked about the probability of rash in Disease 1, although this information is not useful because the probability of rash in Disease 2 could be as high or higher. Given the constraints of the situation, the best solution is to determine the probability of fever in Disease 2, which would permit a comparison: If fever is more likely in Disease 2 than Disease 1, then Disease 2 is more likely. As Schwartz (1994) concluded in an expanded discussion of this example, the physicians seemed to form a tentative hypothesis that the patient had Disease 1, then sought to confirm their hypothesis by finding a high incidence of rash in Disease 1. Because the physicians sought information that would confirm their expectations, their choices exemplified the confirmation bias, or a "positive testing strategy." Positive testing is common in medical diagnosis (Schwartz & Griffin, 1986) although, as Schwartz pointed out, positive testing is "logically useless" (p. 57).

It is easy to see how investigative procedures would be improved by teaching interviewers about the value of disconfirming evidence. For example, imagine that a 2½-year-old girl says that her teenage brother's "pee-pee" makes "white sauce." This spontaneous comment appears to be compelling evidence of sexual abuse, but "white" is not a color term that is learned early by most children, and "sauce" also is an unusual word. Claims that the child did not know these words, or that the family does not use the word "pee pee," could raise doubts about whether the child was describing an experience or was merely mimicking a conversation with another individual. A savvy interviewer might test the child's knowledge of these terms on the spot (by pointing to items in the room and asking her to identify their colors and by labeling various body parts). If the child were to pass this test, the interviewer would be able to counter later attempts to discredit the allegation. In short, interviewers can build a stronger case by asking themselves, "What information would cast doubt on the credibility of this allegation?"

Illusory Correlations

The confirmation bias shows that people ask questions that increase their chances of finding co-occurrences between events (for example, D-3 in the card task) but that limit their chances of finding counterexamples.

In games such as the four-card task, a single occurrence of 7-D proves the rule false. Most judgments are not so precise, however. Rather, physicians and human services professionals generally deal with probabilistic information: Children with strep throat *usually* complain of throat pain; parents with no social supports in the community are *more likely* than socially integrated parents to abuse their children. Thus clinicians rely heavily on the evaluation of correlations between events. Indicators that are highly correlated with conditions are, of course, more useful than indicators that are only weakly correlated.

Do errors in judging the co-occurrence of events disappear when people do not have to search for information (i.e., when people are given all of the information they need)? Unfortunately, the answer is no. Humans use only crude strategies to judge whether events are related, and thus a variety of errors impede the evaluation of correlations. For example, people sometimes perceive correlations between events that are not related, inflate the degree of relationship between events, and fail to detect correlations that do exist (Jennings, Amabile, & Ross, 1982). In short, we have a tendency to develop all sorts of erroneous theories about the associations between events.

Why are humans so limited in detecting correlations? Consider how much information is required to assess the co-occurrence of events accurately. Imagine that a physician has noticed a subtle genital feature in girls referred for sexual abuse evaluations. The question is whether the presence of this feature helps in the substantiation of abuse. Figure 7.5 presents hypothetical data from 260 girls who were hospitalized for a variety of reasons. The children either had experienced sexual penetration within the past 3 months or were not known to have been abused sexually. In all cases, parents granted permission for a brief genital exam, and in each case the

	Sexually Abused	Not Abused
Genital Feature Present	140	60
Genital Feature Absent	42	18

Figure 7.5. Illustration of illusory correlations. The probability of abuse given the presence of the target genital feature is 140/200, or 70%. The probability of abuse given the absence of this feature is 42/60, also 70%. Despite the larger size of the cell indicating "feature present/abuse present," the presence of the genital feature does not help determine abuse status.

presence or absence of the feature was noted. Is the feature related to sexual abuse or, to use another phrase, do the feature and sexual abuse covary?

In such situations, many people report that the two events are related, either because the present–present cell contains the most observations or because the sum of the present–present and absent–absent cells is larger than the sum of the remaining cells (Plous, 1993). These strategies will not always produce an accurate solution, however. In fact, information from all four cells is needed to solve this problem. Notice in Figure 7.5 that the probability of being sexually abused when the feature is present is 140/200, or 70%. The probability of being sexually abused when the feature is absent is 42/60, also 70%. Because the feature is equally distributed among abused and nonabused girls, it is worthless for diagnosing abuse. A tendency to overweight the significance of the present–present cell is evident in a variety of contexts, including medical diagnosis.

The term *illusory correlation* refers to this tendency to perceive relationships where none exist. Illusory correlations occur because we tend to notice when events are paired but fail to notice situations when they are not. Illusory correlations can result when particular pairings of events are especially memorable (Garb, 1994a; Plous, 1993). For example, when the words *bacon*, *lion*, *blossoms*, and *boat* were randomly paired with the words *eggs*, *tiger*, and *notebook*, subjects later reported that when *bacon* appeared, *eggs* was paired with it 47% of the time (Chapman, 1967). The fact that semantically related words were believed to have co-occurred more often illustrates how meaning and expectations can influence judgments by making some pairings more memorable than others.

The notion that memorability of some pairs in random sequences can create illusory correlations is well illustrated by a study conducted by Chapman and Chapman (1967). They gave students Draw-A-Person test protocols that were randomly paired with symptom statements (presumably from the patients who had produced the drawings; e.g., "He is suspicious of other people." or "He is worried about how manly he is."). After inspecting a set of these drawings, the students were asked to describe any apparent relationships they noticed between symptoms and features of the drawings. It is interesting that the relationships they reported from these random pairings were virtually identical to those reported by clinicians examining patient protocols (e.g., that atypical eyes occur more often in the drawings by men who are suspicious of other people). Illusory correlations thus can arise when specific pairings come more readily to mind, perhaps because of preconceived expectations or because specific pairs appear related. These phenomena can create consensus among practitioners regarding relationships that do not exist (see also Chapman & Chapman, 1969). As Garb (1994a) concluded, "Clinicians who attend more to their experiences than empirical research are less likely to make valid judgments" (pp. 76–77).

Just as expectations can lead us to perceive relationships where none exist, semantically neutral events or events that are counter to our expectations may lead us to ignore correlations that do exist (Plous, 1993). Indeed, one wonders how humans manage to stay alive when they predict events so poorly! There are numerous differences between day-to-day living and clinical environments that help explain these findings, however. For example, correlations that influence survival often are perfect (e.g., the correlation between putting your hand in a flame and getting burned), the relevant events are temporally and spatially close (e.g., clouds and rain), or the knowledge is passed down verbally and need not be discovered by each individual (e.g., intercourse and pregnancy; Nisbett & Ross, 1980; Plous, 1993). Furthermore, thinking in the real world does not have to be optimal, it only has to be " 'one up' on competing organisms" (Dawes, 1988, p. viii).

The Availability Heuristic

Humans rarely have the time or resources to scan all available information before forming a judgment. Instead, many everyday decisions are accurately made by conducting a brief search for highly salient or typical examples that relate to the current problem. However, this shortcut can lead to systematic errors in complex environments.

The availability heuristic is the tendency to base judgments on highly salient, memorable, or available events. For example, the frequency of low-probability events is dramatically overestimated when these events are highly memorable (Tversky & Kahneman, 1974). Availability may explain why clinicians who specialize in particular disorders are often criticized for diagnosing those disorders more frequently than is warranted. Similarly, our perceptions of people from "deviant" groups can be biased by availability, because the examples we encounter or remember are not randomly determined. In a discussion of "out groups," such as the homeless and intravenous (IV) drug users, Dawes (1994a) explained how availability increases our perceptions of differences between ourselves and these groups. For example, estimates of the rate of mental illness among homeless persons might be unreasonably high because the bizarre behavior of some homeless people attracts our attention.

The problem of availability also affects the interpretation of research findings. Studies of groups such as child abusers, IV drug users, or delinquents generally are limited to samples that are involved in the legal system or are undergoing treatment, and the characteristics of these groups may be quite unrepresentative of their respective populations. An amusing example involves research on social deficits in delinquent boys. Delinquent boys perform poorly on a variety of perspective-taking tasks, a finding that led some psychologists to hypothesize that an inability to take the perspective of their victims (and therefore to accurately read societal expectations and the intentions of others) is a causal factor in delinquent be-havior. As a result, Chandler (1973) tried to remedy these deficits by training delinquent boys to appreciate other people's perceptions. Because trained boys were less likely to reoffend than untrained boys, social skills training seemed to be a useful remedy for antisocial behavior. Chandler warned, however, that this conclusion was premature because of the avail-ability problem: Perhaps delinquents appear to have poor perspective-taking abilities because we study only those who were limited enough to *get caught*, and training reduces recidivism simply by helping the boys avoid detection. Chandler reasoned that instead of solving the problem of delin-quency, perhaps he might actually have been running a "school for scoun-drels" (p. 331). Similarly, our beliefs about the correlates of child abuse may be distorted by the fact that we tend to study only victims and per-petrators who get involved in the legal and social service systems.

Anchoring and Adjustment

Decisions about children rarely are made by sitting down and review-ing a folder complete with all relevant information. Rather, professionals typically discover information bit by bit. Information that emerges early in an investigation may favor one interpretation of what is in the child's best interests, whereas subsequent information may favor a very different inter-pretation. Research on anchoring and adjustment deals with how initial information biases later decisions, or how skilled humans are at updating their judgments in light of new information.

Many researchers have confirmed that the information people receive first is weighted more heavily than subsequent information (Plous, 1993). In one study of couples who participated in genetic counseling, for ex-ample, risk expectations before counseling were better predictors of post-counseling risk perceptions than the objective knowledge of risk provided during counseling (Shiloh, 1994). Similarly, researchers have shown that the order in which helping professionals receive information influences their decisions, leading Ellis, Robbins, Schult, Ladany, and Banker (1990) to conclude that "salient information presented later will be half as influ-ential as the salient information presented earlier" (p. 347). Clearly, pro-fessionals need to set aside their initial intuitions periodically and reeval-uate the available evidence as a whole.

Ignoring Regression Toward the Mean

People often generate complicated causal theories to explain chance fluctuations in behavior. To avoid such overinterpretations, it is helpful to understand the concept of *regression*, which is easily illustrated by a class-room exercise.

A college professor tells her introductory psychology class that she has found a way to increase students' telepathic sensitivity. She explains that she will think of a number between 1 and 5 and that class members should write down the first number that pops into mind. She repeats this exercise 10 times, reads off the numbers she transmitted, and asks the students to tally their scores. She then indicates that students who scored zero are particularly insensitive to mental phenomena, but that psychological research can help them improve. Specifically, she tells these low-scoring students to switch their pencils to their nondominant hands and to close their eyes. This, the professor claims, will force the nondominant sides of their brains—usually the right (or spiritual) side in humans—to function. She then repeats the exercise and notes that these students are significantly more accurate than they were on the first trial.

Of course, this exercise works every time. Did the professor demonstrate that the nondominant hemisphere is involved in telepathic experience? Not at all. Guessing numbers is an essentially random process (although some numbers are guessed more frequently by adults during such games). Therefore, individuals who were highly inaccurate during the first round of guessing (0) will tend to perform closer to chance (2) on the second round, thereby improving their scores. Similarly, individuals who do particularly well on the first round will do worse on average during the second round. In other words, scores will tend to regress toward the mean, or expected, value.

Because human behavior and test scores also show a degree of random fluctuation, we need to avoid inventing complex reasons to explain simple regression phenomena. In a famous example (Kahneman & Tversky, 1973), experienced flight instructors mentioned that praising students for an exceptionally smooth landing was often followed by a poorer landing on the next try, whereas criticism and correction were associated with improvement. This observation led the instructors to conclude that criticism was an effective teaching strategy. Of course, the instructors overlooked regression effects, or the fact that an exceptionally good landing on one flight is likely to be followed by a somewhat poorer landing the next time around.

Because some children are interviewed numerous times, there often are opportunities for interviewers to ignore regression. If a child is exceptionally verbal during one interview and less so on the next, an interviewer might conclude that the child was being threatened rather than that the change in demeanor was due to random fluctuation or simple boredom with the task. Similarly, a reticent child who suddenly begins to speak might appear to be coached. In fact, there is not enough information in either of these examples to conclude that the change in demeanor was due to anything other than random fluctuation.

Estimating Event Frequencies

Studies of adults' perceptions of risk and risk management provide interesting insights into child protection efforts. Ultimately, child protection is a process of estimating risk from the presence or absence of various indicators or events. Given the number of cognitive biases summarized thus far, it should not be surprising that humans also suffer from a variety of biases when estimating the frequency of events.

An interesting bias that could influence clinical judgment is the conjunction fallacy—the tendency to judge that highly detailed or specific events are more probable or frequent than less detailed events. For example, in a study by Tversky and Kahneman (1982), adults read a description of a woman, Linda, and judged which of several hypotheses about Linda were more likely (e.g., "Linda is a bank teller" vs. "Linda is a bank teller and is active in the feminist movement"). Nearly 90% of the adults believed that Linda is more likely to be a feminist bank teller than a bank teller, although logic tells us that the co-occurrence of two events (feminist and bank teller) cannot be more likely than the probability of either event alone. The conjunction fallacy often leads us to view detailed hypotheses as more likely. As Tversky and Kahneman remarked (1982), "the hypothesis 'the defendant left the scene of the crime' may appear less plausible than the hypothesis 'the defendant left the scene of the crime for fear of being accused of murder,' though the latter account is less probable than the former" (p. 98).

An amusing example of this error involves estimating the rate of alien abductions. Estimates of abduction range as high as 2% of the population, a conclusion Hopkins and Jacobs (1992, cited in Dawes & Mulford, 1993) reached on the basis of affirmative responses to the question, "How often has this happened to you: Waking up paralyzed with a sense of a strange person or presence or something else in the room?" As Dawes and Mulford pointed out, this statement involves the conjunction of two events: a fleeting sense of paralysis and the presence of a stranger. As part of a larger study, Dawes and Mulford asked the same question to 144 adults; 40% answered that this had happened to them at least once. A second sample of 144 adults was asked only how often they remembered waking up paralyzed; only 14% answered that this single event had occurred. Thus, the added detail, "With a sense of a strange person or presence" actually broadened the scope of the question. "Hopkins and Jacobs are, of course, correct in maintaining that the additional phrase *should* 'narrow the scope'" reported Dawes and Mulford, "it's just that the phrase doesn't" (p. 51). It is interesting that children as well as adults are prone to conjunction fallacy errors (Davidson, MacKay, & Jergovic, 1994).

How might the conjunction fallacy affect clinical or interviewing situations? First, children and adults might be more likely to report that an event occurred when the description provided by the interviewer is more detailed. For example, the question, "Did your father ever show you his penis in the house when your mother wasn't home?" might be more likely to elicit a "yes" than the broader question, "Did your father ever show you his penis?" Because of the memory conjunction effect, interviewers who pose highly specific questions based on a priori hypotheses could receive more erroneous "yes" responses.

Problem Framing

Our decisions also are influenced by how information is worded. In a classic article, Tversky and Kahneman (1981) gave adults problems such as the following:

> Problem 1: Imagine that the U.S. is preparing for the outbreak of an unusual Asian disease, which is expected to kill 600 people. Two alternative programs to combat the disease have been proposed. Assume that the exact scientific estimate of the consequences of the programs are as follows:
>
> If Program A is adopted, 200 people will be saved.
> If Program B is adopted, there is $\frac{1}{3}$ probability that 600 people will be saved, and $\frac{2}{3}$ probability that no people will be saved.
>
> Which of the two programs would you favor? (p. 453)

In this problem, the majority (72%) of adults chose Program A. However, consider the following, logically identical alternatives:

> If Program C is adopted, 400 people will die.
> If Program D is adopted, there is $\frac{1}{3}$ probability that nobody will die, and $\frac{2}{3}$ probability that 600 people will die.

When problems were framed in this way, the majority's (78%) choice was for Program D.

The influence of problem framing is very evident in the literature on children's eyewitness testimony. Some investigators emphasize children's accuracy by reporting that, for example, 80% of the children in a particular study were accurate. Other investigators express dismay that 20% of the children in their studies were inaccurate. Experiments on problem framing help us understand why these two classes of articles are cited more often by different groups of investigators and to support different political agendas when, in fact, they say exactly the same thing. To avoid biases due to framing effects, professionals need to adopt a habit of reversing the way in which findings are expressed to consider the flip side of the issue (unless, of course, the findings are expressed as conditional probabilities).

Confidence, Accuracy, and Experience

Intuition leads us to expect that there will be a clear relationship between confidence and decision accuracy: We hope we are more accurate about decisions when we are confident than when we are uncertain. In reality, the relationship between confidence and accuracy is complicated. In some domains (i.e., types of tasks) there seems to be little relationship between expressed confidence and accuracy, whereas in other domains confidence and accuracy are correlated, albeit imperfectly. For example, most studies of eyewitness identification have shown only small correlations, if any, between certainty and accuracy, although a relationship emerges under some circumstances (e.g., long delays; Read et al., 1998). Many discussions of biases in human judgment have emphasized situations in which people are overconfident (e.g., Plous, 1993), but there is no evidence that overconfidence is a ubiquitous cognitive bias that humans apply uniformly across tasks (Dawes & Mulford, 1996). Rather, there are some situations in which people have difficulty judging the likelihood that their decisions are accurate.

Two phenomena related to confidence, accuracy, and experience are worth mentioning in any discussion of "expert" opinion. First, confidence can be a poor indicator of accuracy, especially when judgments are difficult. In an early and telling example, Goldberg (1959) asked 4 clinical psychologists, 10 clinical trainees, and 8 secretaries to judge the presence of brain damage in each of 30 protocols from the Bender-Gestalt test. All groups correctly judged 65–70% of the protocols, and accuracy was not correlated with rated confidence.

Second, both additional information and experience can increase confidence without producing a corresponding increase in accuracy. For example, Plous (1993) reviewed a study by Oskamp in which clinical psychologists, psychology graduate students, and undergraduates read a case study about a 29-year-old man and answered questions that required them to form clinical judgments about the man's personality. Actually, the case study was divided into four parts, with participants answering the question set after each piece of information was presented. After the first part of the case presentation, participants answered 26% of the questions correctly and estimated that they had answered 33% correctly. There was thus good initial agreement between confidence and accuracy. As more information was presented, however, participants became increasingly confident in their judgments without becoming dramatically more accurate. With increased information, the discrepancy between confidence and accuracy grew larger.

As Plous (1993) pointed out, professionals who receive regular and systematic feedback about their performance—such as bridge players, professional oddsmakers, and National Weather Service forecasters—generally show little or no overconfidence. In contrast, professionals whose jobs do not provide opportunities for systematic feedback may gain more confidence in their skills over time, despite the fact that lack of feedback prevents them from actually improving their performance. Dawes (1994b) called this the "illusion of learning" (p. 121). In an excellent discussion of how experience can increase confidence without a concomitant increase in accuracy, Dawes explained why clinical psychologists and professionals who work with abuse victims are unlikely to improve with practice. Simply stated, people learn to categorize (e.g., cancer–no cancer, abuse–no abuse) by receiving immediate feedback when they are wrong. This is possible in medicine, because laboratory tests ultimately land on a physician's desk, but it is an unlikely state of affairs in human services. As Dawes concluded:

> *The feedback most professional clinicians receive about their judgments and decisions is neither immediate nor systematic nor free of probabilistic distortion.* The immediacy problems are obvious: Lacking definitive procedures such as a medical biopsy, the correctness of the diagnosis and predictions that mental health professionals make often cannot be determined for years. Some are intrinsically impossible to evaluate, such as a judgment about who would be a better custodial parent. Knowing whether a good judgment was made would require not just feedback about what happened when one parent was granted custody but knowing what *would* have happened *if* custody had been granted to the other parent. But such hypothetical counterfactuals are unavailable. (p. 120, italics in the original)

This explanation helps explain Wood and Wright's (1995) finding that years of experience or number of sexual abuse cases did not predict performance in judging the likelihood of abuse (see also Horner, Guyer, & Kalter, 1993b). The bottom line is this: Unless the information professionals use to make their decisions is valid (i.e., actually improves decision accuracy), and unless professionals receive error-correcting feedback on their decisions, neither years of experience nor expressed confidence have any forensic relevance whatsoever.

SUMMARY

Familiarity with the common biases and limits of human judgment can be extremely helpful for professionals who interview children. Understanding how to evaluate the evidentiary value of indicators and combine that information with base rates can help mandated reporters decide when information they observe justifies a reasonable suspicion of abuse. Information about indicators and base rates might also guide decisions that investigative interviewers have to make. For example, there is no consensus about whether children should be asked direct abuse questions during investigative interviews, but it *is* clear that younger children are more suggestible in the face of such questions. Interviewers might therefore consider the strength of prior evidence of abuse before deciding how to question specific children. It makes sense to limit explicit prompting when a priori evidence of abuse is extremely weak, for example, but to relax concerns about direct questions when a priori evidence of abuse is compelling (e.g., when there are undisputed physical indicators).

The studies reported in this chapter also warn helping professionals to avoid looking only for confirmatory evidence and instead to test hypotheses that might disconfirm allegations. Studies on judgment and decision making also show how memory limitations influence a variety of interesting phenomena. The tendency to remember instances in which particular events co-occurred can cause illusory correlations, and both the tendency to remember salient or highly available events and the conjunction fallacy can cause us to overestimate the frequency of events. Careful record keeping and familiarity with controlled research are the best defenses against these errors. Informed professionals also know that there is a tendency for initial information to be weighed more heavily in decisions, and they are more open to updating their decisions in the face of new evidence. The studies in this chapter also warn us not to overinterpret chance fluctuations in behavior and to be alert to how the wording of problems can influence our decisions. Finally, many professionals work in environments that provide little opportunity for feedback about their decision accuracy. In these situations, professionals may become increasingly confident without becoming increasingly accurate. It is especially important for professionals in these environments to stay abreast of research that explicitly evaluates the usefulness of alternative decision strategies.

STRATEGIES FOR REDUCING ERRORS

Are humans really as poor at solving problems as students of human judgment contend? Not always. One criticism of research on cognitive biases is that the problems often do not relate to real-world situations, and decision makers in these studies often are not given as much information as they would have in the real world. There is no doubt that humans often display sophisticated cognitive strategies when they solve problems on familiar topics in environments that provide error-correcting feedback. For example, Ceci and Liker (1986, 1988) showed that expert racetrack handicappers used complex algorithms to predict post-time odds. Furthermore, ability on such practical problems is often unrelated to success on formal tests of intelligence (Ceci, 1996).

On the other hand, the cognitive biases we have discussed here are evident even when the subjects are professionals responding to problems in their own fields, such as physicians, neuropsychologists, and judges.

Moreover, errors on many types of problems are not always eliminated when motivational conditions are altered, such as when subjects are offered monetary incentives for accuracy (e.g., Chapman & Chapman, 1967). Although familiarity with a particular problem environment improves some types of problem solving, there is no doubt that cognitive biases can seriously interfere with rational decision making.

How can we avoid these biases? Happily, professionals and organizations can improve their decision making by following a few simple suggestions (Dawes, 1988; Garb, 1994b; Plous, 1993).

- **Attend to conditional probabilities and base rates.** Do not accept anecdotal evidence about which predictors you should use in making your decisions. Ask how well those predictors discriminated between diagnostic groups in empirical reports, and consider how base rates influence the accuracy of your decisions.

- **Consider reasons why you might be wrong.** Realize that once you have a hypothesis about a situation, you are likely to overlook information that is inconsistent with your hypothesis. It is useful to write down your hypothesis, list alternative hypotheses, and consider what information might prove that your preferred hypothesis is incorrect. This exercise can prevent you from overlooking the obvious. Because biases are reduced when individuals are required to justify their decisions (J. Friedrich, 1993), asking professionals to write down evidence for and against various hypotheses may reduce the tendency to confirm preferred hypotheses.

- **Maintain records and refer to them often.** Remember that memory is selective. Do not count on your memory to inform you how frequently events occurred together, how individuals reacted to events, or what outcomes followed your decisions.

- **Follow protocols.** Because of reliance on stereotypes, and problems with the weighing of information, reliability is low when professionals are allowed to make subjective evaluations. In clinical diagnosis, the use of explicit criteria improves diagnostic accuracy. Similarly, structured interviews can force professionals to collect information they might ordinarily overlook.

8

KEEPING PACE WITH CHANGING STANDARDS

Who is wise? One who learns from all persons.

Ben Zoma
In A *Prayerbook for Shabbat, Festivals, and Weekdays*

Readers of this book undoubtedly will have noticed how much of the research on interviewing has been conducted in the last few years and how rapidly professional standards and recommendations have evolved in response to our growing knowledge. New and important findings will continue to emerge, and responsible professionals will want to know, and may be expected to know, about relevant studies and recommendations for practitioners. Our goal in this last chapter is to review the various ways in which professionals can continue to improve their skills and remain abreast of new information.

INTERVIEWER TRAINING

Individuals who train police investigators, CPS workers, or assistants for research projects frequently mention how difficult it is to translate principles into practice. In an illustrative study, Stevenson, Leung, and Cheung (1992) confirmed that interviewing skills do not always improve immediately after training. These researchers evaluated the skills of social workers in Kentucky and California both before and after a 10-day, seven-module training course developed by the American Association for Protecting Children (a division of the American Humane Association). Instead of

239

interviewing alleged victims, the participants interviewed women (trained actresses, human services students, or CPS supervisors) who played the role of 10-year-old girls by modeling their behavior on background information and a demonstration interview from an actual case. The interviewers were given written instructions and a one-page description of the case 10 minutes before the interviews and were told that they had 30 minutes to establish a working relationship with the "child," determine the nature of the abuse, and close the interview.

Raters evaluated the quality of the interviews using a 35-item instrument that tapped three conceptual areas: content-oriented questions (such as the interviewer's ability to state his or her name, determine the name and relationship of the alleged perpetrator, and clarify the child's terminology for private body parts); process skills (such as the ability to sequence questions logically and avoid leading questions); and behavioral skills (such as the ability to make appropriate eye contact and avoid touching the child). Each item was rated on a scale from 0 to 4, with yes–no items scored either 0 (for no) or 4 (for yes). To the researchers' surprise, training had no discernible positive effects on interviews conducted immediately afterward: The average score of the social workers in Kentucky was only slightly higher after training (2.84) than before training (2.72), and the average score in California was somewhat lower after training (3.02 before training vs. 2.77 after training).

Stevenson et al. (1992) offered several explanations for these disappointing results. In the Kentucky sample, both the pre- and posttest interviews used the same case example, and this might have reduced the interviewers' attempts to build rapport and press for details. Because of this, the investigators selected different participants for pre- and posttraining interviews from the California sample. Some of these participants reacted negatively when they were selected for posttraining interviews, however, and their resentment might help explain the lower scores. Alternatively, the need to demonstrate mastery of new information so soon after learning it might have contributed to the surprisingly poor performance of interviewers in both samples immediately after training.

Stevenson et al.'s (1992) findings illustrate a thorny problem for trainers: Information presented in lecture format rarely promotes significant behavior change, particularly when that information involves abstract or general principles (Aldridge, 1992; Doris, Mazur, & Thomas, 1995). Rather, opportunities for practice, together with critical feedback, appear to be essential (Federal Law Enforcement Training Center, 1992). According to R. Fisher (1995), lectures help interviewers perform well on written tests but often do not affect their performance during interviews. While conducting interviews, professionals need to make decisions automatically, without reference to written instructions, and hence interviewing is best viewed as a skill that is gradually acquired after repeated practice and feed-back (R. Fisher, 1995; Fisher & Geiselman, 1992).

Systematic feedback is the key to successful training. In an eye-opening article on the acquisition of expert performance, Ericsson and Charness (1994) explained why deliberate practice leads to improvements in skill, whereas other types of experiences do not have comparable benefits. According to Ericsson and Charness, informal, day-to-day activities often fail to enhance performance because people do not predictably and repeatedly encounter specific difficulties in these situations. It is for this reason that casual conversations with children may not promote improve-ments in interviewing skills unless adults intentionally work on specific skills (e.g., not interrupting) and monitor their success. Similarly, Ericsson and Charness argued that people tend not to learn from their work activ-ities, because the pressures they face at work encourage them to rely on well-entrenched skills. By contrast, *deliberate practice*, in which professional teachers or coaches work on specific aspects of performance through rep-etition and "successive refinement" (p. 738), often is beneficial. Deliberate practice differs from either play *or* work because teachers structure the situation to focus on individual difficulties or skills and they provide im-mediate feedback.

What are the implications of research on expertise for training in-vestigative interviewers? Fisher and Geiselman (1992) suggested that train-ees begin by videotaping a baseline interview—a practice that can humble even experienced interviewers. As Fisher and Geiselman noted,

> After having heard a brief lecture about the use of a particular inter-viewing technique, investigators often felt that they understood the logic of the procedure, and therefore, they did not have to practice. When required to conduct an actual interview, however, many realized that, although they understood the technique, they could not imple-ment it as easily as they expected. (p. 185)

Frequent feedback therefore is necessary throughout the training process to narrow the gap between interviewers' subjective appraisals of their abil-ities or behavior and their actual performance. For example, many of the investigators trained by Fisher and Geiselman claimed that they rarely in-terrupted eyewitnesses but were surprised when recordings of their inter-views indicated otherwise.

Fisher and Geiselman (1992) also suggested that trainers distinguish between primary and secondary skills. Instead of teaching a large number of skills in a single session, it is best to let interviewers master a smaller set of skills in each of several shorter sessions, with opportunities for fre-quent videotaping and feedback.

Researchers and field supervisors alike often lament that some inter-viewers have persistent difficulty pacing their speech, avoiding interruptions, and covering predetermined topics in a spontaneous but thorough fashion. To address this problem, R. Fisher (1995) recommended that agencies acknowledge differences in skill and assign responsibilities appropriately. In an innovative proposal, he suggested that a corps of "superinterviewers" conduct critical interviews in the most difficult cases, just as some types of police work are assigned to specialists (e.g., sharpshooters or hostage negotiators).

Model interviewer training courses recognize that interviewers cannot improve their skills in a matter of several hours or even several days. For example, a 2-week training institute sponsored by Cornell University and the "Just For Kids!" Foundation, Inc. (June, 1996) included background lectures (e.g., the scientific method; language, cognitive, and social development; the anatomy of interviews) and opportunities to interview children. Similarly, the advanced course to train staff for the Child Victim Witness Investigation Pilot Projects in California (July, 1994) was a 40-hour program that included hands-on interviewing experience (see the final report for a description of the training course), and systematic evaluation of interview quality led the Israeli Department of Youth Investigation to recognize the value of mandatory biweekly reviews of interviews following intensive multiday training sessions (Horowitz, Hershkowitz, & Hovav, in press).

Trainers can provide necessary practical experience by asking students to interview other class members about a recent event and then arranging for the students to interview children from the community who have recently witnessed a staged event. When all interviewers talk with children who have experienced the same event, it becomes easier to discuss variability in the behavior of children and interviewers, and a videotape of the original event can be played to compare the children's "testimonies" against the actual event. Whatever training techniques are used, all interviewers, no matter how experienced, benefit from refresher training and opportunities to review and discuss their interviews.

LOCATING REFERENCE MATERIALS

Rapid and continuing changes have made it difficult for helping professionals to stay abreast of new ideas and research findings concerning child development and interview strategies. Most researchers are employed by academic institutions or agencies that provide convenient access to reference materials, including libraries and professional librarians, computer databases for locating materials (often from their offices or even their homes), interlibrary loan services, and secretarial staff who can help with such chores as writing to other researchers for copies of articles. By contrast, helping professionals who do not have ready access to research or professional libraries may find the task of tracking down new information to be enormously frustrating and time consuming. We include this section to assist readers who are not familiar with new information technologies but who nonetheless want to stay abreast of the literature on child development, maltreatment, and interviewing strategies.

Internet Resources

Familiarity with browsing the Internet is fast becoming an essential tool for any professional. Many professional organizations are eliminating the costs associated with paper and postage by placing reference material and announcements on the Internet, and library information systems are gradually becoming integrated with Internet technologies. As a result, it may be impossible to avoid the Internet by visiting a library to use "traditional" resource materials because, depending on the library, visitors may confront the same Web browser screens they were reluctant to use from their homes.

For the uninitiated, the Internet is simply a network of computers around the world, with no single owner or manager (although the Internet Society manages the addresses; consult http://www.isoc.org/ for a brief history of the Internet and information about the Internet Society). Bookstores stock numerous introductions to the origin, terminology, and etiquette of the Internet, as well as manuals on how to connect from home and lists of "hot" sites for users with particular interests. Professionals with children at home often can receive free training from their youngsters, but we caution new users to educate their children about basic safety (e.g., not to give out personal information or make arrangements to meet alone with someone they "met" on the Internet) and to monitor their children's activities (e.g., "chat" rooms may be "visited" by adults trying to solicit children).

Although the lack of central management makes the Internet a somewhat disorganized resource, it still is an invaluable tool for busy professionals who want to access research materials from their homes. There currently are dozens of online journals (browse through the possibilities at http://www.edoc.com/ejournal/); free newspapers (including the *New York Times* and others that provide free online papers to lure readers into buying research services for a fee; click "newspapers" in your favorite search engine, e.g., *Yahoo*); book lists from publishers (e.g., the online catalog for The Association of American University Presses can be found at http://aaup.uchicago.edu/, and individual presses can be found by searching for their home pages); and specialty services (e.g., FindLaw Internet Legal Resources is a source for Supreme Court opinions and state laws, information on legal associations and organizations, and consultants and experts [http:/www.findlaw.com/]; legislative information from the U.S. Congress is available from http://thomas.loc.gov/, named after Thomas Jefferson). For proposed standards for referencing online documents, see the Web extension to American Psychological Association Style at http://www.beadsland.com/weapas/.

The National Clearinghouse on Child Abuse and Neglect Information and CANnet

The National Center for Child Abuse and Neglect (NCCAN) administers and funds resource centers and clearinghouses to meet the information, training, and technical assistance needs of professionals who deal with child abuse and neglect. A hard-copy catalog of services and publications can be obtained by calling (800-FYI-3366) or writing to the NCCAN clearinghouse (National Clearinghouse on Child Abuse and Neglect Information, P.O. Box 1182, Washington, DC 20013-1182; also visit them on the Web at http://www.calib.com/nccanch). The clearinghouse disseminates information on numerous aspects of child maltreatment, including policy and legislation, identification and investigation, treatment, prevention, research, public awareness, training and education, and public and private programs. Included among their materials are manuals, reports, directories, literature reviews, annotated bibliographies, and fact sheets, many available free or at minimal cost.

CANnet is the Child Abuse and Neglect Network, an electronic (Internet) bulletin board operated by the NCCAN clearinghouse to provide professionals in the fields of child maltreatment and child welfare with announcements of upcoming events, access to over 10,000 records in the clearinghouse databases, and opportunities to participate in discussion groups. Prospective users register to receive a user identification and user guide (http://www.calib.com/nccanch/cannet.htm). Other clearinghouse resources are the State Statutes Desk (http://www.calib.com/nccanch/services/statutes.htm), which provides information regarding state laws pertaining to child abuse and neglect; the User Manual Series (http://www.calib.com/nccanch/catalog/umanuals.htm), which currently includes 15 volumes on a range of child maltreatment issues; and numerous other NCCAN-sponsored Web pages (e.g., grant program information, databases).

Other Professional Organizations

Several professional organizations provide materials related to child development and child maltreatment issues. Three prominent organizations are the American Psychological Association (APA), the Society for Research in Child Development (SCRD), and the American Professional Society on the Abuse of Children (APSAC). All three organizations publish professional journals, although most of the articles in the APA and SRCD journals are not directly relevant to investigative interviewing.

Professionals who want to stay abreast of basic research in developmental psychology can subscribe to abstracting services that deliver paragraph-long summaries of articles from selected journals on a regular basis (and at a surprisingly low cost), circumventing time-consuming library research. The American Psychological Association publishes *PsycSCAN: Developmental Psychology*, a service that provides printed abstracts from more than three dozen journals in developmental and general psychology four times a year (call 202-336-5600). *PsycSCAN: Developmental Psychology* deals more with basic research than applied topics (e.g., it does not abstract *Child Abuse and Neglect*), but the Association also publishes two volumes of abstracts specifically on child abuse: *Child Abuse: Abstracts of the Psychological and Behavioral Literature Volume 1 (1967–1985)* and *Volume 2 (1986–1990)*. Topical organization and indices make these volumes especially useful for accessing research articles published prior to 1990. (Visit the APA on the Internet at http://www.apa.org/ to find listings of APA books, journals, and the *PsycINFO* database service.)

SRCD publishes *Child Development Abstracts and Bibliography*, which abstracts articles on numerous basic developmental issues (e.g., health and medicine, cognition, education, psychiatry and clinical psychology, social psychology and personality), including those published in such journals as *Child Abuse and Neglect*. *Child Development Abstracts and Bibliography* also includes book notices and handy author addresses; visit it online at http://www.journals.uchicago.edu/CDAB/. For information about membership and publications, consult http://www.journals.uchicago.edu/SCRD/. APSAC also publishes a catalog of resource materials, including back issues of *The APSAC Advisor* and various practice guidelines. Contact them at 407 South Dearborn, Suite 1300, Chicago, Illinois 60605 (312-554-0166).

Contacting Investigators

Some authors provide copies of their published articles (called *reprints*) or to-be-published articles (called *preprints*) on a first-come-first-served basis. When an article is published, authors have the option of purchasing copies for distribution, and these are available on request as long as they last. Because reprints are costly, however, and investigators or their employers generally pay postage to honor the numerous requests they receive, some authors do not provide copies for distribution. Author addresses are usually printed at the bottom of each article's title page, and most researchers employed by a university can be located through a directory on their college or university Internet Web page (which may include additional information about their work).

Patience and courtesy are important when contacting other overworked professionals. Authors who handle a high volume of reprint requests generally have them processed by an assistant, so it increases the chance of a response to send a simple postcard or letter indicating the desired article (or asking for articles on a specific topic) and including a complete return address. Telephone messages that do not clearly indicate which articles are requested may be given low priority, and unusual requests (e.g., requests for copies of articles by other authors or for large documents such as monographs or training manuals) will likely be ignored.

It is important to know that the publisher of an article, not the author, typically holds copyright to the article. As a result, authors do not mass-produce copies of their own work for distribution, and they do not have the sole right to grant permission for such duplication (e.g., for inclusion in workshop handouts). Special issues (single volumes of journals that include many articles on a particular topic) can be purchased from the publisher at a reasonable cost, as can single articles. Publishers routinely provide permission to reproduce figures or tables from published articles or books, sometimes free and sometimes for a fee. (For online information on copyright and fair use law, browse a resource compiled by Stanford University Libraries at http://fairuse.stanford.edu/).

Navigating an Unfamiliar Research Library

The days when individuals could walk into any research library and find a small and predictable set of reference materials are gone. Instead, libraries currently combine traditional hard-copy reference materials (such as *Books in Print*) with a wide variety of computerized databases. Because computerized services can easily be subscribed to, eliminated, or reprogrammed, individuals who only infrequently visit a particular library often face novel challenges each time they attempt to locate information. Although procedures vary from library to library, the following information applies to the typical university research library.

There are two ways to manage time efficiently when coping with the complexity of a research library. First and most important, ask for guidance from a professional librarian or student staff member at the reference desk before wasting an hour or two exploring. (In many colleges and universities, librarians are members of the faculty who teach and write just as other professors do.) Library staff can provide documentation, such as a map of the library, suggest the most useful databases for locating particular types of materials, and provide handouts that describe how to use specific computer databases. They can also explain what services (such as loan privileges) are available to members of the community who are not affiliated with their institutions. Second, become familiar with a set of general terms and procedures. These terms will help you describe what you need to the library staff and help you make sense of the written documentation the library provides.

Basic Terminology

Most individuals are looking for three basic types of material: books, periodicals, or documents. Hard-copy listings of books that currently are in print can be found in the general reference area of the library (e.g., *Books in Print, Paperbound Books in Print, Forthcoming Books*), and listings of books and book reviews also are available on computer databases. Research libraries have computerized "card catalogs" in which the "call numbers" of the books in their collections can be located using a computer terminal, generally by entering either the author's name or the book's title, but also by searching using a topic or keyword. (Most libraries offer access to other libraries' information systems as well.) Books are organized in libraries using either the Dewey decimal system of classification (an older system still in place in many community libraries that relies on 3-digit codes to represent specific topics) or the Library of Congress classification system. The Library of Congress system uses up to six lines of code, beginning with 1 to 2 letters on the top line (e.g., DB); a number on the second line (e.g., 23); a letter and number represented decimally on the third line (e.g., .B856); and sometimes additional lines that might contain a year and volume number (e.g., N4/1972a/v.2). Library maps indicate where books are housed by these call numbers, so it is important to transcribe these codes exactly as they appear on the database. Computerized catalogs also indicate whether a book is checked out, what its return date is, and whether it currently is housed in an atypical location (such as in the over-sized book section; at the bindery; or at the "reserve" desk, where faculty put materials aside for class readings).

Individuals who want to find books on a particular topic rather than specific books can take advantage of the topical organization of call numbers to browse through the library. One strategy is to use the computerized information system to pull up books whose titles and descriptions seem to be on target, write down their call numbers, and proceed to those areas of the library to browse the shelves. The Library of Congress system is somewhat frustrating (because apparently related books may be housed in different areas of the library), but books on most topics typically are found in one to three general locations, and browsing the shelves is a useful way to explore the types of materials that are available. Because a misplaced book is a lost book, however, libraries prefer that visitors do not reshelve their own books; instead, books should be left on adjacent tables or in marked areas for reshelving by the library staff.

Periodicals are related volumes that are published multiple times a year on a regular basis (e.g., once a month, once every 2 months), including scholarly journals (e.g., *Child Abuse & Neglect*) and magazines (e.g., *Newsweek*). (The term *serials* is a more general term that includes annuals.) Locating articles from periodicals usually involves three steps: identifying relevant articles on a database, using the library's information system to determine whether the library has those particular volumes (if this information is not provided by the database), and consulting a library map or sign that tells where items with those particular call numbers are kept. The key to efficiency is selecting the most appropriate database from the dozens that might be available. Some databases are exhaustive, meaning that they cover all of the major titles in the discipline. *PsycLit*, for example, is a well-known database for psychology and psychology-related professional journals, with *PsycFIRST* and *PsycINFO* available on a service called *FirstSearch*. Psychology journals also appear in numerous other databases, such as the *Expanded Academic Index*. Other reference works, such as the *Social Sciences Index*, are selective. Exhaustive databases are appropriate when you want to identify all of the relevant articles on a topic, but because many of the journals will not be owned by a particular library, users may end up wading through a list that refers to dozens of journals they cannot access that day. In contrast, research libraries often try to subscribe to most of the journals from selective databases such as the *Social Sciences Index*, and therefore it can be less frustrating to use a more selective database if your goal is to read a number of articles in order to become familiar with the relevant literature. Databases also vary with respect to the types of periodicals they review (e.g., just journals, or journals and magazines, newspaper articles, etc.); the number of years they cover (e.g., only the last 3 years or farther back); and whether they provide abstracts (short summaries of the articles), opportunities to order articles online, or even the full text of some articles. Another practical consideration is availability: During times of high-volume use, it may be faster to use a hard-copy reference work than to wait for a terminal to use a database that is in high demand. With all of these choices, it is clear that users who are unfamiliar with their options can save a considerable amount of time by telling a librarian what their goals are and asking for advice.

Once a user identifies an appropriate database, efficiency largely is a function of skill at conducting searches. Although the syntax (specific commands) for searching varies from database to database, there are a few general principles that make it easy to learn a new system. First, databases all allow several basic types of searches, such as searching by subjects, keywords, authors, and sometimes even by date or other field qualifier. Because it is easy to miss articles that appear under a variant of the keyword the user identifies, a useful strategy is to locate a small number of appropriate articles and look to see how they were referenced, using their keywords to conduct the next search. (Many databases also have an online thesaurus to suggest appropriate terms.) Second, databases allow users to broaden or restrict their search using *Boolean operators*. These are commands such as *or* (retrieve all articles pertaining to either the first or second term, as in *abuse or interviewing*), *and* (retrieve only those articles pertaining to both terms, as in *abuse and sexual*), and *not* (eliminate articles on a specific subtopic, as in *abuse not therapy*). If an initial search retrieves too many articles to scan, terms can be combined to restrict the search. Although the specific syntax is dictated by the database, Boolean operators and parentheses often can be combined, for example *(minority or race) and (abuse or neglect)*. In *PsycLit*, for example, combining a keyword with *literature review* will pull up only articles that extensively review the literature on a specific topic. (Ask your reference librarian to explain your options for recording the results of your literature search, which might include printing, copying the information onto a diskette, or using electronic mail to send the results to yourself.)

Documents such as government publications generally are housed in a separate section of the library staffed by documents specialists. This area of the library will have census data, crime statistics, and other government publications, although official materials (e.g., legislation; transcripts of Congressional hearings; and publications from government agencies, including funding agencies such as the National Science Foundation and the National Institutes of Health) are increasingly available on the Internet as well.

Time-Saving Tips

Advance preparation is the key to making the most out of a day at the library. Universities often have more than one library on campus, so a preliminary call to get the location of relevant buildings, find out hours, determine whether appointments are required to use some of the databases, and inquire about high versus low usage times can help with efficient planning. Especially for those who have to travel several hours to reach a research library, the most efficient procedure is to access the college or university's home page on the Internet and click into screens about the library system. These screens often include hours of operation for the various libraries on campus (sometimes with handy maps), telephone numbers for the reference desk and other library services, and access to the information system that often will let prospective users search the library holdings from home to determine which specific buildings house the books or journals needed.

Busy professionals do not have time to return to a library over and over again because lines were too long at the copy machines when they arrived or materials were not available during their first visit. Savvy users know a variety of tricks to circumvent delays. For example, many libraries depend on a type of credit card to charge for use of the copy machines or to print from computer databases, but most libraries still have coin-operated copy machines, which often are in low demand, so a pocket of change can prevent delays. There are numerous reasons why volumes may not be on the shelves: Materials might be at the reserve desk, recent journal volumes might be at the bindery, or volumes simply may not have been reshelved yet. The library's information system will tell you whether a book is checked out or temporarily in another location. If a journal volume seems to be missing simply because it has not been reshelved (journals cannot be checked out), it often is possible to find it by checking nearby tables or copying areas or looking in the reshelving area on that floor (where library staff sort the volumes by call number in preparation for reshelving).

CONCLUDING REMARKS

It is increasingly difficult for professionals to develop and maintain high-quality interviewing skills. New research and recommendations are continually appearing, the number of cases to investigate has increased without commensurate increases in the resources available to investigators, and professionals are being held to increasingly exacting standards. On a positive note, however, recent advances in information technology are making it easier for individuals with different skills and work environments to communicate, share resources, and work together to better understand and protect our children.

EPILOGUE

Over the years, our society gradually has acquired a sense of collective responsibility for the well-being of its children. Currently, most adults believe that all children, regardless of their individual circumstances, have a set of fundamental rights that includes protection from physical abuse, access to education, and an environment that provides emotional support from caring adults. The research we described in this book reflects the more recent idea that children should enjoy yet another right: the right to be understood (Walker, 1994).

Communication failures formerly were blamed on children's inherent inadequacies: their impoverished linguistic skills, their fallible and fragile memories, and their tendencies to fantasize. More recently, we have come to realize that many failures of communication reflect failures in the way adults listen to and question young children. Our goal in this book has been to explain children's tendencies and capacities in such a way that those formally empowered to investigate children's experiences can do a better job of listening, questioning, and understanding so that we might, in turn, intervene where children have been maltreated, protecting them from further exploitation.

Although new interviewing research is continually emerging, the basic guidelines for how professionals should talk with children have changed very little during recent years. There is good agreement that children should be able to describe their lives in their own words, to adults who understand that children do not always use language exactly the same way as an adult would. There are many unanswered questions, but current guidelines reflect developmental phenomena that are unlikely to change dramatically despite broader social changes, and therefore future research probably will refine rather than replace many of the recommendations in this book.

To protect children's right to tell their stories and to be understood, investigators must direct more attention to the study of interviewer training. There are few systematic studies of professionals who interview children, but available data suggest that one-shot training courses do not produce the desired results. Because most graduate training programs and social service agencies will continue to operate with severely limited resources, there is a critical need to develop innovative teaching strategies that will help professionals translate abstract principles into flexible and effective interviewing. A coordinated response to the challenges of interviewing children therefore must include two components: continued research on the many questions we left unanswered in this book (such as when to ask direct abuse questions, how to phrase source monitoring questions, and how to modify the basic interviewing protocol to work most effectively with particular age groups) and the launching of a new research agenda on how to produce expert interviewers.

REFERENCES

Abbeduto, L., & Rosenberg, S. (1985). Children's knowledge of the presuppositions of know and other cognitive verbs. *Journal of Child Language*, *12*, 621–641.

Ackil, J. K., & Zaragoza, M. S. (1995). Developmental differences in eyewitness suggestibility and memory for source. *Journal of Experimental Child Psychology*, *60*, 57–83.

Aldridge, J. (1992). The further training of professionals dealing with child witnesses. In H. Dent & R. Flin (Eds.), *Children as witnesses* (pp. 231–244). New York: Wiley.

American Professional Society on the Abuse of Children. (1990). *Guidelines for psychosocial evaluation of suspected sexual abuse in young children*. Chicago: Author.

American Professional Society on the Abuse of Children. (1993). Press release. *The APSAC Advisor*, *6*(2), pp. 23–24.

American Psychological Association. (1991). Minutes of the Council of Representatives. *American Psychologist*, *46*, 722.

Anderson, D. R., Alwitt, L. F., Lorch, E. P., & Levin, S. R. (1979). Watching children watch television. In G. A. Hale & M. Lewis (Eds.), *Attention and cognitive development* (pp. 331–361). New York: Plenum Press.

Anderson, D. R., Lorch, E. P., Field, D. E., Collins, P. A., & Nathan, J. G. (1986). Television viewing at home: Age trends in visual attention and time with TV. *Child Development*, *57*, 1024–1033.

Anderson, D. R., Lorch, E. P., Field, D. E., & Sanders, J. (1981). The effects of TV program comprehensibility on pre-school children's visual attention to television. *Child Development*, *52*, 151–157.

Baker-Ward, L., Gordon, B. N., Ornstein, P. A., Larus, D. M., & Clubb, P. A. (1993). Young children's long-term retention of a pediatric examination. *Child Development*, *64*, 1519–1533.

Baker-Ward, L., Hess, T. M., & Flannagan, D. A. (1990). The effects of involvement on children's memory for events. *Cognitive Development*, *5*, 55–69.

Barlett, D. L., & Steele, J. B. (1992). *America: What went wrong?* Kansas City, MO: Andrews and McMeel.

Barstow, A. L. (1994). *Witchcraze: A new history of the European witch hunts*. San Francisco: Pandora.

Bauer, P. J., & Fivush, R. (1992). Constructing event representations: Building on a foundation of variation and enabling relations. *Cognitive Development*, *7*, 381–401.

Bauer, P. J., & Mandler, J. M. (1990). Remembering what happened next: Very young children's recall of event sequences. In R. Fivush & J. A. Hudson (Eds.), *Knowing and remembering in young children* (pp. 9–29). New York: Cambridge University Press.

Bauer, P. J., & Wewerka, S. S. (1995). One- to two-year-olds' recall of events: The more expressed, the more impressed. *Journal of Experimental Child Psychology, 59*, 475–496.

Beck, M. (1984, August 20). An epidemic of child abuse. *Newsweek, 104*, 44.

Berliner, L. (1990). Professional exchange: Working with lawyers. *The Advisor, 3*(4), 6–7.

Berliner, L., & Barbieri, M. K. (1984). The testimony of the child victim of sexual assault. *Journal of Social Issues, 40*, 125–137.

Berliner, L., & Conte, J. R. (1993). Sexual abuse evaluations: Conceptual and empirical obstacles. *Child Abuse & Neglect, 17*, 111–125.

Bernthal, J. E., & Bankson, J. W. (1993). *Articulation and phonological disorders* (3rd edition). Englewood Cliffs, NJ: Prentice Hall.

Besharov, D. J. (1990). *Recognizing child abuse.* New York: Free Press.

Best, J. (1989). Dark figures and child victims: Statistical claims about missing children. In J. Best (Ed.), *Images and issues: Typifying contemporary social problems* (pp. 21–37). New York: Aldine de Gruyter.

Bever, T. G. (1970). The cognitive basis for linguistic structures. In J. R. Hayes (Eds.), *Cognition and the development of language* (pp. 279–362). New York: Wiley.

Bjorklund, D. F., & Harnishfeger, K. K. (1995). The evolution of inhibition mechanisms and their role in human cognition and behavior. In F. N. Dempster & C. J. Brainerd (Eds.), *Interference and inhibition in cognition* (pp. 141–173). New York: Academic Press.

Blank, M., & White, S. J. (1986). Questions: A powerful but misused form of classroom exchange. *Topics in Language Disorders, 6*, 1–12.

Boat, B. W., & Everson, M. D. (1986). *Using anatomical dolls: Guidelines for interviewing young children in sexual abuse investigations.* Chapel Hill: University of North Carolina, Department of Psychiatry.

Boat, B. W., & Everson, M. D. (1988). Use of anatomical dolls among professionals in sexual abuse evaluations. *Child Abuse & Neglect, 12*, 171–179.

Boat, B. W., & Everson, M. D. (1993). The use of anatomical dolls in sexual abuse evaluations: Current research and practice. In G. S. Goodman & B. L. Bottoms (Eds.), *Child victims, child witnesses: Understanding and improving testimony* (pp. 47–69). New York: Guilford Press.

Boat, B. W., & Everson, M. D. (1996). Concerning practices of interviewers when using anatomical dolls in child protective services investigations. *Child Maltreatment, 1*, 96–104.

Boat, B. W., Everson, M. D., & Holland, J. (1990). Maternal perceptions of nonabused young children's behaviors after the children's exposure to anatomical dolls. *Child Welfare, 69*, 389–400.

Bottoms, B. L., & Davis, S. L. (1997). The creation of satanic ritual abuse. *Journal of Social and Clinical Psychology, 16*, 112–132.

Bottoms, B. L., Shaver, P. R., Goodman, G. S., & Qin, J. (1995). In the name of God: Religion and child abuse. *Journal of Social Issues, 51*, 85–111.

Boychuk, T. D. (1991). *Criteria-based content analysis of children's statements about sexual abuse: A field-based validation study*. Unpublished doctoral dissertation, Arizona State University.

Bradley, A. R., & Wood, J. M. (1996). How do children tell? The disclosure process in child sexual abuse. *Child Abuse & Neglect, 9*, 881–891.

Bradley-Johnson, S. (1994). *Psychoeducational assessment of students who are visually impaired or blind*. Austin, TX: Pro-Ed.

Bradley-Johnson, S., & Evans, L. D. (1991). *Psychoeducational assessment of hearing-impaired students*. Austin, TX: Pro-Ed.

Brainerd, C. J., & Poole, D. P. (1997). Long-term survival of children's false memories: A review. *Learning and Individual Differences, 9*, 125–151.

Brainerd, C. J., & Reyna, V. F. (1990). Gist is the grist: Fuzzy-trace theory and the new intuitionism. *Developmental Review, 10*, 3–47.

Brainerd, C. J., & Reyna, V. F. (1993). Memory independence and memory interference in cognitive development. *Psychological Review, 100*, 42–67.

Brainerd, C. J., & Reyna, V. F. (1995a). Learning rate, learning opportunities, and the development of forgetting. *Developmental Psychology, 31*, 251–263.

Brainerd, C. J., & Reyna, V. F. (1995b). Autosuggestibility in memory development. *Cognitive Development, 28*, 65–101.

Brainerd C. J., & Reyna, V. F. (1996). Mere testing creates false memories in children. *Developmental Psychology, 32*, 467–476.

Brainerd, C. J., & Reyna, V. F. (in press). Fuzzy-Trace Theory and children's false memories. *Journal of Experimental Child Psychology*.

Brainerd, C. J., Reyna, V. F., & Brandse, E. (1995). Are children's false memories more persistent than their true memories? *Psychological Science, 6*, 359–364.

Brainerd, C. J., Reyna, V. F., Howe, M. L., & Kingma, J. (1990). The development of forgetting and reminiscence. *Monographs of the Society for Research in Child Development, 55*(3–4, Serial No. 222).

Brainerd, C. J., Stein, L., & Reyna, V. F. (in press). On the development of conscious and unconscious memory. *Developmental Psychology*.

Brennan, K. H., & Fisher, R. P. (1998). *Drawing as a technique to facilitate children's recall*. Manuscript in preparation.

Brennan, M., & Brennan, R. E. (1988). *Strange language: Child victims under cross examination* (3rd ed.). Wagga Wagga, New South Wales, Australia: Riverina Literacy Centre.

Briere, J., & Elliott, D. M. (1992). Sexual abuse trauma among professional women: Validating the Trauma Symptom Checklist-40 (TSC-40). *Child Abuse & Neglect, 16*, 391–398.

Bruck, M., & Ceci, S. J. (1996). Issues in the scientific validation of interviews with young children. Comment on "Interviewing young children about body touch and handling." *Monograph of the Society for Research in Child Development, 61*(4–5, Serial No. 248).

Bruck, M., Ceci, S. J., Francoeur, E., & Barr, R. (1995). "I hardly cried when I got my shot!" Influencing children's reports about a visit to their pediatrician. *Child Development, 66,* 193–208.

Bruck, M., Ceci, S. J., Francoeur, E., & Renick, A. (1995). Anatomically detailed dolls do not facilitate preschoolers' reports of a pediatric examination involving genital touching. *Journal of Experimental Psychology: Applied, 1,* 95–109.

Bruck, M., Hembrooke, H., & Ceci, S. (1997). Children's reports of pleasant and unpleasant events. In J. D. Read & D. S. Lindsay (Eds.), *Recollections of trauma: Scientific evidence and clinical practice* (pp. 199–213). New York: Plenum Press.

Brumberg, J. (1982). Chlorotic girls, 1870–1920: A historical perspective on female adolescence. *Child Development, 53,* 1468–1477.

Bull, R. (1992). Obtaining evidence expertly: The reliability of interviews with child witnesses. *Expert Evidence: The International Digest of Human Behaviour Science and Law, 1,* 5–12.

Bull, R. (1995). Innovative techniques for the questioning of child witnesses, especially those who are young and those with learning disability. In M. Zaragoza, J. R. Graham, G. C. N. Hall, R. Hirschman, & Y. S. Ben-Porath (Eds.), *Memory and testimony in the child witness* (pp. 179–194). Thousand Oaks, CA: Sage.

Bull, R., & Cherryman, J. (1995). *Helping to identify skills gaps in specialist investigative interviewing: Enhancement of professional skills.* London: Home Office Police Department.

Burgess, C. A., Kirsch, I., Shane, H., Niederauer, K. L., Graham, S. M., & Bacon, A. (1988). Facilitated communication as an ideomotor response. *Psychological Science, 9,* 71–74.

Burns, R. C., & Kaufman, S. H. (1970). *Kinetic family drawings (K-F-D): An introduction to understanding children through kinetic drawings.* New York: Brunner/Mazel.

Buros, O. K. (1989). *The tenth mental measurements yearbook.* Lincoln: University of Nebraska Press.

Burton, R. V., & Strichartz, A. F. (1992). Liar! Liar! Pants afire! In S. J. Ceci, M. D. Leichtman, & M. E. Putnick (Eds.), *Cognitive and social factors in early deception* (pp. 11–28). Hillsdale, NJ: Erlbaum.

Butler, S. G., Gross, J., & Hayne, H. (1995). The effect of drawing on memory performance in young children. *Developmental Psychology, 31,* 597–608.

Campbell, T. W. (1992). Therapeutic relationships and iatrogenic outcomes: The blame-and-change maneuver in psychotherapy. *Psychotherapy, 29,* 474–480.

Cantlon, J., Payne, G., & Erbaugh, C. (1996). Outcome-based practice: Disclosure rates of child sexual abuse comparing allegation blind and allegation informed structured interviews. *Child Abuse & Neglect, 20,* 1113–1120.

Carey, S. (1978). The child as word learner. In M. Halle, J. Bresnan, & G. A.

Miller (Eds.), *Linguistic theory and psychological reality* (pp. 264–293). Cambridge, MA: MIT Press.

Carter, C. A., Bottoms, B. L., & Levine, M. (1996). Linguistic and socioemotional influences on the accuracy of children's reports. *Law and Human Behavior, 20*, 335–358.

Cassel, W. S., Roebers, C. E. M., & Bjorklund, D. F. (1996). Developmental patterns of eyewitness responses to repeated and increasingly suggestive questions. *Journal of Experimental Child Psychology, 61*, 116–133.

Ceci, S. J. (1995). False beliefs: Some developmental and clinical considerations. In D. L. Schacter (Ed.), *Memory distortion: How minds, brains, and societies reconstruct the past* (pp. 91–125). Cambridge, MA: Harvard University Press.

Ceci, S. J. (1996). *On intelligence: A bioecological treatise on intellectual development.* Cambridge, MA: Harvard University Press.

Ceci, S. J., & Bruck, M. (1993). Suggestibility of the child witness: A historical review and synthesis. *Psychological Bulletin, 113*, 403–439.

Ceci, S. J., & Bruck, M. (1995). *Jeopardy in the courtroom: A scientific analysis of children's testimony.* Washington, DC: American Psychological Association.

Ceci, S. J., Bruck, M., & Rosenthal, R. (1995). Children's allegations of sexual abuse: Forensic and scientific issues. *Psychology, Public Policy, and Law, 1*, 494–520.

Ceci, S. J., Huffman, M. L. C., Smith, E., & Loftus, E. F. (1994). Repeatedly thinking about a non-event: Source misattributions among preschoolers. *Consciousness and Cognition, 3*, 388–407.

Ceci, S. J., Leichtman, M. D., & Putnick, M. E. (1992). *Cognitive and social factors in early deception.* Hillsdale, NJ: Erlbaum.

Ceci, S. J., & Liker, J. K. (1986). A day at the races: A study of IQ, expertise, and cognitive complexity. *Journal of Experimental Psychology: General, 115*, 255–266.

Ceci, S. J., & Liker, J. K. (1988). Stalking the IQ-expertise relation: When the critics go fishing. *Journal of Experimental Psychology: General, 117*, 96–100.

Ceci, S. J., Loftus, E. F., Leichtman, M. D., & Bruck, M. (1994). The possible role of source misattributions in the creation of false beliefs among preschoolers. *International Journal of Clinical and Experimental Hypnosis, 42*, 304–320.

Ceci, S. J., Ross, D. F., & Toglia, M. P. (1987). Suggestibility of children's memory: Psycholegal implications. *Journal of Experimental Psychology: General, 116*, 38–49.

Chandler, M. J. (1973). Egocentrism and antisocial behavior: The assessment and training of social perspective-taking skills. *Developmental Psychology, 9*, 326–332.

Chapman, L. J. (1967). Illusory correlation in observational report. *Journal of Verbal Learning and Verbal Behavior, 6*, 151–155.

Chapman, L. J., & Chapman, J. P. (1967). Genesis of popular but erroneous psychodiagnostic observations. *Journal of Abnormal Psychology, 72*, 193–204.

Chapman, L. J., & Chapman, J. P. (1969). Illusory correlation as an obstacle to the use of valid psychodiagnostic signs. *Journal of Abnormal Psychology, 74*, 271–280.

Chess, S., & Hassibi, M. (1986). *Principles and practice of child psychiatry* (2nd ed.). New York: Plenum Press.

Child Abuse Prevention and Treatment Act (P.L. 93-247). (1974).

Child Victim Witness Investigative Pilot Projects. (1994, July). *Research and evaluation final report*. Sacramento: California Attorney General's Office.

Cicchetti, D., & Carlson, V. (Eds.). (1991). *Child maltreatment: Theory and research on the causes and consequences of child abuse and neglect*. New York: Cambridge University Press.

Cohen, J. A., & Mannarino, A. P. (1988). Psychological symptoms in sexually abused girls. *Child Abuse & Neglect, 12*, 571–577.

Cohen, R. L., & Harnick, M. A. (1980). The susceptibility of child witnesses to suggestion. *Law and Human Behavior, 4*, 201–210.

Cohn, D. S. (1991). Anatomical doll play of preschoolers referred for sexual abuse and those not referred. *Child Abuse & Neglect, 15*, 455–466.

Conte, J. R., Sorenson, E., Fogarty, L., & Rosa, J. D. (1991). Evaluating children's reports of sexual abuse: Results from a survey of professionals. *American Journal of Orthopsychiatry, 61*, 428–437.

Cook County Task Force on Intake and Interviewing. (1996). *Cook County procedural manual for criminal child abuse intake and forensic interviewing for children's advocacy centers and victim sensitive intervention programs*. Unpublished manuscript.

Coons, P. M. (1994). Reports of satanic ritual abuse: Further implications about pseudomemories. *Perceptual and Motor Skills, 78*, 1376–1378.

Cornah, D., & Memon, A. (1996, February). *The effects of peer support and suggestibility on children's testimony*. Paper presented at the meeting of the American Psychology-Law Society, Hilton Head, SC.

Cosmides, L. (1989). The logic of social exchange: Has natural selection shaped how humans reason? Studies with the Wason selection task. *Cognition, 31*, 187–276.

Coulton, C. J., Korbin, J. E., Su, M., & Chow, J. (1995). Community level factors and child maltreatment rates. *Child Development, 66*, 1262–1276.

Cronin, Ó., Memon, A., Eaves, R., Küpper, B., & Bull, R. (1992, June). The Cognitive Interview: A child-centered approach? Paper presented at *The Child Witness in Context: Cognitive, Social, and Legal Perspectives*, NATO Advanced Study Institute, Lucca, Italy.

Daly, M., & Wilson, M. I. (1996). Violence against stepchildren. *Current Directions in Psychological Science, 5*, 77–81.

Davidson, D., MacKay, M., & Jergovic, D. (1994). The effects of stereotypes on children's use of decision heuristics. In L. Heath, R. S. Tindale, J. Edwards, E. J. Posavac, R. B. Bryant, E. Henderson-King, Y. Suarez-Balcazar, & J. Myers

(Eds.), *Applications of heuristics and biases to social issues* (pp. 241–257). New York: Plenum Press.

Davies, G., & Wilson, J. C. (1996, March). *Effect of hearsay on jurors' reactions in abuse cases*. Paper presented at the meeting of the American Psychology-Law Society, Hilton Head, SC.

Davies, G., Wilson, C., Mitchell, R., & Milsom, J. (1996). *Videotaping children's evidence: An evaluation*. London: Home Office.

Dawes, R. M. (1986). Representative thinking in clinical judgment. *Clinical Psychology Review, 6,* 425–441.

Dawes, R. M. (1988). *Rational choice in an uncertain world*. New York: Harcourt Brace Jovanovich.

Dawes, R. M. (1994a). AIDS, sterile needles, and ethnocentrism. In L. Heath, R. S. Tindale, J. Edwards, E. J. Posavac, R. B. Bryant, E. Henderson-King, Y. Suarez-Balcazar, & J. Myers (Eds.), *Applications of heuristics and biases to social issues* (pp. 31–44). New York: Plenum Press.

Dawes, R. M. (1994b). *House of cards: Psychology and psychotherapy built on myth*. New York: Free Press.

Dawes, R. M. (1995). Standards of practice. In S. C. Hayes, V. M. Follette, R. M. Dawes, & K. E. Grady (Eds.), *Scientific standards of psychological practice: Issues and recommendations* (pp. 31–43). Reno, NV: Context Press.

Dawes, R. M. (1996). *Daubert, Rule 401, and Bayes Theorem*. Draft of a letter since revised to the Honorable James H. Brickey, Chief Justice, Michigan Supreme Court, sent September 9.

Dawes, R. M. (in press). Behavioral decision making and judgment. In D. Gilbert, S. T. Fiske, & G. Lindzey (Eds.), *The handbook of social psychology* (Vol. 1, 4th ed.). New York: McGraw-Hill.

Dawes, R. M., Faust, D., & Meehl, P. E. (1989). Clinical versus actuarial judgment. *Science, 243,* 1668–1674.

Dawes, R. M., & Mulford, M. (1993). Diagnoses of alien kidnappings that result from conjunction effects in memory. *Skeptical Inquirer, 18,* 50–51.

Dawes, R. M., & Mulford, M. (1996). The false consensus effect and overconfidence: Flaws in judgment or flaws in how we study judgment? *Organizational Behavior and Human Decision Processes, 65,* 201–211.

DeLoache, J. S. (1990). Young children's understanding of models. In R. Fivush & J. A. Hudson (Eds.), *Knowing and remembering in young children* (pp. 94–126). New York: Cambridge University Press.

DeLoache, J. S. (1995a). Early understanding and use of symbols: The model model. *Current Directions in Psychological Science, 4,* 109–113.

DeLoache, J. S. (1995b). The use of dolls in interviewing young children. In M. S. Zaragoza, J. R. Graham, G. C. N. Hall, R. Hirschman, & Y. S. Ben-Porath (Eds.), *Memory and testimony in the child witness* (pp. 160–178). Thousand Oaks, CA: Sage.

DeLoache, J. S., & Marzolf, D. P. (1995). The use of dolls to interview young children: Issues of symbolic representation. *Journal of Experimental Child Psychology, 60,* 155–173.

DeLoache, J. S., Miller, K. F., & Rosengren, K. S. (1997). The credible shrinking room: Very young children's performance with symbolic and nonsymbolic relations. *Psychological Science, 8,* 308–313.

Dennis, M., Sugar, J., & Whitaker, H. A. (1982). The acquisition of tag questions. *Child Development, 53,* 1254–1257.

Dent, H. R. (1986). Experimental study of the effectiveness of different techniques of questioning mentally handicapped child witnesses. *British Journal of Clinical Psychology, 25,* 13–17.

Dent, H. R. (1991). Experimental studies of interviewing child witnesses. In J. Doris (Ed.), *The suggestibility of children's recollections* (pp. 138–146). Washington, DC: American Psychological Association.

Dent, H. R., & Stephenson, G. M. (1979). An experimental study of the effectiveness of different techniques of questioning child witnesses. *British Journal of Social and Clinical Psychology, 18,* 41–51.

deVilliers, J. G., & deVilliers, P. A. (1973). Development of the use of word order in comprehension. *Journal of Psycholinguistic Research, 2,* 331–341.

deVilliers, J. G., & deVilliers, P. A. (1978). *Language acquisition.* Cambridge, MA: Harvard University Press.

de Young, M. (1988). The indignant page: Techniques of neutralization in the publications of pedophile organizations. *Child Abuse & Neglect, 12,* 583–591.

Dietze, P. M. (1994). *An evaluation of the utility of mental reinstatement in enhancing children's recall.* Doctoral dissertation, Monash University, Australia.

Dietze, P. M., & Thomson, D. M. (1993). Mental reinstatement of context: A technique for interviewing child witnesses. *Applied Cognitive Psychology, 7,* 97–108.

Doris, J., Mazur, R., & Thomas, M. (1995). Training in child protective services: A commentary on the amicus brief of Bruck and Ceci (1993/1995). *Psychology, Public Policy, and Law, 1,* 479–493.

Downs, J. F. (1972). *The Navajo.* Prospect Heights, IL: Waveland Press.

Dubowitz, H., Black, M., Harrington, D., & Verschoore, A. (1993). A follow-up study of behavior problems associated with child sexual abuse. *Child Abuse & Neglect, 17,* 743–754.

Edwards, M. L. (1974). Perception and production in child phonology: The testing of four hypotheses. *Journal of Child Language, 1,* 205–219.

Eisen, M. L., Goodman, G. S., & Qin, J. (1995, July). Eyewitness testimony in victims of child maltreatment: Stress, memory, and suggestibility. In J. Parker (Chair), *Children's eyewitness memory: Stress and arousal.* Symposium conducted at the meeting of the Society for Applied Research on Memory and Cognition, Vancouver, British Columbia, Canada.

Eisen, M. L., Goodman, G. S., Qin, J., & Davis, S. (in press). Memory and suggestibility in maltreated children: New research relevant to evaluating allegations of abuse. In S. L. Lynn & K. McConkey (Eds.), *Trauma and memory*. New York: Guilford Press.

Elliott, A. N., O'Donohue, W. T., & Nickerson, M. A. (1993). The use of sexually detailed dolls in the assessment of sexual abuse. *Clinical Psychology Review, 13*, 207–221.

Elliott, D. J., & Tarnowski, K. J. (1990). Depressive characteristics of sexually abused children. *Child Psychiatry and Human Development, 21*, 37–48.

Elliott, D. M., & Briere, J. (1994). Forensic sexual abuse evaluations of older children: Disclosures and symptomatology. *Behavioral Sciences and the Law, 12*, 261–277.

Ellis, M. V., Robbins, E. S., Schult, D., Ladany, N., & Banker, J. (1990). Anchoring errors in clinical judgments: Type I error, adjustment, or mitigation? *Journal of Counseling Psychology, 37*, 343–351.

Ericsson, K. A., & Charness, N. (1994). Expert performance: Its structure and acquisition. *American Psychologist, 49*, 725–747.

Everson, M. D., & Boat, B. W. (1989). False allegations of sexual abuse by children and adolescents. *Journal of the American Academy of Child and Adolescent Psychiatry, 28*, 230–235.

Everson, M. D., & Boat, B. W. (1990). Sexualized doll play among young children: Implications for the use of anatomical dolls in sexual abuse evaluations. *Journal of the American Academy of Child and Adolescent Psychiatry, 29*, 736–742.

Everson, M. D., & Boat, B. W. (1994). Putting the anatomical doll controversy in perspective: An examination of the major uses and criticisms of the dolls in child sexual abuse evaluations. *Child Abuse & Neglect, 18*, 113–129.

Ewing, C. P. (1994, January). Judicial notebook: Child's disclosure of sexual abuse held tainted by repeated exposure to suggestive book. *APA Monitor*, p. 14.

Faller, K. (1988). Criteria for judging the credibility of children's statements about their sexual abuse. *Child Welfare, 67*, 389–401.

Faller, K. (1991). Possible explanations for child sexual abuse allegations in divorce. *American Journal of Orthopsychiatry, 61*, 86–91.

Fallon, T. J., & Pucci, L. (1994). *Forensic interviewing techniques with young children*. Handout for a workshop sponsored by the Wisconsin Department of Justice.

Faludi, S. (1991). *Backlash: The undeclared war against American women*. New York: Crown.

Farrar, M. J., & Goodman, G. S. (1990). Developmental differences in the relation between scripts and episodic memory: Do they exist? In R. Fivush & J. A. Hudson (Eds.), *Knowing and remembering in young children* (pp. 30–64). New York: Cambridge University Press.

Faust, D., Hart, K., & Guilmette, T. J. (1988). Pediatric malingering: The capacity of children to fake believable deficits on neuropsychological testing. *Journal of Consulting and Clinical Psychology, 56*, 578–582.

Faust, D., Hart, K., Guilmette, T. J., & Arkes, H. R. (1988). Neuropsychologists' capacity to detect adolescent malingers. *Professional Psychology: Research and Practice, 19*, 508–515.

Feagans, L. (1980). Children's understanding of some temporal terms denoting order, duration, and simultaneity. *Journal of Psycholinguistic Research, 9,* 41–57.

Federal Law Enforcement Training Center. (1992). *Validation of 9-week basic law enforcement for land management agencies (9-PT) report.* Glynco, GA: Department of the Treasury.

Feld, A. (1994). *MSW education: Where is the content on memory?* Paper presented at the 40th Annual Program Meeting of the Council on Social Work Education, Atlanta.

Finkelhor, D., & Baron, L. (1986). High-risk children. In D. Finkelhor & Associates (Eds.), *Sourcebook on child sexual abuse* (pp. 60–88). Newbury Park, CA: Sage.

Finkelhor, D., Hotaling, G., Lewis, I. A., & Smith, C. (1990). Sexual abuse in a national survey of adult men and women: Prevalence, characteristics, and risk factors. *Child Abuse & Neglect, 14,* 19–28.

Finkelhor, D., Hotaling, G. T., & Sedlak, A. (1990). *Missing, abducted, runaway, and thrownaway children in America: First report.* Washington, DC: Juvenile Justice Clearinghouse.

Finkelhor, D., Williams, L. M., & Burns, N. (1988). *Nursery crimes: Sexual abuse in day care.* Newbury Park, CA: Sage.

Fisher, C. B. (1995). American Psychological Association's (1992) ethics code and the validation of sexual abuse in day-care settings. *Psychology, Public Policy, and Law, 1,* 461–478.

Fisher, R. P. (1995). Interviewing victims and witnesses of crime. *Psychology, Public Policy, and Law, 1,* 732–764.

Fisher, R. P. (1996). Misconceptions in design and analysis of research with the Cognitive Interview: Commentary on Memon & Stevenage on Witness-Memory. *Psycholoquy, 7,* witness-memory.12.fisher

Fisher, R. P., & Geiselman, R. E. (1992). *Memory-enhancing techniques for investigative interviewing: The Cognitive Interview.* Springfield, IL: Thomas.

Fisher, R. P., Geiselman, R. E., & Amador, M. (1989). Field test of the cognitive interview: Enhancing the recollection of actual victims and witnesses of crime. *Journal of Applied Psychology, 74,* 722–727.

Fisher, R. P., Geiselman, R. E., & Raymond, D. S. (1987). Critical analysis of police interview techniques. *Journal of Police Science and Administration, 15,* 177–185.

Fisher, R. P., Geiselman, R. E., Raymond, D. S., Jurkevich, L. M., & Warhaftig, M. L. (1987). Enhancing enhanced eyewitness memory: Refining the cognitive interview. *Journal of Police Science and Administration, 15,* 291–297.

Fisher, R. P., & McCauley, M. R. (1995). Improving eyewitness testimony with the Cognitive Interview. In M. S. Zaragoza, J. R. Graham, G. C. N. Hall, R. Hirschman, & Y. S. Ben-Porath (Eds.), *Memory and testimony in the child witness* (pp. 141–159). Thousand Oaks, CA: Sage.

Fisher, R. P., McCauley, M. R., & Geiselman, R. E. (1994). Improving eyewitness testimony with the Cognitive Interview. In D. F. Ross, J. D. Read, & M. P. Toglia (Eds.), *Adult eyewitness testimony: Current trends and developments* (pp. 245–269). New York: Cambridge University Press.

Fivush, R., Haden, C., & Adam, S. (1995). Structure and coherence of preschoolers' personal narratives over time: Implications for childhood amnesia. *Journal of Experimental Child Psychology, 60,* 32–56.

Fivush, R., & Hamond, N. R. (1990). Autobiographical memory across the preschool years: Toward reconceptualizing childhood amnesia. In R. Fivush & J. A. Hudson (Eds.), *Knowing and remembering in young children* (pp. 223–248). New York: Cambridge University Press.

Fivush, R., & Schwarzmueller, A. (1995). Say it once again: Effects of repeated questions on children's event recall. *Journal of Traumatic Stress, 8,* 555–580.

Fivush, R., & Shukat, J. (1995). What young children recall: Issues of content, consistency and coherence of early autobiographical recall. In M. S. Zaragoza, J. R. Graham, G. C. N. Hall, R. Hirschman, & Y. S. Ben-Porath (Eds.), *Memory and testimony in the child witness* (pp. 5–23). Thousand Oaks, CA: Sage.

Flanagan, O. (1992). Other minds, obligation, and honesty. In S. J. Ceci, M. D. Leichtman, & M. Putnick (Eds.), *Cognitive and social factors in early deception* (pp. 111–126). Hillsdale, NJ: Erlbaum.

Flin, R., Boon, J., Knox, A., & Bull, R. (1992). The effect of a five-month delay on children's and adults' eyewitness memory. *British Journal of Psychology, 83,* 323–336.

Flin, R. H., Bull, R., Boon, J., & Knox, A. (1990). *Child witnesses in criminal prosecutions.* Edinburgh: Scottish Home and Health Department.

Flin, R., Davies, G., & Tarrant, A. (1988). *The child witness.* Edinburgh: Scottish Home and Health Department.

Foley, M. A., & Johnson, M. K. (1985). Confusions between memories for performed and imagined actions: A developmental comparison. *Child Development, 56,* 1145–1155.

French, L. A., & Nelson, K. (1985). *Young children's knowledge of relational terms.* New York: Springer-Verlag.

Friedman, W. J. (1991). The development of children's memory for the time of past events. *Child Development, 62,* 139–155.

Friedman, W. J., Gardner, A. G., & Zubin, N. R. E. (1995). Children's comparisons of the recency of two events from the past year. *Child Development, 66,* 970–983.

Friedrich, J. (1993). Primary error detection and minimization (PREDMIN) strategies in social cognition: A reinterpretation of confirmation bias phenomena. *Psychological Review, 100,* 298–319.

Friedrich, W. N. (1993). Sexual victimization and sexual behavior in children: A review of recent literature. *Child Abuse & Neglect, 17,* 59–66.

Friedrich, W. N., Grambsch, P., Broughton, D., Kuiper, J., & Beilke, R. L. (1991). Normative sexual behavior in children. *Pediatrics, 88,* 456–464.

Friedrich, W. N., Grambsch, P., Damon, L., Hewitt, S. K., Koverola, C., Lang, R. A., Wolfe, V., & Broughton, D. (1992). Child Sexual Behavior Inventory: Normative and clinical comparisons. *Psychological Assessment, 4*, 303–311.

Garb, H. N. (1984). The incremental validity of information used in personality assessment. *Clinical Psychology Review, 4*, 641–655.

Garb, H. N. (1989). Clinical judgment, clinical training, and professional experience. *Psychological Bulletin, 105*, 387–396.

Garb, H. N. (1992). The *trained* psychologist as expert witness. *Clinical Psychology Review, 12*, 451–467.

Garb, H. N. (1994a). Cognitive heuristics and biases in personality assessment. In L. Heath, R. S. Tindale, J. Edwards, E. J. Posavac, F. B. Bryant, E. Henderson-King, Y. Suarez-Balcazar, & J. Myers (Eds.), *Applications of heuristics and biases to social issues* (pp. 73–90). New York: Plenum Press.

Garb, H. N. (1994b). Judgment research: Implications for clinical practice and testimony in court. *Applied & Preventive Psychology, 3*, 173–183.

Garb, H. N. (1996). The representativeness and past-behavior heuristics in clinical judgment. *Professional Psychology: Research and Practice, 27*, 272–277.

Gardner, R. A. (1996). *Psychotherapy with sex-abuse victims: True, false, and hysterical*. Cresskill, NJ: Creative Therapeutics.

Garnica, O. K. (1973). The development of phonemic speech perception. In T. E. Moore (Ed.), *Cognitive development and the acquisition of language* (pp. 215–222). New York: Academic Press.

Garven, S., Wood, J. M., Malpass, R. S., & Shaw, J. S. (in press). More than suggestion: The effect of interviewing techniques from the McMartin Preschool case. *Journal of Applied Psychology*.

Gee, S., & Pipe, M.-E. (1995). Helping children to remember: The influence of object cues on children's accounts of a real event. *Developmental Psychology, 31*, 746–758.

Geiselman, R. E., & Padilla, J. (1988). Cognitive interviewing with child witnesses. *Journal of Police Science and Administration, 16*, 236–242.

Geiselman, R. E., Saywitz, K. J., & Bornstein, G. K. (1993). Effects of cognitive questioning techniques on children's recall performance. In G. S. Goodman & B. L. Bottoms (Eds.), *Child victims, child witnesses: Understanding and improving testimony* (pp. 71–93). New York: Guilford Press.

Gibson, E., & Radner, N. (1979). Attention: The perceiver as performer. In G. A. Hale & M. Lewis (Eds.), *Attention and cognitive development* (pp. 1–21). New York: Plenum Press.

Giovannoni, J. (1991). Definitional issues in child maltreatment. In D. Cicchetti & V. Carlson (Eds.), *Child maltreatment* (pp. 3–37). New York: Cambridge University Press.

Glaser, D., & Collins, C. (1989). The response of young, non-sexually abused children to anatomically correct dolls. *Journal of Child Psychology & Psychiatry & Allied Disciplines, 30*, 547–560.

Gleason, J. B. (1977). Code switching in children's language. In E. M. Hetherington & R. D. Parke (Eds.), *Contemporary readings in child psychology* (pp. 138–143). New York: McGraw-Hill.

Goldberg, L. R. (1959). The effectiveness of clinicians' judgments: The diagnosis of organic brain damage from the Bender-Gestalt Test. *Journal of Consulting Psychology, 23*, 25–33.

Goodman, E. (1996, July 18). Tennis shorts of dubious origin. *The Boston Globe*.

Goodman, G. S. (1984). The child witness: An introduction. *Journal of Social Issues, 40*, 1–8.

Goodman, G. S., Aman, C., & Hirschman, J. (1987). Child sexual and physical abuse: Children's testimony. In S. J. Ceci, M. P. Toglia, & D. F. Ross (Eds.), *Children's eyewitness memory* (pp. 1–23). New York: Springer-Verlag.

Goodman, G. S., Bottoms, B. L., Schwartz-Kenney, B. M., & Rudy, L. (1991). Children's testimony about a stressful event: Improving children's reports. *Journal of Narrative and Life History, 1*, 69–99.

Goodman, G. S., & Clarke-Stewart, A. (1991). Suggestibility in children's testimony: Implications for sexual abuse investigations. In J. Doris (Ed.), *The suggestibility of children's recollections* (pp. 92–105). Washington, DC: American Psychological Association.

Goodman, G. S., Hirschman, J. E., Hepps, D., & Rudy, L. (1991). Children's memory for stressful events. *Merrill-Palmer Quarterly, 37*, 109–158.

Goodman, G. S., Quas, J., Batterman-Faunce, J. M., Riddlesberger, M. M., & Kuhn, J. (1994). Predictors of accurate and inaccurate memories of traumatic events experienced in childhood. *Consciousness and Cognition, 3*, 269–294.

Goodman, G. S., Rudy, L., Bottoms, B. L., & Aman, C. (1990). Children's concerns and memory: Issues of ecological validity in the study of children's eyewitness testimony. In R. Fivush & J. A. Hudson (Eds.), *Knowing and remembering in young children* (pp. 249–284). New York: Cambridge University Press.

Gopnik, A., & Graf, P. (1988). Knowing how you know: Young children's ability to identify and remember the sources of their beliefs. *Child Development, 59*, 1366–1371.

Gordon, B. N., Schroeder, C. S., & Abrams, J. M. (1990a). Age and social-class differences in children's knowledge of sexuality. *Journal of Clinical Child Psychology, 19*, 33–43.

Gordon, B. N., Schroeder, C. S., & Abrams, J. M. (1990b). Children's knowledge of sexuality: A comparison of sexually abused and nonabused children. *American Journal of Orthopsychiatry, 60*, 250–257.

Gordon, P., & Chafetz, J. (1990). Verb-based versus class-based accounts of actionality effects in children's comprehension of passives. *Cognition, 36*, 227–254.

Gould, S. J. (1996). *The mismeasure of man*. New York: Norton.

Grant, J. P. (1995). *The state of the world's children 1995*. New York: Oxford University Press for UNICEF.

Gray, E. (1993). *Unequal justice: The prosecution of child sexual abuse*. New York: MacMillan.

Greenstock, J., & Pipe, M.-E. (1996). Interviewing children about past events: The influence of peer support and misleading questions. *Child Abuse & Neglect, 20,* 69–80.

Gross, A. M., Stern, R. M., Levin, R. B., Dale, J., & Wojnilower, D. A. (1983). The effect of mother-child separation on the behavior of children experiencing a diagnostic medical procedure. *Journal of Consulting and Clinical Psychology, 51,* 783–785.

Grove, W. M., & Meehl, P. E. (1996). Comparative efficiency of informal (subjective, impressionistic) and formal (mechanical, algorithmic) prediction procedures: The clinical-statistical controversy. *Psychology, Public Policy, & Law, 2,* 293–323.

Gruppen, L. D., Wolf, F. M., Billi, J. E. (1991). Information gathering and integration as sources of error in diagnostic decision making. *Medical Decision Making, 11,* 233–239.

Hackbarth, S. G., Murphy, H. D., & McQuary, J. P. (1991). Identifying sexually abused children by using kinetic family drawings. *Elementary School Guidance & Counseling, 25,* 255–260.

Hagen, J. W., & Hale, G. A. (1973). The development of attention in children. In A. D. Pick (Ed.), *Minnesota symposium on child psychology* (Vol. 7, pp. 117–140). Minneapolis: University of Minnesota Press.

Harker, C. (1986, September/October). Japanese. *The Iowa Alumni Review,* pp. 16–20.

Harlow, J. (Ed.). (1985). *A prayerbook for Shabbat, festivals, and weekdays.* New York: The Rabbinical Assembly, The United Synagogue of America.

Harner, L. (1975). Yesterday and tomorrow: Development of early understanding of the terms. *Developmental Psychology, 11,* 864–865.

Haskett, M. E., Wayland, K., Hutcheson, J. S., & Tavana, T. (1995). Substantiation of sexual abuse allegations: Factors involved in the decision-making process. *Journal of Child Sexual Abuse, 4,* 19–47.

Haugaard, J. J. (1993). Young children's classification of the corroboration of a false statement as the truth or a lie. *Law and Human Behavior, 17,* 645–659.

Haugaard, J. J. (1996). Sexual behaviors between children: Professionals' opinions and undergraduates' recollections. *Families in Society, 77,* 81–89.

Hernandez, D. J. (1994). Children's changing access to resources: A historical perspective [Monograph]. *Social Policy Report, 8*(1).

Hershkowitz, I. (1997). *The dynamics of interviews yielding plausible and implausible allegations of child sexual abuse.* Manuscript in preparation.

Hershkowitz, I., Lamb, M. E., Sternberg, K. J., & Esplin, P. W. (1997). The relationships among interviewer utterance type, CBCA scores, and the richness of children's responses. *Legal and Criminological Psychology, 2,* 169–176.

Hershkowitz, I., Orbach, Y., Lamb, M. E., Sternberg, K. J., Horowitz, D., & Hovav, M. (in press). Visiting the scene of the crime: Effects on children's recall of alleged abuse. *Legal and Criminological Psychology.*

Higgins, L. C. (1973). *Classification in the congenitally blind*. New York: American Foundation for the Blind.

Home Office. (1992). *Memorandum of good practice on video recorded interviews with child witnesses for criminal proceedings*. London: Author, with Department of Health.

Honts, C. R. (1994). Assessing children's credibility: Scientific and legal issues in 1994. *North Dakota Law Review, 70,* 879–903.

Horner, T. M., Guyer, M. J., & Kalter, N. M. (1993a). Clinical expertise and the assessment of child sexual abuse. *Journal of the American Academy of Child and Adolescent Psychiatry, 32,* 925–933.

Horner, T. M., Guyer, M. J., & Kalter, N. M. (1993b). The biases of child sexual abuse experts: Believing is seeing. *Bulletin of the American Academy of Psychiatry and Law, 21,* 281–292.

Horowitz, D., Hershkowitz, I., & Hovav, M. (in press). The effect of using a scripted interview protocol and training of youth investigators on the quality of interviewing child victims of sexual abuse [Hebrew]. In Y. Vozner, M. Golan, & M. Hovav (Eds.), *Evaluation of interventions in correctional services*. Tel Aviv: Shirikova Press.

Horowitz, S. W., Lamb, M. E., Esplin, P. W., Boychuk, T., & Reiter-Lavery, L. (1997). Reliability of criteria-based content analysis of child witness statements. *Legal and Criminological Psychology, 2,* 11–26.

Horowitz, S. W., Lamb, M. E., Esplin, P. W., Boychuk, T., Reiter-Lavery, L., & Krispin, O. (1995). Establishing the ground truth in studies of child sexual abuse. *Expert Evidence: The International Digest of Human Behaviour Science and Law, 4,* 42–51.

Howe, M. L., & Courage, M. L. (1993). On resolving the enigma of infantile amnesia. *Psychological Bulletin, 113,* 305–326.

Howe, M. L., Kelland, A., Bryant-Brown, L., & Clark, S. L. (1992). Measuring the development of children's amnesia and hypermnesia. In M. L. Howe, C. J. Brainerd, & V. F. Reyna (Eds.), *Development of long-term retention* (pp. 56–102). New York: Springer-Verlag.

Hudson, J. A. (1988). Children's memory for atypical actions in script-based stories: Evidence for a disruption effect. *Journal of Experimental Child Psychology, 46,* 159–173.

Hudson, J. A. (1990). The emergence of autobiographical memory in mother-child conversation. In R. Fivush & J. A. Hudson (Eds.), *Knowing and remembering in young children* (pp. 166–196). New York: Cambridge University Press.

Hudson, J. A., Fivush, R., & Kuebli, J. (1992). Scripts and episodes: The development of event memory. *Applied Cognitive Psychology, 6,* 483–505.

Huffman, M. L., & Ceci, S. J. (1997). *Can criteria-based content analysis discriminate between accurate and false reports of preschoolers? A validation attempt*. Submitted for publication.

Huffman, M. L., Warren, A. R., & Frazier, S. (1997, November). *The effect of a truth/lie discussion on children's accuracy and competence.* Paper presented at the 23rd annual conference of the Association for Moral Education, Atlanta.

Hughes, M., & Grieve, R. (1980). On asking children bizarre questions. *First Language, 1,* 149–160.

Hulse, D. A. (1994). *Linguistic complexity in child abuse interviews.* Unpublished masters thesis, University of Tennessee at Chattanooga.

Huston, A. C. (1994). Children in poverty: Designing research to affect policy [Monograph]. *Social Policy Report, 8*(2).

Idaho v. Wright, 116 Idaho 382, 775 P-2d 1224. (1989).

Jacobson, J. W., Mulick, J. A., & Schwartz, A. A. (1995). A history of facilitated communication: Science, pseudoscience, and antiscience. *American Psychologist, 50,* 750–765.

Jampole, L., & Weber, M. K. (1987). An assessment of the behavior of sexually abused and nonsexually abused children with anatomically correct dolls. *Child Abuse & Neglect, 11,* 187–192.

Jennings, D. L., Amabile, T. M., & Ross, L. (1982). Informal covariation assessment: Data-based versus theory-based judgments. In D. Kahneman, P. Slovic, & A. Tversky (Eds.), *Judgment under uncertainty: Heuristics and biases* (pp. 211–230). New York: Cambridge University Press.

Johnson, C. N., & Wellman, H. M. (1980). Children's developing understanding of mental verbs: Remember, know, and guess. *Child Development, 51,* 1095–1102.

Johnson, M. K., Hashtroudi, S., & Lindsay, D. S. (1993). Source monitoring. *Psychological Bulletin, 114,* 3–28.

Jones, D., & Krugman, R. (1986). Can a three-year-old bear witness to her sexual assault and attempted murder? *Child Abuse & Neglect, 10,* 253–258.

Jones, D., & McGraw, J. M. (1987). Reliable and fictitious accounts of sexual abuse in children. *Journal of Interpersonal Violence, 2,* 27–45.

Jones, D. P. H., & Seig, A. (1988). Child sexual abuse allegations in custody or visitation cases: A report of 20 cases. In E. B. Nicholson (Ed.), *Sexual abuse allegations in custody and visitation cases: A resource book for judges and court personnel.* Washington, DC: American Bar Association National Legal Resource Center for Child Advocacy and Protection.

Jones, R. J., Gruber, K. J., & Freeman, M. H. (1983). Reactions of adolescents to being interviewed about their sexual assault experiences. *Journal of Sex Research, 19,* 160–172.

Kahneman, D., & Tversky, A. (1973). On the psychology of prediction. *Psychological Review, 80,* 237–251.

Kalichman, S. C. (1993). *Mandated reporting of suspected child abuse: Ethics, law, & policy.* Washington, DC: American Psychological Association.

Keary, K., & Fitzpatrick, C. (1994). Children's disclosure of sexual abuse during formal investigation. *Child Abuse & Neglect, 18,* 543–548.

Keenan, E. O. (1977). Making it last: Repetition in children's discourse. In S.

Ervin-Tripp & C. Mitchell-Kerman (Eds.), *Child discourse* (pp. 125–138). New York: Academic Press.

Kempe, C. H., Silverman, F., Steele, B., Droegemueller, W., & Silver, H. (1962). The battered child syndrome. *Journal of the American Medical Association, 181*, 17–24.

Kendall-Tackett, K. A., & Watson, M. W. (1992). Use of anatomical dolls by Boston-area professionals. *Child Abuse & Neglect, 16*, 423–428.

Kenyon-Juma, R., Burnette, M. M., & Robertson, M. (1991). Comparison of behaviors of suspected sexually abused and nonsexually abused preschool children using anatomical dolls. *Journal of Psychopathology and Behavioral Assessment, 13*, 225–240.

Kessen, W. (1965). *The child.* New York: Wiley.

Kihlstrom, J. F. (in press). Exhumed memory. In S. J. Lynn & N. P. Spanos (Eds.), *Truth in memory.* New York: Guilford Press.

Kinsey, A. C., Pomeroy, W. B., & Martin, C. E. (1948). *Sexual behavior in the human male.* Philadelphia: Saunders.

Kohl, J. (1993). School-based child sexual abuse prevention programs. *Journal of Family Violence, 8*, 137–150.

Kohlberg, L., LaCrosse, J., & Ricks, D. (1972). The predictability of adult mental health from childhood behavior. In B. B. Wolman (Ed.), *Manual of child psychopathology* (pp. 1217–1284). New York: McGraw-Hill.

Köhnken, G. (1993). *The Structured Interview: A step-by-step introduction.* Unpublished manuscript.

Köhnken, G. (1995). Interviewing adults. In R. Bull & D. Carson (Eds.), *Handbook of psychology in legal contexts* (pp. 215–233). Chichester, England: Wiley.

Köhnken, G., Finger, M., Nitschke, N., Höfer, E., & Aschermann, E. (1992, March). *Does a Cognitive Interview interfere with a subsequent Statement Validity Analysis?* Paper presented at the American Psychology and Law Society meeting, San Diego.

Köhnken, G., Milne, R., Memon, A., & Bull, R. (1994, March). *Recall in cognitive interviews and standard interviews: A meta-analysis.* Paper presented at the biennial meeting of the American Psychology-Law Society, Santa Fe, New Mexico.

Koocher, G. P., Goodman, G. S., White, C. S., Friedrich, W. N., Sivan, A. B., & Reynolds, C. R. (1995). Psychological science and the use of anatomically detailed dolls in child sexual-abuse assessments. *Psychological Bulletin, 118*, 199–222.

Korbin, J. E. (1994). Perpetrators of fatal child maltreatment. *The APSAC Advisor, 7*(4), 45–46.

Kuehnle, K. (1996). *Assessing allegations of child sexual abuse.* Sarasota, FL: Professional Resource Press.

Lamb, M. E. (1994). The investigation of child sexual abuse: An interdisciplinary consensus statement. *Child Abuse & Neglect, 18*, 1021–1028.

Lamb, M. E., Hershkowitz, I., Sternberg, K. J., Boat, B., & Everson, M. D. (1996). Investigative interviews of alleged sexual abuse victims with and without anatomical dolls. *Child Abuse & Neglect, 20,* 1239–1247.

Lamb, M. E., Hershkowitz, I., Sternberg, K. J., Esplin, P. W., Hovav, M., Manor, T., & Yudilevitch, L. (1996). Effects of investigative utterance types on Israeli children's responses. *International Journal of Behavioral Development, 19,* 627–637.

Lamb, M. E., Sternberg, K. J., & Esplin, P. W. (1994). Factors influencing the reliability and validity of statements made by young victims of sexual maltreatment. *Journal of Applied Developmental Psychology, 15,* 255–280.

Lamb, M. E., Sternberg, K. J., & Esplin, P. W. (1995). Making children into competent witnesses: Reactions to the amicus brief *in re Michaels. Psychology, Public Policy, and the Law, 1,* 438–449.

Lamb, M. E., Sternberg, K. J., & Esplin, P. W. (in press). Conducting investigative interviews of alleged sexual abuse victims. *Child Abuse & Neglect.*

Lamb, M. E., Sternberg, K. J., Esplin, P. W., Hershkowitz, I., & Orbach, Y. (1997). Assessing the credibility of children's allegations of sexual abuse: Insights from recent research. *Learning and Individual Differences, 9,* 175–194.

Lamb, M. E., Sternberg, K. J., Esplin, P. W., Hershkowitz, I., Orbach, Y., & Hovav, M. (1997). Criterion-based content analysis: A field validation study. *Child Abuse & Neglect, 21,* 255–264.

Lamb, S., & Coakley, M. (1993). "Normal" childhood sexual play and games: Differentiating play from abuse. *Child Abuse & Neglect, 17,* 515–526.

Lane, D. M., & Pearson, D. A. (1982). The development of selective attention. *Merrill-Palmer Quarterly, 28,* 317–337.

Laumann, E. O., Gagnon, J. H., Michael, R. T., & Michaels, S. (1994). *The social organization of sexuality.* Chicago: University of Chicago Press.

Leichtman, M. D., & Ceci, S. J. (1995). The effects of stereotypes and suggestions on preschoolers' reports. *Developmental Psychology, 31,* 568–578.

Lempert, H. (1978). Extrasyntactic factors affecting passive sentence comprehension by young children. *Child Development, 49,* 694–699.

Lepore, S. J., & Sesco, B. (1994). Distorting children's reports and interpretations of events through suggestion. *Journal of Applied Psychology, 79,* 108–120.

Levine, M., & Doueck, H. J. (1995). *The impact of mandated reporting on the therapeutic process.* Thousand Oaks, CA: Sage.

Lidz, C. W., Mulvey, E. P., & Gardner, W. (1993). The accuracy of predictions of violence to others. *Journal of the American Medical Association, 269,* 1007–1011.

Lindsay, D. S., Gonzales, V., & Eso, K. (1995). Aware and unaware uses of memories of postevent suggestions. In M. S. Zaragoza, J. R. Graham, G. C. N. Hall, R. Hirschman, & Y. S. Ben-Porath (Eds.), *Memory and testimony in the child witness* (pp. 86–108). Thousand Oaks, CA: Sage.

Lindsay, D. S., Johnson, M. K., & Kwon, P. (1991). Developmental changes in memory source monitoring. *Journal of Experimental Child Psychology, 52,* 297–318.

Lindsay, D. S., & Read, J. D. (1994). Psychotherapy and memories of childhood sexual abuse: A cognitive perspective. *Journal of Applied Cognitive Psychology, 8,* 281–338.

Loftus, E. F. (1975). Leading questions and the eyewitness report. *Cognitive Psychology, 7,* 560–572.

Loftus, E. F., & Ketcham, E. (1994). *The myth of repressed memory: False memories and allegations of sexual abuse.* New York: St. Martin's Press.

Loftus, E. F., & Palmer, J. C. (1974). Reconstruction of automobile destruction: An example of the interaction between language and memory. *Journal of Verbal Learning and Verbal Behavior, 13,* 585–589.

Lowry, D. T., Love, G., & Kirby, M. (1981). Sex on the soap operas: Patterns of intimacy. *Journal of Communication, 31,* 90–96.

Luria, A. R. (1973). *The working brain: An introduction to neuropsychology.* New York: Basic Books.

MacFarlane, K. (1986). Child sexual abuse allegations in divorce proceedings. In K. MacFarlane & J. Waterman (Eds.), *Sexual abuse of young children.* New York: Guilford Press.

Marche, T. A., & Howe, M. L. (1995). Preschoolers report misinformation despite accurate memory. *Developmental Psychology, 31,* 554–567.

Marxsen, D., Yuille, J. C., & Nisbet, M. (1995). The complexities of eliciting and assessing children's statements. *Psychology, Public Policy, and Law, 1,* 450–460.

Mason, M. A. (1991). A judicial dilemma: Expert testimony in child sex abuse cases. *Journal of Psychiatry and Law, 19,* 185–219.

Mason, M. A. (1995). The child sex abuse syndrome: The other major issue in *State of New Jersey v. Margaret Kelly Michaels. Psychology, Public Policy, and Law, 1,* 399–410.

McCauley, M. R., & Fisher, R. P. (1995). Facilitating children's eyewitness recall with the revised Cognitive Interview. *Journal of Applied Psychology, 80,* 510–516.

McGarrigle, J., & Donaldson, M. (1974). Conservation accidents. *Cognition, 3,* 341–350.

McGough, L. S. (1994). *Child witnesses: Fragile voices in the American legal system.* New Haven, CT: Yale University Press.

McGough, L. S. (1995). For the record: Videotaping investigative interviews. *Psychology, Public Policy, and Law, 1,* 370–386.

McGough, L. S. (1996). Commentary: Achieving real reform—The case for American interviewing protocols. *Monographs of the Society for Research in Child Development, 61*(4–5, Serial No. 248), 188–203.

McGough, L. S., & Warren, A. R. (1994). The all-important investigative interview. *Juvenile and Family Court Journal, 45,* 13–29.

Medin, D. L., & Ross B. H. (1992). *Cognitive psychology.* New York: Harcourt Brace Jovanovich.

Memon, A., & Bull, R. (1991). The Cognitive Interview: Its origins, empirical support, evaluation and practical implications. *Journal of Community and Applied Social Psychology, 1,* 291–307.

Memon, A., Cronin, O., Eaves, R., & Bull, R. (1996). An empirical test of the mnemonic components of the Cognitive Interview. In G. Davies, S. Lloyd-Bostock, M. McMurran, & C. Wilson (Eds.), *Psychology, law, and criminal justice: International developments in research and practice* (pp. 135–145). New York: Walter de Gruyter.

Memon, A., Holley, A., Wark, L., Bull, R., & Koehnken,[1] G. (1996). Reducing suggestibility in child witness interviews. *Applied Cognitive Psychology, 10,* 416–432.

Memon, A., & Stevenage, V. S. (1996). Interviewing witnesses: What works and what doesn't? *Psycholoquy, 7,* witness-memory.1.memon.

Memon, A., & Vartoukian, R. (1996). The effects of repeated questioning on young children's eyewitness testimony. *British Journal of Psychology, 87,* 403–415.

Memon, A., Wark, L., Bull, R., & Koehnken, G. (1997). Isolating the effects of the cognitive interview. *British Journal of Psychology, 88,* 179–197.

Memon, A., Wark, L., Holley, A., Bull, R., & Köhnken, G. (1995, September). *Eyewitness performance in cognitive and structured interviews.* Paper presented at the meeting of the British Psychological Society Cognitive Section Conference, Bristol, England.

Memon, A., Wark, L., Holley, A., Bull, R., & Koehnken, G. (1997). Eyewitness performance in cognitive and structured interviews. *Memory, 5,* 639–656.

Merritt, K. A., Ornstein, P. A., & Spicker, B. (1994). Children's memory for a salient medical procedure: Implications for testimony. *Pediatrics, 94,* 17–23.

Mesibov, G. B., Schroeder, C. S., & Wesson, L. (1977). Parental concerns about their children. *Journal of Pediatric Psychology, 2,* 13–17.

Michael, R. T., Gagnon, J. H., Laumann, E. O., & Kolata, G. (1994). *Sex in America.* Boston: Little, Brown.

Michaels, S. (1981). "Sharing time": Children's narrative styles and differential access to literacy. *Language in Society, 10,* 423–442.

Miller, R. L., Jr. (1995). *Indiana practice: Vol. 13. Indiana Evidence.* St. Paul, MN: West.

Miller, T. W., Veltkamp, L. J., & Janson, D. (1987). Projective measures in the

---

[1]This is a variant spelling of *Köhnken.* The name appears herein according to the form published in the original source.

clinical evaluation of sexually abused children. *Child Psychiatry and Human Development, 18,* 47–57.

Milne, R., & Bull, R. (1996). Interviewing children with mild learning disability with the cognitive interview. In N. K. Clark & G. M. Stephenson (Eds.), *Investigative and forensic decision making* (pp. 44–51). Leicester, England: British Psychological Society.

Milne, R., Bull, R., Koehnken, G., & Memon, A. (1995). The Cognitive Interview and suggestibility. In G. M. Stephenson & N. K. Clark (Eds.), *Criminal behavior: Perceptions, attributions and rationality* (Division of Criminological & Legal Psychology Occasional Papers, No. 22, pp. 21–27). Leicester, England: British Psychological Society.

Moerk, E. L. (1974). Changes in verbal child-mother interactions with increasing language skills of the child. *Journal of Psycholinguistic Research, 3,* 101–116.

Montoya, J. (1995). Lessons from *Akiki* and *Michaels* on shielding child witnesses. *Psychology, Public Policy, and Law, 1,* 340–369.

Morey, L. C., & Ochoa, E. S. (1989). An investigation of adherence to diagnostic criteria: Clinical diagnosis of the DSM-III personality disorders. *Journal of Personality Disorders, 3,* 180–192.

Morgan, M. (1995). *How to interview sexual abuse victims.* Thousand Oaks, CA: Sage.

Moston, S. (1987). The suggestibility of children in interview studies. *First Language, 7,* 67–78.

Moston, S., & Engelberg, T. (1992). The effects of social support on children's eyewitness testimony. *Applied Cognitive Psychology, 6,* 61–75.

Mulder, M. R., & Vrij, A. (1996). Explaining conversation rules to children: An intervention study to facilitate children's accurate responses. *Child Abuse & Neglect, 20,* 623–631.

Munro, J. K., & Wales, R. J. (1982). Changes in the child's comprehension of simultaneity and sequence. *Journal of Verbal Learning and Verbal Behavior, 21,* 175–185.

Myers, J. E. B. (1987). *Child witness law and practice.* New York: Wiley.

Myers, J. E. B. (1993). Expert testimony regarding child sexual abuse. *Child Abuse & Neglect, 17,* 175–185.

Myers, J. E. B., Bays, J., Becker, J., Berliner, L., Corwin, D. L., & Saywitz, K. L. (1989). Expert testimony in child sexual abuse litigation. *Nebraska Law Review, 68,* 1–145.

Nathan, D., & Snedeker, M. (1995). *Satan's silence: Ritual abuse and the making of a modern American witch hunt.* New York: Basic Books.

National Center for Prosecution of Child Abuse, American Prosecutors Research Institute, National District Attorneys Association. (1993). *Investigation and prosecution of child abuse* (2nd ed.). Alexandria, VA: American Prosecutors Research Institute.

Nelson, K. (1990). Remembering, forgetting, and childhood amnesia. In R. Fivush

& J. A. Hudson (Eds.), *Knowing and remembering in young children* (pp. 301–316). New York: Cambridge University Press.

Nelson, K. (1991). The matter of time: Interdependencies between language and thought in development. In S. A. Gelman & J. P. Byrnes (Eds.), *Perspectives on language and thought* (pp. 278–318). New York: Cambridge University Press.

Newcombe, P. A., & Siegal, M. (1996). Where to look first for suggestibility in young children. *Cognition, 59*, 337–356.

Newcombe, P. A., & Siegal, M. (1997). Explicitly questioning the nature of suggestibility in preschoolers' memory and retention. *Journal of Experimental Child Psychology, 67*, 185–203.

Nisbett, R., & Ross, L. (1980). *Human inference: Strategies and shortcomings of social judgment.* Englewood Cliffs, NJ: Prentice-Hall.

Ofshe, R., & Watters, E. (1994). *Making monsters: False memories, psychotherapy, and sexual hysteria.* New York: Scribner.

Ornstein, P. A., Gordon, B. N., & Larus, D. M. (1992). Children's memory for a personally experienced event: Implications for testimony. *Applied Cognitive Psychology, 6*, 49–60.

Osofsky, J. D. (1995). The effect of exposure to violence on young children. *American Psychologist, 50*, 782–788.

Paivio, A. (1971). *Imagery and verbal processes.* New York: Holt, Rinehart, & Winston.

Paris, S. C., & Lindauer, B. K. (1982). The development of cognitive skills during childhood. In B. B. Wolman (Ed.), *Handbook of developmental psychology* (pp. 333–349). Englewood Cliffs, NJ: Prentice-Hall.

Parker, J. F. (1995) Age differences in source monitoring of performed and imagined actions on immediate and delayed tests. *Journal of Experimental Child Psychology, 60*, 84–101.

Pear, T., & Wyath, S. (1914). The testimony of normal and mentally defective children. *British Journal of Psychology, 3*, 388–419.

People v. Miller, 165 Mich. App. 32, 418 N.W.2d 668 (1987).

People v. Naugle, 152 Mich. App. 227, 235 (1986).

Pence, D., & Wilson, C. (1994). *Team investigation of child sexual abuse.* Thousand Oaks, CA: Sage.

Perry, N. W., McAuliff, B. D., Tam, P., Claycomb, L., Dostal, C., & Flanagan, C. (1995). When lawyers question children: Is justice served? *Law and Human Behavior, 19*, 609–629.

Perry, N. W., & Teply, L. L. (1984–1985). Interviewing, counseling, and in-court examination of children: Practical approaches for attorneys. *Creighton Law Review, 18*, 1369–1426.

Perry, N. W., & Wrightsman, L. S. (1991). *The child witness: Legal issues and dilemmas.* Newbury Park, CA: Sage.

Peterson, C., & Bell, M. (1996). Children's memory for traumatic injury. *Child Development, 67,* 3045–3070.

Peterson, C., & Biggs, M. (1997). Interviewing children about trauma: Problems with "specific" questions. *Journal of Traumatic Stress, 10,* 279–290.

Pezdek, K., & Roe, C. (1995). The effect of memory trace strength on suggestibility. *Journal of Experimental Child Psychology, 60,* 116–128.

Phillips, J. R. (1973). Syntax and vocabulary of mothers' speech to young children: Age and sex comparisons. *Child Development, 44,* 182–185.

Phillips, K. (1990). *The politics of rich and poor.* New York: Harper Perennial.

Piaget, J. (1929). *The child's conception of the world.* London: Routledge & Kegan Paul.

Pillemer, D. B., Picariello, M. L., & Pruett, J. C. (1994). Very long-term memories of a salient preschool event. *Applied Cognitive Psychology, 8,* 95–106.

Pipe, M.-E., Gee, S., & Wilson, C. (1993). Cues, props, and context: Do they facilitate children's event reports? In G. S. Goodman & B. L. Bottoms (Eds.), *Child victims, child witnesses: Understanding and improving testimony* (pp. 25–45). New York: Guilford Press.

Pipe, M.-E., & Wilson, J. C. (1994). Cues and secrets: Influences on children's event reports. *Developmental Psychology, 30,* 515–525.

Plous, S. (1993). *The psychology of judgment and decision making.* Philadelphia: Temple University Press.

Polusny, M. A., & Follette, V. M. (1996). Remembering childhood sexual abuse: A national survey of psychologists' clinical practices, beliefs, and personal experiences. *Professional Psychology: Research and Practice, 27,* 41–52.

Poole, D. A. (1995). Strolling fuzzy-trace theory through eyewitness testimony (or vice versa). *Learning and Individual Differences, 7,* 87–94.

Poole, D. A., & Lindsay, D. S. (1995). Interviewing preschoolers: Effects of nonsuggestive techniques, parental coaching, and leading questions on reports of nonexperienced events. *Journal of Experimental Child Psychology, 60,* 129–154.

Poole, D. A., & Lindsay, D. S. (1996, June). Effects of parental suggestions, interviewing techniques, and age on young children's event reports. Paper presented at *Recollections of Trauma: Scientific Research and Clinical Practice,* NATO Advanced Study Institute, Port de Bourgenay, France.

Poole, D. A., & Lindsay, D. S. (1997, April). Misinformation from parents and children's source monitoring: Implications for testimony. In K. P. Roberts (Chair), *Children's source monitoring and eyewitness testimony.* Symposium conducted at the meeting of the Society for Research in Child Development, Washington, DC.

Poole, D. A., & Lindsay, D. S. (1998). Assessing the accuracy of young children's reports: Lessons from the investigation of child sexual abuse. *Applied and Preventive Psychology, 7,* 1–26.

Poole, D. A., Lindsay, D. S., Memon, A., & Bull, R. (1995). Psychotherapy and the recovery of memories of childhood sexual abuse: U.S. and British practitioners' opinions, practices, and experiences. *Journal of Consulting and Clinical Psychology, 63*, 426–437.

Poole, D. A., & White, L. T. (1991). Effects of question repetition on the eyewitness testimony of children and adults. *Developmental Psychology, 27*, 975–986.

Poole, D. A., & White, L. T. (1993). Two years later: Effects of question repetition and retention interval on the eyewitness testimony of children and adults. *Developmental Psychology, 29*, 844–853.

Poole, D. A., & White, L. T. (1995). Tell me again and again: Stability and change in the repeated testimonies of children and adults. In M. S. Zaragoza, J. R. Graham, G. C. N. Hall, R. Hirschman, & Y. S. Ben-Porath (Eds.), *Memory and testimony in the child witness* (pp. 24–43). Thousand Oaks, CA: Sage.

Powell, M. B., & Thomson, D. M. (1996). Children's memory of an occurrence of a repeated event: Effects of age, repetition, and retention interval across three question types. *Child Development, 67*, 1988–2004.

Powell, M. B., & Thomson, D. M. (1997a). Contrasting memory for temporal-source and memory for content in children's discrimination of repeated events. *Applied Cognitive Psychology, 11*, 339–360.

Powell, M. B., & Thomson, D. M. (1997b). The effect of an intervening interview on children's ability to remember one occurrence of a repeated event. *Legal and Criminological Psychology, 2*, 247–262.

Powell, M. B., Thomson, D. M., & Dietze, P. M. (1997). Children's ability to remember an occurrence of a repeated event. *Expert Evidence, 5*, 133–139.

Pratt, C. (1990). On asking children—and adults—bizarre questions. *First Language, 10*, 167–175.

Priestley, G. K., & Pipe, M. E. (1997). Using toys and models in interviews with young children. *Applied Cognitive Psychology, 11*, 69–87.

Quinton, D., Rutter, M., & Gulliver, L. (1990). Continuities in psychiatric disorders from childhood to adulthood in the children of psychiatric patients. In L. Robins & M. Rutter (Eds.), *Straight and deviant pathways from childhood to adulthood* (pp. 259–278). New York: Cambridge University Press.

Rand Corporation. (1975). *The criminal investigative process* (Vols. 1–3; Rand Corporation Technical Report R-1777-DOJ). Santa Monica, CA: Author.

Raskin, D. C., & Esplin, P. W. (1991). Statement validity assessment: Interview procedures and context analysis of children's statements of sexual abuse. *Behavioral Assessment, 13*, 265–291.

Raskin, D. C., & Yuille, J. C. (1989). Problems in evaluating interviews of children in sexual abuse cases. In S. J. Ceci, D. F. Ross, & M. P. Toglia (Eds.), *Perspectives on children's testimony* (pp. 184–207). New York: Springer-Verlag.

Read, J. D., & Lindsay, D. S. (1997). *Recollections of trauma: Scientific research and clinical practice*. New York: Plenum Press.

Read, J. D., Lindsay, D. S., & Nicholls, T. (1998). The relationship between accuracy and confidence in eyewitness identification studies: Is the conclusion changing? In C. P. Thompson, D. Herrmann, J. D. Read, D. Bruce, D. Payne,

& M. P. Toglia (Eds.), *Eyewitness memory: Theoretical and applied perspectives* (pp. 107–130). Mahwah, NJ: Erlbaum.

Realmuto, G. M., Jensen, J. B., & Wescoe, S. (1990). Specificity and sensitivity of sexually anatomically correct dolls in substantiating abuse: A pilot study. *Journal of the American Academy of Child & Adolescent Psychiatry, 29,* 743–746.

Realmuto, G. M., & Wescoe, S. (1992). Agreement among professionals about a child's sexual abuse status: Interviews with sexually anatomically correct dolls as indicators of abuse. *Child Abuse & Neglect, 16,* 719–725.

Reese, E., Haden, C. A., & Fivush, R. (1993). Mother-child conversations about the past: Relationships of style and memory over time. *Cognitive Development, 8,* 403–430.

Reich, P. A. (1986). *Language development.* Englewood Cliffs, NJ: Prentice-Hall.

Reyna, V. F. (1995). Interference effects in memory and reasoning: A fuzzy-trace theory analysis. In F. N. Dempster & C. J. Brainerd (Eds.), *Interference and inhibition in cognition* (pp. 29–59). New York: Academic Press.

Reyna, V. F., & Brainerd, C. J. (1995). Fuzzy-trace theory: An interim synthesis. *Learning and Individual Differences, 7,* 1–75.

Richards, M. M. (1976). Come and go reconsidered: Children's use of deictic verbs in contrived situations. *Journal of Verbal Learning and Verbal Behavior, 15,* 655–665.

Richards, M. M. (1982). Empiricism and learning to mean. In S. Kuczaj, II (Ed.), *Language development, Vol. 1: Syntax and semantics* (pp. 365–396). Hillsdale, NJ: Erlbaum.

Riordan, R. J., & Verdel, A. C. (1991). Evidence of sexual abuse in children's art products. *The School Counselor, 39,* 116–121.

Roberts, K. P., & Blades, M. (1996, February). *Do children confuse memories of events seen on television and events witnessed in real life?* Paper presented at the biennial meeting of the American Psychology-Law Society, Hilton Head, SC.

Robin, M. (1991). The social construction of child abuse and "false allegations." In M. Robin (Ed.), *Assessing child maltreatment reports: The problem of false allegations* (pp. 1–34). Binghamton, NY: Haworth Press.

Robins, L. N. (1966). *Deviant children grown up: A sociological and psychiatric study of sociopathic personality.* Baltimore: Williams & Wilkins.

Rogoff, B., & Mistry, J. (1990). The social and functional context of children's remembering. In R. Fivush & J. A. Hudson (Eds.), *Knowing and remembering in young children* (pp. 197–222). New York: Cambridge University Press.

Romaine, S. (1984). *The language of children and adolescents: The acquisition of communicative competence.* New York: Basil Blackwell.

Rosenthal, R. (1995). *State of New Jersey v. Margaret Kelly Michaels:* An overview. *Psychology, Public Policy, and Law, 1,* 246–271.

Rosner, S. R., & Poole, D. A. (1978, May). *A longitudinal study of category item judgments.* Paper presented at the meeting of the Midwestern Psychological Association, Chicago.

Rosner, S. R., & Poole, D. A. (1981, April). *Category attributes and item inclusion.* Paper presented at the meeting of the Society for Research in Child Development, Boston.

Rosner, S. R., & Poole, D. A. (1985, August). *Children's comprehension of subsets and supersets.* Paper presented at the meeting of the American Psychological Association, Los Angeles.

Rovee-Collier, C. (1995). Time windows in cognitive development. *Developmental Psychology, 31,* 147–169.

Rovee-Collier, C., & Hayne, H. (1987). Reactivation of infant memory: Implications for cognitive development. *Advances in Child Development and Behavior, 20,* 185–238.

Russell, B. (1969). *The autobiography of Bertrand Russell: 1944–1969* (Vol. 3). New York: Simon & Schuster.

Salmon, K., Bidrose, S., & Pipe, M.-E. (1995). Providing props to facilitate children's event reports: A comparison of toys and real items. *Journal of Experimental Child Psychology, 60,* 174–194.

Salmon, K., & Pipe, M.-E. (1997). Props and children's event reports: The impact of a 1-year delay. *Journal of Experimental Child Psychology, 65,* 261–292.

Salmon, K., & Pipe, M.-E. (1998). *Do props and drawings facilitate children's event recall following very long delays?* Unpublished manuscript.

San Diego County Grand Jury. (1994, June 1). *Analysis of child molestation issues* (Report No. 7). San Diego: County of San Diego.

Santrock, J. W. (1993). *Adolescence: An introduction* (5th ed.). Madison, WI: Brown & Benchmark.

Saywitz, K. J. (1988). The credibility of child witnesses. *Family Advocate, 10*(3), 38–41.

Saywitz, K. J. (1989). Children's conceptions of the legal system: "Court is a place to play basketball." In S. J. Ceci, D. F. Ross, & M. P. Toglia (Eds.), *Perspectives on children's testimony* (pp. 131–157). New York: Springer-Verlag.

Saywitz, K. J., Geiselman, R. E., & Bornstein, G. K. (1992). Effects of cognitive interviewing and practice on children's recall performance. *Journal of Applied Psychology, 77,* 744–756.

Saywitz, K. J., Goodman, G. S., Nicholas, E., & Moan, S. F. (1991). Children's memories of a physical examination involving genital touch: Implications for reports of child sexual abuse. *Journal of Consulting and Clinical Psychology, 59,* 682–691.

Saywitz, K. J., Moan, S., & Lamphear, V. (1991, August). *The effect of preparation on children's resistance to misleading questions.* Paper presented at the meeting of the American Psychological Association, San Francisco.

Saywitz, K. J., & Snyder, L. (1993). Improving children's testimony with preparation. In G. S. Goodman & B. L. Bottoms (Eds.), *Child victims, child witnesses: Understanding and improving testimony* (pp. 117–146). New York: Guilford Press.

Schacter, D. L., Kagan, J., & Leichtman, M. D. (1995). True and false memories in children and adults: A cognitive neuroscience perspective. *Psychology, Public Policy, and Law, 1,* 411–428.

Schwartz, S. (1994). Heuristics and biases in medical judgment and decision making. In L. Heath, R. S. Tindale, J. Edwards, E. J. Posavac, F. B. Bryant, E. Henderson-King, Y. Suarez-Balcazar, & J. Myers (Eds.), *Applications of heuristics and biases to social issues* (pp. 45–72). New York: Plenum Press.

Schwartz, S., & Griffin, T. (1986). *Medical thinking: The psychology of medical judgment and decision making.* New York: Springer-Verlag.

Shatz, M. (1978). On the development of communicative understandings: An early strategy for interpreting and responding to messages. *Cognitive Psychology, 10,* 271–301.

Shatz, M., & McCloskey, L. (1984). Answering appropriately: A developmental perspective on conversational knowledge. In S. Kuczaj (Ed.), *Discourse development: Progress in cognitive development research* (pp. 19–36). New York: Springer-Verlag.

Shiloh, S. (1994). Heuristics and biases in health decision making: Their expression in genetic counseling. In L. Heath, R. S. Tindale, J. Edwards, E. J. Posavac, F. B. Bryant, E. Henderson-King, Y. Suarez-Balcazar, & J. Myers (Eds.), *Applications of heuristics and biases to social issues* (pp. 13–30). New York: Plenum Press.

Siegal, M. (1991). *Knowing children: Experiments in conversation and cognition.* London: Erlbaum.

Siegal, M., & Peterson, C. C. (1996). Breaking the mold: A fresh look at children's understanding of questions about lies and mistakes. *Developmental Psychology, 32,* 322–334.

Siegal, M., Waters, L. J., & Dinwiddy, L. S. (1988). Misleading children: Causal attributions for inconsistency under repeated questioning. *Journal of Experimental Child Psychology, 45,* 438–456.

Sigelman, C. K., Budd, E. C., Spanhel, C. L., & Schoenrock, C. J. (1981). Asking questions of retarded persons: A comparison of yes-no and either-or formats. *Applied Research in Mental Retardation, 2,* 347–357.

Sink, F. (1988). Studies of true and false allegations: A critical review. In E. B. Nicholson (Ed.), *Sexual abuse allegations in custody and visitation cases: A resource book for judges and court personnel* (pp. 37–47). Washington, DC: American Bar Association.

Slusser, M. M. (1995). Manifestations of sexual abuse in preschool-aged children. *Issues in Mental Health Nursing, 16,* 481–491.

Smith, J. (1991). Aftermath of a false allegation. *Issues in Child Abuse Accusations, 3,* 203.

Sorensen, T., & Snow, B. (1991). How children tell: The process of disclosure in child sexual abuse. *Child Welfare, 70,* 3–15.

Sorenson, E., Bottoms, B., & Perona, A. (1997). *Intake and forensic interviewing in the children's advocacy center setting: A handbook.* Washington, DC: National Network of Children's Advocacy Centers.

Spence, D. P. (1984). *Narrative truth and historical truth*. New York: Norton.

Spock, B. (1976). *Baby and child care*. New York: Pocket Books.

State v. DBS, 700 P.2d 630, 634 (Mont. 1985).

Steller, M., Raskin, D. C., & Esplin, P. W. (1989, March). *Interviewing and assessment techniques in child sexual abuse cases*. Workshop sponsored by the University of Utah, Department of Psychology and Division of Continuing Education, Denver, CO.

Stern, P. (1992). Videotaping child interviews. *Journal of Interpersonal Violence, 7*, 278–284.

Sternberg, K. J., Lamb, M. E., & Hershkowitz, I. (1996). Child sexual abuse investigations in Israel. *Criminal Justice and Behavior, 23*, 322–337.

Sternberg, K. J., Lamb, M. E., Hershkowitz, I., Esplin, P. W., Redlich, A., & Sunshine, M. (1996). The relationship between investigative utterance types and the informativeness of child witnesses. *Journal of Applied Developmental Psychology, 17*, 439–451.

Sternberg, K. J., Lamb, M. E., Hershkowitz, I., Yudilevitch, L., Orbach, Y., Esplin, P. W., & Hovav, M. (1997). Effects of introductory style on children's abilities to describe experiences of sexual abuse. *Child Abuse & Neglect, 21*, 1133–1146.

Stevenson, K. M., Leung, P., & Cheung, K-f. M. (1992). Competency-based evaluation of interviewing skills in child sexual abuse cases. *Social Work Research & Abstracts, 28*, 11–16.

Steward, D., Farquhar, L., Driskill, J., & Steward, M. S. (1996). Child and interviewer behaviors in drawing and computer-assisted interviews. *Monograph of the Society for Research in Child Development, 61*(4–5, Serial No. 248), 137–143.

Steward, M. S., Bussey, K., Goodman, G. S., & Saywitz, K. J. (1993). Implications of developmental research for interviewing children. *Child Abuse & Neglect, 17*, 25–37.

Steward, M. S., & Steward, D. S. (with L. Farquhar, J. E. B. Myers, M. Reinhart, J. Welker, N. Joye, J. Driskill, & J. Morgan). (1996). Interviewing young children about body touch and handling. *Monograph of the Society for Research in Child Development, 61*(4–5, Serial No. 248).

Strawn, J. (1992). The states and the poor: Child poverty rises as the safety net shrinks [Monograph]. *Social Policy Report, 6*(3).

Summit, R. C. (1983). The child sexual accommodation syndrome. *Child Abuse & Neglect, 7*, 177–193.

Sutker, N. P., & Adams, H. E. (1993). *Comprehensive handbook of psychopathology* (2nd ed.). New York: Plenum Press.

Tavris, C. (1992). *The mismeasure of woman*. New York: Touchstone.

Taylor, M., Esbensen, B. M., & Bennett, R. T. (1994). Children's understanding of knowledge acquisition: The tendency for children to report they have always known what they have just learned. *Child Development, 65*, 1581–1604.

Thoennes, M., & Tjaden, P. G. (1990). The extent, nature, and validity of sexual abuse allegations in custody/visitation disputes. *Child Abuse & Neglect, 14,* 151–163.

Thoennes, N., & Pearson, J. (1988). Summary of findings from the sexual abuse allegations project. In E. B. Nicholson (Ed.), *Sexual abuse allegations in custody and visitation cases: A resource book for judges and court personnel.* Washington, DC: American Bar Association.

Tobey, A. E., & Goodman, G. S. (1992). Children's eyewitness memory: Effects of participation and forensic context. *Child Abuse & Neglect, 16,* 779–796.

Tower, C. C. (1996). *Child abuse and neglect.* Boston: Allyn and Bacon.

Tucker, A., Mertin, P., & Luszcz, M. (1990). The effect of a repeated interview on young children's eyewitness testimony. *Australian and New Zealand Journal of Criminology, 23,* 117–124.

Tversky, A., & Kahneman, D. (1974). Judgment under uncertainty: Heuristics and biases. *Science, 185,* 1124–1131.

Tversky, A., & Kahneman, D. (1981). The framing of decisions and the psychology of choice. *Science, 211,* 453–458.

Tversky, A., & Kahneman, D. (1982). Judgments of and by representativeness. In D. Kahneman, P. Slovic, & A. Tversky (Eds.), *Judgment under uncertainty: Heuristics and biases* (pp. 84–98). New York: Cambridge University Press.

Underwager, R., & Wakefield, H. (1990). *The real world of child interrogations.* Springfield, IL: Thomas.

Undeutsch, U. (1982). Statement reality analysis. In A. Trankell (Ed.), *Reconstructing the past: The role of psychologists in criminal trials* (pp. 27–56). Stockholm: Norstedt & Sons.

Undeutsch, U. (1989). The development of statement reality analysis. In J. C. Yuille (Ed.), *Credibility assessment* (pp. 101–120). Dordrecht, The Netherlands: Kluwer.

U.S. Department of Health and Human Services, National Center on Child Abuse and Neglect. (1995). *Child maltreatment 1993: Reports from the states to the National Center on Child Abuse and Neglect.* Washington, DC: U.S. Government Printing Office.

U.S. Department of Justice. (1978). *Sourcebook of criminal justice statistics: 1978.* Washington, DC: Bureau of Justice Statistics.

U.S. Department of Justice. (1992). *Sourcebook of criminal justice statistics: 1992.* Washington, DC: Bureau of Justice Statistics.

Veith, I. (1965). *Hysteria: A history of a disease.* Chicago: University of Chicago Press.

Wakefield, H., & Underwager, R. (1991). Sexual abuse allegations in divorce and custody disputes. *Behavioral Sciences and the Law, 9,* 451–468.

Wakefield, H., & Underwager, R. (1994a). *Return of the furies: An investigation into recovered memory therapy.* Chicago: Open Court.

Wakefield, H., & Underwager, R. (1994b). The alleged child victim and real victims of sexual misuse. In J. J. Krivacksa & J. Money (Eds.), *The handbook of forensic sexology: Biomedical & criminological perspectives* (pp. 223–264). Amherst, NY: Prometheus Books.

Wales, R. J. (1979). Deixis. In P. Fletcher & M. Garman (Eds.), *Language acquisition: Studies in first language development* (pp. 241–260). New York: Cambridge University Press.

Walker, A. G. (1994). *Handbook on questioning children: A linguistic perspective.* Washington, DC: American Bar Association Center on Children and the Law.

Walker, A. G. (1995, October). *Understanding the language of children.* Workshop presented at the fall conference on child abuse sponsored by the Indiana Prosecuting Attorneys Council, Indianapolis, IN.

Walker, A. G., & Warren, A. R. (1995). The language of the child abuse interview: Asking the questions, understanding the answers. In T. Ney (Ed.), *True and false allegations of child sexual abuse: Assessment and case management* (pp. 153–162). New York: Brunner/Mazel.

Walker, N. E., & Hunt, J. S. (1998). Interviewing child victim-witnesses: How you ask is what you get. In C. P. Thompson, D. Herrmann, J. D. Read, D. Bruce, D. Payne, & M. P. Toglia (Eds.), *Eyewitness memory: Theoretical and applied perspectives* (pp. 55–87). Mahwah, NJ: Erlbaum.

Walker, N. E., Lunning, S. M., & Eilts, J. L. (1996, June). Do children respond accurately to forced choice questions? Yes or no. Paper presented at *Recollections of Trauma: Scientific Research and Clinical Practice*, NATO Advanced Study Institute, Port de Bourgenay, France.

Ward, M. L. (1995). Talking about sex: Common themes about sexuality in the prime-time television programs children and adolescents view most. *Journal of Youth and Adolescence, 24,* 595–615.

Warren, A. R. (1992, May). Interviewing child witnesses: Some linguistic considerations. Paper presented at *The Child Witness in Context*, NATO Advanced Study Institute, Lucca, Italy.

Warren, A. R. (1997, January). *Forensic interviewing in child welfare.* Workshops for the State of Maine Department of Human Services in Bangor and Augusta.

Warren, A., Hulse-Trotter, K., & Tubbs, E. C. (1991). Inducing resistance to suggestibility in children. *Law and Human Behavior, 15,* 273–285.

Warren, A. R., & Lane, P. (1995). Effects of timing and type of questioning on eyewitness accuracy and suggestibility. In M. S. Zaragoza, J. R. Graham, G. C. N. Hall, R. Hirschman, & Y. S. Ben-Porath (Eds.), *Memory and testimony in the child witness* (pp. 44–60). Thousand Oaks, CA: Sage.

Warren, A. R., & McCloskey, L. A. (1997). Language in social contexts. In J. B. Gleason (Ed.), *The development of language* (4th ed., pp. 210–258). New York: Allyn and Bacon.

Warren, A. R., & McGough, L. S. (1996). Research on children's suggestibility: Implications for the investigative interview. *Criminal Justice and Behavior, 23,* 269–303.

Warren, A. R., Perry, N. W., Nelson, D. H., Porter, C., Elliott, K., Komori, L.,

Hunt, J., Gleason, T., Galas, J., & Kellen, L. (1995, June). *Interviewing children: Questions of structure and style.* Paper presented at the Third National Colloquium of the American Professional Society on the Abuse of Children, Tucson, AZ.

Warren, A. R., Woodall, C. E., Hunt, J. S., & Perry, N. W. (1996). "It sounds good in theory, but . . .": Do investigative interviewers follow guidelines based on memory research? *Child Maltreatment, 1,* 231–245.

Warren-Leubecker, A., Tate, C. S., Hinton, I. D., & Ozbeck, N. (1989). What do children know about the legal system and when do they know it? First steps down a less traveled path in child witness research. In S. J. Ceci, D. F. Ross, & M. P. Toglia (Eds.), *Perspectives on children's testimony* (pp. 158–183). New York: Springer-Verlag.

Wason, P. C., & Johnson-Laird, P. N. (1972). *Psychology of reasoning: Structure and content.* Cambridge, MA: Harvard University Press.

Westcott, H. L. (1991). The abuse of disabled children: A review of the literature. *Child: Care, Health and Development, 17,* 243–258.

Westcott, H. L. (1994). The *Memorandum of Good Practice* and children with disabilities. *Journal of Law and Practice, 3,* 21–32.

Westman, J. C. (1979). *Child advocacy: New professional roles for helping families.* New York: Free Press.

Whitcomb, D. (1992). *When the victim is a child.* Washington, DC: National Institute of Justice.

White, S. (1988). Should investigatory use of anatomical dolls be defined by the courts? *Journal of Interpersonal Violence, 3,* 471–475.

Whitehead, B. D. (1994, October). The failure of sex education. *The Atlantic Monthly, 274*(4), 55–80.

Whittaker, S. J., & Robinson, E. J. (1987). An investigation of the consequences of one feature of teacher-child talk for children's awareness of ambiguity in verbal messages. *International Journal of Behavioral Development, 10,* 425–438.

Wilkinson, J. (1988). Context in children's event memory. In M. M. Gruneberg, P. E. Morris, & R. N. Sykes (Eds.), *Practical aspects of memory: Current research and issues* (Vol. 1, pp. 107–111). Chichester, England: Wiley.

Wilkinson, K. M., Dube, W. V., & McIlvane, W. J. (1996). A crossdisciplinary perspective on studies of rapid word mapping in psycholinguistics and behavior analysis. *Developmental Review, 16,* 125–148.

Wimmer, H., Gruber, A., & Perner, J. (1984). Young children's conception of lying: Lexical realism-moral subjectivism. *Journal of Experimental Child Psychology, 37,* 1–30.

Winer, G. A., Rasnake, L. K., & Smith, D. A. (1987). Language versus logic: Responses to misleading classificatory questions. *Journal of Psycholinguistic Research, 16,* 311–327.

Wolfner, G., Faust, D., & Dawes, R. M. (1993). The use of anatomically detailed dolls in sexual abuse evaluations: The state of the science. *Applied & Preventive Psychology, 2,* 1–11.

Wood, B., Orsak, C., Murphy, M., & Cross, H. J. (1996). Semistructured child sexual abuse interviews: Interview and child characteristics related to credibility of disclosure. *Child Abuse & Neglect, 20,* 81–92.

Wood, J. M. (1996). Weighing evidence in sexual abuse evaluations: An introduction to Bayes's theorem. *Child Maltreatment, 1,* 25–36.

Wood, J. M., McClure, K. A., & Birch, R. A. (1996). Suggestions for improving interviews in child protection agencies. *Child Maltreatment, 1,* 223–230.

Wood, J. M., & Wright, L. (1995). Evaluation of children's sexual behaviors and incorporation of base rates in judgments of sexual abuse. *Child Abuse & Neglect, 19,* 1263–1273.

Woodall, D. E. (1996). *The effects of linguistic question form on children's recall accuracy.* Unpublished master's thesis, University of Tennessee at Chattanooga.

Wright, L. (1994). *Remembering Satan: A case of recovered memory and the shattering of an American family.* New York: Knopf.

Yapko, M. D. (1994). *Suggestions of abuse: True and false memories of childhood sexual trauma.* New York: Simon & Schuster.

Yates, A., Beutler, L. E, & Crago, M. (1985). Drawings by child victims of incest. *Child Abuse & Neglect, 9,* 183–189.

Yuille, J. C. (1988). The systematic assessment of children's testimony. *Canadian Psychology, 19,* 247–261.

Yuille, J. C. (1991). *The Step-Wise Interview: A protocol for interviewing children.* Unpublished manuscript, University of British Columbia.

Yuille, J. C., & Farr, V. (1987, Fall). Statement validity analysis: A systematic approach to the assessment of children's allegations of child sexual abuse. *British Columbia Psychologist,* 19–27.

Yuille, J. C., Hunter, R., Joffe, R., & Zaparniuk, J. (1993). Interviewing children in sexual abuse cases. In G. S. Goodman & B. L. Bottoms (Eds.), *Child victims, child witnesses: Understanding and improving testimony* (pp. 95–115). New York: Guilford Press.

Zaragoza, M. S., Dahlgren, D., & Muench, J. (1992). The role of memory impairment in children's suggestibility. In M. L. Howe, C. J. Brainerd, & V. F. Reyna (Eds.), *Development of long-term retention* (pp. 184–216). New York: Springer-Verlag.

Ziff, P. (1972). *Understanding understanding.* Ithaca, NY: Cornell University Press.

Zigler, E., & Hall, N. W. (1991). Physical child abuse in America: Past, present, and future. In D. Cicchetti & V. Carlson (Eds.), *Child maltreatment* (pp. 38–75). New York: Cambridge University Press.

INDEX

Fitzpatrick, C., 70–71
Fivush, R., 40–41, 49
Flin, R., 51
Follow-back studies, 217
Forensic interviewing, nonforensic vs., 106–112
Four-card task, 225–226
Framing, problem, 234
Francoeur, E., 63, 187
Frazier, S., 47
Free narrative, 136
Friedman, W. J., 164
Friedrich, W., 224–225
Frontal lobe development, 36, 43–44

Gardner, R. A., 195
Garnica, O. K., 158
Garven, S., 62
Gee, S., 197
Geiselman, R. E., 83–88, 90, 142, 241
Gleason, J. B., 76
Goals of interviewing, 36–37
Goldberg, L. R., 235
Goodman, E., 10n2
Goodman, G. S., 51, 58, 60, 61
Grant, J. P., 7
Gray, E., 16
Greece, ancient, 11
Gross, J., 183–184
Ground rules, interview, 126–130, 145
Gruppen, L. D., 226–227

Hackbarth, S. G., 182
Hamond, N. R., 41
Harker, C., 178
Harnick, M. A., 58
Haskett, M. E., 118
Hassibi, M., 28–29
Haugaard, J. J., 47–48
Hayne, H., 183–184
Hearing impairments, interviewing children with, 200–201
Hepps, D., 51
Hernandez, D. J., 21–22
Hershkowitz, I., 192–193
Hinton, I. D., 160–161
Hirschman, J. E., 51
Hispanic children, 176–177
Holland, J., 188

Holley, Angela, 92–94
Honesty, 107–108
Huffman, M. L., 47, 203
Hulse, D. A., 173
Hulse-Trotter, K., 127
Humpty-Dumpty effect, 15
Hunt, J. S., 103–104, 204
Hutcheson, J. S., 118
Hypothesis testing, in forensic interviewing, 109

Idaho v. Wright, 112
Illusory correlations, 227–230
Incest, 11
Income levels, 21
Indexicals, 171
Internet resources, 243–244, 249
Interviewer(s)
    behavior/demeanor of, 108–109, 121
    bias of, 67
    clothing of, 122
    number of, 119–120
    training of, 8, 30–32, 239–242. *See also* Professional development
Introduction of topic, 133–136
Intuition, in forensic vs. nonforensic interviewing, 108
Investigators, contacting, 245–246
Israel, 130

Johnson-Laird, P. N., 225–226
Journals, professional, 245, 248
Judgment/decision making, 209–238
    accuracy in, 216
    anchoring/adjustment in, 231
    availability heuristic in, 230–231
    base rates, ignoring of, 220–222
    case studies involving, 209–212
    conditional probabilities, reversal of, 216–218
    and confidence–accuracy relationship, 235–236
    confirmation bias in, 225–227
    and estimation of event frequencies, 233–234
    faulty expert opinion (example), 213–215
    illusory correlations in, 227–230
    and odds form of Bayes's theorem, 222–225

problem framing in, 234
regression toward mean, ignoring of, 231–232
representativeness heuristic in, 218–220
strategies for reducing errors in, 237–238
three principles of, 212–213
"Just For Kids!" Foundation, Inc., 242

Kagan, J., 43–44
Kahneman, D., 218–219, 233, 234
Karniel, I., x
Keary, K., 70–71
Keenan, E. O., 175
Kempe, C. H., 10
Kessen, W., 9–10
Kinsey, A. C., 29n11
Kinship terms, 167
Knox, A., 51
Kohlberg, L., 217, 219
Köhnken, G., 92–93
Koocher, G. P., 186, 195
Kuehnle, K., 135

LaCrosse, J., 217
Ladany, N., 231
Lamb, M. E., x, 34, 69, 103, 125, 132–133, 137, 139, 192–193, 202–203
Lamphear, V., 127
Lane, P., 58
Language
  adult-to-child, 76–78
  with child witnesses, 78–79
Language development, 153–180
  and attentional development, 37
  and conversational competence, 174–176
  and culture, 176–178
  and inappropriate questioning, 154–157
  phonology, 157–160, 179
  and pragmatics, 173–174, 180
  syntax, 168–173, 179
  vocabulary, 160–168, 179
Laws, reporting, 10–11
Leading questions, 140, 147
Left-branching, 170

Legal language, 154–155, 167–168
Legal system, increased involvement of young children in, 15–16
Leichtman, M. D., 43–44, 61, 63–64, 67
Lepore, S. J., 62
Leung, P., 239–240
Libraries, 246–250
  terminology, 247–249
  time-saving tips for using, 249–250
Lies, truth vs., 45–48, 124–127
Likelihood ratio, 223
Liker, J. K., 237
Lindsay, D. S., 43n2, 44, 54, 59, 60, 64, 66, 123
Loftus, E. F., 61, 67–68
Lunning, S. M., 53

MacFarlane, K., 19–20
Malpass, R. S., 62
Martin, C. E., 29n11
McCauley, M. R., 88, 91
McCloskey, L. A., 174–175, 176
McClure, K. A., 204
McGough, L. S., 15, 16, 105
Media, conservative politics in, 23–24
Memon, A., 56, 92–93, 94, 95n2, 127
Memorandum of Good Practice, 100–101
Memories, first, 41
Memory source monitoring, 42–45
Michaels, K., 19, 64
Michigan Court of Appeals, 141
Miller, R. L., Jr., 124n3
Milne, R., 92–93
Milsom, J., 101
Misleading information, encountered prior to interviews, 62–66
Misleading questions, explicitly, 57–60
Mispronunciation, 159
Mitchell, R., 101
Mixed series multiple questions, 156
Moan, S., 127
Montoya, J., 118
Morgan, M., 112, 131, 134
Moston, S., 127
Mr. Science, 64–66
Mulder, M. R., 127
Mulford, M., 233
Multiple-choice questions, 139, 146
Multiple questions, 170
Myers, J. E. B., 207n1

closure phase, 144
Cognitive Interview. *See* Cognitive Interview
and discussion of truth vs. lies, 124–127
for forensic vs. nonforensic interviewing, 106–112
free narrative, use of, 136–137
ground rules, establishment of, 126–130
in *Guidelines for Psychosocial Evaluation of Suspected Sexual Abuse in Young Children*, 101–102
introductory comments, 121–124
and language addressed to child witnesses, 78–79
and *Memorandum of Good Practice*, 100–101
need for formal, 75
NICHD interview protocol, 98–99
open-ended vs. specific questions, 52–55
phases, interview, 145
and planning for interview, 112–120
practice interview, 130–133
questioning phase, 137–138
and rapport building, 121–124, 130–133
Step-Wise Interview, 95–98
strategies for constructing, 81–82
and structure of adult–child conversations, 76–78
summary statements on, 100–103
topic, introduction of, 133–136
Pucci, L., 140n4

Qin, J., 60
Questioning
child development and appropriate level of, 154–157
suggestive, 60–61
witness-compatible, 86
Questioning phase, of interview, 137–138
Questions
closed, 139, 146
explicitly misleading, 57–60
leading, 140, 147
mixed series multiple, 156
multiple, 170
multiple-choice, 139, 146

negation, 170–171
open-ended, 52, 67, 138, 146
repeat, 55–57, 175
repetition of, 154
specific, 52
tag, 170–171
unrelated, 156
wh-, 54, 172–173
yes–no, 54, 139, 146, 199

Rand Corporation, 83
Rapport, building, 86–87, 96
with drawing, 183
with practice interview, 130–133
Raskin, D. C., 107, 139
Realmuto, G. M., 188
Recreation, context, 85
Reference materials, 242–250
Internet resources, 243–244
investigators, direct contact with, 245–246
libraries, 246–250
professional organizations, 244–245
Regression toward the mean, 231–232
Reich, P. A., 77, 159, 162n2, 167
Religion, 24
Remembering, conversational, 37–42
Renick, A., 187
Repeated questions, 55–57, 175
Repetition, 55–57, 154, 175
Reporting laws, 10–11
Reporting of abuse, by children. *See also* Testimony
accuracy in, 48
anatomically detailed dolls, as alternative to verbal reporting, 193–195
and attentional development, 35–37
and conversational remembering, 37–42
and memory source monitoring, 42–45
and suggestibility, 48–49
and time since event, 49–52
and understanding of between lies and truth, 45–48
Representativeness heuristic, 218–220
Reprints, 245
Retrieval, 85
Reversing conditional probabilities, 216–218
Reyna, V. F., 44
Ricks, D., 217

ABOUT THE AUTHORS

Debra A. Poole, PhD, is a professor of psychology at Central Michigan University. She received her PhD in developmental psychology from the University of Iowa and served on the faculty of Beloit College for 7 years before relocating to Michigan with her family. Dr. Poole's recent publications span a variety of topics, including memory development and memory theory, gender differences in scientific knowledge, and the concept of heritability. Her studies of children's eyewitness testimony, funded by grants from the National Institute of Mental Health and the National Science Foundation, have been widely cited in articles, textbooks, and interviewing protocols. In addition, she drafted the interviewing protocol and workshop materials for the Child Investigative Interviewing Pilot Project in Michigan, sponsored by the Michigan Family Independence Agency. Dr. Poole is a Fellow of the American Psychological Society.

Michael E. Lamb, PhD, is Head of the Section on Social and Emotional Development at the National Institute of Child Health and Human Development in Bethesda, Maryland. Prior to that, he was Professor of Psychology, Pediatrics, and Psychiatry at the University of Utah in Salt Lake City, and he has also served on the faculties of the Universities of Wisconsin, Michigan, Hokkaido (Japan), Haifa (Israel), Osnabruck (Germany), and Halle (Germany) since receiving his PhD from Yale University. Dr. Lamb's current research is concerned with the evaluation, validation, and facilitation of children's accounts of sexual abuse; the effects of domestic violence on children's development; the effects of contrasting patterns of early child care on children and their families; and the description of early patterns of infant care in diverse sociocultural ecologies. He is the coauthor or editor of more than two dozen books on various aspects of child development; the recipient of an honorary degree from the University of Göteborg, Sweden and of numerous research awards; and a Fellow of the American Psychological Society.